W9-APO-091

A SYSTEMS ANALYSIS OF POLITICAL LIFE

John Wiley & Sons, Inc., New York • London • Sydney

A Systems Analysis of Political Life

DAVID EASTON

UNIVERSITY OF CHICAGO

Library of Congress Catalog Card Number: 65-12714
Printed in the United States of America

To Sylvia

Preface

THIS is the third work in a long-range project on empirically oriented political theory. The first, *The Political System,* sought to present the case for general theory in political science. The second, *A Framework for Political Anaylsis,* laid out the major categories in terms of which it has seemed to me that such a theory might be developed. In the present book, the task will be to put that structure of concepts to work and, in doing so, to elaborate them further so that they can be more readily applied to empirical situations.

But this book remains a work confined to the theoretical level. Its primary objective is to elaborate a conceptual structure and suggest, where possible, some theoretical propositions. Its goal is not to undertake the validation of the statements or to demonstrate definitively the applications of such concepts. Testing is closely interwoven with theory construction; each feeds and grows on the other. But for sustained periods of time it is vital, in the development of a discipline, that particular attention be given to the separate needs and problems of each. In the specialization of labor that inevitably takes place, I have chosen to devote my efforts in this book to the elaboration of empirical theory. It is significant that although, until the last decade, empirical theory had received the blessings of but a small minority and the attention of only an isolated few, it is now increasingly becoming a special field of teaching, training, and research in political science.

This book picks up where *A Framework for Political Anaylsis* left off. Here I explore in detail what may be called the life processes of a political system, those kinds of functions through which it performs its characteristic work as a political system. I continue to view political life as a system surrounded by a variety of environments. Because it is an open system, it is constantly subject to possible stress from these environments. Yet, in spite of these dangers to political life, many systems are able to take the measures necessary to assure their own persistence through time. Our problem will be the deceptively simple one: How does it come about that any type of system can persist at all, even under the pressures of frequent or constant crises?

In seeking an answer to this central problem of empirical political theory, we are led to inquire into the exact nature of these stresses, to examine concepts for describing precisely the way in which they are communicated to the political system, and to explore in considerable detail the various means through which a system may respond so as to cope with the stress. The very notion that political systems are capable of seizing fate by the forelock and shaping it to their own purposes will lead us to probe the means at their disposal for doing so.

In the outcome, we shall not have a theory in the full-blown sense of the term. We shall have a conceptual structure which, for various reasons to be elaborated later, is the most that we can expect in the area of general theory today. Some generalizations will inevitably emerge, but only as by-products.

Since we shall be concerned with general theory, we must constantly bear in mind what theory building at this level requires. The character of a theory will always hinge on how closely we decide to scrutinize a political system or on how far back we stand. If we are too remote, we can see only the broadest of outlines and this can be of little guidance to relevant research; and yet, if we remain too close, we will see details in such profusion and confusion that we will scarcely be better off. As a discipline, we have perhaps tended to be myopic in the past and to be inclined to peer too intently at our subject matter. I propose in this book to stand back, quite far compared to what our distance has been in the past, but not so far as to lose all sense of detail. At times, indeed, we may wish to take a very close look but only to illustrate a point here and there.

Those who have been accustomed to the microscopic research characteristic of political science will feel uneasy at so much that is being left out, and at such broad and rapid sweeps of the eyes across the empirical horizon. But unless I do this, I cannot fulfill my major objectives —to isolate the critical variables within the system, to identify some of their most significant relationships, and to present a coherent image of a theoretical approach.

In a way, theory building is like good photography. The details make better sense if we have first shot the broad scene so that we can see the proportions and better fit the bits and pieces of close-ups into a wider and more coherent frame. This is the very task of macroanalysis, the kind to be undertaken here.

In the preface to *A Framework for Political Analysis* I indicated the indebtedness I have incurred to others in the many years during which the present ideas were being worked over, and I would refer the reader to those comments. They apply here with equal force and justice.

But once again, I wish to express my appreciation for the financial assistance made available by the Social Science Research Committee of the Division of the Social Sciences at the University of Chicago, and for the free time and funds put at my disposal by a Ford Research Professorship in Governmental Affairs (1960–1961). A year as a fellow at the Center for Advanced Study in the Behavioral Sciences at Stanford, California (1957–1958) provided a unique systems-specific environment in which to think through many of the problems with which this book deals. In the past year, at Chicago, Vicky I. Meyer and Ruth Butzloff performed Herculean feats of labor in deciphering and transforming many rough drafts into finished, clearly typed manuscripts and in organizing the footnotes with painstaking attention to detail. I am also especially indebted to Mrs. Rosemary Smith for her meticulous skill in proofreading a long manuscript and in keeping an orderly hand on its final stages of preparation for publication.

The dedication of my book to my wife acknowledges in only token fashion her active participation in every phase of my intellectual, editorial, and administrative work.

David Easton

December, 1964

Contents

DIAGRAMS

TABLES

A SYSTEMS ANALYSIS OF POLITICAL LIFE

Part One

The Mode of Analysis

I

The Form of Theoretical Analysis

THEORIES, IT HAS BEEN SAID, ARE CHEAP; THEY COST ONLY THE TIME and effort of the theorists and these can be had quite inexpensively. With the cost so low, we might expect to find the study of politics inundated with a flood of theories. Yet a perusal of research literature reveals that they are strangely rare and infrequent. Of course, if we were to interpret theories to mean speculation about political matters, Western civilization has never suffered for lack of them. But if in theories we seek tools for the analysis and reliable understanding of the way political systems operate, it is apparent that scarcity prevails. And the more general or broader the kind of theory we seek, the greater the dearth.

I shall be concerned with the formulation of theory at its most inclusive level, what may be called general theory. Is there a need for such theories to explain the functioning of political systems? This is a question to which I have already addressed myself in the volume *The Political System*.[1] The need is apparent and its utility undeniable. Is it possible to construct such a theory at the present stage of development in political and social science? This presents an entirely different and more challenging problem, one that will command our immediate attention in this chapter. What form might it take? Grappling with this question will occupy the bulk of this study.

The Changing Image of Political Theory

Before I venture a reply to what is possible in the way of general theory or inquire into a plausible structure for it, or even suggest a strategy for theoretical analysis appropriate to and feasible at the present stage of political research, I must discuss in some detail the kind of image we may hold of political theory and the role of general theory within it. What we expect or feel we ought to expect from

[1] (New York: Knopf, 1953).

theory will help to set the criteria in terms of which we judge the adequacy of any efforts in this direction.

Political theory is in the throes of a major revolution. In the past, any mention of political theory would have been likely to rouse an image of it in the grand philosophical tradition of Plato, Aristotle, Rousseau, Mill, or Dewey rather than any set of ideas that could even vaguely be called general theory. So entrenched has this traditional model of theory become that it would be confusing and even seemingly arbitrary to begin to describe my objectives with regard to the formulation of general theory without first having examined the relationship of this kind of theory to traditional conceptions, at least briefly.[2]

In most of the social and natural sciences, reference to theory would be understood with reasonable ease and clarity; the measure of consensus about the meaning of the concept is considerable. To the extent that differences of interpretation may exist, they involve refinements of detail rather than doubt about the basic premises. In political research, the state of affairs is radically different. Dispute is widespread about the basic tasks of theory, the relative emphasis on its parts and the merits of its innovations. To the casual observer, the confusion might seem to run rampant, with every man his own theorist or, what is worse, with every man the apparent founder of his own school of theory, at least as long as attention is confined to traditional theory alone. If we add newer interpretations of the task of theory and its functions within political science, confusion seems to be confounded.

There are sound reasons why this should be so in the field of theory. It deals in part with basic philosophical assumptions; we cannot expect that the present generation will achieve any greater consensus on these than those of the past. But some share of the responsibility for the particular apparent disorder that greets us currently in theory must be attributed, not to the intrinsic nature of the traditional kinds of questions with which theory has dealt, but to the fact that our image of theory and of its relationship to the rest of political research is undergoing a profound and rapid change. One of the not-so-hidden costs of this rate of change is ambiguity and uncertainty of direction, at least for those who still strongly entertain traditional expectations.

Recent developments in the overall orientation of political science, largely characterized by its reception of more rigorous methods of research and analysis,[3] have led to a radical transformation in concep-

[2] For a fuller description, see *ibid.*

[3] A full discussion appears in *A Framework for Political Analysis* (New York: Prentice-Hall, 1965) chapter I.

tions of the tasks and functions of theory. Not that this change involves rejecting or discarding any of the historical concerns of theory or for that matter of adding any entirely new dimensions. Rather, it has led to the injection of a new and stronger emphasis on concerns that have always found some place within traditional theory but that out of neglect and untimeliness have been allowed to lie unattended.

The aspect that has thus remained concealed and which now rises to shatter the old image of the nature and tasks of theory may be described as descriptive, empirically-oriented, behavioral, operational or causal theory. The variety and indeterminacy of terms used to identify this kind of theory indicate how recently it has appeared on the horizon of political research.[4] But to all intents and purposes, the terms are synonymous and will be so used here.

Until recently, it has not at all been customary for political theorists to avow an interest in causal theory or to accept its development as one of their major responsibilities. Traditionally, political theory, interchangeable here with political philosophy, has held and propagated an image of itself as narrowly engaged in and committed to the quest for an understanding of the nature of the good life or at least an understanding of the way others have viewed it. Analysis of the moral rather than of the strictly empirical world has stood at the peak of theory's hierarchy of priorities.

In the last decade, however, for the first time this limiting image has begun to change decisively and there can be little doubt, permanently. It now becomes possible for theory to escape the shackles imposed by so narrow a perspective and to broaden its scope to include a serious and systematic concern for descriptive theory. To the extent that theory takes advantage of this opportunity, it holds out the promise of sharing the study of political life much more intimately with the rest of political science and of measuring up to the expectations always inherent in the very idea of theoretical research itself.

If in this volume we seek to encourage and hasten the processes that will enable political theory to broaden its horizons and enrich its value for the rest of political research, we shall not be seeking to impose upon it goals that are entirely alien to its historically developed character. If only in recent years, it has become transparently clear that political theory is not, need not be and ought not to be a monolithic subject confined exclusively to moral and philosophical inquiry. It includes such varying patterns of thought and analysis as those involved in creative moral inquiry, linguistic analysis, the interpretation of the nature and determinants of political belief systems

[4] *Ibid.*

or ideologies and the discovery and formulation of empirically oriented theories.[5] Although these different aspects of political theory may be found woven into a single web within the thought of any single political theorist, this need not and has not prevented others from treating one or another aspect as an intellectual enterprise worthy of special and concentrated attention.

Today there can be no doubt that recurrent efforts to squeeze theory into a narrow intellectual mold in which moral concerns, vital as they are and must always be, are made peremptory and exclusive, must fail. Descriptive theory has begun to take its first steps in earnest and as its experience accumulates, it promises an exponential rate of development.[6] Even though this approach to theory has been primarily a post-World War II development, there has already been so substantial an effort in this direction, that we can now say that traditional political theory has been joined by a new field of concern and instruction which may be called causal or descriptive political theory.

The Properties of General Theories

Even if we are ready to accept the fact that in recent years causal theory has shattered the prevailing traditional image of political theory, this would offer us little help in appreciating the specific place in political research of the kind of theory with which this volume is concerned, namely, of general theory. Casual theory itself takes many shapes among which general theory represents only one kind and it is a kind that has certainly not received most attention in the emerging empirical science of politics. Since my objective will be to take one step in the direction of such a general theory, it will be helpful to inquire into some of its properties.

In the social sciences, terminology is not stabilized with respect to what is to be designated as causal theory. In the popular usage of social research, causal theory covers a broad miscellany of subjects: conceptual clarification, methodology, inventive and speculative explanations of empirical subjects, informed guesses with respect to the application of knowledge and generalizations in the strict sense. This variety of intellectual pursuits associated with the term undoubtedly

[5] For an analysis of the various components of theory, see D. Easton, "La naturaleza de la teoría política," 3 *Revista de Ciencias Sociales* (1959) 555–562.

[6] For references, see *A Framework for Political Analysis*, chapter I, footnote 1.

reflects, in part, the broad scope of interest included within it; but it also indicates the prestige and authority that the idea of theory itself commands. Many intellectual activities seek to bask in its glory.

In order to escape the complications involved in an over-refinement of vocabulary, I propose somewhat arbitrarily, but without damage to the intrinsic meaning of the term, to describe a theory as any kind of generalization or proposition that asserts that two or more things, activities, or events covary under specified conditions. A theory or generalization that has been well-confirmed would be called a law; one that awaits confirmation through further testing would be an hypothesis.

A general theory, on the other hand, is one that differs from other kinds of theories with respect to two characteristics in terms of which all theories might be classified: the scope or generality of its subject matter and its coherence or interrelatedness. The scope refers to the range of subject matter that the theory embraces, varying from very limited data to the most inclusive kind. The coherence of a theory refers to the degree of consistency among the component propositions.

Using these criteria elsewhere, I have shown that theories would fall into three categories: singular generalizations, narrow gauge or partial theories, and general theories.[7] Singular generalizations encompass only a very limited body of data. Political research is well-supplied with generalizations of this sort, which apply to limited types of behavior at a given time and place or to relatively few kinds of events. From the point of view of their consistency or logical coherence, they are distinctive by virtue of their relative isolation in the whole web of political generalizations. At times they may well find a place among components of broader theories. But until that occurs, that is, until someone sees a relationship that is not intuitively apparent, the disproof of one such generalization need have no serious consequences for the validity or reliability of the others. This reflects their essential singularity and theoretical isolation from one another.

If we conceive of generalizations to lie on a scale of generality and consistency, as we move further along it, we find sets of propositions that are somewhat more inclusive in the data to which they refer and more consistent in their relationship to each other. These narrow-gauge generalizations are partial theories. They isolate some part or aspect of behavior in a political system, less than the whole and yet greater than some isolated fragment, which experience or intuition suggests is related significantly. Such a partial theory seeks to help us

[7] D. Easton, *The Political System*, pp. 52–59.

understand why this part of the political system hangs together in the way it does. The very fact that the assumption is made that the behavior in a given segment or type of activity in the political system can be selected for unified analysis indicates an aspiration on the part of the investigator to develop an integrated set of generalizations about this substantive area.

There have been efforts to develop partial theories about such selected and presumably coherent areas of political life as parties, organizations, interest groups, legislative behavior, federalism, leadership, authority, administrative behavior, decision-making or coalitions. The task of the theorist is to identify sharply the particular aspect or segment of the political system on which he is focusing and to construct a body of logically interrelated propositions adequate for explaining behavior in this area. But it does not include the effort to fit each of these partial theories into a larger logical or theoretical whole. The varying degrees of success that have been achieved in formulating coherent partial theories is a matter that goes beyond my interest here. But at least the intention of their formulators is to present some kind of unified analysis of a somewhat broad area of political life.

What is left logically indeterminate or ambiguous and inconsistent is the relationship among such partial theories. The area between these theories forms an intellectual no-man's-land. It is this region that general theory helps to plot.

A general theory is a type of causal theory that differs from singular generalizations and partial theories, in scope at least, by virtue of its presumed application to the whole of a field of inquiry. In politics, it seeks to illuminate the functioning of political systems in their entirety. It would not be confined to any special aspect of a political system or any of its segments. It would not be concerned with understanding the way in which any single system operates, such as the American, French, or Indonesian; nor would it be specifically restricted to explaining the differences among mutually exclusive classes of systems, such as those found in peasant as against industrial societies, modernized as compared to traditional systems, or democratic as contrasted with authoritarian political orders. A useful method for classifying systems might well find an important place in such a general theory, but its primary objectives would be otherwise. The main objectives are threefold: to establish criteria for identifying the important variables requiring investigation in all political systems; to specify the relationships among these variables; and to achieve these goals through a set of generalizations that hang together with greater rather than lesser logical coherence and interdependence.

Strategies in Theorizing

The utility of a general theory for explaining the behavior of the empirical system to which it applies increases directly with the degree of logical coherence and consistency that obtains among its component concepts and generalizations. In its ideal and most powerful form, a general theory achieves maximal value when it constitutes a deductive system of thought so that from a limited number of postulates, assumptions and axioms, a whole body of empirically valid generalizations might be deduced in descending order of specificity. It is for this reason that mathematical formulation of general theory is often cited as the optimum mode of expression, even where quantification may not yet be possible, since mathematics is uniquely the science of rigorous deduction.

It would indeed be an astonishing feat if from the present relatively barren theoretical soil of political research, a full-blown deductive theory were to spring up overnight, even if we are willing to yield that the nights of scientific investigation may extend over many generations. Nevertheless, awareness of the existence of even this improbable ideal helps to set the stage for the recognition and reception of what can be attained at this juncture in the evolution of political science. Ideals give purpose and direction to more limited probabilities.

If a general deductive theory is too remote to be taken seriously at present, this does not imply that all analysis at the level of general theory is beyond our grasp. There are a number of ways of working the theoretical soil short of using the tools of pure deductive analysis. The task is to find and select one that is most practical and promising at this juncture in the history of political science. As von Neumann has suggested with regard to another area of knowledge, if early in the game, we cannot hope to offer a rounded theory, it is certainly possible to make some proposals that will serve to bring the range of theoretical inquiry within manageable bounds.[8]

We can conceive of attempts to develop types of general theories by linking together, into a logically loose system of thought, a variety of generalizations pertaining to various areas of political life. Presumably these might have been some of the aspirations underlying the efforts in recent years to accumulate inventories about what is known in the so-

---

[8] J. von Neumann, *The Computer and the Brain* (New York, Yale University Press, 1958).

cial sciences, including political science.[9] We might even assume that there was a latent hope that the collection of inventories of discrete generalizations in various sub-fields of political science, if carried through in all areas and linked together in one grand design, might have spawned some suggestions for an overarching, integrative theory.

It is highly unlikely that the construction of general theory occurs in this way although certainly not enough is known about the processes of theoretical innovation to be able to exclude any approach, however unpromising it may appear to be on the surface. But the probability of being able to assemble the miscellaneous generalizations in political research into even a logically loosely integrated body of general theory seems highly remote at the present day. As in most of the other social sciences, there is a severe shortage of generalizations to begin with; and those that do exist have arisen episodically, frequently without much interest in or relationship to hypotheses already in existence. Social science as a whole and political science in particular have been lacking in accumulative research. This leaves us with extremely few generalizations of sufficient breadth and significance upon which we could build even a theory with minimal logical coherence.[10]

If the only alternatives open to political theory were either to search for a deductive body of propositions or for a loosely connected set of generalizations with just sufficient coherence to mark it off from mere bead-stringing or stock-taking, there would indeed be little left to engage the attention of a serious student of theory. But more modest steps are indeed available which, if taken successfully, would open the way for major and richly rewarding strides in the direction of general theory. These steps lead to efforts to construct a useful and comprehensive framework of concepts for the analysis of political systems.

The Invention of Conceptual Structures

What frequently passes for theory in social research consists largely of the investigation of alternative concepts, dispute about their utility, their clarity, and implications. There is good reason why this should be so. One of the major stumbling blocks in the discovery of uniformities has not been only the lack of techniques for empirical research but

---

[9] As, for example, in H. D. Lasswell and A. Kaplan, *Power and Society* (New Haven: Yale University Press, 1950) and H. Hyman, *Political Socialization* (Glencoe, Illinois: Free Press, 1959).

[10] Most recent efforts at theory construction remain at the level of partial theory. See the works referred to in footnote 6 of this chapter.

the great difficulty in discovering units of analysis that have the degree of stability and definiteness or lack of ambiguity in their boundaries necessary for the kind of propositions expected of an exact science. To some extent such units are available with regard to very selected aspects of political life; the discovery of the vote, for example, has led to a vast and still growing literature on the way in which such choices are made in popular elections, committees, legislatures, or organizations. But there are few other areas of political life in which an equally well-defined and limited unit of research has been discovered. Functions, decision-making, power, and interest groups are today central and broad concepts lying at the crossroads of political research and yet little success has been achieved in clarifying their meaning.

This lack of adequate units of analysis accounts for the inordinate amount of space and time given over to the argument about concepts and their meaning. Contrary to superficial criticism often leveled at those who argue about meaning, the inability to exorcise the conceptual demon from social research as a whole is not a function of inadequate skills in or knowledge about scientific method but a natural outcome of the state of research at the present time. Each age in a science has its peculiar problems, and a major one in ours is the discovery and definition of stable units for understanding human behavior in its political, as well as in many of its other aspects.

It is for this reason that what we call theory in political research often takes the form of conceptual analysis rather than the formulation of generalizations. Not that the latter are ignored or downgraded in importance as objectives; and it is not that the theorizers are unaware of their ultimate goals. But the meaning of such generalizations and their acceptance rest on their clarity and consequent verifiability. Where the concepts of which they are composed remain ambiguous, there is little possibility of passing on to consider the interrelationship among concepts. Discussion is bound to be tied up by differences with regard to the referents of the concepts.

A great deal of what labels itself theory at this stage in the development of political science cannot help but be concerned centrally with the formation and evaluation of concepts. Although hard-headed scientists might protest, it is certainly not erroneous to place such conceptual discussion in the area of general theory. It would be a mistake, however, to assume that this exhausts the subject. It is just a preliminary, albeit an inescapable major step toward the development of such theory.

The reason for this is that even though a full-fledged general theory is probably beyond the reach of political science at this stage, however urgent the need for it may be, the development of a logically related set of concepts, an integrated conceptual framework at the highest level of abstraction, is vital if we are to establish the limits in subject matter. Concepts point to the variables that may be included as relevant to some ultimate theory. "The foremost task of science, that is, the continuous one, is to find the right concepts by which to conduct the analysis . . ." [11] If it will do nothing else, such a conceptual structure would at least indicate first, the part of reality to be included within a systematic study of political life and second, those elements of this broad area that ought to command our prior attention if we are to understand the major determinants of political behavior. If concept formation does nothing else, it at least provides criteria of political relevance to guide us in the distribution of our attention to matters of theoretical, and thereby, of explanatory and ultimately, of practical importance. At the very least it helps to promote the preliminary description of what are selected as significant phenomena.

This is not to say our conceptual analysis will in fact be neglectful or devoid of theoretical propositions or generalizations. As we shall see, they cannot be avoided, any more than concept formation and theoretical propositions can be entirely ignored in strictly empirical research. But where such generalizations occur, and to the extent that they do, they can be accepted as welcome unanticipated dividends of the efforts to establish a logically integrated set of criteria of significance for empirical research.

These dividends will themselves lead research directly toward a broader general theory. Precisely because of this, as we shall clearly see, the discovery of useful categories of analysis really carries us more than just a short step toward the fuller general theory about which I have been speaking as an ultimate ideal. But in spite of the deliberate inclusion of many generalizations, what I shall be consciously striving toward in this volume is not a fully matured general theory or even a close approximation to one. Rather, I shall be exploring a conceptual framework around which the more complex structure of a theory may possibly, in the slowness of time, be added.

There is another limitation in my objectives that will become evident in due course. Even with respect to the categories of theoretical analysis, I do not intend to be comprehensive in this volume. Concepts, we shall find, may identify two fundamentally but analytically distinguishable parts of political life. One reflects the kinds of activities that go on in a political system, what we might at other times and

[11] A. R. Radcliffe-Brown, *A Natural Science of Society* (Glencoe, Illinois: The Free Press and The Falcon's Wing Press, 1957), p. 28.

places have called the political functions, if this concept itself had not become virtually unusable because of the enormous variety of slippery meanings currently attached.[12] The other refers to the way these activities are performed; that is, it deals with the structure and processes of political life as particular modes for expressing these activities.

In this volume I shall not be directly concerned with exploring a conceptual framework for the analysis of political structures and their interrelationships. My objective will be to extricate from the total political reality those aspects that can be considered the fundamental processes or activities without which no political life in society could continue.[13]

The Central Problem of General Theory

Various kinds of orientations to theory may be adopted, whether the theory be general or only partial. In recent political research, as empirical theory has begun to attract more attention, one of the dominant approaches has been to select some value as the organizing principle and to construct a body of concepts and propositions around it. Normative rather than purely descriptive theory has been the outcome. In characterizing such theories as normative I am not implying that they stand in the tradition of ethical political philosophy. At its best, ethical theorizing seeks to warrant or justify alternative ethical positions, not to explain behavior.[14] Normative theory, however, adopts a value as its objective and evolves an explanation in terms of the conditions necessary to maximize the selected value. This theoretical strategy is not unknown in social research and has indeed paid considerable dividends, whatever its important limitations may be. It is well represented by economic theory which has been indebted to the primary value, "maximizing profit," as the peg on which its conceptualization has hung.

In political research a variety of normative theories has taken shape

[12] As K. Davis has pointed out in "The Myth of Functional Analysis as a Special Method in Sociology and Anthropology," 24 *American Sociological Review* (1959) 757–773, functional analysis, so-called, is not a theory but a concept intrinsic to all scientific research. Indeed, it is fundamentally devoid of theoretical content. It is a great and unnecessary arrogation, attributable ultimately to Malinowski, to take an idea central to all social research and to claim that it represents the point of departure for a special theory.

[13] The reasons for confining my attention to this aspect of general theory have already been developed in *A Framework for Political Analysis*.

[14] For a discussion of ethical theory, as such, see *The Political System, ad hoc.*

around a parallel diversity of values. In some cases, the perpetuation of democracy as a preferred type of political system has served as the ethical focus.[15] In others, the concern has been with the efficient allocation of resources, as in organizational theories, or, as in various species of game theories, the alternative strategies logically appropriate for the attainment of specified ends under varying conditions.

From the point of view of understanding political life as such, regardless of the particular objectives that may be attributed to or associated with it, each of these perspectives of necessity looks out upon a relatively narrow prospect, however important they may be as partial theories. The very fact that some value has been adopted as the principle that gives coherence and relevance to the theory restricts the range of interests to particular classes of phenomena and of systems. What is lacking is a broad way of formulating a theoretical question, one that will deliberately refrain from fixing on specific goals or even upon the vital matters of democratic systems but one that will extend its scope and address itself to the permanent and enduring problems faced by all types of political systems. Just as we may have a general theory of motion in physics or of life in biology, we require a general theory of the vital processes in politics.

It was from a starting point such as this that in *A Framework for Political Analysis,* I sought to demonstrate that within the context of a systems analysis could there be found an intellectual approach that would lead us to pose the most comprehensive kind of question. It is a question that can open a window on political life at its most general level, where we may temporarily even overlook differences among the structures of systems and bring within our view all and any forms that political life may take.

Once we affirm that all political life in its varied manifestations may properly become our universe, the substance of a theoretical inquiry would have to change radically. It would no longer suffice to assert some central value that is associated with an interest bred by the historical experience of Western civilization. Rather, our attention will be directed, of necessity, to the most general kind of matter that must be faced by all political systems regardless of time or place, from the most democratic to the most dictatorial, from the most primitive to the most industrialized, from the most traditional to the most modern.

The perspectives of a systems analysis of political life impel us to

[15] See, as examples, R. A. Dahl, *A Preface to Democratic Theory* (Chicago: University of Chicago Press, 1956); J. M. Buchanan and G. Tullock, *The Calculus of Consent* (Ann Arbor: University of Michigan Press, 1962); and A. Downs, *An Economic Theory of Democracy* (New York: Harper, 1957).

address ourselves to the following kind of question. How can any political system ever persist whether the world be one of stability or of change? It is comparable to asking with respect to biological life: How can human beings manage to exist? Or for that matter, what processes must be maintained if any life is to persist, especially under conditions where the environment may at times be extremely hostile?

With respect to political systems, this order of question has an added advantage. It helps us to prevent research from remaining exclusively and narrowly preoccupied, at least implicitly, with one type of system, namely, democracy as it has developed in the West. Even where non-democratic systems are under scrutiny, it is seldom for the sake of understanding and explaining political systems as such but, through contrast with Western democracies, to shed a stronger light on the conditions surrounding the existence or emergence of democracies. The designation of exotic systems as developing or transitional suggests a norm toward which they are moving, and seldom does this standard represent anything other than Western democracies as we know them today. The prevalence of the concept "modernity" further reflects this marked cultural limitation.

The primary motivation of scholarship today, including most theorizing, is to know more about democratic systems and the way in which they come about, with the fundamental and virtually unquestioned assumption that the quickest and best way to do this is to study democratic systems directly as a type or to examine other systems with democracies as a latent model. But even if we were to adopt this assumption explicitly and organize theory around it as the dominant value of a normative theory—in this case related to the attainment and perpetuation of a democratic way of political life—we might still wish to question whether we can ever secure the most reliable understanding of how democracies emerge and function unless we are able to invent a conceptual framework that applies to a much broader range of system types. As in many efforts at scientific explanation, it may be that the longest route home will ultimately prove to be the quickest.

Broadening the kind of problems to which we address ourselves also has significant secondary consequences. It helps to enlarge the sample of political systems upon which we may draw. From an interest in democratic and near-democratic or international political systems, we would now have to move to embrace all types of systems, past as well as present. Size, which has always been an implicit consideration, recedes into a less dominant position. Since we would be concerned with the processes underlying all political life, whatever form it takes, we would have to be prepared to test the general utility of concepts by their applicability to systems as small as a band of fifty Bushmen or as large as an international system encompassing hundreds of millions of persons.

But what is a systems analysis of political life that can thus help us to break the constricting bonds that tradition has imposed on the theoretical perspectives of political research? Although, as I have indicated, I have discussed this fully elsewhere, here if I am to elaborate this mode of analysis into a relatively detailed framework of concepts, it will be necessary to begin, in the next chapter, by describing, at least in broad outlines, the commitments imposed by a decision to interpret political life in systems terms.

2

Some Fundamental Categories of Analysis

IN *A Framework for Political Analysis* I SPELLED OUT IN CONSIDERABLE detail the assumptions and commitments that would be required in any attempt to utilize the concept "system" in a rigorous fashion. It would lead to the adoption of what I there described as a systems analysis of political life. Although it would certainly be redundant to retrace the same ground here, it is nonetheless necessary to review the kinds of basic conceptions and orientations imposed by this mode of analysis.[1] In doing so, I shall be able to lay out the pattern of analysis that will inform and guide the present work.

Political Life as an Open and Adaptive System

As I suggested at the end of the last chapter, the question that gives coherence and purpose to a rigorous analysis of political life as a system of behavior is as follows. How do any and all political systems manage to persist in a world of both stability and change? Ultimately the search for an answer will reveal what I have called the life processes of political systems—those fundamental functions without which no system could endure—together with the typical modes of response through which systems manage to sustain them. The analysis of these processes, and of the nature and conditions of the responses, I posit as a central problem of political theory.

Although I shall end by arguing that it is useful to interpret political life as a complex set of processes through which certain kinds of inputs are converted into the type of outputs we may call authoritative policies, decisions and implementing actions, at the outset it is useful to take a somewhat simpler approach. We may begin by viewing polit-

[1] Where it seems appropriate, I shall reiterate, without benefit of quotation marks, a few paragraphs from *A Framework for Political Analysis*. At times I find that what then seemed like the very best way to formulate my thoughts continues to be so and there seems little point in modifying the phrasing for the sake of novelty alone. Permission of the publishers, Prentice-Hall, is acknowledged.

ical life as a system of behavior imbedded in an environment to the influences of which the political system itself is exposed and in turn reacts. Several vital considerations are implicit in this interpretation and it is essential that we become aware of them.

First, such a point of departure for theoretical analysis assumes without further inquiry that political interactions in a society constitute a *system* of behavior. This proposition is, however, deceptive in its simplicity. The truth is that if the idea "system" is employed with the rigor it permits and with the implications currently inherent in it, it provides a starting point that is already heavily freighted with consequences for a whole pattern of analysis.

Second, to the degree that we are successful in analytically isolating political life as a system, it is clear that it cannot usefully be interpreted as existing in a void. It must be seen as surrounded by physical, biological, social and psychological *environments*. Here again, the empirical transparency of the statement ought not to be allowed to distract us from its crucial theoretical significance. If we were to neglect what seems so obvious once it is asserted, it would be impossible to lay the groundwork for an analysis of how political systems manage to persist in a world of stability or change.

This brings us to a third point. What makes the identification of the environments useful and necessary is the further presupposition that political life forms an *open* system. By its very nature as a social system that has been analytically separated from other social systems, it must be interpreted as lying exposed to influences deriving from the other systems in which empirically it is imbedded. From them there flows a constant stream of events and influences that shape the conditions under which the members of the system must act.

Finally, the fact that some systems do survive, whatever the buffetings from their environments, awakens us to the fact that they must have the capacity to *respond* to disturbances and thereby to adapt to the conditions under which they find themselves. Once we are willing to assume that political systems may be adaptive and need not just react in a passive or sponge-like way to their environmental influences, we shall be able to break a new path through the complexities of theoretical analysis.

As I have elsewhere demonstrated,[2] in its internal organization, a critical property that a political system shares with all other social systems is this extraordinarily variable capacity to respond to the conditions under which it functions. Indeed, we shall find that political systems accumulate large repertoires of mechanisms through which

[2] See *A Framework for Political Analysis*, especially chapter 8.

they may seek to cope with their environments. Through these they may regulate their own behavior, transform their internal structure, and even go so far as to remodel their fundamental goals. Few systems, other than social systems, have this potentiality. In practice, students of political life could not help but take this into account; no analysis could even begin to appeal to common sense if it did not do so. Nevertheless it is seldom built into a theoretical structure as a central component; certainly its implications for the internal behavior of political systems have never been set forth and explored.[3]

Equilibrium Analysis and Its Shortcomings

It is a major shortcoming of the one form of inquiry latent but prevalent in political research—equilibrium analysis—that it neglects such variable capacities for systems to cope with influences from their environment. The equilibrium approach is seldom explicitly elaborated, yet it infuses a good part of political research, especially group politics [4] and international relations. Of necessity an analysis that conceives of a political system as seeking to maintain a state of equilibrium must assume the presence of environmental influences. It is these that displace the power relationships in a political system—such as a balance of power—from their presumed stable state. It is then customary, if only implicitly so, to analyze the system in terms of a tendency to return to a presumed pre-existing point of stability. If the system should fail to do so, it would be interpreted as moving on to a new state of equilibrium and this would need to be identified and described. A careful scrutiny of the language used reveals that equilibrium and stability are usually assumed to mean the same thing.[5]

Numerous conceptual and empirical difficulties stand in the way of

[3] K. W. Deutsch in *The Nerves of Government* (New York: Free Press of Glencoe, 1963) has considered the consequences of the response capacity of political systems with regard to international affairs, although still in very general terms; some work has been done with regard to formal organizations as in the case of J. W. Forrester, *Industrial Dynamics* (New York: M.I.T. Press and Wiley, 1961); see as well, W. R. Dill, "The Impact of Environment on Organizational Development" in S. Mailick and E. H. Van Ness, *Concepts and Issues in Administrative Behavior* (Englewood Cliffs, New Jersey: Prentice-Hall, 1962), pp. 94–109 and the references there.

[4] See D. Easton, *The Political System*, chapter 11.

[5] In "Limits of the Equilibrium Model in Social Research," 1 *Behavioral Science* (1956) 96–104, I discuss difficulties created by the fact that social scientists typically fail to distinguish between stabilitiy and equilibrium. We often assume that a state of equilibrium must always refer to a stable condition whereas there are at least two other kinds of equilibria: neutral and unstable.

an effective use of the equilibrium idea for the analysis of political life.[6] But among these there are two that are particularly relevant for my present purposes.

In the first place, the equilibrium approach leaves the impression that the members of a system are seized with only one basic goal as they seek to cope with change or disturbances, namely, to re-establish the old point of equilibrium or, at most, to move on to some new one. This is usually phrased, at least implicitly, as the search for stability as though this were sought above all else. In the second place, little if any attention is explicitly given to formulating the problems relating to the path that the system takes insofar as it does seek to return to this presumed point of equilibrium or to attain a fresh one. It is as though the pathways taken to manage the displacements were an incidental rather than a central theoretical consideration.

But it would be impossible to understand the processes underlying the capacity of some kind of political life to sustain itself in a society if either the objectives or the form of the responses are taken for granted. A system may well seek goals other than those of reaching one or another point of equilibrium. Even though this state were to be used only as a theoretical norm that is never achieved,[7] it would offer a less useful theoretical approximation of reality than one that takes into account other possibilities. We would find it more helpful to devise a conceptual approach that recognized that at times members in a system may wish to take positive actions to destroy a previous equilibrium or even to achieve some new point of continuing disequilibrium. This is typically the case where the authorities may seek to keep themselves in power by fostering internal turmoil or external dangers.

Furthermore, with respect to these variable goals, it is a primary characteristic of all systems that they are able to adopt a wide range of actions of a positive, constructive, and innovative sort for warding off or absorbing any forces of displacement. A system need not just react to a disturbance by oscillating in the neighborhood of a prior point of equilibrium or by shifting to a new one. It may cope with the disturbance by seeking to change the environment so that the exchanges between the environment and itself are no longer stressful; it may seek to insulate itself against any further influences from the environment; or the members of the system may even transform their own relationships fundamentally and modify their own goals and practices so as to improve their chances of handling the inputs from the environment.

⁶ *Ibid.*

⁷ J. A. Schumpeter, *Business Cycles* (New York: McGraw-Hill, 1939), especially chapter 2, uses the idea of equilibrium as a theoretical norm.

In these and other ways a system has the capacity for creative and constructive regulation of disturbances as we shall later see in detail. It is clear that the adoption of equilibrium analysis, however latent it may be, obscures the presence of system goals that cannot be described as a state of equilibrium. It also virtually conceals the existence of varying pathways for attaining these alternative ends. For any social system, including the political, adaptation represents more than simple adjustments to the events in its life. It is made up of efforts, limited only by the variety of human skills, resources, and ingenuity, to control, modify or fundamentally change either the environment or the system itself, or both together. In the outcome the system may succeed in fending off or incorporating successfully any influences stressful for it.

Minimal Concepts for a Systems Analysis

A systems analysis promises a more expansive, more inclusive, and more flexible theoretical structure than is available even in a thoroughly self-conscious and well-developed equilibrium approach. To do so successfully, however, it must establish its own theoretical imperatives. Although these were explored in detail in *A Framework for Political Analysis,* we may re-examine them briefly here, assuming, however, that where the present brevity leaves unavoidable ambiguities, the reader may wish to become more familiar with the underlying structure of ideas by consulting this earlier volume. In it, at the outset, a system was defined as any set of variables regardless of the degree of interrelationship among them. The reason for preferring this definition is that it frees us from the need to argue about whether a political system is or is not really a system. The only question of importance about a set selected as a system to be analyzed is whether this set constitutes an interesting one. Does it help us to understand and explain some aspect of human behavior of concern to us?

To be of maximum utility, I have argued, a *political* system can be designated as those interactions through which values are authoritatively allocated for a society; this is what distinguishes a political system from other systems that may be interpreted as lying in its environment. This environment itself may be divided into two parts, the intra-societal and the extra-societal. The first consists of those systems in the same society as the political system but excluded from the latter by our definition of the nature of political interactions. Intra-societal systems would include such sets of behavior, attitudes and ideas as we might call the economy, culture, social structure or personalities; they are functional segments of the society with respect to which the political system at the focus of attention is itself a component. In a given society the systems other than the political system constitute a source of many influences that create and shape the conditions under which the political system itself must operate. In a world of newly emerging political systems we do not need to pause to illustrate the impact that a changing economy, culture, or social structure may have upon political life.

The second part of the environment, the extra-societal, includes all those systems that lie outside the given society itself. They are functional components of an international society or what we might describe as the supra-society, a supra-system of which any single society is part. The international political systems, the international economy or the international cultural system would fall into the category of extra-societal systems.

Together, these two classes of systems, the intra- and extra-societal, that are conceived to lie outside of a political system may be designated as its total environment. From these sources arise influences that are of consequence for possible stress on the political system. The total environment is presented in Table 1 as reproduced from *A Framework for Political Analysis*,[8] and the reader should turn to that volume for a full discussion of the various components of the environment as indicated on this table.

Disturbances is a concept that may be used to identify those influences from the total environment of a system that act upon it so that it is different after the stimulus from what it was before. Not all disturbances need strain the system. Some may be favorable with respect to the persistence of the system; others may be entirely neutral with respect to possible stress. But many can be expected to lead in the direction of stress.

When may we say that *stress* occurs? This involves us in a rather complex idea, one that has been treated at length.[9] But since it does stand as a major pillar underpinning the analysis to be elaborated in the succeeding chapters, I must at least broadly sketch out its implications. It embodies several subsidiary notions. All political systems as such are distinguished by the fact that if we are to be able to describe them as persisting, we must attribute to them the successful fulfillment of two functions. They must be able to allocate values for a society; they must also manage to induce most members to accept these alloca-

[8] Chapter V.
[9] In *A Framework for Political Analysis*.

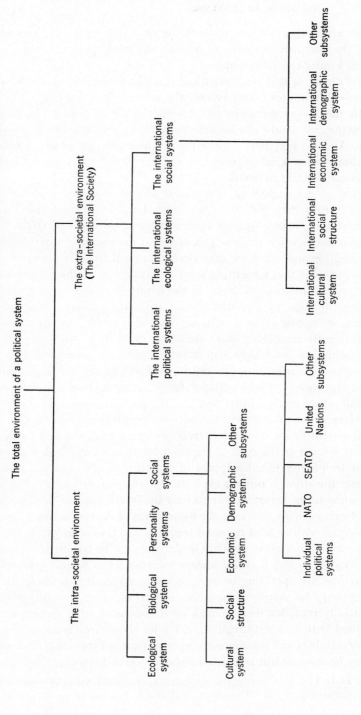

TABLE 1   COMPONENTS OF THE TOTAL ENVIRONMENT OF A POLITICAL SYSTEM

tions as binding, at least most of the time. These are the two properties that help us to distinguish most succinctly political systems from other kinds of social systems.

By virtue of this very fact these two distinctive features—the allocations of values for a society and the relative frequency of compliance with them—are the *essential variables* of political life. But for their presence, we would not be able to say that a society has any political life. And we may here take it for granted that no society could exist without some kind of political system; elsewhere I have sought to demonstrate this in detail.[10]

One of the important reasons for identifying these essential variables is that they give us a way of establishing when and how the disturbances acting upon a system threaten to stress it. Stress will be said to occur when there is a danger that the essential variables will be pushed beyond what we may designate as their *critical range*. What this means is that something may be happening in the environment— the system suffers total defeat at the hands of an enemy, or widespread disorganization in and disaffection from the system is aroused by a severe economic crisis. Let us say that as a result, the authorities are consistently unable to make decisions or if they strive to do so, the decisions are no longer regularly accepted as binding. Under these conditions, authoritative allocations of values are no longer possible and the society would collapse for want of a system of behavior to fulfill one of its vital functions.

Here we could not help but accept the interpretation that the political system had come under stress, so severe that any and every possibility for the persistence of a system for that society had disappeared. But frequently the disruption of a political system is not that complete; the stress is present even though the system continues to persist in some form. Severe as a crisis may be, it still may be possible for the authorities to be able to make some kinds of decisions and to get them accepted with at least minimal frequency so that some of the problems typically subjected to political settlements can be handled.

That is to say, it is not always a matter as to whether the essential variables are operating or have ceased to do so. It is possible that they may only be displaced to some extent as when the authorities are partially incapacitated for making decisions or from getting them accepted with complete regularity. Under these circumstances the essential variables will remain within some normal range of operation; they may be stressed but not in a sufficient degree to displace them beyond

[10] In D. Easton, *A Theoretical Approach to Authority*, Office of Naval Research, Technical Report No. 17 (Stanford, California: Department of Economics, 1955).

a determinable critical point. As long as the system does keep its essential variables operating within what I shall call their critical range, some kind of system can be said to persist.

As we have seen, one of the characteristic properties of every system is the fact that it has the capacity to cope with stress on its essential variables. Not that a system need take such action; it may collapse precisely because it has failed to take measures appropriate for handling the impending stress. But it is the existence of a capacity to respond to stress that is of paramount importance. The kind of response actually undertaken, if any, will help us to evaluate the probabilities of the system's being able to ward off the stress. In thus raising the question of the nature of the response to stress, it will become apparent, in due course, that the special objective and merit of a systems analysis of political life is that it permits us to interpret the behavior of the members in a system in the light of the consequences it has for alleviating or aggravating stress upon the essential variables.

The Linkage Variables between Systems

But a fundamental problem remains. We could not begin the task of applying this kind of conceptualization if we did not first pose the following question. How do the potentially stressful conditions from the environment communicate themselves to a political system? After all, common sense alone tells us that there is an enormous variety of environmental influences at work on a system. Do we have to treat each change in the environment as a separate and unique disturbance, the specific effects of which for the political system have to be independently worked out?

If this were indeed the case, as I have shown in detail before,[11] the problems of systematic analysis would be virtually insurmountable. But if we can devise a way for generalizing our method for handling the impact of the environment on the system, there would be some hope of reducing the enormous variety of influences into a relatively few, and therefore into a relatively manageable number of indicators. This is precisely what I have sought to effect through the use of the concepts "inputs" and "outputs."

How are we to describe these inputs and outputs? Because of the analytic distinction that I have been making between a political system and its parametric or environmental systems, it is useful to interpret the influences associated with the behavior of persons in the

[11] Chapter VII of *A Framework for Political Analysis*.

environment or from other conditions there as *exchanges* or *transactions* that cross the *boundaries* [12] of the political system. Exchanges can be used when we wish to refer to the mutuality of the relationships, to the fact that the political system and those systems in the environment have reciprocal effects on each other. Transactions may be employed when we wish to emphasize the movement of an effect in one direction, from an environmental system to the political system, or the reverse, without being concerned at the time about the reactive behavior of the other system.

To this point, there is little to dispute. Unless systems were coupled together in some way, all analytically identifiable aspects of behavior in society would stand independent of each other, a patently unlikely condition. What carries recognition of this coupling beyond a mere truism, however, is the proposal of a way to trace out the complex exchanges so that we can readily reduce their immense variety to theoretically and empirically manageable proportions.

To accomplish this, I have proposed that we condense the major and significant environmental influences into a few indicators. Through the examination of these we should be able to appraise and follow through the potential impact of environmental events on the system. With this objective in mind, I have designated the effects that are transmitted across the boundary of a system toward some other system as the *outputs* of the first system and hence, symmetrically, as the *inputs* of the second system, the one they influence. A transaction or an exchange between systems will therefore be viewed as a linkage between them in the form of an input-output relationship.

Demands and Supports as Input Indicators

The value of inputs as a concept is that through their use we shall find it possible to capture the effect of the vast variety of events and conditions in the environment as they pertain to the persistence of a political system. Without the inputs it would be difficult to delineate the precise operational way in which the behavior in the various sectors of society affects what happens in the political sphere. Inputs will serve as *summary variables* that concentrate and mirror everything in the environment that is relevant to political stress. Thereby this concept serves as a powerful tool.

The extent to which inputs can be used as summary variables will depend, however, upon how we define them. We might conceive of

[12] For a detailed analysis of boundaries see *A Framework for Political Analysis*, chapter V.

them in their broadest sense. In that case, we would interpret them as including any event external to the system that alters, modifies or affects the system in any and every possible way.[13] But if we seriously considered using the concept in so broad a fashion, we would never be able to exhaust the list of inputs acting upon a system. Virtually every parametric event and condition would have some significance for the operations of a political system at the focus of attention; a concept so inclusive that it does not help us to organize and simplify reality would defeat its own purposes. We would be no better off than we are without it.

But as I have already intimated, we can greatly simplify the task of analyzing the impact of the environment if we restrict our attention to certain kinds of inputs that can be used as indicators to sum up the most important effects, in terms of their contributions to stress, that cross the boundary from the parametric to the political systems. In this way we would free ourselves from the need to deal with and trace out separately the consequences of every different type of environmental event.

As the theoretical tool for this purpose, it is helpful to view the major environmental influences as coming to a focus in two major inputs: demands and support. Through them a wide range of activities in the environment may be channeled, mirrored, and summarized and brought to bear upon political life, as I shall show in detail in the succeeding chapters. In this sense they are key indicators of the way in which environmental influences and conditions modify and shape the operations of the political system. If we wish, we may say that it is through fluctuations in the inputs of demands and support that we shall find the effects of the environmental systems transmitted to the political system.

Outputs and Feedback

In a comparable way, the idea of outputs helps us to organize the consequences flowing from the behavior of the members of the system rather than from actions in the environment. Our primary concern is, to be sure, with the functioning of the political system. In and of themselves, at least for understanding political phenomena, we would have no need to be concerned with the consequences that political

[13] I am confining my remarks here to external sources of inputs. For the possibility of inputs deriving from internal sources and therefore constituting "withinputs," see *A Framework for Political Analysis*, chapter VII.

actions have for the environmental system. This is a problem that can or should be handled better by theories seeking to explore the operations of the economy, culture, or any of the other parametric systems.

But the fact is that the activities of the members of the system may well have some importance with respect to their own subsequent actions or conditions. To the extent that this is so, we cannot entirely neglect those actions that do flow out of a system into its environment. As in the case of inputs, however, there is an immense amount of activities that take place within a political system. How are we to sort out the portion that has relevance for an understanding of the way in which systems manage to persist?

Later we shall see that a useful way of simplifying and organizing our perceptions of the behavior of the members of the system, as reflected in their demands and support, is in terms of the consequences of these inputs for what I shall call the political outputs. These are the decisions and actions of the authorities. Not that the complex political processes internal to a system, and that have been the subject of inquiry for so many decades in political science, will be considered in any way irrelevant. Who controls whom in the various decision-making processes will continue to be a vital concern since the pattern of power relationships helps to determine the nature of the outputs. But the formulation of a conceptual structure for this aspect of a political system would draw us into a different level of analysis. Here I am only seeking economical ways of summarizing the outcomes of these internal political processes—not of investigating them—and I am suggesting that they can be usefully conceptualized as the outputs of the authorities. Through them we shall be able to trace out the consequences of behavior within a political system for its environment.

There would be little point in taking the trouble to conceptualize the results of the internal behavior of the members in a system in this way unless we could do something with it. As we shall see, the significance of outputs is not only that they help to influence events in the broader society of which the system is a part; in doing so, they help to determine each succeeding round of inputs that finds its way into the political system. As we shall phrase it later, there is a *feedback loop* the identification of which will help us to explain the processes through which the authorities may cope with stress. This loop has a number of parts. It consists of the production of outputs by the authorities, a response on the part of the members of the society with respect to them, the communication of information about this response to the authorities and finally, possible succeeding actions on the part of the authorities. Thereby a new round of outputs, response.

information feedback and reaction on the part of the authorities is set in motion and is part of a continuous never-ending flow. What happens in this feedback loop will turn out to have the deepest significance for the capacity of a system to cope with stress.

A Flow Model of the Political System

It is clear from what has been said that this mode of analysis enables and indeed compels us to analyze a political system in dynamic terms. Not only do we see that it gets something done through its outputs but we are also sensitized to the fact that what it does may influence each successive stage of behavior. We appreciate the urgent need to interpret political processes as a continuous and interlinked flow of behavior.

If we apply this conceptualization in the construction of a rudimentary model of the relationship between a political system and its environment, we would have a figure of the kind illustrated in Diagram 1. Readers of *A Framework for Political Analysis* are already familiar with this figure but it is useful to recall its details. In effect it conveys the idea that the political system looks like a vast and perpetual conversion process. It takes in demands and support as they are shaped in the environment and produces something out of them called outputs. But it does not let our interest in the outputs terminate at this point. We are alerted to the fact that the outputs influence the supportive sentiments that the members express toward the system and the kinds of demands they put in. In this way the outputs return to haunt the system, as it were. As depicted on the diagram, all this is still at a very crude level of formulation. It will be our task to refine these relationships as we proceed in our analysis.

But let us examine the model a little more closely since in effect this volume will do little more than to flesh out the skeleton presented there. In interpreting the diagram, we begin with the fact that it shows a political system surrounded by the two classes of environments that together form its total environment. The communications of the many events that occur here are represented by the solid lines connecting the environments with the political system. The arrowheads on the lines show the direction of flow into the system. But rather than attempting to discuss each disturbance in the environment uniquely or even in selected groups or classes of types, I use as an indicator of the impact that they have on the system, the way in which they shape two special kinds of inputs into the system, demands and support. This is

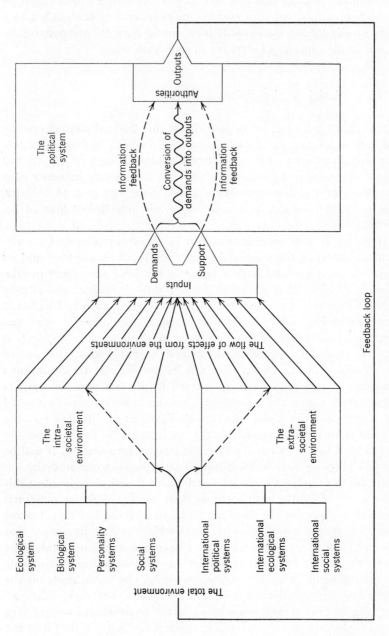

DIAGRAM 1   A DYNAMIC RESPONSE MODEL OF A POLITICAL SYSTEM

why the effects from the environment are shown to flow into the box labelled "inputs." We must remember, however, that even though the desire for simplicity in presentation does not permit us to show it on the diagram, events occurring within a system may also have some share in influencing the nature of the inputs.[14]

As is apparent, the inputs provide what we may call the raw materials on which the system acts so as to produce something we are calling outputs. The way in which this is done will be described as a massive conversion process cavalierly represented on the diagram by the serpentine line within the political system. The conversion processes move toward the authorities since it is toward them that the demands are initially directed. As we shall see, demands spark the basic activities of a political system. By virtue of their status in all systems, authorities have special responsibilities for converting demands into outputs.

If we were to be content with what is basically a static picture of a political system, we might be inclined to stop at this point. Indeed much political research in effect does just this. It is concerned with exploring all those intricate subsidiary processes through which decisions are made and put into effect. This constitutes the vast corpus of political research today. Therefore, insofar as we were concerned with how influence is used in formulating and putting into effect various kinds of policies or decisions, the model to this point would be an adequate if minimal first approximation.

But the critical question that confronts political theory is not just the development of a conceptual apparatus for understanding the factors that contribute to the kinds of decisions a system makes, that is, for formulating a theory of political allocations. As I have indicated, theory needs to know how it comes about that any kind of system can persist long enough to continue to make such decisions. We need a theory of systems persistence as well. How does a system manage to deal with the stress to which it may be subjected at any time? It is for this reason that we cannot accept outputs as the terminal point either of the political processes or of our interest in them. Thus it is important to note on the diagam, that the outputs of the conversion process have the characteristic of feeding back upon the system and shaping its subsequent behavior. Much later I shall seek to demonstrate that it is this feature together with the capacity of a system to take constructive actions that makes it possible for a system to seek to adapt or to cope with possible stress.

On the diagram, this feedback is depicted by the line that shows the

[14] See footnote 13 of this chapter.

effects of the outputs moving directly back to the environments. As the broken lines within the environmental boxes indicate, the effects may reshape the environment in some way; that is to say, they influence conditions and behavior there. In this way the outputs are able to modify the influences that continue to operate on the inputs and thereby the next round of inputs themselves.

But if the authorities are to be able to take the past effect of outputs into account for their own future behavior, they must in some way be apprised of what has taken place along the feedback loop. The broken lines in the box labeled "The political system" suggest that, through the return flow of demands and support, the authorities obtain information about these possible consequences of their previous behavior. This puts the authorities in a position to take advantage of the information that has been fed back and to correct or adjust their behavior for the achievement of their goals.

It is the fact that there can be such a continuous flow of effects and information between system and environment, we shall see, that ultimately accounts for the capacity of a political system to persist in a world even of violently fluctuating changes. Without feedback and the capacity to respond to it, no system could survive for long, except by accident.

In this brief overview, I have summarized the essential features of the analytic structure to be developed in the following chapters. If we condensed the diagram still further, we would have the figure shown on Diagram 2. It reduces to its bare essentials the fundamental proc-

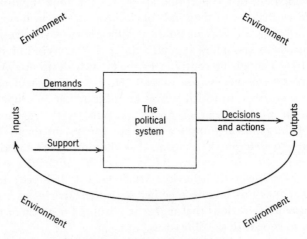

DIAGRAM 2   A SIMPLIFIED MODEL
OF A POLITICAL SYSTEM

esses at work in all systems and starkly reveals the source of a system's capacity to persist. It may well stand temporarily as the simplest image, to carry in our minds, of the processes we are about to discuss in detail.

To summarize the conceptualization being reviewed here, our analysis will rest on the idea of a system imbedded in an environment and subject to possible influences from it that threaten to drive the essential variables of the system beyond their critical range. To persist, the system must be capable of responding with measures that are successful in alleviating the stress so created. To respond, the authorities at least must be in a position to obtain information about what is happening so that they may react insofar as they desire or are compelled to do so.

In *A Framework for Political Analysis* each of these concepts and interrelationships was attended to in varying degrees of detail. Here it will be my task to begin to apply them in an effort to construct a much more elaborate structure for the analysis of political systems.

In doing so, we shall find ourselves confronted with a series of major questions. What precisely are the nature of the influences acting upon a political system? How are they communicated to a system? In what ways, if any, have systems typically sought to cope with such stress? What kinds of processes will have to exist in any system if it is to acquire and exploit the potential for acting so as to ameliorate these conditions of stress?

In posing this series of questions I have in effect outlined the major topics that will be dealt with in the rest of this volume. To begin, therefore, we shall have to turn directly to one set of influences that move toward a political system and that can be revealed through the impact that they have upon demands, the first of the inputs that needs to be considered. We shall need to explore the varying consequences that these demands, in turn, may have for the persistence of a system.

Part Two

The Input of Demands

3

Demands as the Inputs of a System

SINCE POLITICAL LIFE IS TO BE CONCEIVED AS AN OPEN SYSTEM, DEMANDS, I have suggested, offer us a key to understanding one of the ways in which the total environment will leave its impress upon the operations of the system. The demands sum up a wide range of conditions and events that are transmitted to the system.

But I am not proposing to select demands as a variable that merits our attention just because they do influence the operations of a system in some generalized way. Rather, the purpose is much more specific and directed. I am assuming something that will later become an object of special inquiry: that the demands flowing into a system constitute one of the major sources of stress acting on its essential variables. This is the primary criterion for selecting demands or, for that matter, any other input, for particular attention.

Another way of putting this is that the very reason for conceptualizing one of the major inputs in this way has been the explicit assumption that under the appropriate circumstances the demands may become a potential danger to the persistence of any kind of system at all. If this is so, to the extent that some kind of system has managed to survive historically, it will in itself be evidence that the members of the system must have been able to devise some means for handling potential dangers from this direction. When in the next chapter we finally come to consider the primary forms of such stress, I shall suggest that the capacity of a system to make binding decisions will be threatened under those conditions when demands are substantively of a type that consume excessive time in their processing or when they exceed an empirically ascertainable volume.

The identification of the breaking point for a system, when stress becomes so great that no system for allocating values authoritatively can endure, would have to wait upon empirical evidence; theoretically it could not be established in any precise way.[1] But two general conditions can be indicated. First, the point at which stress from the input

[1] See *A Framework for Political Analysis,* chapter VII, for the elaboration of "stress" as a central concept.

of demands begins to make itself felt will depend upon the type of system under examination. Some systems will be more resistant to specific kinds of stress than others. Second, whether the system founders or manages to escape the dangers will turn upon the measures that the members of the system adopt to cope with the stress. The way in which the system responds is as vital to the outcome as the nature of the initial stress itself.

The relevant sequence here is stimulus-system-response-outcome, a pattern that will apply to the input of support as well. Demands set up a disturbance, the system feels the impact, its members respond or fail to do so, and the resultant state of affairs reveals the effectiveness with which the system has managed to cope with the strain so occasioned. It is this sequence that our conceptualization will be designed to analyze and understand.

The Concept Defined

The Scope of Demands

Since the concept of "demands" [2] is so central to the mode of analysis being developed, it is imperative at the outset to clarify the meaning to be attributed to it. This task will constitute the burden of the present chapter; it will put us in a position to trace out, in the next chapter, the functions that demands perform.

A demand may be defined as an expression of opinion that an authoritative allocation with regard to a particular subject matter should or should not be made by those responsible for doing so.[3] As

[2] This concept was an integral part of a model that was initially explored several years ago in "An Approach to the Analysis of Political Systems," 9 *World Politics* (1957) 383–400. This essay has since been reproduced in a number of volumes of readings including: S. Ulmer (ed.), *Introductory Readings in Political Behavior* (New York: Rand McNally, 1961); R. Macridis and B. E. Brown (eds.), *Comparative Politics* (Homewood, Illinois: Dorsey, 1961); N. J. Smelser and S. M. Lipset (eds.), *Sociology: The Progress of a Decade* (New York: Prentice-Hall, 1961); M. L. Barron, *Sociology: A Textbook of Readings in Contemporary Classics* (New York: Dodd, Mead, 1964); and it was included in the Italian edition of *The Political System* (Milan: Edizioni di Comunità, 1963). It is pleasing to note that since the publication of this article, demands as a concept has been employed by others (see the Preface to *A Framework for Political Analysis*), although not at all times with a meaning and purpose that I can fully share.

[3] This is not to be confused with the use to which H. D. Lasswell and A. Kaplan, *op. cit.*, chapter 2, put the same concept. They describe a demand statement as "one expressing a valuation by the maker of the statement" (p. 17). For my purposes it

such, a demand may be quite narrow, specific, and simple in nature as when grievances and discontents, relevant to a given experience, are directly expressed. A flood may stimulate a demand of this type, as for a specific dam; exposure of corruption in government may give rise to a demand for improved control over lobbying.

But a call for a binding decision is no less a demand if it is highly general, vague, and complex. Broad pleas for better government, for a more vigorous defense policy, or for greater attention to the under-privileged, without specification of the exact steps to be taken, represent such highly generalized demands. Ideologies frequently embody ill-defined, all encompassing programs of action that can be realized only through binding decisions. To the extent that they do so, they can be interpreted as sets of demands.

The Direction of Demands

Demands also have a built-in direction and it takes two forms. Those who voice the demands will intend that those persons normally perceived as responsible for the day-to-day business of acting on behalf of or in the name of society shall take the desired action. In addition, the demands may be directed toward these persons but not as a suggestion that they act in a certain way. Rather, if it is thought that the current incumbents of the roles burdened with this responsibility are unlikely to be responsive to the demands, the voicers of the demands may support an overriding demand which calls for the replacement of these members.[4] But whichever form the demands take, they are directed toward the authorities.

Directionality of demands is vital. It is the expectation that the

is not necessary that the one who voices a demand impress upon it his preferences. Demands may be utilized in a purely Machiavellian way, as instruments toward power with respect to which the utterer is affectively neutral. Indeed, demands may be used to conceal the demand-maker's preferences. This happens, for example, in the case where a power-seeking counter-elite may deliberately falsify its program as a quick and efficient way to build up sufficient support to oust the incumbents. Furthermore, as I interpret Lasswell's usage, demands in his sense need not be utterances directed toward influencing authoritative allocations whereas in my conceptualization this goes to the heart of the matter.

[4] Although at a later point the concept "authorities" will identify those who have this day-to-day responsibility for governing, this does not imply that all political systems must have structurally differentiated government in our sense of the term. Nevertheless, all systems do make some distinction between those who share this responsibility and others who do not, even if these others include only the women and children, as in those tribal systems in which the authorities consist of all male adults in the group.

resolution of the differences will be accepted as binding that distinguishes political demands from other kinds.[5] Not all demands need to be satisfied in this way. Indeed, most differences in demands, even in a socialist society, are probably not negotiated through political means. Out of the enormous body of differences that members of a society may experience, the vast majority are satisfied privately by the persons involved. As I have put it elsewhere, "demands for prestige may find satisfaction through the status relationships of society; claims for wealth are met in part through the economic system; and aspirations for power find expression in fraternal, labor, educational, and similar private organizations" in our society.[6] But demands assume a political complexion when an effort is made to bring the weight of society on one's side. In such cases, efforts to influence the allocation of the values involved must ultimately be directed toward those who hold positions of authority.[7]

The Explicitness of Demands

Demands may be expressed or implied. In the first case, we may detect them most easily if they are clearly enunciated orally or in writing. In many systems, members typically engage in efforts to clarify and distribute information about demands and rally support around them.

But demands are often only implied in actions and these may at times speak as loudly as words. Voting for a candidate, the decision to assume membership in an organization and indeed, most kinds of support for others in a political context often indicates the substitution of the demands of others for one's own. Whether or not we may interpret such behavior in this way, however, would have to be demonstrated by the evidence since adherence to organizations and move-

[5] For a description of the political aspect of social life see D. Easton, *The Political System*, chapter 5 and *A Framework for Political Analysis*, chapter IV.

[6] D. Easton, "An Approach to the Analysis of Political Systems," p. 387.

[7] Changes in the direction of demands will themselves be decisive indicators of profound changes taking place in a system with regard to the location of political power. Legal claims may be viewed as demands for varying types of protection or rules. Thus, in the Middle Ages, as the relevant members took their cases out of the baronial courts and placed themselves under a developing King's law, this shift in the object toward which the demands were directed both provided evidence of the growing power of the monarchy as against the lords and barons and, at the same time, hastened the unification of modern nations and the centralization of formal power.

ments may at times be motivated by reasons other than preference for their political positions.[8]

The General Content of Demands

It may be objected that by its very nature, demands as a concept seem to attribute an imperative, self-seeking quality to political differences, as though we must interpret these inputs of a political system as an expression of the sentiment that government owes one a living. This would be true only if we confused the normal nuances of the term with its technical use here. In our special usage, a demand may call for the attainment of self-centered aims or it may well seek political decisions that impose duties and onerous obligations upon all members of the system. A demand may be inspired by a desire for private gain; but it may also be stimulated by the highest of public motives and require the most noble sacrifices.

Exclusions from the Category of Demands

If we look at what we must exclude from the category of political demands we can get a better idea of what they do in fact embrace. At the same time this procedure will enable us to examine the connection between demands and some of their determinants.

Expectations

Expectations are not to be confused with political demands. A member of a society may expect others to behave in given ways and yet he may not raise a political demand that they do so. In American society, we expect others to abide by certain conventions in social relationships, to preserve the amenities in ordinary dealings with others, to act according to certain rules of compromise and negotiation, and to strive for success in whatever we may undertake. But failure of these expectations to be fulfilled does not necessarily mean that we demand

[8] For example, members of organizations may be unaware of the objectives to which they are presumed to commit themselves. They may even be hostile to many objectives, as in the case of political parties where the member may disagree with the party platform and the position of the leadership on specific issues. Belonging may indicate only adoption of broad assumptions with regard to policy or it may offer other rewards such as prestige, association with friends and neighbors, or feelings of acceptance.

that the authorities do something about it. Only under certain conditions will frustrated expectations lead to an outcry for political action to remedy the situation. An unmet expectation may well be the stimulus for a member to put a demand into the political system. But many expectations, whether fulfilled or otherwise, never become converted into demands.[9]

Public Opinion

Strange as it may seem at first glance, public opinion need not represent public demands. If we describe public opinion as a set of attitudes on matters of public importance or concern, it is not at all unusual for members of a political system to feel, for example, that they should have more public housing and yet, in the political context of the moment, they may also hold the opinion that they ought not to press for government action. They may recognize the urgent need for housing, express themselves in an opinion survey as being in favor of having something done about it. But because of the state of the economy or the priorities of other urgent matters, they may not be prepared to take a position one way or another as to whether political action should be taken, that is, to state their position as a demand. Thus public opinion on political matters need not always be identical with political demands.

Yet public opinion may ultimately be quite influential in stimulating and shaping demands. The stability of public opinion over time, the strength of feeling behind it, and the extent to which it reflects a readiness to act are all significant determinants of the demands which a person may subsequently adopt or advocate as his own. But before an opinion can be activated as a political demand, it may need to wait for the position of a recognized leader to become known or for an issue to be formed by others. Thereby latent sentiment may be brought to a focus on possible alternatives to action and attach itself to one or another of them.

Motivations

There are other determinants of demands that exist as states of mind and that may be confused with demands. Motives, for example, may give rise to demands but are not necessarily identical with them. Members may be motivated by a desire for status, power, or release

[9] See W. C. Mitchell, *The American Polity* (New York: Free Press of Glencoe, 1962), p. 270 ff. for a fuller discussion of expectations as precursors of demands.

from boredom, by deep-seated social sympathies or patriotism. These may form the motivational matrix out of which political demands arise. But they are different from the demands in that they provide only the incentive to express an opinion for political decisions or action.

Conversely, the utterance of a demand or its vigorous defense and pursuit need not always indicate any strong sentiment directly in its favor. A political leader need have little feeling for the unemployed, in fact may be repelled by them as a group. Yet for obvious strategic reasons he may be willing to adopt their demands as his own. Sharing of demands may but need not necessarily invite sharing of motivations.

Ideology

Ideology usually covers more than a set of demands, although it may be influential in shaping them. We may here disregard the level of generality of the ideology or the scope of its concerns. It may refer narrowly to economic beliefs, such as liberalism and conservatism, or to convictions about the role of freedom, as in the case of libertarianism and authoritarianism. It may cast its net broadly, setting forth beliefs about the total organization of society including the political system, as in the case of democratic, totalitarian or authoritarian doctrines. But regardless of the scope and general content of belief systems, they may be classified according to their demand content.

At the one extreme, an ideology may be formulated as a pattern of goals for immediate or future action in which positive statements are made with respect to the kind of general program political authorities ought to pursue. In that event, the ideology may be interpreted as a very complicated set of statements incorporating varied demands in some more or less consistent or coherent pattern. At the other extreme, we can conceive of an ideology that helps members of society to orient themselves to the future and to assess the past, indicating the hope and aspirations of the adherents with regard to the organization of society but excluding any program for authoritative political action. It is doubtful whether any ideological position ever falls wholly into the one or other extreme class, whether it is entirely devoid of political demands or entirely committed to demanding that its image of the world be realized through political means. Rather, it is likely that any given ideology will just lean more or less in one or the other direction.

For example, the set of beliefs represented in contemporary economic liberalism, of nineteenth century vintage, tends toward the exclusion of political demands from its vocabulary however it might turn out if it were applied. It envisages a world in which government has withdrawn from most social spheres and proposes a policy of future political restraint, a moratorium upon additional political intervention and, among its most radical adherents, a withdrawal from most major areas of current governmental concern, including public education and postal services.

To the degree that it would require authoritative action to undo what has already been done, this ideology certainly includes demands, even though these are of a negative character. That is to say, the demands would require decisions to refrain from doing what is currently being done. Nevertheless, in its broadest ideals, this brand of conservative ideology envisages a society that requires no further action on the part of the authorities other than the protection of the members of the society from fraud, theft, and violence, and the provision of minimal kinds of services, such as defense, that are thought to be inappropriate for commitment to the hands of private enterprise. Hence, aside from the major demand for a reversal of actions already taken, this set of beliefs inclines specifically in the direction of those ideologies that do not seek the fulfillment of demands. As an ideology it could not be equated with demands; its objectives can be best attained through the operations of the politically unrestrained interactions among the members of society themselves.

Socialist ideology, however, together with the less easily labeled varied belief systems of most developing and transitional societies, move in the opposite direction. They are highly infused with political demands. Since, as belief systems, they are products of circumstances that have dictated fundamental changes in social and political relationships, it would be surprising if this dependence upon political action did not show up in the ideologies in the form of demands. Indeed, in these cases it is very difficult to separate out any elements of the ideology from demands; the ideology as a whole may be described as a broad spectrum of demands for authoritative decisions to help achieve the ideals also incorporated in the ideology. National unity, freedom, economic growth, social security, peace are all envisioned as attainable through actions that ultimately involve large scale governmental participation. In this type of ideology, therefore, we might accept the ideals as a statement of demands at the most general level, even though in each specific circumstance it would still be necessary to relate the ideals to the particular demands through which they might be implemented.

The major point here is that we cannot assume that the identification of a set of beliefs automatically reveals the political demands which a member or collectivity in the political system is putting into the political process. In each case we would still need to inquire into the extent to which the ideology embodied demands or simply pictured some future state of affairs with respect to which no immediate demands were implicated or contemplated.

Interests

Interests might easily be confused with demands. However close a connection there may be between the two, it is important to recognize that, conceptually, they are quite separate.

Interests is itself a conceptually ambiguous term in political research. It might be used to refer to the fundamental value system of an individual or group, his basic goals, hopes and aspirations in life. To use it so broadly is to destroy any specific analytic significance it may have. It is more helpful to abandon this possible meaning and retain "basic goals" or "fundamental values" as concepts for this purpose. Interests can then be more narrowly defined to refer to instrumental values, those means through which a person or group seeks to implement what may be considered to be his or its fundamental goals. In this sense, a person may speak of a law or administrative decree or policy as being in his interest. It helps him to fulfill his basic goals.

In this instrumental sense, we may describe interest as either subjective or objective. From the subjective point of view, the interest of a person is to be found in his own interpretation of what is necessary if he is to realize his broader goals. In the case of a farmer, for example, the needs he feels for a minimal income, in the face of possible crop failures or fluctuations in world market conditions, would represent his interpretation of the means necessary for him to attain the kind of life he considers necessary or fundamentally desirable. More usually, in politics, subjective interests would be attributed to groups, as where they are perceived and voiced by an organization that presumes to speak for its membership at the very least.

An objective interest may be described as those instrumental needs which others attribute to a person or group according to criteria quite independent of the subjective perceptions of that person or group. To determine what the objective interests of a person, such as a farmer, are, the observer would probably need to take into account both the long-range life situation in which the agricultural sector of society finds itself and its identified or presumed goals and values. But whatever the criteria adopted, an objective observer could then offer a judgment as to the requirements of agriculture. That is to say, the observer could specify the nature of the interests of farmers as dictated by the circumstances, regardless of what the personal awareness of farmers or farm organizations might be as to their own interests.

Thus, the farmer might seek subsidies of one sort or another to ease his concern for financial security; they would represent subjectively perceived interests. But a student of agricultural politics might argue that even if he adopts the same basic goals as does the farmer himself, the objective interests of farmers would be better served by the complete withdrawal of public support. In order to offer such a statement, the observer would have to assume certain basic goals, possess knowledge of the circumstances, profess some knowledge of the consequences of price supports or other financial aid and be able to spell out the effect of these consequences themselves on the ultimate goals of the farmer.

Due to ignorance, incompetence or other cause, the objective observer might possibly be in gross error. The subjectivity or objectivity of the interest is no certain indicator of the degree of reliability to be attached to the judgment of where a person's or group's interests lie, even if we ignore a far more complex question of how ultimate goals are to be established with reliability or sorted out from instrumental ones. But the difficulties hinted at here do not damage the principle requiring us to distinguish between subjective and objective interests.

Whether we accept a subjective or objective interpretation of interests or recognize them as mutually compatible ways of delineating and classifying interests, my point is that we cannot automatically conclude either that interests are synonymous with demands or that every interest must become incorporated into a demand. It is not difficult to appreciate the distinction between interests and demands in the case of objective interests. The persons most affected by these interests need not be aware of them; and since this is the case, they or others may not undertake to convert them into demands.

Thus we may say it is objectively in the interests of the citizens in a modern democratic system, under conditions of international crises, to seek the free flow of accurate information about foreign affairs. Yet it is doubtful that many members of democratic systems are sensitive to the existence of such a problem; much less are they likely to raise political demands in relation to it.

But even subjectively felt interests need not always be elevated to the level of potential political discussion as a demand. There are many areas of life that members of a system will not consider to be appropriate matters for political settlement. In the United States many physicians feel a keen sense of responsibility about strengthening the code of conduct in their profession for the protection of the patient as well as for the long-run maintenance of trust and confidence in the patient-doctor relationship. Yet this interest in medical ethics and the deeply felt need to do something about it may not be and, typically, is not accompanied by a demand for authoritative decisions.

The expression of an interest in a matter is not identical with the input of a demand. To become a demand, there needs to be voiced a proposal that authoritative action be taken with regard to it.

Preferences

Finally, many kinds of preferences are stated with respect to behavior in a political system that need not fall into the category of demands. Members of a system might well desire to see political leaders act more honestly, consistently, effectively or with greater drive. They might prefer a political structure that lends itself to more responsible action on the part of the authorities or that more readily permits members to identify those who are to blame. But as we have seen in the case of public opinion, it is one thing to wish that something were different; it is quite another to assert that there ought to be authoritative action in the matter. It is thus possible that members may express many more preferences, wishes or desires for a different state of affairs than they are prepared to support, if only verbally, as a possible basis for political decision.

Demands as the Major Informational Input

In the use to which the term "demand" is being put here, we can readily apprehend that it assumes a quite technical meaning. If we wish, we may conceive of many kinds of information being put into a political system other than what I am designating as demands. Members also put in expectations, opinions, expressions of motivations, ideologies, interests and statements of preferences. At times these may be identical with demands; at others they may be just partial determinants of these demands. The probability of a demand arising and the content given to it will be strongly shaped by the nature, intensity, and persistence of expectations, opinions, beliefs, interests and the like. And the demands, once voiced, may in turn react back upon and modify the very opinions, ideologies, and interests that gave them birth.

From among some of the numerous possible informational inputs already indicated, why should we select out demands to the exclusion of others, at least as our central dependent variable, that with which we shall be particularly concerned? The reply to this question requires our close attention.

The Further Function of Demands

In the first place, I have already discussed the vital role that demands play as a summary variable that enables us to join economically many of the happenings in the environment of a system to processes within the system itself. I shall pursue this boundary exchange function much more fully in the immediately succeeding chapters.

In the second place, in the selection of demands as a central variable, I shall be focusing on a main point of contention in political life. Conflicts over demands constitute the flesh and blood of all political systems, from the smallest to the largest and from the simplest to the most complex. Not that we shall be disinterested in preferences, expectations, interests, ideologies, or other possible informational inputs. But they can be excluded from the category of inputs without any loss of power in dealing with them. They will assume relevance for our analysis only if they turn out to be significant for an understanding of what some or all of the members of a system think that the authorities should do or if, as we shall later see, they influence the input of support.

Demands may be conceived as a central variable for the simple fact that without them there would literally be no occasion to undertake the making of binding decision for a society. For example, if we could find a political system in which the input of demands shrank to zero, we could be certain that the system was in process of disintegrating. There would be no reason for its continued existence except for some limited time as a cultural remnant or an historical anomaly.

The reason for this is that without some inflow of demands there would be no raw material for the system to process, no conversion work for it to do. What a political system does or what is done in its name, it does not do or is not done without some incentive. Something has to spark a decision or action. It must take the form of a suggestion, proposal, invitation, or insistent and voiced concern on someone's part for authoritative decisions or actions.

It is true, some political ideologies, such as philosophical anarchism, foresee the deliquescence of all political structure if men lived up to their presumed potential for the cooperative resolution of all their differences through bilateral or multilateral negotiation among individual members or collectivities. But short of the attainment of this millennium, the inability of the members of a society to meet all their wants, needs, and desires through independently cooperative activity compels them to call upon the resources of society as a whole to settle differences. For some limited purposes at least, they must seek to commit the whole society to supporting action in favor of these unsatisfied desires.[10]

Regardless of the purposes which might be pursued in the name of a system, there is nothing so magical or esoteric about the activities of its members that enables them to make authoritative decisions out of the thin air. They must have before them some range of alternatives from which a selection may be made. Without the assertion of demands the politically dominant members of a system could not orient themselves to the major problems requiring their attention nor could they bring their energies to a focus. Whether these problems involve the defense of the society, the survival of a ruling class, the perpetuation of a bureaucracy, provision of public service, someone must bring the cause or need for action to the attention of those primarily responsible for making decisions.

At times these receptors through which problems are transmitted to the various decision centers may consist of any one in the system at all, if the operating rules and structure of the system permit. In a democracy this is at least formally true. It provides for the broadest sweep of members who may voice demands for political action. But in an autocracy, only a member of the inner circle of rulers may be permitted this privilege, and then perhaps under very limited conditions that sharply restrict the content of what may be introduced and the propagation of the demand itself.

But in all systems, some one or group must be able to say: this ought to be done. And if there is instantaneous agreement, some one must also be in a position to say: it ought to be done in this way, not that way. This is the direction-yielding consequence of the airing of demands, whether they are being presented to the Central Committee of the Party in the USSR, to the American public, or to a council of elders in a tribe. Only in the limiting and extraordinary case where

[10] The nature of the purposes for which political decisions are sought will vary with time and place. It is true, as we shall have occasion to note in chapter 22, that students of politics have drawn up lists of goals assumed to be common to all systems, such as the pursuit of peace, justice, welfare, or defense. But surveys of even broader ranges of political systems than those of the Western world have indicated, as we shall see, that not even these highly general objectives can be included among the demands of all systems.

one member of a system and he alone could raise matters for consideration, consider them by himself in isolation, arrive at a decision and act upon them, could we say that demands played no part.

Not even a small consanguineous band of Eskimos can decide when and where to move in its search for food without entertaining the suggestions of one or another of the elders with regard to possible alternatives. However spontaneously a small group may appear to behave, it would be only under atypical conditions that even a relatively homogeneous small society would speak with one voice, excluding at least some deliberation and consultation with regard to alternatives. It is these alternatives, in a very simple, undifferentiated political system, that constitute the demands being fed into it as a basis for decision and action, however informal and indistinct the process may be to the observer. The more complex, heterogeneous and differentiated a political structure, the more likely it is that the members will speak in many separate voices, given the opportunity.

The Rationality of Demands

Not that all men are so rational that they insist upon a careful weighing of alternatives before participating in collective action. A demand need not be a rationally calculated position designed to maximize one's advantage and minimize those of a possible opponent or conflicting claimant. A demand may well express a deep emotional response toward a problem. On the other hand, it may also emerge from a thorough, disinterested examination of a situation by the most highly qualified experts, as in the case of proposals for reform of fiscal policy in modern systems.

The Relationship of Demands to Support

The conceptualization of demands in this way implies the possibility of separating them from support, at least for analytic purposes. For the present, support can be understood in its ordinary, commonsense meaning. The fact that demand and support may be analytically independent does not mean that they appear separately in political interaction. On the other hand, the fact that we may not be able to pare off a demand from the support associated with it in the phenomenal world cannot and will not prevent us from looking for the independent effects that variations in demands—or for that matter, of support —have upon a system. The voltage and amperage of an electric current are closely interrelated and never appear separately. Yet each of them describes and accounts for a very different effect of electricity. In much the same way we may view demands and support as normally appearing together, although with much less interdependence than in the case of the mentioned components of an electric current.

Although in later chapters I shall devote considerable attention to exploring the special significance of support, we can shed further light on the characteristics of demands as inputs if at this point we examine their relationship to support. In the normal course of events, by the very act of voicing a demand or proposing it for serious discussion, a member will imply that he supports it in some measure. Hence the problem here is not one of showing that demands are usually accompanied by an expression of support. Rather, we need to draw attention to the further condition that wherever we find some support for a position, it is both possible and useful to abstract the position itself, that is, the demands, for separate analysis. Whatever the reasons may be, there has been an unmistakable tendency in political research to lose sight of demands as such an independent analytic factor. Insofar as there has been theoretical research in this area, it has dwelt on the support side of political interaction; [11] demands represent the other side of the coin and they merit at least equal and independent attention.

Although demands are analytically distinct from support, they may at times appear empirically as points of considerable concentration in the activities of the members of a system. Such extreme instances indicate the practicality of treating demands as possible independent sources of stress on a system. For example, at party conferences and conventions, demands are formulated, revised, fought over, and negotiated in the construction of a party platform. Ever present is the effect that one as against another version will have upon the popular success of the party or its ability to hold its component groups together. This is a problem of the support potentialities of the program and this includes the formal demands.

Temporarily, however, the focus at party conventions is on what shall be said, what shall be proposed as the course of action for the coming period, what shall be the demands. This is a problem of the

[11] See most of the large volume of voting studies. The limited theory emerging from these studies relates to who supports whom and why. Even to this degree, the emphasis is very narrowly restricted to one kind of support, that flowing to competitors for the leadership positions among the political authorities. Support of those fundamental aspects of a political system that I shall call the regime and political community has drawn negligible interest and attention.

content and volume of demands. It is conceivable, although not likely, that a party's activities could stop here; having hammered together a platform, it could decide to do nothing about rallying support behind it. Typically however, once the platform is adopted, the emphasis shifts. There may still be differences with regard to the interpretation of what the platform means in whole or part, and individual leaders may inject new issues into a popular debate. But at least in those political systems in which party platforms are taken with some measure of seriousness as an indication of party intention and commitment, the shift is in the direction of carrying the message, that is, the set of demands, to those who count in the system, in order to build up support.

Although parties are typically devices for generating support, and, therefore, the image that both they themselves and others have of them militates against parties confining themselves exclusively to the formulation of programs of action, there are many groups in democratic systems that conceive of their task in precisely these more limited terms. They examine social problems, say with regard to the economy or foreign affairs, and then issue documents, statements or formal proposals outlining what they consider to be appropriate policies in a given area. They may carefully refrain from engaging in a campaign to stimulate support on behalf of their proposals. They conceive their job well done when they have given voice to a carefully considered set of demands, say, with regard to government policy, and have communicated this information to others. With respect to groups such as these, the injection of demands into the political system constitutes, if not their sole function, at least their major and most visible one.

In industrially advanced societies there has developed some institutional differentiation between those who seek to formulate and propose alternatives for action and those who see their task as that of participating in building up support around these demands. The presence of such structural differences in some systems testifies even more forcefully that it makes sense to view demands as an input separate from support, at the very least analytically, and, at times, even as a reflection of what happens phenomenally.

The Meaning of the "Input" of a Demand

Before we can consider the stress that inputs of demands as such may impose upon a system, we must also decide how we are to determine when a demand has been "put into" the political system. The accident of language and the constraints of diagrams make it seem that there is something appearing on the outside of a political system that is then inserted into it. What sense does it make to use such imagery?

As a first approximation this is precisely the kind of impression that needs to be created. But we cannot take this literally. It is just conceptual imagery for purposes of helping us to understand the process taking place. In fact, it is quite obvious that neither inputs nor members of society literally step out of the economy or culture into the political system and back again as though they were moving to and fro among the rooms of some societal mansion. What this formulation seeks to convey, rather, is the idea that political demands may arise as a result of experiences persons undergo in sectors of society that are not directly concerned with politics. If any movement or oscillation occurs, it is between political and non-political roles. To say that a person puts in a demand is an elliptical way of indicating that momentarily, at least, he is participating in a political act.

For example, a social phenomenon occurs such as the gradual transformation of the structure of industrial organizations, the onset of a depression, a sudden and unregulated spurt in urban growth. Each may lead persons to call upon political leaders to take kinds of action hitherto uncontemplated; or the changes may induce political leaders to initiate proposals for such action themselves long before other members of the system have an inkling as to what might or should be done. The initial stimulus for the expression of the view that an authoritative allocation of some sort should be adopted emerges in this instance from experiences in non-political sectors of life. Events related to the non-political roles of members of society lead to changes in the things that they want, expect, need, prefer or believe in. The changes in these social determinants of existence help to induce and shape the expression of what members of society consider politically desirable or necessary.

When such a process occurs, resulting in members giving voice to a demand, we shall conceive that a demand has been "put into" the political system. As we shall later see, this may be conceptualized as the starting point of the political processes. The input thereby acts as that concrete link, about which I have already spoken, between what happens in other aspects of social life and in politics. Demands bridge the gap between political and non-political sectors of life and, as we have seen, are therefore also vital for helping us to understand the way in which transformations in the one affect the other.

The Sources Stimulating Inputs of Demands

Inputs of demands cannot be narrowly restricted only to those that are stimulated in the non-political sectors of society, that is, in the intra-societal environments as in the illustration just used. A political system exists in multiple environments [12] and our focus on demands is a convenient and theoretically acceptable way of linking events in any one of these environmental systems to the political system. Persons acting in and stimulated by their roles in any environmental system may thereby be led to demand binding decisions of some sort. In formal terms, independent variations of varied types of parameters of the political system will influence the input of demands.[13]

For example, at times demands may originate in that part of the extra-societal environment that lies in other political systems, as in the case where an American law firm or lobby acts for a foreign industry or government to mold or defeat a bill before the American legislature.[14] Such demands may be viewed as intakes of the American political system flowing from separate political systems at the same level of analysis. The interaction is between two analytically equivalent political systems from different societies so that the input is from society to society as well as from political system to political system.

In addition, frequently what people demand may derive from wants, opinions, preferences or interest bred within the political system itself. In this case, demands can be said to originate directly among persons acting in their political as against some other type of social role or as against a political role in a political system of a different society.

For example, from his own experiences in politics, a legislative representative or political executive might be led to suggest modifications to the political structure, a kind of demand that only someone who had intimate contact with political life might be led to espouse.

[12] The idea of multiple environments appears in W. R. Dill, *op. cit.*, especially at p. 106. For the differences between intra- and extra-societal environments, see *A Framework for Political Analysis*, chapter V.

[13] In chapter 23 I shall deal with the theoretical problems created by the fact that through feedback response political outputs may influence these apparently independent variables and thereby, indirectly at least, help to shape the inputs themselves.

[14] In 1953, an American law firm acted for the Chamber of Commerce of a foreign oil producing country to defeat an oil bill which would have restricted the import of foreign residual oil into the United States.

In the United States, proposals for revision of the procedures for the nomination of Presidential candidates or for the organization of political parties are of this sort.

Similarly in transitional societies, it is common to witness the birth of new counter-elites out of a previously existing leadership or spawned by some newly emerging social groups. Counter-elites frequently voice demands for reform of the existing political structure so as to improve their chances of obtaining power. Their proposals may take the form of demands for increased liberalization of electoral laws or for firmer adherence to the rule of law, especially in recognition of broader limits for freedom of speech and organization. In instances such as these, to the extent that demands can be shown to arise out of and reflect dissatisfaction with the current structure of the political system, we can say that they are internally generated.

We can scarcely insist that demands such as these have been "put into" the political system in the same sense as we have been using the idea to this point. These demands do not arise from the experiences of persons who have acted in roles outside the political sector of society. They emerge directly out of political roles themselves, that is, from within the system. I have already proposed the awkward term "withinputs" to describe those demands formed through experiences and activities in strictly political roles.[15] Demands such as these differ from the inputs we have been discussing in that the latter are shaped by such parameters as culture, economy, social structure, and the like, whereas withinputs are politically determined.

From a methodological point of view, the idea of withinputs presents us with a boundary problem. Whereas the externally influenced demands must cross the boundary from parameters to political system—thereby creating an exchange between the social environment and the system—the internally shaped demands may just flow from one subsystem within a political system to another. Demands may move from a party subsystem to the legislative subsystem, as in the case of a party proposal to the legislature for an amendment to an electoral law. Boundaries need not be relevant for all purposes and consequently they may be ignored when the occasion requires it without impeding the analysis or creating any logical inconsistencies. For tracing out the effect of variations in demands on a political system, the fact that demands are determined by variables within the political system is quite irrelevant. Both inputs and withinputs press themselves in the same way upon members of the system as a possible agenda for discussion. Their implications for stress on the system are

[15] See chapter 2, footnote 13.

identical. We may therefore assimilate them both under the one category that I am calling inputs. For this limited purpose we may conceptually ignore the boundary of political systems even though for other purposes it may be necessary to insist upon awareness of the existence of such a boundary.

This chapter has offered a more elaborate description of the meaning of demand as a central concept, distinguished it from other objects with which it could easily be confused such as expectations, public opinion, motivations, ideology, interests and preferences, and has sought to demonstrate the validity of peeling it away analytically from support. In the process it has been possible to seek to allay any lingering doubts about the central importance of demands in the analysis of political life and about the utility of conceptualizing such demands as inputs of a political system.

But this discussion has been largely preliminary to the main thrust of our conceptual formulation. It has been necessary to clear away these kinds of ambiguities or obscurities so that we may move unhampered by unnecessary reservations into a discussion first, of the way in which demands may act as stressors of a system and second, of the kinds of responses typically available to political systems regardless of their general or specific type.

4

Demands as Source of Stress

REGARDLESS OF THE TYPES OF SYSTEM WE CONSIDER, I SHALL PROPOSE in this chapter that demands have the capacity to impose strains on a system by driving its essential variables toward their critical limits. If the inflow of demands is so heavy as to require excessive time for processing, or if substantively the demands are of such a kind as to lead toward a similar condition, I shall argue that this will tend to undermine the capacity of a system to produce its characteristic outputs, authoritative decisions.

Types of Demand Stress

Demand-Related Stress

Demands may act as stressors on a system in two different ways. First, to the extent that the demands remain unfulfilled, they may lead to the decline of support for a system in one or another of several aspects yet to be discussed. As we shall see, the relationship between demands and outputs may be so far out of balance as to stimulate active opposition, not only to the existing authorities but to the regime or political community as well.

The reasons for the failure to satisfy demands may be quite varied. The resources may not be equal to the task, as is the case in many developing nations today. Contact with the West has stimulated an interest in and desire for many of the benefits available only after a high level of wealth and economic growth have been achieved, a condition still in the distant future for these nations. But even in those systems in which the means may be available, the authorities may be quite unresponsive to the demands of various politically potent segments of the population. This can be as true of a democracy as of a totalitarian regime. The social origins, ideological perspectives, accessibility to pressure from different social groups in the system and the perceptiveness of the authorities all help to determine the groups to which the authorities will be more likely to make concessions or to whose wishes they will listen more attentively and grant greater consideration.

But the stress occasioned for a system as a result of such dissatisfaction with the way in which or degree to which demands are fulfilled is due to a decline in support, and not strictly to the character of the demands themselves. There certainly is a connection with demands; but for the kinds of demands being voiced, there would be no incentive even to seek to meet them and there would be no disappointment at failure to do so. But the threat for the system derives directly from the failure, for reasons only indirectly associated with characteristics of the demands, to maintain an adequate level of support. We can, therefore, conveniently postpone discussion of this kind of stress to a much later point, when we consider outputs.

Stress Due Directly to Demands

Demands may induce stress in a second and this time direct way. On the one hand, in any given state, a system is able to accept and process only a determinate amount of information with respect to what is demanded, at least in a specified interval of time. It is certainly impossible to conceive of a system that could absorb and give consideration to any and every number of demands. Every political system must have some finite capacity with respect to the number of demands it can accept for processing into decisions or consider as a possible basis of choice. It will have only some finite amount of time available to devote to settling differences politically. Neither the channels along which information flows nor the time available for processing such demands are infinitely expansible. In principle, what we may designate as *demand input overload* [1] could be said to describe a system if, within a specified time interval, the number of demands exceeded an empirically determinable limit. In excess of these numbers, we would expect that unprocessed demands would begin to pile up, some might get no attention at all and others might ultimately be dealt with but too late to do any good.

When a system is confronted with a situation in which the input of information conveying demands becomes too great for the responsible members of the system to process for possible conversion to decisions, the system cannot help but operate under the danger of collapse. This

---

[1] Compare with J. G. Miller, "Information Input Overload" in M. C. Yovits, G. T. Jacobi and G. D. Goldstein (eds.), *Self-Organizing Systems 1962* (Washington, D.C.: Spartan, 1962), pp. 61–78.

condition I shall designate as *excessive volume stress*. As in all other cases of stress, the point at which the volume begins to disturb a system seriously will vary with the structures and operating rules within the system. The danger point from any stress may always be different, within a broad range, for each class of system and even for each specific system within that class.

But on the other hand, volume is not the sole characteristic of demands that may induce stress. The kinds of demands, as determined by their content, would also have an important bearing upon the capacity of a system to provide for their processing.

Not all demands are substantively the same. Some lead to far greater contention among the members of the system or are far more complex in terms of the conditions that their fulfillment would create. In the normal course of events, such demands would require considerably more time for processing than others about which there is greater consensus or that are simpler in their implications.

In any interval of time, the content of the demands would have a vital bearing on the amount of time that would need to be expended in processing them. We must, of course, continue to postulate that no system has an infinite amount of time at its disposal for formulating and converting demands into outputs. This seems reasonable since at the very least there are many other things to be done in a political system aside from processing demands. If, at some point, the content of the demands requires an amount of time excessive for the system, it could not help but experience stress. Its capacity to produce outputs would be seriously impaired, if not destroyed. It would have the same effect as too large a volume in a specified interval of time. I shall designate this kind of strain on a system as *content stress* although, where it seems appropriate, I shall feel free to include it within volume stress since it is a subtype of such stress.

Demand Stress and Output Failure

To explain the stress caused by excessive volume and the time-consuming substance of demands, it is not enough to say that they would prevent the authorities from producing outputs. We must pose a further question: why is it that the failure to produce outputs might prevent some or any kind of political system from persisting?

The reason is that to the extent that demands remain unfulfilled, it is strongly possible, although not inevitable, that what I shall designate as output failure, will occur. This is a condition in which outputs

prove insufficient to hold the minimal support of the politically significant members. Output failure is a complex phenomenon and our
analysis is not as yet sufficiently advanced to be able to explore it in
detail. But it will be enough to say here that the stress associated with
it is due to the fact that under certain circumstances, the failure to
meet the demands of at least the politically powerful members in a
system will undermine the basic support for the system.

Not that we need ever find a system that we can say has succumbed
as a result of its inability to cope with a given volume of demands or
with substantively stressful sorts. Even if every system were able to
handle its demands with greater or lesser success, the fact that it has
been able to do so, regardless of time requirements, must itself be explained. That is to say, many of the activities and structures within
political systems could not be fully understood unless we saw their
relationship to demands as a potential source of stress.

Thus two separate problems present themselves. We must explore
the nature of those tendencies in the input of demands that become
possible sources of strain on a system. This we shall deal with in the
present chapter. We must then inquire into illustrative and typical
ways in which political systems have been able to handle these kinds of
stressful conditions so as to protect the system from collapse. These we
shall discuss in the immediately succeeding chapters.

Volume Stress

The Reality of Volume Stress

What is implied in the idea of stress due to an increasing volume of
demands, to the overloading of a system with demands? Speculatively,
we might think it possible for a system to deal with any number of
demands and this might be true if a system had an unlimited amount
of time to devote to them. But once we introduce the constraint of
restricted time, the need to process demands within some interval of
time, the magnitude of the task confronting systems becomes apparent.

A system is not an undifferentiated aggregate of human beings. It
has structure and in all but the smallest systems, it will consist of many
subsystems. In characterizing a system as being subject to the stress of
excessive volume in demands, the overload need not affect each subsystem in identical ways. Any subsystem may be affected differentially
and may respond in its own way to the stress so occasioned.

If we consider only the special case of democratic systems for the moment, it has frequently been observed that the great increase in issues, especially in recent years, threatens to tax the machinery for organizing an agenda for public discussion. It becomes increasingly difficult to bring public attention to a focus on the critical issues of the day.

In the first place, even the individual member may be threatened with demand input overload. Indeed, voting research has shown that one of the services performed by ideologies or belief systems and stable party identification is that they help to structure underlying attitudes. They represent a psychological economizing mechanism that frees the individual from the onerous need to evaluate each demand or issue separately. On logical grounds, it has also been suggested, it would be quite irrational for members of a system to attempt to do so.[2]

In the second place, those responsible on a day-to-day basis for converting demands into decisions and actions—the authorities—constitute another subsystem typically exposed to demand overload. Under modern conditions they are frequently confronted with such an array of demands that any effort to consider all of them would impose virtually insuperable burdens. The volume of bills appearing before the American federal legislature, for example, has increased enormously, exposing it constantly to demand input overload.[3] One Senator has complained that even in the short interval of about fifteen years, the "Congressional workload" has increased about 60 per cent in terms of the number of bills or resolutions initiated.[4] Our current awareness of the load that the volume of demands imposes on authorities in most industrialized societies testifies to the plausibility of the idea that this is a major source of stress.

Indeed we may go further. It will be possible to demonstrate in the next chapters that no system really leaves the matter of volume (or content) of demands to chance. The converse is clearly the case. Every system, from the smallest Bushman band to the most complex industrialized society must provide some method for regulating the number of demands if the system is to persist in any form at all.

Measurement of the Volume of Demands

If we are to speak intelligibly about the overload of demands put into a system, our first task is to indicate how we shall go about measuring the number of demands present at any moment of time.

[2] A. Downs, *op. cit.*

[3] See the table presented by W. C. Mitchell, *op. cit.*, p. 393.

[4] Senator H. H. Humphrey, "To Move Congress Out of Its Ruts," *The New York Times*, Magazine Section, April 7, 1963, p. 129.

Can we assume that each demand counts as one regardless of the differing significance that each person attributes to the content? Can we sum demands at all? [5]

If we tried to consider each expressed demand as equivalent, for counting purposes, to any other demand, it might seem that we would be letting ourselves in for serious difficulties. If a member of a system argues that there ought to be more housing and stops at this indication of what he thinks government ought to do, shall we count this as one expressed demand? If someone else holds the same conviction but is better informed, he may express himself in a series of demands for slum clearance, Cabinet status for housing and improved availability of cheap mortgage money. Is the more detailed specification of steps sought for adding to the supply of housing to be counted as a greater number of demands or simply as elements of one larger demand? The particularity or generality of specification of a demand or set of demands seems to have some bearing upon the number put into a system. Yet the content of the more general but single demand for increased housing may imply as much as, if not more than the specific detailing of varied demands in the second case.

These illustrations suggest that many demands are so broad in nature that we might feel disposed to break them down into the larger number of subsidiary demands that are obviously implied within them. Such implicit demands would have to be satisfied before the overarching, general demand itself could be fulfilled.

But there are compelling reasons for taking voiced demands at their face value and refusing to read into them a numerical value for unexpressed but potential future demands. Implied demands cannot properly be counted as existing ones. It may be helpful to recognize that such demands may be forthcoming at a later stage; one can prepare for them, especially if the nature of the initial demand is such as to indicate clearly that secondary demands must quickly be entertained once the original demand has been adopted. But until such follow-up demands are in fact made, they are only implicit or future demands

[5] For a suggestion about indicators of demand volume, see K. W. Deutsch, *op. cit.*, pp. 125–126 who argues that "it might be possible to estimate very roughly the rise in the volume of political demands made upon the government from the rate of social mobilization, that is, the rate at which people leave the seclusion of subsistence agriculture and village life, their control of tradition, and the isolation of illiteracy and lack of contact with mass communications. The rates at which people leave these conditions and enter the ambit of the money economy, wage labor, urban life, literacy, exposure to mass media, and partial acculturation to modernity have been in part measured, and average estimates for the over-all process have been derived from them."

rather than actual or present ones. It would be premature to include them in any count of the current demand load on the system. Since they are unexpressed, they are not commanding the efforts of the members and therefore do not contribute to the workload of the system.

Kinds of Countable Demand Units

The demands being put into a system may be totaled in two different ways. We could count the frequency with which a single demand is repeated in the specified interval under consideration and we could also make a tally of the number of different kinds of demands that occur. Frequency of repetition of a single demand and the absolute variety of demands both contribute to the total of all demands relevant for system stress.

Frequency of repetition of the same demand may account for a large part of the demand load on a system. In measuring this, we would have to sum all demands voiced on behalf of the same output or policy. It would itself include two component elements: all the demands voiced by all those members who are expressing views in favor of the same policy as well as the total number of times with which any single member or group voiced a separate demand for this policy.

Thus, many members may each be putting in a demand once and only once for housing; or a single member may be expressing a demand for housing repeatedly over the interval of time under consideration. Both kinds of utterances on behalf of housing would have to be included among the total number of demands being expressed.

Frequency of repetition is an important indicator of the number of demands being put into a system. Without it, we would find it impossible to give due weight and consideration to the addition to the workload of a system contributed by the persistence of any single demand over a period of time. Some demands appear once, linger on for a while and disappear. Others, such as proposals in the United States for medical care, are repeated year after year and have increased their number of adherents with time. If we were to count any demand only once, at the time it appears, it would prove impossible to give the necessary added weight to those demands which, through frequent repetition, persist and in doing so, add to the load that the information channels in the system must bear.

The quantity of demands may also be made up, in part, of a number of demands being voiced with respect to different kinds of content or subject matter, that is, of a variety of demands. From the point of view of their stressful qualities, it is important to include and weigh separately the contribution made by the variety of demands to the total number being put into a system. A thousand expressions of demands for the same outputs would not be as stressful as an expression of a thousand different demands, assuming for the moment some equivalence of support behind these demands. The time and resources necessary to process the varied demands would greatly exceed that required for the single constant demand.

There can be little doubt that variety of demand input has become a major problem in the twentieth century. And here we may postpone consideration of the impact of the substantive content of these varied demands; we shall come to content in a moment. It has frequently been noted that with the growth of industrialism in the West—and now in the non-Western developing nations as well—popular participation has not only led to a marked increase in the number of persons able to voice support for the same demand, but in addition, it has brought about a revolutionary change in the variety of demands being made upon government. The increase already noted with respect to democratic legislatures is only in part one of having many persons put pressure on their legislators for action with respect to the same area of policy. It also reflects the enormous growth in the variety of things that members of these systems feel the authorities ought to undertake. Demands in the fields of health, social security, transportation facilities, preservation of natural resources, civil rights or special benefits for various interest groups were virtually unknown as little as fifty years ago.

This variety adds another dimension to the total number of demands being put into these systems. The input load competing for the attention of the authorities not only includes many demands, but also many different types of demands. In this way, the increased number imposes variety as an added load on the authorities. They may need to diversify their interests, knowledge, allocations of time and the like in order to be able to handle the increased kinds of demands being directed toward them.

Sources of Volume Stress

Volume stress, we have seen, will stem from the fact that those in a system primarily involved in processing demands through to decisions and actions can handle only a certain number of demands in any period of time. More than that, it is not unreasonable to assume that they will have to take some measures to make it possible to regulate the inputs if the system is to persist. What these are we shall see in succeeding chapters.

But we can improve our conceptualization of how excessive volume incapacitates the members of a system for processing demands if we now conceive of demands as information or messages that flow through political channels. From this point of view, it is obvious that every political system must have some finite channel capacity for transmitting information about demands to the various points where they require processing, as they proceed to the output stage. That there are such definable points will appear in the next few chapters.

This conceptualization offers us another way of interpreting volume stress. Stress from a large number of demands will occur if they require greater channel space than is available or that can be readily produced by the system. For example, if the channel is a newspaper or a legislative representative, the paper can carry only so much printed material and the representative can handle only a certain amount of mail or listen to only a limited number of persons in his office or, in developing nations, at the bazaar.[6] As the number of demands flowing along the information channels in a system begins to exceed their carrying capacity, the overloading means neglect of some, superficial attention to others and so on, as we shall see.

But at the moment I am not concerned with how such overloading is handled; neglect or inadequate attention are only two possible ways of coping with such a situation. Rather, I wish to establish what it is that is taking place that leads to stress on the system.

Perhaps a good illustration of the effects of excessive volume is to be found in the analogy with an airport traffic control tower. The controllers in the tower may be stressed in at least two different ways and a glance at these will help us to understand better what happens in a political system. In the first place, if messages from aircraft are viewed as demands being made upon the controllers, the traffic system would break down if so many messages were coming through, during any specified interval of time, that the controllers could not process them under the prevailing structure and operating rules. Output failure would result not because of the inadequacy of the channels; they are able to carry the flow of information. But it is the recipients who are unable to process them in the time at their disposal. It is one form of stress and we shall return to it in a subsequent chapter.

But in the second place, regardless of the capacity of the controllers

[6] Comments on the limited absorptive capacity of Congressmen are offered by R. A. Bauer, I. Pool, and L. A. Dexter, *American Business and Public Policy* (New York: Atherton Press, 1963), especially Part V.

to handle incoming messages about location, speed and direction of aircraft under their jurisdiction, messages being sent to the tower are clearly dependent upon the number and capacity of the available air channels. Where the volume of incoming messages is excessive, the frequencies become clogged as the messages seek to move toward the decision centers. Whereas we might characterize the incapacity of the decision-makers to handle the flow of information as response failure, in this instance we could describe what happens as channel failure.

Although some political systems such as those composed of small consanguineous bands—among the Eskimo, for example—may possess a much simpler set of communication channels than a traffic control center at a large modern airport, in most cases political systems are transparently far more complex. Nevertheless, since it is certainly valid to interpret demands as messages and since we can and do talk about there being more or less of them, we therefore do in fact measure their quantity, at least ordinally. We shall soon see, too, that they flow through a system. If we wish, we may choose to describe the paths they take as channels. It would then become realistic to visualize the possibility of these channels becoming overloaded due to an excessive volume.

In the case of the control towers, it seldom happens that conditions are allowed to deteriorate to the point where the system actually collapses; measures are usually taken far enough in advance to avoid this. Yet unless we recognized that there is constantly present the danger that the messages or demands may exceed the capacity of the channels, it would be impossible to understand the function of many of the structures and operating rules in the traffic control system. Similarly with regard to political systems, the mere fact that we cannot point to any system that may have collapsed due to demand input overload does not thereby indicate that the conceptualization of possible stress upon processing channels is inconsequential for understanding what happens in a political system. Neither can its structures or operating rules be understood without relating them to the way in which volume stress is avoided.

Content Stress

Demands may vary along another dimension critical for an appreciation of their stressing capacity, that of content. Variations in content with respect to such properties as complexity, contentiousness, drain upon limited resources, or capacity to enlist the interest of politically potent members means that some demands may require far more time to process than others.

For example, in France today it might seem strange to equate the three demands for a new post office in a town, better roads in a department and increased family allowances, with three such time and re-source-consuming demands as increased nationalization of industry, greater solidarity with NATO or a more cooperative attitude toward the cessation of nuclear testing. The first set of demands could conceivably be dealt with in a matter of a few weeks or even days. In the case of the second set, the demands might endure for years and be reinforced by many ancillary demands.

It would impose a gross oversimplification on the data to consider all such demands as equivalent units, even if for purposes of measuring their numbers it was helpful so to homogenize them. There can be no doubt that a single demand, the content of which requires several months or many years to process and implement, represents a greater imposition on the time and energies of the members of the system than one that takes only a few weeks. If input overload is to make sense, it would have to take into consideration the lack of time and energy to attend to other matters as long as the major efforts of the authorities were being directed toward a limited number of major demands. Too frequently today is it argued that the necessities of foreign affairs prevent authorities from giving the kind of time and attention really required for effective handling of many domestic matters. Any count of demands that held content constant would subsequently have to devise some means for weighting demands so as to give due consideration, in terms of their stressfulness for a system, to variations in the time-consuming quality of demands as dictated by the policies they proposed.

Time and Stress

In speaking of input overload due to volume or content, I have repeatedly qualified my remarks by indicating that stress would prevail only if we were limiting our observations to a given time interval. If a system had all the time in the world to deal with an increased volume or time-consuming content, there would be little reason for any overload to evolve. Alternatively, as we shall see, one of the ways of coping with overload is to extend the available time.

What this suggests is that in addition to any absolute level of numbers or content, there is involved a problem of the rate of input.

Overload may result not from there being an excess as such, but from the way in which the inputs are spaced over time.

If we can return to the traffic control tower analogy, this can be simply shown. Let us assume that such a control center can handle three hundred messages of a given content in an hour, if they are evenly spaced at the rate of five every minute. If the rate of input of the same volume of messages is increased, say to twenty-five a minute and spaced at five minute intervals, the same volume would arrive over the total hour, but for twelve different minutes the rate of input would be twenty-five messages and for the remaining forty-eight minutes it would remain at zero. If the channel capacity permitted the absorption of only five messages a minute, unless means were found to delay the arrival of the excess twenty at each of the twelve active minutes of message flow, many messages would simply not get through. Channel failure would prevail. The traffic system would be operating under stress.

Although with regard to a political system, the analysis does not lend itself to such easy and simple numerical analysis for obvious reasons, the principle remains the same. An increase in the rate of input over determinate intervals of time must lead to the growth of structural changes or new operating rules if the increased demands are to be processed. And we have numerous instances of such increased rates today. The so-called revolution in rising expectations associated with the emergence of the developing nations and the growing strength of popular participation or popular orientation of the authorities in most political systems are certain indicators of the great surge of new demands seeking attention from political authorities.

Explicit in the analysis of demand stress has been the general hypothesis that the more time-consuming the demands, due to volume or content, the more threatening they are to the viability of any political system at all. If there were no ways of limiting volume and regulating content, even in the smallest political systems, large numbers of demands might go unsatisfied. If these were from politically significant members, the consequences for a system would without doubt be stressful.

Social structures are, in this respect at least, better off than individuals. Social structures normally have considerably greater flexibility in responding to information input overload than the individual organism. Although individuals can adapt in many ways, they are finally limited by the fact that human beings can rearrange the organization of the external world only, not of their own internal physiological system.

A social structure, on the other hand, is able to utilize individual and cooperative human ingenuity to adapt to conditions in which it finds itself both by altering its own parts fundamentally and by actively seeking to modify those conditions. Nevertheless, like the human organism, social structures, including political structures, I have postulated, must have a maximal absorptive capacity with respect to the input of demands, at least for any given state of the structure and over any interval of time. This has led us to the further hypothesis that in finding itself subject to an excessive number of demands, a political system must devise some means for ordering their reception, reducing their numbers, or regulating their content, if it is to persist.

It is to an extended and detailed exploration of these means of response and regulation that I shall immediately turn. In the process, we shall discover that we cannot escape the need to chart a new course in political analysis.

Part of the utility of the mode of analysis under way here is not only that it will help to shed light on the fundamental processes contributing to the persistence of political systems. It also reveals the political system in its most dynamic aspects. Central to the analysis will be the idea that a political system gets something done; it processes demands. To do so, there must be a flow of demands through the system and in tracing and interpreting the nature of the flow patterns so created, I shall be viewing a political system as it performs part of its characteristic work. It will help us to grasp fully the significance of my earlier remarks that a political system is not just a set of structures and activities that react supinely to stimuli.[7] It is rather a set of interactions through which positive and constructive efforts may be taken to cope with situations that threaten to destroy its integrity as a system.

[7] See Chapter 2.

5

Conversion of Wants to Demands

S TRESS ON POLITICAL SYSTEMS IS A FUNCTION OF THE INTERRELATION-
ship between the volume and content of demands, on the one hand,
and the responses available to a system for meeting and handling such
demands, on the other. I have been looking at the first component of
this equation and it is now time to turn to the second.

In doing so, what must be my objective? It should be clear by this
time that from the present analytic stance, my purpose cannot be to
demonstrate how any specific system manages to cope with potential
stress. Rather it must be to clarify the nature of the relevant processes
and variable structures that make it possible for any or all political
systems to contain or regulate threatening stress.

As we shall find, the major types of processes through which regulation takes place are similar in all systems, from the smallest and structurally least differentiated to the largest and most complex. Structures
and subordinate processes that constitute the exact form that the response takes in any system may also on occasion be the same; but we
can expect to find that they usually vary. What we shall have, then,
will be constant regulative processes fulfilled through variable structures and subordinate processes. Although it will be impossible to
speak of regulative means without exploring the varied structures
through which they are performed, nevertheless discussion of different
kinds of structures will be only incidental to my main purposes. Instead I shall be seeking to identify, describe and explain the relationship of universal regulative processes to the stress they may help to
avert.

The Flow of Demands

To help us understand how regulation of demand input takes place,
I propose to construct a model of the kinds of pathways that demands
pursue from the moment they enter a system and as they make their
way through various stages to their point of exit as binding decisions

and related actions. This model will enable us to trace through typical career or flow patterns of a demand from its inception to its termination—and the terminal point will vary from early and complete extinction to ultimate embodiment in an output.[1]

Empirically, it is most difficult to extricate any single demand and watch its progress through a system in the way one might trace a message as it moves through a telephone network. Unlike the standardized structures of most telephone systems, the structural types of political systems are enormously varied; in the last analysis each system is *sui generis*—and not in any trivial sense. The result is that political demands in each system appear to follow a web of pathways peculiar to that system. Within any given system itself, in fact, it might also be argued that no two demands will take the same course.

There can be no doubt that in the last analysis each system would be unique and each demand would take a unique course. Nevertheless, it is quite feasible to abstract, from the multiplicity of reality, a typical pattern for demand networks in all political systems, from the moment demands are given birth in the form of an ambiguous, restless want, felt need, hope or desire, to the time they ultimately find their way to points of political decision and implementation. In spite of the individual peculiarities, we shall be able to extricate the common and universal patterns underlying the multiplicity of differences.

Wants

As I am depicting the demand network, fundamentally it forms part of what resembles a giant conversion process whereby wants and the like are transformed into binding decisions, the final outcome or resultants of which are actions based upon and implementing the decisions. The factors that shape demands, we earlier saw to be such ideas and attitudes as expectations, opinions, motivations, ideologies, interests and preferences. In order to be able to refer generically to this aggregate background of attitudes and ideas out of which demands arise, I shall henceforth describe them as *wants*. They represent what it is that the members of a system may want as contrasted with demands. Demands refer to those wants that the members would wish to see implemented through political outputs of some sort.

The wants will themselves be a function of many social determi-

---

[1] For another use of flow charts, with respect to organizations, see J. W. Forrester, *op. cit.,* p. 109 ff. R. E. Lane offers an informal description of the flow of demands as generated by some of his fifteen subjects in *Political Ideology* (New York: The Free Press of Glencoe, 1962), pp. 442–445.

nants but for our purposes they can be taken as givens. Not that this means that we need to assume that they are static; indeed the opposite tends to be the case. Expectations, opinions, motivations, interests and the other wants will keep pace with the varied social, economic and cultural changes in society. But the conditions of the wants, whether they are static or changing, will be accepted as parameters of the system. Our task will be to explain how any or all wants manage to enter a system, the first step on the way to being processed, possibly, into outputs.

The Conversion Processes

If my imagery will not be mistaken for a concrete description of what takes place, but is simply accepted for what it is, an analogy, we might compare a political system to a huge and complex factory in which raw material in the form of wants, in our generalized sense, are taken in, worked upon and transformed into a primary product called demands. Some few of these are then found to be appropriate for additional processing through a variety of intermediary operations until they are ready to be converted into finished products or outputs, called binding decisions and their implementing actions. These finished products leave the system to act upon the society as a whole, with consequences that may make themselves felt subsequently through the generation of additional demands that seek entry into the system. This forms a closed-loop process that I shall later characterize as feedback.

Alternatively, we may visualize a political system as a gigantic communications network into which information in the form of demands is flowing and out of which a different kind of information we call a decision emerges. If such an output is to be possible, there must be various intermediary processes the consequences of which are to permit passage of, winnow out, combine and recombine the incoming messages so as to mold them into a number and kind that can be conveniently managed by the decision-makers. Our task is to examine and understand the way in which the conversion process moves this information along the network from the point of entry to exit, regulating any possible stress on the system that might emerge.

Both analogies are of course artificial and vast oversimplifications. But whether we adopt the imagery of a factory, of a communciations network or of any other set of analogous processes, is immaterial. The significant point is that demands just do not suddenly become transformed into outputs nor are they just inexplicably blocked. They must run the gauntlet of a number of preliminary processes before they can influence the nature of or become incorporated into binding decisions.

As we shall see, one major effect of the processes is that they serve to regulate the volume and content of demands. Not that they must always do so in a way that prevents the essential variables of a system from moving beyond their critical range. We need adopt no eufunctional bias.[2] But regardless of whether the regulative mechanisms are effective in assuring the persistence of a system, our immediate task is to identify and explore the operation of those intermediate processes that stand between the inflow of demands and the outputs. Thereby we shall see how any stressful effects from demands may be or are typically minimized, circumscribed or even eliminated. This is the immediate use to which we shall put the model; but as we proceed, we shall have frequent occasion to refer back to it.

The Flow Model

To help in understanding the processes at work and their related variable structures, Diagram 3 depicts the logical alternatives with regard to flow patterns of demands in any system, regardless of type, time and place. Of necessity, the diagram presents a crude and highly oversimplified approximation of the possible paths taken by demands as they move through the system. Nevertheless, using it as a point of departure, the box stands for the political system; and outside it is the total environment, intra-societal and extra-societal. In the environment, the general, nonpolitical opinions, preferences, interests, ideologies and similar ideas and attitudes, what we shall be calling wants, are formed. As members of society express these wants in the form of expectations or desires that binding decisions should be taken with respect to them, they are by definition converted into demands and have become part of the political processes of that society. The conversion of wants takes place at the boundary and is identified by the shaded arrows.

Inside the box, the various solid arrow lines represent pathways or channels along which demands are borne as they move from their first emergence on the scene to their crystallization, in whole or part, into binding decisions and implementing actions. But by virtue of their flow through the network of channels, demands undergo a number of preparatory or pre-processing phases through which they become mod-

[2] For the meaning of eufunctional, see M. J. Levy, Jr., *The Structure of Society* (Princeton, New Jersey: Princeton University Press, 1952), p. 77.

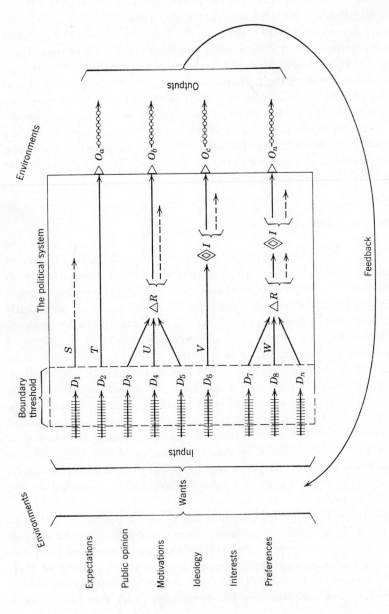

DIAGRAM 3 TYPES OF DEMAND FLOW PATTERNS

LEGEND AND EXPLANATIONS

Environments: These include the intra- and extra-societal environments indicated on Table 1, in Chapter 2.

Boundary threshold: This is shown as a broad band, indefinite as to limits, in order to indicate that it matters little whether we interpret the conversion of wants as taking place in the environments or in the system.

Wants: By definition this term refers to expectations, opinions, motivations, ideology, interests and preferences, out of which demands arise or by which demands are shaped.

Conversion points:

Symbol	Reference	Interpretation
╫╫╫╫➤	D_{1-n}	*Voicing of demands:* The shaded arrows represent the points of entry and inflow of demands. They indicate that varying wants have been voiced as demands. The letters D and their subscripts identify different demands.
➤➤➤	S to W	*Flow channels and patterns:* The solid arrows represent the channels along which demands flow, and the broken arrows suggest the disappearance of the demands. The letters identify the five basic types of flow patterns that demands may take.
△	R	*Reduction and combining points:* Once a demand is part of the political processes, it may be modified or combined with others, thereby reducing the total number of demands in the system. *Reducing units:* These are not shown but may consist of any individuals or groups in the system. Typically, in modern systems they take the form of parties, opinion leaders, elites, interest groups, legislators, administrators, and the like.
◇	I	*Conversion to issues:* At some stage demands are transformed into issues; from these a selection is ultimately made for conversion to outputs.
△	O_{a-n}	*Conversion to outputs:* Demands in their original or processed form are turned into decisions and associated actions. The subscripts identify different outputs. The circled arrows represent the flow of the outputs into the environments.
		Output units: Outputs are produced and implemented by the authorities.

Feedback: Although this is shown as a single line, in fact it represents extremely numerous feedback channels. They represent the paths taken through the environment by outputs as they influence prior wants and demands.

ified in content or reduced in numbers. As a result of these processes each persisting system is able to guarantee that by the time the demands reach the areas where binding decisions are made and implemented, there is a reasonable chance that those who are responsible for these final stages will be able to cope with what might otherwise have been an overwhelming welter of time-consuming demands.

The diagram traces five logically possible channels along which a want may travel after it has been converted to a demand. These flow paths are labeled S to W. Although they are derived logically, it also turns out that phenomenally all these patterns appear, if not together in the same system, at least individually or in various combinations in one or another system. Through them the inflow and processing of demands are regulated.

The Logical Modes of Regulation

The five logical alternatives were derived by hypothesizing that there are only three major types of regulatory mechanisms standing athwart the flow channels: the conversion of wants to demands, their reduction through combination, modification or elimination, and their transformation into issues. Let us look at these briefly.

In the first place, to enter a system, a want must be converted to a demand. This serves as the first major mechanism through which the numbers and contents of demands may be restricted. The points in the diagram, marked D with a subscript, indicate that conversion is a boundary transaction. The boundary itself is vaguely defined by broken lines, as a broad threshold. The purpose for depicting the boundary in this way is that its location is simply a matter of usefulness.[3] We may move the boundary in one direction or another, as required, so as to include or exclude want conversion, without hindering or upsetting our analysis.

In the second place, the points indicated by a triangle and marked R stand for the fact that usually more demands enter any system than could possibly be processed. They need to be modified in content and reduced in number. The letter R suggests that this reduction is achieved by combining single demands with others, as when all manner of demands for medical care may find themselves appeased by a single bill, even though the wishes of any single advocate are not completely fulfilled. Regulation may also take the form of elimination, and this is indicated by a broken arrow. It is used to signify that the demand has disappeared, either naturally, because it has not elicited

---

[3] See *A Framework for Political Analysis*, chapter V.

enough interest or as a result of some identifiable reduction and combination process.

In the third place, regulation may take the form of conversion to issues. Many of those demands that fail to become issues, never reach the output stage. We shall discover that the probabilities of pre-processed demands surviving and reaching the output stage will be increased enormously if they first become converted to issues; that is, if they are seriously entertained by the members of the system as possible binding decisions. This is the point of regulation marked with a double diamond and labeled *I*. The converse, of course, is what makes it a regulatory device. Those demands that fail to become converted to issues are less likely to remain around in the system. Thereby demands may be substantially reduced, especially when it is known that a system is able to handle only a limited number of issues at any moment of time.

If we now vary the combination of these modes of regulation as they appear in any channel or flow path that a demand may take, we find that there is a total of fourteen logically derivable patterns of regulation to which a demand may be exposed as it flows from input toward output as a binding decision. These can be listed schematically, as in Table 2, with *O* designating outputs. For ease of identifying the paths on Diagram 3 that correspond to the logical types presented here, the second column of the table may be consulted.

TABLE 2   LOGICAL TYPES OF FLOW CHANNELS

Logical Types	Identification on Diagram 3
1. *D* to its disappearance before reaching *O*	*S*
2. *D* to *O*	*T*
⎰3. *D* to *R* to *O*	*U*
⎱4. *D* to *R* to disappearance	*U*
⎰5. *D* to *I* to *O*	*V*
⎱6. *D* to *I* to disappearance	*V*
⎰7. *D* to *R* to *I* to *O*	*W*
⎱8. *D* to *R* to *I* to disappearance	*W*
9. *R* to *O*	
10. *R* to disappearance	
11. *I* to *O*	
12. *I* to disappearance	
13. *R* to *I* to *O*	
14. *R* to *I* to disappearance	

D = demand; *O* = output; *I* = issue conversion; *R* = reduction.

Of these fourteen possible patterns of regulation that may limit the number and content of demands getting through to outputs, the last six, separated in the table from the first eight, represent empty sets. The reason for this is that if a demand is to be regulated, it must first exist. In the last six patterns of the logical types, this empirical stipulation could not be met; neither reduction nor issue formulation could occur. The want has never been transformed into a demand. Hence these types can be omitted and they do not appear in the diagram.

With regard to the remaining types, 3 and 4, 5 and 6, as well as 7 and 8 form dyads the members of each of which have patterns of regulation identical to the other, except that the demand in one of the pair of channels disappears before it can become an output. In the other member of the pair of channels, the demand is successful in surviving to the output stage. In the diagram, for the sake of simplicity, these dyads are combined as alternative legs of the same channel; they are therefore bracketed together. But they might easily have been represented as different types of channels without any damage beyond that of complicating the presentation of the diagram itself. Hence, if we now combine into their pairs the empirically possible alternatives indicated by items 1 through 8 in Table 2, they give us the five different regulative channels to which a demand may be subjected and these are identified by the letters S through W on Diagram 3.

We shall now glance briefly at these with the knowledge that the next several chapters will be devoted to a full elaboration of their significance.

Channel S: This is the most frequent possibility. A demand enters the system and withers on the vine almost immediately. The solid line denotes that someone has voiced a demand; but its transformation into a broken line indicates that the demand quickly disappears from the political scene.

Channel T: This presents the polar extreme type of regulation as compared to channel S. Here the demand is voiced by someone and without any further ado, it moves to the output stage. It is as though the proverbial great leader had expressed a wish that something be done politically and others among the authorities had adopted it as their command. We shall see that in a democracy, there is a class of demands, the grassroots type, that fits this category and thereby manages to avoid all regulation.

Channel U: In this regulatory pattern, the demand has been voiced but at some stage it is combined with other demands of like character. Alternatively, it may be that it is modified in character and content as when a member of an interest group may express a wish for a very high tariff and at a conference, the other members modify it to bring it into closer alignment with realistic possibilities. But even then, two courses are open to the demand. It may achieve no success in winning approval as an output; in this case it may linger around for some time, ultimately to disappear. But it may also finally be successful. The broken and solid lines symbolize these outcomes respectively.

Channel V: The significance of this mode of regulation is that the demand bypasses the reduction and combination stage. Once it is put into the system, it is immediately transformed into an issue. Although issues have received considerable attention in voting research, here our interest in them will be with regard to the function they serve as regulators. To the extent that demands find it difficult to move to the output stage without taking the form of issues, this imposes some restrictions on the number of demands that may get through. However, as the solid and broken lines indicate, the fact of having been converted into an issue is no guarantee that the demand will indeed be adopted as an output.

Channel W: This alternative flow path demonstrates that it is possible for a number of demands to experience regulation by being combined or modified together. Many political parties typically serve this function by drawing together a *mélange* of demands and working them into a common platform, that is, into a single set of demands. These may fail to move to the next processing stage; in this case, as shown by the broken line, they disappear. But alternatively, if they do continue, they may be converted to an issue or set of issues in the system. Here too, the probabilities are that in the selection of one set of demands as against another to form the political issues, the range of demands getting through will be drastically reduced. Similarly, we can expect that the processes of the system may frequently work to shape the content so that the demands do not irreparably divide the system. Once again, after having been fought out as an issue in the system, the demand may die or it may finally reach the output stage.

With regard to the three modes of regulation cutting across the channels, although I have mentioned some structures that will be associated with each of them, we shall quickly discover that every major processing point represents only a function that is performed. It is not designed to specify the nature of the structure that fulfills this function or to suggest that in any system there are necessarily specialized structures of given kinds that carry out that function and nothing else. Indeed, it will quickly become apparent, and I shall have occasion to stress it, that a single structure, such as a political party, may be found at all processing points, especially in modern political systems.

The last stage in the life of a demand is that in which it is trans-formed into an output. But as we shall see much later, this does not terminate our interest in it. An output has important feedback conse-quences for existing and future demands in a system, as the feedback channel indicates. Although this channel stands as a single line, it is very deceptive to represent it thus. There are innumerable feedback channels through which outputs carry back their effects on the wants and, through them, on the demands of the members of the system.

The Voicing of Demands

After this cursory survey of alternative channels open to a demand, depending upon time and place, we shall now begin to probe with considerably greater detail into the typical career line of a demand as it courses from its point of entry to its moment of exit from a system. Since we are examining a model, no particular system can correspond exactly to this pattern—the channels will only approximate and repre-sent elements common to all systems. Any and every type of system will be used for exemplification whenever it seems appropriate. In this and the succeeding chapter my remarks will be confined to the first stage, the introduction of the demand as it begins its flow through the system. It is a critical stage since here wants are regulated as they seek conversion to demands and no greater number or different kinds can find their way into a system other than those that are permitted through the regulatory mechanisms operating at this stage. An outer limit is set on the number and kind of demands, however broad it may be.

Somewhere at the outset of its career, before a demand first appears as such, it is preceded by a general opinion, preference, interest, ideol-ogy, motive or the like—what I have denoted generically as a want—which may or may not be articulated in some form. If a want is to pass from this stage and become transformed into a demand, a person or group must be brought to the point of giving voice to the idea that the members charged with the responsibility for making binding decisions ought to act so as to fulfill this want. When this happens, we shall say that the want has been *converted* into a demand and it has therefore been put into the political system. The want has become politicized.[4]

It matters little whether the demand so stated has been voiced to a

[4] This way of characterizing the conversion process also appears in W. C. Mitchell, *op. cit.*, p. 279.

friend over cocktails, to a fellow worker between bites of a sandwich on the end of an I-beam, to fellow sufferers before a meeting of the local ratepayers association or as a complaint, in a traditional society, to a neighboring hawker at a bazaar. Nor does it matter whether the demand has been uttered in public to rouse popular support or in secret to get the ear of an effective official or powerful person. It may be voiced by the ordinary member of a political system, by an eminent political leader in the name of an interest group or political party, or even by a dictator. Where it is voiced, who articulates it, who hears it, how widely it is diffused are all matters of signal importance for the future stages of the demand's career. But before it can have a future, it must have a present beginning. This requires that at some stage, a want, broadly defined in our sense, has been strong enough to stir such a demand into existence. It thereby becomes an input of the system.

This establishes the first point of regulation. The wants of all people, at all times and places, have not got equal probability of being converted into a demand. From the point of view of the effect upon the system, this means that if there are factors that impose some restrictions on the number and character of wants that can be converted, we have here the first major process that might be consequential for warding off potential stress from demand inputs. As we shall see, the importance of this point of regulation will vary with the type of system under scrutiny.

The Conversion of Wants to Demands

What factors help to determine the volume and kinds of wants seeking conversion to demands? We shall be examining here the wants that present themselves in the neighborhood of the points marked D on our diagram. As soon as wants pass this point, we consider that they have crossed the boundary from the rest of society to the political system and have begun to flow along the internal demand network.

The number and kinds of wants that are injected into the political processes will in part be a function of the number and kinds of wants generated in society and, of course, seeking entry. We can imagine any number of parametric changes which might increase the volume and variety of wants held by members of society. Almost any significant social change dislocates at least a few members considerably and all members to some extent, frequently enough so as to stimulate the politicizing of wants. Parametric changes may alter the hopes and expectations of a member and this may be reflected in changing demands on the authorities.

Not that change need always lead to an increase in the volume of demands. It may at times work in an opposite direction. In the case of the decline of mercantilism and the substitution of laissez faire policies in a number of European political systems in the nineteenth century, there was a distinct reversal of the tendency to seek amelioration of trade conditions through governmental action.

There is no reason to believe that the universal contemporary trend toward an increase in the volume of demands is irreversibly set. There may be a long range trend toward such an increase but, as in the past, important fluctuations will undoubtedly appear over the centuries. Certainly at the present time, however, change seems to bring with it an increased politicizing of wants. In fact, such an increase is often itself an index of the presence of rapid change.

The effects of the diffusion of Western culture, technology and industrial organization has led to the spectacular spread of Western types of wants. In the developing nations, these have become transformed into widespread expressed expectations that the new authorities should meet these wants by experimenting with directed economies of various sorts, progressive taxation, public aid for the sick, poor and unemployed, public ownership of the mass media and transportation systems and government-financed industrialization.

Nor have the less tangible wants, shaped by broad ideological considerations found in many Western systems, been neglected in those areas where change has been most strongly felt. The sense of purpose necessary to mobilize hitherto quiescent masses has been provided through the growth of Western inspired ideologies that have stimulated the desire for freedom, popular welfare, widespread suffrage, mass education, and racial and economic equality. From broad goals such as these, there has burst forth a rank and virtually uncontrollable growth of demands.

As one author has phrased it, "Economic progress is thus likely to be accompanied by a rise in organized demands . . . The argument that economic growth provides government with greater revenue, thus enabling it to satisfy more of the demands made on it, assumes a constancy in demand for which there is neither historical precedent nor theoretical justification." [5] But this irresistible tendency toward in-

---

[5] M. Weiner, *op. cit.,* pp. 238–239. See also K. W. Deutsch, "Social Mobilization and Political Development," 55 *American Political Science Review* (1961) 493–514. Here the author argues that "the growing need for new and old government services usually implies persistent political pressures for an increased scope of government

creasing the rate of conversion of wants to demands was equally true of Western society itself in the past. During its early developmental phases it underwent comparable major transformations through the bureaucratization of vast areas of life, rapid industrialization and technological innovation, cleaving shifts in the basic power relationships among nations, and the spread of new religions. Empirically it can be shown that these changes, many of which have not yet spent their force, have led to great spurts in the volume and kinds of wants converted into demands.

Not that those who hold new wants need inevitably seek to convert them all into demands. Indeed, if all the wants held by members of a society clamored for admission to the political system, we might suspect that two conditions had occurred both of which are equally improbable.

On the one hand, we might suspect that no other sector of social behavior could satisfy or was in fact able to meet the wants of the members of the society. Speculatively this is a possible condition; but empirically, it is probably impossible to find a society in which all wants are met exclusively through the political sphere.

On the other hand, such a condition might also signify that the mechanisms for protecting the political system against input overload had broken down or did not come into operation until a later stage, one beyond the conversion of wants, at some time after they had been injected into political life as a demand. Empirically it would be difficult to find an instance to fit into this hypothetical situation. Most political systems do have some major means to ward off input overload from the very beginning.

How does regulation occur at those points in the system where wants are in process of being converted into demands for the first time?

and a greater relative size of the government sector in the national economy. In the mid-1950s, the total government budget—national, regional and local—tended to amount to roughly 10 per cent of the gross national product in the very poor and poorly mobilized countries with annual per capita gross national products at or below $100. For highly developed and highly mobilized countries, such as those with per capita gross national products at or above $900, the corresponding proportion of the total government sector was about 30 per cent. If one drew only the crudest and most provisional inference from these figures, one might expect something like a 2.5 per cent shift of national income into the government sector for every $100 gain in per capita gross national product in the course of economic development. It might be more plausible, however, to expect a somewhat more rapid expansion of the government sector during the earlier stages of economic development, but the elucidation of this entire problem—with all its obvious political implications— would require and reward a great deal more research." (p. 498).

There are two major means for regulating this initial inflow of demands. One is bound up with the kind of political structure prevailing in the system; it determines *who* converts wants to demands and therefore their number and content. The other relates to the cultural norms. These establish *what* is allowed through; they consist of those rules of behavior that deal with what is or is not permissible in the system. In the next chapter I shall consider the way in which the structural determinants operate to shape the volume and content of demands. Thereafter the cultural aspects of regulation will command our attention.

6

Regulation of Want Conversion:

Structural Mechanisms

WANTS DO NOT APPEAR ON THE POLITICAL SCENE AS DEMANDS IN SOME mysterious or inexplicable way. Members of the system must do the converting. They must give voice to a want in such a way as to indicate that they feel it ought to be handled through the formulation of binding decisions. Every demand will, therefore, have a concrete and in principle, determinable point of entry into a system through some member or group. This is our anchor point and although it may appear to be emphasizing the obvious, we can easily lose sight of the fact that the input of demands is the product of identifiable, observable behavior on the part of a person or a group.

But if this is so, who can be expected to voice wants as demands, introducing them into the system for the first time? In principle there is no reason why the selection of such members could not be a totally random process. In practice, we find that there are stable points of entry for demands. We shall be able to identify loci in the political structure where it is more rather than less likely that conversion of wants will take place.

If it is true that wants do gain entry to systems through determinable and stable points in the political structure, clearly we have here a specific class of means for regulating the inflow of demands. In thus turning to the structural means whereby conversion takes place, we shall acquire the added dividend of putting ourselves in a position to sharpen our conceptualization of the demand input process, the first stage in the whole chain of events whereby demands may be shunted aside or become transformed into outputs.[1]

---

[1] For a suggestive statement of the conditions under which wants are likely to be converted to demands, see W. C. Mitchell, *op. cit.*, p. 280 ff. There is an interesting and relevant discussion of the conversion process in R. E. Lane, *Political Life: Why People Get Involved in Politics* (Glencoe, Illinois: Free Press, 1959), chapters 5 and 6.

Types of Structural Regulators

I shall define structure in the broadest sense to include, on the one hand, the interrelationships among all political roles, individually considered, and on the other, such goal-oriented collections and combinations of roles as are embodied in groups and organizations. All members of a political system occupy some political role if only that of "general member of the system" who may be called a citizen, subject or in primitive systems, a kinsman or tribesman. Insofar as a member of a system has any regularized voice in the conversion of wants to demands, the role in which he is acting will have some significance for the input of demands. We may not be able to identify a role that is exclusively or even largely devoted to the tasks of want conversion. It will be enough to establish that, in some roles, an appreciable part of the activities are devoted to voicing wants as demands. If this turns out to be the case, the occupants of these roles in the political structure will have some say over the kinds of demands that become part of political life. They will thereby help to regulate the inflow of demands.

In most political systems that have any degree of structural differentiation, regulators fall into two types. First, in all but the simplest political systems, intrasystem structural differentiation is such that there are a number of kinds of roles functionally distinct from that of general member of the system. In this event, it will be worth considering the part that such internally differentiated political roles play in the initial stages of processing demands. As we shall see, such components of a political structure as parties, interest groups, legislators, opinion leaders, administrators, executives, or tribal chiefs represent elements of political structures that have many and varied consequences for the operation of a system. Among them, however, the expression of wants as political demands plays an unmistakable part.

But there is a second type of structural regulation in which the points of entry of demands are far more diffusely spread throughout a system. This occurs particularly in those systems in which the cultural norms permit or conduce to popular involvement. However, few systems can avoid it to some limited extent. To the degree that relatively large numbers in a system are able to convert their wants to demands directly, conversion is the result of a more widely spread and less easily located set of processes. In principle, every occupant of the role "general member of the political system" is a potential converter. To establish the point of entry of any want empirically is more difficult than in the case where demands enter through specific and numerically more limited political roles such as those of leaders, parties and the like.

But if it is not practical to specify the precise point of entry of a demand in cases where the conversion takes place in relatively undifferentiated sectors of the political system, at least we should be able to identify the type of structural component that is activated. Specifically, for this second type of structural regulation, even though we cannot locate the exact member who first politicizes a want, under certain circumstances we should be able to identify the type of source. We will be able to say that it is the membership of the system at large that does the converting or some isolable segment of it. For the first class of structural regulator, however, we can always pinpoint some special roles or role combinations such as legislator, political activist, party, interest group, or mass medium.

What this discussion brings out is that persons who engage in converting wants to demands, those who put demands into the system by being the first to give expression to them, may be located in different parts of the political structure, depending upon the rules of the regime. At the extremes, conversion may be permitted to all or it may be restricted to a few leaders or even one chief extraordinary. In reality, any system will fall somewhere between these two poles.

Gatekeeping

If we now recall Diagram 3 we can fit the preceding discussion more sytematically into our general scheme of analysis. To anticipate briefly what will later be dealt with more fully, as wants are transformed into demands, some of them may have an extremely abbreviated life. They may move no further in the system than their point of entry. Having been asserted, they expire. Typically, however, at least some demands must flow right through the system to points of decision and implementation, otherwise the system could get no political work done. If this is so, the point of entry into a system may be viewed analytically as the beginning of a pathway, network or what I shall usually call a channel, along which demands may move.

We may now re-interpret what each position marked with a D, R or I stands for in the diagram. Structurally, it represents a check point on the channel where, through the role activities of specific or general members of the system, a demand may find itself stopped completely from continuing on to other points and where it may be modified in some way as to content. Perhaps the most appropriate way to characterize these structural points in the system is to designate them as gateways regulating the flow along the demand channels. The occupants of the roles, whether they are individuals or groups, are the gatekeepers. They form the key structural elements in determining what the raw materials of the political process will be. As we shall see, gatekeepers are not only those who initiate a demand by first voicing it; the term also designates those whose actions, once a demand is moving through the channels of the system, at some point have the opportunity to determine its destiny.

Bypassing the Gatekeepers

Later chapters will analyze the functions of those gatekeepers who are located well along the communication channels in a system. Here I shall restrict my remarks to those at the boundary.

Before anything can be said about them, it is important to recognize that there are rare moments in the history of political systems when it is possible to bypass them entirely. Wants may then be converted to demands without falling into the hands of these gatekeepers. Conversion of wants may occur spontaneously, entirely without benefit of gatekeepers, unless we attenuate the meaning of the word so thinly that it loses its specific content.

For example, in the case of popular upheavals, gatekeepers may find themselves unceremoniously swept aside or their regulative powers seriously impaired. Since the conversion of wants occurring in this way would be direct, we might describe the demands they spawn as *unmediated inputs*. Unmediated demands will normally reflect popular responses to special situations of distress, emergency or catastrophe, a common reaction to similar conditions that leads to the contagious and widespread popular conversion of wants almost instantaneously. The want is transmitted as a demand directly from its holders to the authorities without formal or informal intermediaries.

In the United States such a conversion took place at the end of World War II when a spontaneous grassroots movement arose around the feeling that the government ought to "bring the boys back home." Swift decisions were taken in the wake of this popular outcry; the want was almost instantaneously transformed into a demand and soon thereafter into an output.[2]

[2] "In 1945 the very memory of this war was sickening, and in America there began a dash to dismantle the greatest military force the world had known. Angry mothers

The decision need not be favorable, however. Historically, spontaneous demands may pour forth in the form of uprisings, jacqueries or
other manifestations of discontent that are genuinely unorganized and
unpremediated—rare occurrences in politics. In such cases the outputs
may be of a negative character, rejecting or suppressing the demands
entirely.[3]

Genuinely spontaneous grassroots movements are quite extraordinary but they do represent one kind of conversion of wants in which,
at the very least, the gatekeeping kind of regulation is minimal. There
are other cases of popular political expression of wants that appear to
be equally spontaneous and unmediated but which, upon close scrutiny, turn out to be spurious.

At one time or another every system has witnessed the apparent
direct expression of wants through the medium of violent outbursts,
street demonstrations, assassinations, or other types of militant and
direct action. In many transitional systems today, this has come to be
the expected mode of behavior and in some, where the regular and
free expression of demands may be difficult, it may be the only kind
available.

But appearances are frequently misleading. Popular outbreaks such
as these seldom partake of the character of a groundswell of sentiment,
uninspired and essentially undirected. Inquiry into the origins and
patterns of diffusion of these mass demonstrations frequently reveals a
concealed, underlying leadership that guides and manipulates larger
aggregates, giving point and content to the outpouring of sentiments.

marched on Washington demanding that their sons be returned home . . . Everywhere Americans were clamoring for an end to the austerity of war and the high
cost of maintaining a large military establishment to oversee the peace. In 1946, a
Congressional year, few men ran for office on platforms of continued wartime controls. By the end of that year the U.S. Army had been effectively emasculated . . .”
R. Leckie, *Conflict: The History of the Korean War, 1950–1953* (New York: Putnam,
1962), p. 28.

[3] If we inflexibly insisted upon theoretical rigor, however artificial its outcome,
we could interpret unmediated inputs as instances in which the tenders of the gates
in the communication channels are maximally diffused through the system. In that
event we could describe the situation as one in which virtually each person was his
own gatekeeper. His actions would represent a common response to similar circumstances. Each gatekeeper could be seen as opening the gate to a similar want and
converting it to an identical political slogan. But an intellectually more relaxed
construction might be put upon the matter. Where popular sentiments swell to
overwhelming strength in a short span of time, the gatekeepers are simply swamped
in the flood of demands and find themselves helpless to stem it even if they so desired. Each person genuinely raises his voice in unison with others; the conversion of
demands is direct and unmediated.

In such cases, we may designate these unobtrusive persons as the real gatekeepers.

The Power of the Gatekeepers

Without a closer examination of the role of those gatekeepers who stand at the boundary of a political system, it would be difficult to understand one essential source of control and power over the numbers and kinds of demands entering a system and, thereby, over the agenda for discussion in the system. Even if many and varied wants are created in the environment of the system and even if the political culture, to be examined next, permits their conversion to demands, whether or not they do gain admission will hinge on the characteristics and behavior of these gatekeepers who straddle the channels of admission to the system.

From a structural point of view, the probability that a want will be converted to a demand will be closely tied to the number of alternative gatekeepers who regulate the admission process and the rules under which they operate. Where the gatekeepers are widely distributed throughout a membership, less control over conversion will exist and there will be greater danger of input overload, discounting entirely, for the moment, restraints imposed by the political culture. At the same time, if the conversion of wants falls into relatively few and specialized hands, the opportunities for keeping the input of demands within critical limits increases enormously.

Here our analysis leads us to consider the consequences of different structural arrangements only from the perspective of the persistence of some kind of system, regardless of its type or ethical merit. But it is clear from what I have just said that the control over inputs has major consequences for the achievement of the ideals of democratic systems. With respect to them, we find that effects move in conflicting directions. From the point of view of the persistence of the system, some means must be found to keep the input of demands below a critical level. But in the light of the objectives of democratic systems, the intent is to maximize the expression of every point of view on Colonel Rainboro's maxim in the Putney Debates during the Puritan Revolution that "the poorest he that is in England hath a life to live as the richest he." [4] We shall discover in the following chapter that the ten-

---

[4] Cited by A. D. Lindsay, *The Modern Democratic State* (New York: Oxford University Press, 1943), vol. 1, p. 118.

sion between these two requirements is eased by the emergence in democratic systems of cultural means to inhibit the flow of demands into the system.

The Distribution of Gatekeepers

Each type of system—democratic, non-literate, and dictatorial—has different sets of rules applying to the input of demands. But if we hold these constant for the moment, fundamentally the overall distribution and numbers of gatekeepers will be a function of the degree of specialization as between the political system and the rest of society as well as within the political system itself. Where the degree of structural differentiation between a political system and the rest of society is low, the capacity to convert wants to demands will be widely distributed throughout the system. Typically this is the case in those traditional systems in which there is even very little structure in the way of a well-defined set of authorities. In small, non-literate systems composed of lineages, clans, and tribes, the communication and formulation of demands is no more distinctively associated with a given role than is the case of most other activities. Elders, councils, lineages, clans, age-sets, occupational and craft organizations, villages, and similar groups perform many different kinds of social activities, religious, economic, and ritualistic, as well as political. Among these will be included want-conversion.

Where political roles are thus imbedded in other social roles and scarcely distinguishable from them, there is likely to be maximal diffusion of the capacity to convert wants to demands. There are few structural check-points for limiting the input of demands. Cultural restraints, to which we shall come, must bear the whole burden, at least at this point in the network of demand channels. There are no structural barriers to anyone voicing a demand and, in fact, in these societies each adult member tends to his own gate. This is what gives all life in small non-literate societies an intense and overriding political character seldom if ever achieved in structurally more differentiated societies.

Keesing has put this well when he comments that "a distinction may be noted between a traditionally habituated society such as Samoa and the modern Western setting in the degree to which specific issues are institutionally assigned or delegated. This is not just a function of size or massiveness of organization, though this factor undoubtedly is influential. In Samoa problems are easily referable to the responsible decision-makers." [5] The fact that members of traditional systems of this sort are able to turn naturally and constantly to the authorities in the society for the resolution of differences has meant that in the dislocations occasioned by contact with Western civilization, the tendency has been great to politicize problems rather than to seek extra-political solutions. This customary ease of converting new wants into political demands has made an important contribution to the enormous increase in the volume of demands already noted with regard to transitional societies today.

The Effects of Structural Differentiation

Where, however, structural differentiation prevails, whatever other source there may be for an increase of the inflow of demands, the fact that conversion may fall into specialized hands provides an important means for regulating volume and content. Among the varied roles arising in those systems that are structurally well-differentiated from the rest of society and that manifest considerable internal role specialization as well, we shall be able to identify roles with respect to which want conversion is particularly closely associated. By thus narrowing the points of entry into the system, the regulation of conversion is more readily facilitated.

The Impact of Rules Governing the Freedom to Convert Wants

Although reduction of the number of converters automatically reduces the input load that gatekeepers as a class can transmit to the system, nevertheless the volume they do let through will be inextricably bound up with the rules under which they operate. Strictly speaking, we should put off discussion of these rules until the next chapter. They consist of part of the response mechanism that I shall call cultural regulation. But it would be artificial to postpone consideration of this element of political culture since it fits logically at this point. It would be awkward to attempt to analyze the effects flowing from structural differentiation in and of itself. We need to discuss it with respect to two kinds of cultural rules: the regime rules that forbid conversion to all but a few members in the system and those rules that throw conversion open to any and all members of the system. Although we

[5] F. M. and M. M. Keesing, *Elite Communication in Samoa* (Stanford: Stanford University Press, 1956), p. 97.

cannot examine all structural types of systems that conform to these criteria, I shall be able to illustrate the consequences for the conversion process by citing two cases, dictatorial and democratic systems under conditions of modern industrialism.

Gatekeepers in Dictatorial Systems

Modern totalitarian or dictatorial systems present an instance of structural differentiation as related to want conversion that is about as divergent from the small traditional systems we have been looking at, as we can expect to find empirically. In such dictatorial systems the capacity to set the agenda for political discussion is a crucial instrument of control. If the regime is to endure, its rules must carefully and drastically restrict the number and variety of gatekeepers.

The operating rules of regimes such as these require that any want seeking political expression must secure validation through the approval of the leadership or of cadre groups in an approved political party which is close enough to the leadership to be able to interpret its desires and intentions. By thus imposing limits on those who may act as gatekeepers in the conversion of wants to demands, access to the political process is limited and the leadership is able effectively to help regulate the entry of demands. In systems such as these, based as they are on the limitation of want conversion, input overload would scarcely be likely to occur or even threaten.

Diffuse Gatekeepers in Democratic Systems

Democracies, under conditions of structural differentiation such as we find in industrialized societies, present us with a type of system that falls somewhere between the least inhibited expression of demands typical of small non-literate systems and the severely restricted range in dictatorial systems. In democracies as we know them today, the formal capacity to convert wants to demands is broadly diffused throughout the system. Each person may tend to his own gate, is even encouraged to do so by injunctions to participate actively in politics, always of course within the permissible limits of the other aspects of the political culture.

Although nominally each person may be able to cry out politically when the shoe pinches, in fact only certain kinds of persons or groups are likely to do so. Even where the rules impose few formal restrictions upon conversion, whether it be a small intimate system or a mass democracy, the political structure is likely to create differential opportunities. Some roles will provide greater power over the conversion process than others. Furthermore, it is utopian to believe that each member in a democracy is interested enough in politics, sufficiently well-informed and aware of what is possible, or endowed with a sufficiently vibrant sense of efficacy to desire to express his wants as political demands or to feel able to do so. The number of persons able and willing to voice demands is undoubtedly drastically lower than those formally entitled to do so.

If not every man becomes his own converter, even in a democracy, those who in fact do engage in this activity will help to set the content and level of input of demands. To be sure, as long as we continue to consider the popular gatekeepers, we shall be looking at members who are diffuse, ill-defined and low in visibility, dispersed as they are through the system. But in spite of this, they cannot be ignored if we are not to neglect one of the important points of regulation over the input of demands.

In the following chapter I shall discuss the cultural rules in conformity with which such popular gatekeepers will operate. These will serve to limit the range and number of demands that they are likely to convert. But here we must recognize that in spite of limits imposed by realistic considerations, popular gatekeepers do constitute numerous, widespread structural points through which demands may enter a system. Because of the potentially large number of gatekeepers that they represent, they are a possible source of stress for democratic systems.[6]

[6] If we move from the theoretical to the empirical level, we have some clues as to who the converters are likely to be. Coleman refers to the fact that there is a direct relationship between the degree of involvement of members in a community and the frequency with which they raise issues. J. S. Coleman, *Community Conflict* (Glencoe, Illinois: Free Press, 1957), p. 3.

In an unpublished Master's dissertation, *The Conversion of Wants into Demands: A Theoretical Statement and An Exploratory Case Study* (University of Chicago, 1959), Elliott White reports on a study specifically directed to the problems of conversion of the kind raised in this chapter. In this study, a survey was conducted in Marshfield, a pseudonym for a small neighborhood housing development in the city of Chicago. Using this as a democratic political subsystem, White sought to discover the characteristics of those who are most likely to voice the grievances, wants and discontents of the persons of Marshfield. The developer of the community had provided for a Council, resembling a ratepayers association, with some legal powers, and it is here that grievances were typically raised and negotiated.

White found that those persons who became converters of wants held by themselves and others usually had the following characteristics. (1) The person must himself adhere to the want with a minimal intensity of conviction. Since he is not usually a professional politician he has little to gain aside from status and satisfaction of achieving his own purposes. (2) He must be able to recognize similar wants on the part of others and if he is to express their wants, he must feel that he

Implicit here is the suggestion that, other things being equal, the greater the number of gatekeepers or points of entry for demands, the greater are the number of demands that can gain entry into a system. Accordingly, the greater is the importance that must attach to non-structural regulatory means in a democratic system, the special signifi-cance of which I shall consider in the next chapter.

Well-Defined Gatekeepers in Democratic Systems

To some minimal extent then, especially in a democracy in which conditions encourage popular interest rather than apathy, each person is his own converter. But there are no data as yet that would permit us to hazard a guess as to the proportion of wants that are converted at the hands of the general members, natural spokesmen of this sort, who occupy no special or clearly differentiated role as converters of wants. However little data we may have of the extent to which they contrib-ute toward the conversion of wants, there can at least be much less doubt that a very considerable amount of this activity is performed by others, namely by those who do hold well-defined political roles such as that of opinion leader, politician, legislator, or administrator, or by organizations such as an interest group, legislature, political party, or newspaper.

Stable roles and organized centers of political discussion and action of which these are representative, perform many kinds of tasks in a political system. The conversion of wants need not even reflect the

speaks for them as well as for himself. (3) He must be able to generalize on the basis of this awareness so that the want can be validated by reference to others favoring the same one. (4) He must have such minimal knowledge of political life that he is at least aware of the fact that there are political units to which he can direct his wants. (5) He must feel efficacious, that his voice can be made to count in some way.

This study suggests that the members of the small political system under consider-ation who were more likely to possess these characteristics, were those who had a greater number and variety of interpersonal and organizational contacts, especially with regard to the area of life in which the wants being traced lay, that is, in the broader community adjacent to the neighborhood itself. The interpretation is that the broader the range of relevant contacts, the more likely is a person to be aware of the means available for meeting a want, to assess its possibilities realistically, and to feel able to do something about them, given the total cultural and political context. It may also enable him to anticipate wants sensitively even before those who have the needs become aware of them.

Finally, it is suggested that the skills and responses so developed by want con-verters tend to reinforce themselves. Habit, success and self-confidence will encour-age increased reliance on such persons as gatekeepers of wants. In this way some stability for the occupant of the role of want converter ensues.

major contribution of any one of the roles or groups just mentioned. Yet even the low salience of a function in the total behavior does not necessarily reduce the significance of this part of the political structure for the operation of the system as a whole. Regardless of whether or not want conversion is dominant, one of the characteristic activities of the occupants of these roles and members of these organizations is that they reflect the wants of others as well as their own, by voicing them as demands.

Thus, a labor organization not only sums up the demands of its membership in the area of politics; it may also sort out, summarize and evaluate their wants, anticipate their needs, and decide what political demands can be formulated around them. Indeed, interest groups, and in some systems, although not usually the American, political parties, may conceive it as part of their task to sense in advance what the wants of their followers and sympathizers may be and to formulate these as a program for political discussion and action.

Certainly such highly differentiated structures as interest groups are constantly searching for expressed or latent wants that, within the framework of their beliefs, they can appropriately adopt and around which they may formulate political policy alternatives. In modern industrialized systems, interest groups are specific structures for the conversion of wants. In fact, it is well known that the bureaucracies of such groups require a constant flow of dissatisfactions and complaints to justify the organization's continued existence. An alert leadership of an interest group will anticipate wants, at times even attempt to create them when they do not exist, if it seems necessary to assure the active survival of the group as a political instrument.

Within the limits of their positions and roles, parties, opinion leaders, the intelligentsia—where they are a political force—and the mass media similarly may search out the wants of what may in this context appropriately be called the silent ones in the system, the less articulate. And as in the case of interest groups, each of these units may also initiate demands as a reflection of their own, independently felt wants.

Hence, these members or organizations are critical gatekeepers standing at the boundary of the system, at the point marked D in Diagram 3, and controlling the initiation of demands. As we shall see, it is possible for the same unit to play a significant part at quite different points along the flow channels of demands. The fact that I locate them at the boundary for purposes of conversion will not prevent us from recognizing that they may also appear at other loci well within the system. How much more they do with regard to the passage of demands through the system—and it is considerable—and at what other points in the system, will appear in later chapters.

The Authorities as Specific Converters

In modern systems to a considerable extent and in transitional types to an even greater extent, demands may be initiated by government bureaucracies such as the administrative services, the military establishment, political leaders in the role of the executive, and by the legislative representatives.[7] These are differentiated structural elements that, collectively, make up the authorities. Indeed, we can generalize this proposition by stating that wherever the authorities constitute a distinguishable set of roles, part of their activities is inevitably devoted to want conversion.

A variety of reasons may motivate them to put in demands. It may be that they are responding to direct pressure from citizens or subjects. They may undertake to convert what they view as the wants of members in the system in the anticipation that if they did not, they would be subject to considerable pressure to do so in any event. Thereby they anticipate and abort the input of demands on the part of others.

But aside from inspiration under the threat of sanctions of others, the authorities may convert wants quite independently, in response to internal moral norms that inspire them to live up to the ideal expectations of the culture with regard to what is expected of the authorities in the system. For example, the absolute monarchs of seventeenth century Europe were not entirely capricious or arbitrary in the selection of demands that they sought to fulfill. They were limited to some extent by compelling expectations of others with respect to how the authorities ought to behave. And what is true of such systems as these is equally the case, in some degree, of all political systems. In primitive systems, the paramount chief may by convention be expected to take the initiative to propose moving out of the hills down into the river valleys in simple anticipation of the dry season.

Numerous other reasons may induce the authorities to generate demands themselves and introduce them into the system for consideration according to the normal rules of the regime. The government leaders may be responding to their own image, not of what is expected of them, but of what they view in any event to be necessary. They may

---

[7] Cf. L. W. Pye, *Politics, Personality and Nation Building* (New Haven: Yale University Press, 1962), p. 43: "Indeed, the initiative for change [in transitional societies] more often than not comes from those in command of the arbitrarily introduced structures [of government], and instead of the government responding to pressures from the society, the process is in many respects essentially reversed."

state demands as formal proposals for legislation if prior economic projections or developmental studies show such policies to be a necessary step in the achievement of agreed-upon ends.

At times, the authorities may simply be adjusting to the logic of previous actions which imposes upon them the need to voice certain demands. For example, a developing nation that commits itself to a large military establishment thereby sets in motion a whole chain of inescapable demands. To consummate such a policy, one or another segment of the authorities must be prepared to raise the request for a program and funds for training technological experts, for the purchase of modern equipment, for the education of medical personnel to maintain the health of the armed forces, and for equipment to make possible the use of advanced methods of communication and transportation.[8] Like so many other types of demands, the demand for a capable military force proves to be a breeder demand under modern conditions of military competition. Once it has been introduced, it gives birth to vast second and third generation sets of wants.

But whatever the source of inspiration for authorities to convert wants to demands, it is a task that is always closely associated with their roles in any system. It is easy to neglect the fact that the authorities, no less than any general or specific member of the system, are to be found among the structural regulators of the input of demands. We tend to think of them only as producers of binding decisions; but as an intrinsic part of this task, authorities at all times and places have themselves taken the initiative in proposing action.

The authorities must, therefore, be viewed as spanning the boundary between a system and its environment, on the input side. Later we shall see that they perform the same function on the output side. What this demonstrates once again is that it will not be inconsistent with our analysis to locate a structure at more than one point along the flow channels. This is just another, but theoretically more precise way, of observing that a given structure may perform many functions in a system.

In this chapter I have been identifying the gatekeepers who stand athwart the demand channels at the very beginning. Theoretically, there are many other matters regarding the gatekeepers that have to be answered before we can understand the regulative power and control of variable types of structures over the volume and content of demands.

[8] F. W. Riggs, "Prismatic Society and Financial Administration," 5 *Administrative Science Quarterly* (1960) 1–46, especially on pp. 15–6.

In the first place, the number and content of wants themselves, as validated by the general culture and influenced by historical events, would determine the reservoir from which a selection could be drawn. But since we consider that wants are formed in the environment, we may take them as givens, even if these givens themselves are subject to considerable change over time.

In the second place, which of whose wants are likely to be converted, what the gatekeepers read into the situation and interpret as a want, which of these are selected for conversion, and how many they are ready to act upon and convey to the political system will depend upon more than the general structure of gatekeeping as already described.

In the third place, a number of other factors need to be taken into consideration. Among these it would be important to look at the characteristics of the gatekeepers as related to their socio-economic origins, the processes through which they arrive as gatekeepers, the ideological perspectives within which they operate, the motivations underlying their actions, the communication processes through which the wants of others may be impressed upon them, the resources for conversion at their disposal, and their differential responsivenesss to the wants of others as compared to their own goals.

But among all of these factors operating on the gatekeepers, one type looms large as a major category of regulative means relevant to input overload. This is what we may call the cultural norms that inhibit or promote conversion. Without minimizing the importance of those that have just been mentioned, nevertheless many of them are themselves derivative of the kind of culture of which the gatekeepers are part. The norms act as the operating rules according to which behavior in the system is expected to take place. Which wants get through as demands and which never assume this form will therefore be decisively influenced by the kind of cultural rules prevalent in the political system. We shall concern ourselves with this in the following chapter.

7

Regulation of Want Conversion:

Cultural Mechanisms

OUR EXAMINATION OF THOSE WHO RESTRICT THE INFLOW OF DEMANDS has enabled us to see only half the picture with respect to the conversion of wants to demands. The other half is that regardless of who the gatekeepers may be, their behavior in regulating the flow of demand will be conditioned by the cultural context within which they act. In no system is it even theoretically possible for any member to express his wants as demands automatically, without any restrictions at all. At the very least, every system provides for built-in restraints in the form of norms that inhibit the gatekeepers from seeking a political solution for all discontents, interests or desires.

Within any one system, no two gatekeepers need be ready and able to convert the same kinds of wants to demands. Even in the same system, subcultural variations may induce different gatekeepers to voice different kinds of wants, however similar the circumstances might be. If we look at whole systems, we would have even greater expectations that no two would operate under identical cultural norms and, accordingly, that the gatekeepers in such systems would also be acting under different kinds of cultural inhibitors or releasers with respect to the conversion of wants to demands. In passing, we have already seen, in the last chapter, the impact of some cultural norms on the behavior of gatekeepers, but this has referred exclusively to the numbers of gatekeepers permitted within a given type of system. In this chapter I wish to broaden my scope by taking into account the consequences of cultural norms for other aspects of converting behavior.

Examination of the influence of cultural norms on the want conversion processes will help us to understand how a system regulates the volume and content of wants that are ultimately transformed into demands. It is these norms that constitute the second of the two major means for regulating conversion, as I indicated earlier. The first means was described as the structural mechanisms in a system, those that we have just discussed in the preceding chapter.

The Significance of Cultural Norms as Regulators

It is commonplace to observe that systems vary with respect to the subject matters that are incorporated into binding decisions. What may be considered an appropriate topic for political action in one system will be entirely excluded from political consideration in another. That Nepal should limit the age gap between spouses to no more than twenty years is a want that the members of few other societies would contemplate converting into political demands, much less into a binding output. We could easily draw up lists of demands that are culturally taboo for one system but quite acceptable in another.

But what is not so commonplace is the realization that such variations in what are to be considered culturally appropriate areas for political decision have major consequences for the input load of demands. What is culturally prohibited or frowned upon in a system will tend to stifle any inclination, even if it should arise, to express a want, outside of these areas, as a political demand. And conversely, those subjects deemed proper for political consideration will encourage any inclination to voice a want as a demand.

The Need for Cultural Inhibitors

Even in the most intimate political system, consisting of an extended family band, as among the Eskimo or the Bushmen, cultural norms help to restrain and, as we shall see, sometimes to release the members with regard to the wants they would seek to settle through the intervention of the group. It is true, in such small societies observers have noted that anything can be the subject of group discussion. There is good reason for this ease in being able to politicize even trivial matters, at least when compared with the far greater barriers standing in the way in modern societies. In small traditional systems, social relationships are closely intermeshed. Individuals are simultaneously related to each other by a complex web of ties, through blood, marriage, ritual, production and exchange, and residence. A breach in one of these ties may threaten the whole fabric of community relationships, so interdependent are all of them. A quarrel between two men may easily spread to engage the energies of the whole society, often in the form of bitter feuds that are hard to eradicate, an outcome that the elders must bear constantly in mind as they seek to resolve disputes.[1]

In modernized systems, however, the high degree of structural differentiation and specialization compels relationships among members to become much more specific and compartmentalized. A violation of an economic tie between worker and employer need not disturb the friendship or other relationships that each has in his own neighborhood, church or kinship group. The contagious quality of a disturbance is much lower.

But in spite of the manifest integrative value, at least in small undifferentiated societies, of leaving the conversion of wants into demands as easy a process as possible, even here some restrictions exist, although they are at the very low end of the continuum. Not all matters automatically come up as the elders foregather in the field of an evening to talk over and, thereby, to attempt to resolve some of the problems of the day. Relatively static cultural traditions dictate certain expectations with regard to what is considered to be acceptable behavior in bringing a matter up for common discussion. A man should try to settle small things of life before he troubles his kin with them, especially if there are more urgent matters to talk about. Nevertheless, in this kind of political system we approach the one extreme where a minimum of constraints is imposed upon the conversion of wants to demands for collective decision and action if necessary.

In political systems of societies more complex than the simple familial band or lineage segment, we expect without question that even under conditions of maximum government responsibility for human affairs, as in the case of modern communism, there will be vast areas of day-to-day life with respect to which wants are met through other than political means. It would otherwise be impossible for any modern complex system, based upon a mass society, to cope with the resulting demand overload.

The Consequences of Cultural Norms

The effect of cultural norms in political life is to impose some kind of outer limits on the number and kinds of wants seeking entry as demands. The political culture in a system will, of course, usually offer

[1] This is discussed in P. Bohannan, *Justice and Judgment Among the Tiv* (London: Oxford University Press, 1957) and in M. Gluckman, *Judicial Process Among the Barotse of Northern Rhodesia* (Manchester: Manchester University Press, 1955), pp. 20–21.

a rather unique combination of elements; in no two systems will it restrict or ease the conversion of the same kinds of wants. Furthermore, even within a single system, gatekeepers will abide by varying cultural rules, depending on their ethnic, class, regional or other characteristics.

But the point here is that however diverse or homogeneous the cultural norms within a system or as between different systems may be, they do fulfill a common function in all systems. They serve to dampen or ease the inflow of demands as the case may be. The cultural norms, transmitted across the generations, dictate and regulate which wants a member is expected to solve for himself or in cooperation with others, and which it is acceptable in the society for the members to seek to fulfill through political action. The values and biases of a political culture will prevent many demands from ever arising. In anticipation, members of the system know that either they would not get a hearing or that, in seeking to politicize a want, they might indeed suffer considerable social humiliation or even legal penalties. The cultural norms serve as rules guiding the converting decisions of the gatekeepers in a given system, regardless of who they are. By providing such decision rules for the gatekeepers, norms help to regulate the number and content of demands gaining admission to the system.

To illustrate the way in which such cultural rules operate, it is clear that conventions arise in each system about the kinds of areas of social life that may be subject to governmental intervention and, therefore, that may be made the focus of demands. Although like any other cultural norms, there may be considerable room to challenge and change these restrictive rules, each historical epoch tends to be colored or dominated by definable types of norms.

Historically, the cultural rules regulating the conversion of wants have varied markedly in those systems which today have become modernized. The key terms by which we often characterize the attitudes toward government intervention in Western political systems mirror such changing cultural rules. Mercantilism, laissez faire, welfare state and socialism serve as symbols, it is true, of the part that government has played in the economy of a society. But they also suggest a cultural orientation in which it is felt to be appropriate and even expected that for the satisfaction of many kinds of material wants, a member may or may not pose them as demands.

In addition to such well labeled attitudes toward want-conversion, each system establishes conventions relating to the complete exclusion of certain areas of life from political intervention. These may become so deeply rooted in the mores of the society that the members no longer expect them to be questioned. They represent culturally sensitive areas withdrawn from the region of political conflict either because they might generate excessive cleavage or because tradition dictates that they are zones for the operation of private preferences. To a considerable extent, these limits upon the conversion of wants to demands remain purely at the informal cultural level—although in some cases they may be embodied in laws or constitutions—but they are nonetheless effective regulators of wants for that reason.

In the United States, for example, as in many other systems, members may have wants with respect to the style of clothing they think ought to prevail—the length of the hemline on women's dresses perhaps, the way in which people ought to spend their vacations, the kind of religion they ought to practice, the political party to which they ought to adhere, or the providence members ought to display in the disbursement of their income. In many systems, the likelihood of a member turning his ideals, opinions, or interests in such matters into a demand that government take some action is very low and remote. This is entirely aside from the question of the chances that the demand might have of being taken seriously as a possible basis for political action or of the probability that the ignominy and humiliation of being considered political oddities or cranks might await those who violate such cultural standards.

The fact, however, that suggestions for political action in these areas might be received in this way is a further indication of the restraining effects imposed by the culture on those who might otherwise be inclined to voice them as demands. Over the generations we are socialized to inhibit automatically the utterance of demands with regard to large segments of life. The prevalence of a learned cultural norm that differences in religious doctrine are matters inappropriate for political decision reduces the probability that members will even think of politics as a way of handling the consequences of religious variety. In this way cultural norms help to reduce the number of demands and limit their controversiality or time-consuming character.

More generally speaking, the types of wants converted to political demands will depend on the image prevailing in the political culture of the purposes for which political processes may be used. The conception a member holds of the nature of political instrumentalities, of his role in political life and the role of others will condition the kinds of claims that he feels justified in politicizing. A composite picture of the nature of the varying conceptions members hold of the purposes to which political processes may be put would help us to estimate the limits in the contents of wants that can readily be converted. Inherited or newly cultivated cultural norms and the general images they create of the purpose to which political action may be put can easily be overlooked as a decisive means for regulating overload due to demand inputs.

Conflicting Consequences of Cultural Norms

Here as elsewhere, when we speak of regulation there is no reason to believe that the cultural criteria must always operate to reduce the input of demands or modify their cleaving effects. To do so would be to commit the eufunctional fallacy of assuming that all mechanisms in a system must always contribute to its persistence. Some cultural rules may serve as input releasers and encourage the input of demands and aggravate their controversiality by enlarging and intensifying differences. We shall discuss a special one of these rules regarding popular involvement, in a later section of this chapter.

Furthermore, no system is so homogeneous or consensual that all the members necessarily conform to precisely the same norms. Conflict about what is appropriate may and usually does exist. At the opposite extreme, even in traditional systems, however much we may perhaps somewhat nostalgically assume that rules of behavior are known and fixed, the fact is that there is frequently room for doubt and there are interstices among which members may escape the dominant rules. We can anticipate, therefore, that in most systems there will be doubt and dispute in some cases as to whether a matter may appropriately be broached for political consideration.

As usual, where we have a single class of mechanisms, such as cultural norms, that simultaneously moves in competing directions, we are compelled to look at the net effect of its operation. In the present case we must conclude that if a system is not to be exposed to possible stress from demand overload, the net effect of the cultural norms must serve to reduce the number and modify the content of the wants that would otherwise be politicized. At the same time, however, we must remember that if the cultural regulators fail to produce this net outcome, the system may still be spared from collapse. What is not accomplished at this point in the inflow channels may be compensated for at later points and these we have yet to consider.

Content Sensitivity: Central Values

A major impetus in a system toward the cultural restriction of want conversion derives from the special sensitivity of the members to the content of some wants. The substance of some wants may be more disturbing or stressful for a system than others and by providing means for restricting the conversion of these, the cultural rules in a system may manage to limit the volume seeking entry. But even more significantly from the point of view of demand overload, by restricting the input of subject matters that threaten to generate considerable cleavage among the members, such rules may also help to reduce the time required to process demands. Overload, we will remember, results not only from an excessive volume but from some fewer demands, the content of which may be the equivalent, in time consumed, of a much larger volume.

However free a society may claim to be, it will nevertheless place some limits on the substantive kinds of demands a member may raise because of their socially disruptive potential. Tolerance in a society cannot permit the unrestricted challenge to any and every value if only because of the effort that would be required to meet each challenge and re-assert a belief in its desirability or presumed necessity. Some of the premises of behavior—its basic rules and goals—must be taken for granted if constant turmoil is to be avoided. These are what we might call the central values of a society or what from time to time, with respect to the political sphere alone, students of politics have termed the "agreement on fundamentals."

The notion here is not that the central values are forever inaccessible to dispute and discussion. If this were the case, a system would be contained within a permanent mold. It scarcely needs to be said that the history of societies shows fundamental transformations over the ages, including the alteration of many of the central value premises, political and otherwise.

But unless a society is caught in the throes of rapid change, we can adopt as an operating assumption, the idea that its members will seek to protect themselves from those who would be constantly chipping away at the characteristic foundations of that society. Whatever the particular values that are thus protected, empirically we know of no case in which a society has given absolute and unrestricted free play to those who would challenge any or all of its premises. Every society has its politico-cultural totems and taboos, its goals and assumptions that it treats as sacrosanct and inviolable.[2] Normally these will lie outside the realm of dispute and thereby wants with respect to them will find it difficult to become incorporated into demands. In the process of socialization, the members will have so internalized attachment to these values that they will be reluctant to tolerate any challenge to them. Informal sanctions, through social disparagement and embarrassment, will keep deviant members in line; or special formal sanctions as in laws of treason and sedition will impose serious penalties upon those rash enough to violate the taboo.[3]

Although central values have many consequences for a society, especially with regard to its general cohesion and stability, from the point of view of our concern with the input of demands, the basic significance of such values is that they help to set real limits on the content of political controversy. Ethically, the preservation of some central values may be anathema to the observer, as in the case of societies with dictatorial systems. But theoretically, it is important to recognize that by withdrawing some subjects from the realm of political disputation or by making it difficult for a member to raise such a subject as a controversial demand, a system, whether it be democratic or otherwise, will help to reduce the time spent in processing demands. To that

[2] It can be taken for granted that there are probably no systems in which complete consensus exists with regard to the values that are to be considered central. This in itself would do no violence to our discussion. Not all members of a system need consider the same values to lie beyond the pale of dispute. But the greater the number that do or the more dominant or influential the upholders of the values are, the less likely is it that their content will become part of a political demand. The discovery of just what the central values of a society are would be an empirical rather than a theoretical problem, at least in this context.

[3] "Even in a relatively well-integrated country such as Turkey, legislators have resorted to a long list of specific prohibitions on political articulation that might endanger national unity. A law of association, adopted in the late Ottoman period and continued with little modification to the present day, specifically prohibits political associations based on distinctions of race, language, religion, locality or social class. But this legal provision is reinforced by psychological taboos dating back to the formative years of the Republic. Census data record the proportion of Muslim Turkish citizens who speak Kurdish, Arabic, Circassian, Laz or other dialects. Yet while practical politicians are keenly aware of the importance of these groupings, any open reference to such distinctions in the press or in public speech would meet with cries of indignation. In addition, the distinction between Sunni and Alevi (or Shi'i) Muslims seems to be of considerable social and political significance in some localities of Anatolia. But here the inhibition against admitting to any sectarian differences among the Muslim population is so strong that even elementary census data on the proportion of Alevis in Turkey are lacking." D. A. Rustow, "The Politics of the Near East" in G. A. Almond and J. S. Coleman, *The Politics of the Developing Areas* (Princeton: Princeton University Press, 1960), pp. 369–454 at p. 431.

extent the relevant cultural norms will alleviate the demand load that might otherwise be imposed on the system.

Regulation under Conditions of Popular Involvement

But to return to a point mentioned earlier, some kinds of rules in the political culture may tend to aggravate rather than to ameliorate the stress threatened by demand input overload. They serve as demand input releasers rather than inhibitors. Later when we discuss in some detail the characteristics of that aspect of a system that we may call the regime, we shall see that a major part of it is composed of the so-called rules of the game, the constitutional norms. These norms, describing as they do, the actual pattern of relatively basic political interrelationships, are clearly part of the political culture. The significance of these regime rules is that they will affect the number and percentage of members of a society who are permitted to participate in political life, especially but not exclusively through active involvement in the selection of the authorities and in their control through other means. The percentage of a population that is able to take part in political processes in this way will correlate highly with the volume and variety of wants presenting themselves for conversion. That is to say, the demand input load will vary directly with the degree of popular involvement.

We have already discovered this relationship in our general discussion of demand inputs; here we are able to broaden our understanding of it by suggesting that the regime norms governing the extent of popular involvement will thereby serve as regulators of demand input. Unlike the other cultural norms that tended to reduce the conversion of wants, however, regime norms of this kind will have an opposite effect, to the extent that they permit and encourage popular participation in political life. They will, therefore, throw the burden of regulation on other stages in the processing of demands through the system.

The degree of popular involvement in political processes will be able to retard or stimulate an increase in the conversion of wants for two reasons. First, norms to this effect will influence the number of persons who are inspired and able to express their wants in political terms, as became evident from our earlier discussion. But second, the extent of popular involvement also affects the degree of pressure on the leadership itself, encouraging it to anticipate, express and represent the wants of its followers in the form of political demands.

Effects of Numbers of Political Participants on Input of Demands

To take the first point, in those non-democratic systems where active political life is restricted to the few, as in many traditional societies or in Western civilization prior to the rise of democratic movements, limitations in the numbers of persons who could be expected to voice political opinions and judgments automatically restricted the transformation of wants into demands. To take an extreme case, one that approaches the limit in this direction, in some traditional societies the uneducated peasant and hard-pressed town worker know only exclusion from political power. They are accustomed to accepting the legitimacy of their rulers in broad traditional areas of life. Under the pressure of the need to use most of their energies for mere physical survival, they may be satisfied to be free of the cares of state.

Under these conditions, a frame of mind may develop, present but declining in many traditional areas of the world today, in which the members could not conceive that any wants of theirs would be important or significant enough for the socially distant rulers to take into account. It represents more than apathy. Apathy suggests that political interest and involvement is a realistic possibility. But in many traditional systems only the political elite, such as an autocracy or aristocracy, have a right to become involved, not the masses. What we have, rather, under these conditions, is a kind of political impermeability, a long suffering patience on the part of the general membership that leads to the acceptance of one's fate and either a complete absence of any thought of politicizing one's wants or an unquestioned stifling of any urge to do so.[4]

Although this close approximation to total exclusion from the process of converting wants to demands still describes the state of large sections of traditional peasant societies in particular, it does not imply that without popular suffrage, most of the wants of the members must fail to become transmuted into demands. Few traditional societies conform wholly to the pattern just depicted. At the very least, the markets and bazaars have provided a forum for the expression of discontent and most traditional systems have allowed some means for the communication of grievances from the membership to the authorities.

[4] See L. Binder, *Iran* (Berkeley and Los Angeles: University of California Press, 1962), and D. Lerner, *The Passing of Traditional Society* (Glencoe, Illinois: Free Press, 1958).

Certainly, in the case of large-scale political systems under conditions of modern industrialism, it would be impossible to exclude all expression of demands. At the very least the need for some feedback from the members forces this upon modern complex and bureaucratized government. Even under the severe restrictions upon popular participation that we find in modern totalitarianism, there is still room for the articulation of political demands, although the range of content and the modes of expression are strictly confined to a framework of policies laid down by the authorities.

But even though most systems provide some avenues through which wants may be voiced, if the operating rules of the regime permit members of a system to become involved in its political life and to exercise some measure of control or supervision over policies, we can expect an increase in the frequency with which members seek to convert their wants to demands. Indeed, the experience of many traditional societies as they move along the road to modernization includes the adoption of some form of democracy, at least in the initial stages. One man, one vote becomes the familiar slogan. With freedom from colonial status or the emergence of a new elite in the case of already autonomous systems, the formal adoption of popular suffrage amply demonstrates how quickly a new frame of mind will arise with respect to who has the right and expectation of having his wants converted to demands.

As against the standard view in traditional systems, reinforced frequently by the total culture, including the dominant religion, that the authorities have the unique responsibilities for governing and the general membership is not expected to have an opinion or to intervene, democratic ideology has promoted the idea that every person's opinion is apparently as good as his fellow's. With this idealization of the common man and the diffusion of the sentiment that the voicing of demands or the right to be heard belongs to everyone as an adjunct of the vote, a universally sharp rise in the conversion process has occurred.

In the outcome, many transitional systems have quickly found themselves confronted with the so-called revolution in rising expectations. We can interpret this as nothing less than the breakdown of the old and reliable regulators of the pre-existing regimes, that is, the norms and rules of the traditional or colonial regimes that restricted the expression of wants as demands. With the disappearance of these inhibitors and the emergence of positive encouragement to participate in the political process—required for mobilizing the energies of the masses for the overthrow of the domestic or colonial oppressors—the increase in the rate of conversion has taken on dramatic proportions. This does not mean that these new systems must necessarily succumb. As I have repeatedly pointed out, other mechanisms may step in to prevent the initial input overload from continuing very far along the demand processing channels.

Effects on Demand Inputs from Leadership

Part of the increase in the conversion of wants arises from the effect on the individual members themselves of their own emerging interest and involvement in political life. They are now more prone to have opinions about what government ought to do and to express these opinions as demands.

But part of the increase can also be attributed to the inputs of competing elites and this brings us to the second point mentioned earlier. The rise in the degree of political involvement of the membership is often refracted through competing leaderships, especially but not exclusively in societies in which a single elite formerly dominated the political processes. Even with the growth of popular participation, the tendency is for the support groups to form around leaders either because they are esteemed in proportion to their perceived capacity to express and anticipate the needs and wants of their followers or because they are successful in manipulating their followers through the use of demands formulated by the leaders themselves. Members may seek out leaders to express their wants; or leaders may locate followers necessary to the fulfillment of their own ambitions.

All political leaders need to possess some capacity to sense the wants of their support groups and to give open expression to them or to give the appearance of doing so. In large-scale developing or transitional systems, due to the lower levels of literacy and political experience on the part of the masses and to their traditional reliance on the authority of their rulers, the function of the new authorities in converting wants becomes especially critical. Under pressure from below and in competition for political office, even if the bulk of the members did not themselves articulate their own demands, the leaders could be expected to do so in their stead. Under conditions of increasing popular involvement in political life, the new leadership may itself, therefore, form a second vital source from which will spring an increase in the volume and controversial content of wants seeking conversion to demands.

Cultural Inhibitors on Popular Involvement

If popular involvement were the single factor responsible for regulating the level and quality of conversion at any time, we can readily appreciate that, with the spread of democratic institutions, we ought to find democratic systems under constant threat of input overload from the influx of new demands. But this danger need not occur in practice. Political systems are capable of responding creatively and constructively to threatening situations and need not accept them as inescapable. Before we can state definitely that the stress is more than latent, we need to inquire into the way in which a system may respond to any threatened or actual increase, at least at this first point in the input channels.

In the first place, it is always possible to leave the gates open to any volume or content of demands and to deal with a threatened overload by regulation at a later point. In part this is exactly what does happen and very shortly we shall discuss modes of regulative response to such demands as do cross the boundary into the system.

But in the second place, new and supplementary regulative means may arise that result in reducing the inflow at its source, as wants are in process of being formulated into political demands. In the evolution of Western democratic systems, the degree of popular interest and participation has been high, relative at least to other types of systems, so it is instructive to see what happens in this general type of system.

As we might expect from our previous discussion, perhaps the most critical kind of regulation at the boundary is to be found in the growth of a special set of inhibiting norms with which the members of the system are imbued. In the face of the speculatively unlimited wants that members of a regime as permissive as a democracy might seek to have their authorities satisfy, cultural imperatives have gradually grown up side by side with the slow development of democratic institutions. These cultural norms have encouraged the leadership to exercise a socially defined sense of responsibility in promoting demands as they seek to mobilize support on their own behalf. The sky is not the limit and the leadership generally tends to shy away from outrageous demagoguery; the very term indicates the disrepute in which rash, excessive, and extreme promises are held.

These cultural inhibitors act not only upon the leadership but upon the membership as well. The average member is expected to display self-restraint in the expression of his wants and to take into account not only what is necessary but also what is possible. Ham-and-eggs schemes, by their very designation, are seen as quixotic and not to be taken too seriously; or if they are approved, it would not surprise most members to find that they are seriously modified before efforts are made at implementation.

Further, ideally, members are expected to be prepared to sacrifice the present for the future and to accept the exclusion from the realm of political conflict of exceptionally tender and sensitive issues that might destroy the cohesive tissue of the political community. The evolution of democratic institutions has been protracted over a long enough time for such norms to be worked out through trial and error and for them to become invisibly woven into the texture of political socialization in most democratic systems.

The significance of such cultural regulators is not a matter of conjecture or logical inference. Perhaps the most dramatic instance of their failure to operate and the effect this has on other parts of the regime are revealed in many contemporary transitional systems. In these, the exigencies of the struggles for national independence have compelled the indigenous leadership to rouse large segments of hitherto politically disinterested members to vigorous action, however sporadic and uneven the nature of the participation on the part of the members at large. To mobilize the kind of large scale action that was necessary as a leverage against the colonial powers meant encouragement of the appetites of the members of the system for the fulfillment both of long quiescent wants and of wants newly created by changing economic and social conditions.

To the point of independence, these latent demands could be held in abeyance or postponed in the universally accepted belief that national freedom must be achieved first. But with the attainment of this freedom has come the insistent desire to obtain payment on the promissory notes. Not that the bulk of the people themselves need seek this payment. It may arise from a competing or counter-elite that sees in the failure to deliver on the promises of the pre-independence days, a means and opportunity to obtain power for itself.

Out of this extremely fluid kind of situation, which differs in details for each transitional system but which is very much alike in general outline for most, has emerged what has so frequently been characterized as "the revolution in rising expectations." Whether this phrase adequately describes all that is happening need not concern us here. But that it does draw attention to the vast influx of demands being put into post-independence systems and to the equally vast conversion of dormant wants into active demands, cannot be overlooked.

To the members of the former colonial territories, national independence has been painfully slow in arriving. But if we bear in mind the long period it took the Western democracies to evolve, the democratically inclined transitional systems today have virtually mushroomed forth overnight. In part, the appeal of democratic ideologies has been a product of their obvious usefulness in helping to mobilize the masses against the colonial powers. To obtain the support of the democratic nations of the world or of groups within them, it also made sense to appeal against the colonial powers on the grounds of ideals that frequently their own systems were supposed to incorporate.

In espousing democratic ideologies, dominant groups in the transitional systems were unwittingly committing themselves to a complex kind of political system, in many cases with very little previous experience and true understanding of the conditions required for its operation. One of the consequences has been that members in these systems have lacked the time and historical experience that would have permitted them to develop, absorb, and transmit over the generations, those cultural inhibitors that, under other conditions, have helped to reduce the flow of demands at their source. A second consequence is that they have not had the opportunity to learn how to regulate the content of demands for the sake of minimal internal cohesion. From the perspectives of history, it may be that today, with the various oscillations between autocratic and democratic regimes in numerous transitional systems, we are witnessing the way in which the members of a system gradually build up a cultural tradition, that, among other things, serves to restrain the inflow of demands.

However complex the circumstances surrounding the sudden achievement of independence, underwritten in part by democratic ideologies, the experience in new nations demonstrates that without regulators at the level of want conversion, a system will typically find itself in grave straits from demand overload. Indonesia is a case in point, although she is not alone. In Indonesia, as in many developing systems, the norms of self-restraint and of a willingness to balance present satisfactions against future requirements, are lacking or in their infancy. These norms have been as rare in the general population as among the varied segments of the national and local leadership. Competing leaders have been able to mobilize support around the desire to obtain more of what are viewed as the just fruits of independence, and yet typically these leaders may show considerable indifference to or lack of understanding of what may in fact be possible. Immediately after independence, in particular, considerable pressure was exerted upon competing elites to offer ever rasher but economically quite unfeasible promises.

As one kind of response to this increase in the quantity and variety of demands, Sukarno was finally led to reinterpret the theory of democracy in a more limited vein which he embodied in the idea of "guided democracy." Whatever ambiguity surrounds this notion and whatever other manipulative motives underlie it, in consequence of its enunciation the general members of the system were encouraged to yield the task of generating demands or of passing upon their appropriateness, to the leadership.

In other systems, as in Ghana, the response to demands has taken a structural form labeled "one-party democracy." Whether or not such a phrase is a contradiction in terms, it reduces the number of organized, specialized groups (parties), which, among other tasks in developing nations, typically undertake to sense the wants of their followers and to convert these wants to demands. Regardless of the underlying intentions of a leadership—such as a desire to maintain its grip on the reins of authority—the idea of "guided democracy" and a one-party "democratic" structure both represent attempts of a hard-pressed leadership to cope with demand input overload. Ideas and practices like these constitute responses that are closely geared to limiting and controlling the conversion process.

It is apparent that those rules of the regime that discourage popular involvement in the political processes have as one of their major consequences the reduction of the volume and control of the content of the wants converted into demands. By the same reasoning, the diffusion throughout a system of an interest and involvement in political life will have the opposite effect; it is equivalent to opening the sluice gates to the political system as far as wants are concerned. In this sense the regime's rules for popular participation and involvement can be described as regulators of want conversion.[5]

[5] It may appear strange to include cultural norms, such as the rules of a regime, among the regulative means available to keep a political system within its critical limits. In ordinary language the idea of regulation often implies positive and voluntary effort on the part of some person to change the course of events under consideration, through a means under his control. This is certainly the case with respect to a mechanical device such as the governor on a motor, the gates of a sluice, or the automatic pilot on a ship. Each of these regulators is intended to keep the system of which it is part within prescribed or predetermined limits and each is amenable to modification, in operation or basic structure, at the hands of its designer or other person.

But not all regulators need be mechanical or humanly manipulate contrivances. In biological systems regulation may take place without conscious intervention as when appropriate physiological devices in the organism automatically, or autonom-

In concluding this chapter, I must emphasize that even though structural arrangements and cultural norms may regulate the entry of wants so as to exclude excessively large numbers from seeking conversion through existing structures, the degree of stress on the system will hinge on other conditions as well. Stress may be reduced or even aborted if the members of the system are willing and able to undertake measures to change the behavior of existing role incumbents, the structure of the system, or the cultural rules. If changes such as these were to occur, they would provide other or alternative modes of conversion. That is to say, the members of a system have the opportunity to respond to threatened stress by modifying the way in which the structural or cultural regulators operate even though they need not always take advantage of it.

Furthermore, even though a given volume and variety of demands may gain admission to the system, become part of the subsequent political processes and thereby raise the spectre of input overload, this is no certain indication that these demands will move far enough along the channels of the system to deliver on this threat. Much can and does happen between input and output to reduce volume and modify content. I shall shortly turn to these intervening possibilities.

---

ically, respond to threatened loss of sugar level, blood pressure, or oxygen, by activating other parts of the system. This suggests that in applying the concept "regulation" to social systems, it matters little whether the activity or structures that serve to keep a system within its critical limits are the result of deliberate and conscious activity or whether they arise spontaneously or even accidently in the course of events. In some cases, as through the construction or modification of a political constitution, very deliberate and rational efforts may be involved in creating regulative devices that will help to keep a given regime or whole system within its critical limits. In other cases, as in the slow and imperceptible modification of rules of behavior laid down through time in a political culture, regulators that help to keep a political system within its critical limits may be the product of the intricate play of history.

8

Regulation of the Flow of Demands:
The Communication Channels

ALL WANTS ARE NOT AUTOMATICALLY CONVERTED INTO DEMANDS AND large numbers may be excluded by the structural and cultural means of regulation available at the beginning of the flow paths. Nonetheless, many systems are probably faced with a larger volume of demands than they are prepared or able to process into decisions. If a system is to cope with a situation like this, some means must be available to regulate the demands *after* they have entered the system so as to prevent at least the major decision and action subsystems from being overloaded with matters requiring attention. In this chapter, we will begin to discuss the typical ways in which potential stress from demands is handled once the demands have become part of the activities within a system.

The Flow Channels of Demands

To appreciate what is involved in these kinds of overload, we must recall that demands do not flow randomly through a system.[1] They represent vector forces with a directionality that derives from the fact that the articulators of demands must orient themselves toward the subsystem that produces authoritative decisions. If they did not do so, the demands would have little chance of being fulfilled. Even if the originator of a demand were unaware of this fact—a highly unlikely situation for most members of a society—his political desires would be quite ineffectual unless in fact they did find their way ultimately to the authorities.

This is not to say that demands are always voiced with the expectation that they will be acted upon by the authorities. Frequently demands may be aired for their socially therapeutic value, to provide a

[1] See chapter 3.

focus of discussion that will help clear away tensions and discontents. But even in such instances, the members would have to feel that the authorities were at the psychological focus of the demands.

If the demands were not so oriented to the authorities, an air of unreality would surround them. Only if the authorities are somehow aware of them, can the demands be met. Accordingly, whenever demands appear in such numbers that the system is unable to absorb and transmit them, through various channels, to the authorities, stress on the system must result. The demands would of necessity remain unfulfilled. This output failure, persisting over time, must lead to the loss of support for a system, a point that I have mentioned before but which will be elaborated in a much later chapter.

To appreciate the way in which such stress is related to channel capacity, we must consider once again the idea of channels along which progenitor wants flow, once they have become transformed into demands. Later we shall also have to revive the companion notion of gatekeepers who stand astride these channels and by whom ultimately the rate, quantity, and content of the current of demands are conditioned.

As we saw in Chapter 4, demands may be conceived as messages or units of information that pass from one subsystem to another, indicating that certain members in the system seek to have their wants fulfilled through authoritative outputs. The paths of flow I have designated "channels," and the whole complex of them in any system I have designated "a network of channels." Every political system incorporates such a demand network. It is a communication structure, with differential power associated with different parts of it, through which demands are accumulated, interpreted, and then passed from one set of members or subsystem to another. It is a conveyance mechanism for funneling communications with regard to what members of a system want in the way of authoritative decisions.

Empirically, the network of channels will vary enormously from system to system and it would be both impossible and, fortunately, unnecessary for our purposes, to attempt to delineate the whole range. In small-scale, simple primitive societies, for example, the channels are diffuse and unspecialized. They are composed of the regularized communication structure of the whole primary group of which the system is composed. The absolute dominance of face-to-face relationships suggests that no organized groups stand athwart the channels as gatekeepers between an individual and the authoritative decision-makers.

But in modern societies, the communication channels for demands are highly diversified and structurally very differentiated. In addition to the primordial underlay of face-to-face communications, empirically the channels consist of the interrelationships among such familiar secondary political structures as interest groups, parties, opinion leaders, mass media, political leaders, legislatures, and relevant unorganized publics. What permits us to describe connections among these structures in a political system as channels is that regardless of where a demand is initiated, it becomes a message that may move from and through one of these subsystems to another, depending on the demand's particular career. Each subsystem may modify the demands coming to it, both as to their numbers and content, or it may stop them entirely under appropriate circumstances. As we shall later see, it is thereby capable of performing an intrasystem gatekeeping function.

Input overload may occur under one of two general circumstances, once demands have passed into a system. In the first place, the very capacity of the channels may be such that they cannot handle the volume of demands coming in.[2] I shall describe this as channel failure and we shall discuss it fully in this chapter. But in the second place, the channels may handle demands only too well and allow far more to reach the authorities than the latter can possibly handle. Overload may therefore be attributable to the way in which the intrasystem gatekeepers, standing athwart the channels at various points, handle the flow of demands. Consideration of this source of stress will be reserved for the next chapter. These two factors, the state and organization of channel capacity and the activities of intrasystem gatekeepers, will share the major influence over the extent of overload threatening a political system.

Channel Capacity

The capacity to handle demands once they have entered a system is a function of the volume of demands and existing channel capacity.

[2] Cf. H. A. Simon, "Political Research: The Decision-Making Framework," a paper delivered to the annual meeting of the American Political Science Association, New York, September, 1963: "The body politic is composed of very large numbers of human beings . . . Some of the crucial political processes—in particular, legislative and institutional changes that affect important, conflicting values—occur only in the presence of the simultaneous attention of large numbers of members of the political community. If one such issue is on the active agenda, most others are crowded off. A simple example of this is the postponement, by mutual consent, of most consideration of vital domestic issues during wartime. One reason, of course, for the bottleneck of attention is that most important changes call for action by the President or Congress, or other specific one-of-a-kind institutions. The Congress has a modest capacity for parallel action through its committee system, but largely for routine, low-temperature matters. Moreover, the formal and informal communications channels of the society appear to be capable of handling only a very few topics at any given moment in history."

The members of a system can cope with overload either by reducing the volume in some way or by increasing the capacity of the system to handle the existing volume. These are the two basic types of possible responses. In looking at the effects of structural and cultural regulation of wants, although the emphasis was not exclusively on the restrictive consequences of these mechanisms, nevertheless it was largely so. In now undertaking to explore the regulation of demands through modification of the capacity of the demand network, the emphasis is shifted to the other possibility. I shall be seeking to show that by creative adjustment of its channel capacity, a system may strive to handle a greater load of demands, thereby ameliorating overload stress. Subsequently I shall inquire into the various ways in which any excessive volume may be modified through measures restricting the flow of demands.

Sources of Channel Failure

Demand overload due to inadequate channel capacity may develop in a system as the result of a host of factors no one of which was designed or intended to interfere with the capacity of the system to handle demands. Because of the way in which the political structure of a system has emerged historically, it may prove difficult for the volume of demands with which the system has to deal to move along in a clear and orderly fashion to the points of consideration, decision, and action. The major problems here would be a matter of the number of channels and their carrying capacities, whether there are enough channels along which demands may move or whether each of the existing ones is capable of handling a large enough load so as to process the total volume entering the system.

This is not to say constriction of the flow of demands is always the unwitting and undesired outcome of general political processes. It may frequently be part of the deliberate policy or intention of the authorities to block off some demands by creating conditions that prevent them from being expressed or carried along to points of influence in the system. Channel inadequacy may be a calculated policy to maintain a group in power. The elimination of plural groups as competitors to a ruling elite, the curbing of free speech for those groups that remain, the subjection of political units, such as parties, to strict control, the close supervision of the mass media where they exist, will all contribute to the total effect of blocking and reducing the channels of communication for the flow of demands. It is a characteristic and decisive way whereby elites, fearful of popular pressure and, therefore, unwilling to entertain popular demands but unable to stifle their expression entirely, can prevent the demands from becoming disseminated through the system.

But impediments in the way of the communication of demands need not always occur only as the result of the purposeful behavior of a fearful ruling group seeking to obtain or retain power. In modern societies, the historical shift from a traditional social structure with a low volume of demands to one in which due to technological, economic, and other changes, demands have multiplied enormously, took place slowly over the centuries. Because of the slowly paced transformations, it was possible for these societies to invent channels to bring demands to a focus at the points where they could be of most use in enlightening the decision-makers. Channeling mechanisms such as parliaments, interest groups, parties, or responsive administrative organizations did not just emerge as ways of absorbing, communicating and processing demands. They were social inventions, gradually worried through, to deal with specific sources of tension, one of which involved the increasing rate of demand input and the need to devise ways of handling it.

In transitional societies today, for well-known reasons, the rapid pace of change would not have permitted the members of the relevant political systems to devise and experiment with alternative mechanisms for the collection and transmission of demands appropriate for the culture, even if they had wished to do so. Nor has it offered the time required, through slow trial and error, as in the West. Particularly in those transitional systems that are developing large-scale structures, local communities are typically and frequently cut off from the national centers. A local leadership may emerge as the brokers between local communities and the center, as in Indonesia where communal leaders serve as the major communication links between central and local subsystems.

But this one type of channel has been less than what would be necessary to handle the volume of demands to which change has given rise. Few effective alternative channels may be available. Mass media covering the society as a whole may be non-existent; parties, interest groups, or administrative agencies, which offer competing channels for the flow of demands may be absent, poorly operative, or strictly controlled. Under such conditions of limited channels, many demands may be blocked, restricted or what amounts to the same thing, grossly distorted.

The Consequences of Channel Failure

The stressful consequences attending the blockage of demands through insufficient channel capacity will manifest themselves in a variety of ways. In transitional systems, for example, at least in those in which the masses are politically mobilized or becoming involved, channel inadequacy, if not outright failure, is reflected in the build-up of a backlog of latent demands that periodically threaten to break through to the surface. In many modern systems, differentiated structures for voicing and transmitting demands, such as interest groups, legislatures, mass media, or parties, will serve as input channels that are continuously open, at least for those that are influential. In many non-Western systems, however, the lack of such institutionalized structures for carrying the growing volume of demands to the decision centers, has meant that demands can be introduced only intermittently.

This condition has helped to produce a style of politics notable for its dependence on violence and mass action. Demonstrations, riots, mass rallies, and the like have become important mechanisms for expressing and communicating demands. Blockage of demands in these cases has not served to obliterate them. Its consequence has been to transform what might have been a pacific continuous flow of demands into a spasmodically violent, eruptive one.

In modern systems, channel failure has also revealed itself through violent modes of expressing demands or pacific marches and demonstrations to the seat of the legislative and executive authorities. But in addition, it is manifest in the confusion among the members of the system with regard to the nature of the issues at stake or in the faulty and insufficient information that may reach the authorities with regard to the sources of discontent. As we shall discover much later, when we come to consider the feedback processes, information failure of this kind also tends to create an unfavorable balance between inputs of demands and outputs and will thereby adversely affect the support for major aspects of a system.

It is important in every system, therefore, that the demands formed out of wants can be presented to those who are involved in making a selection among them and converting them into binding outputs. In a democratic system, for example, this will mean that the network along which demands flow must be large and extensive enough to be able to bring demands before the relevant publics, for their discussion, as well as to the attention of the political leaders and authorities. In a dictato-

rial system, the network need only be linked to the general membership in an asymmetric way providing the authorities alone with sufficient information for the achievement of their independently determined goals.

Responses to Channel Failure

The rise of demands is a phenomenon clearly associated with the
growth of democracy and popular involvement. But it is equally an
outcome of the increase in the size of populations in political systems
and of the growth in technology and complexity of life through industrialization and its accompanying social and economic interdependence. How have systems historically managed to cope with an increasing flood of demands? What kind of responses in a system will increase
the volume of demands that its network of channels is able to carry?

Increase in the Number of Channels:
Political versus Social Structures

Historically, one major mode of response to a heavy input of demands is to be found in the specialization of political labor. The
greater the structural differentiation within a political system becomes,
the greater the variety and frequency of demands that can be processed.

Such structural differentiation may take several forms. In the first
place, it may involve differentiation of the political from the other
kinds of social roles. If the communication of demands through the
system to the point of authoritative decision were the general responsibility of all members in the system, the information load that each
person would have to carry and the time consumed in discussing the
demands would under most conditions become intolerable. Only
where the input of demands was small in proportion to the number of
members might this arrangement be less than stressful. Thus, it would
be feasible for each member to be equally responsible for the processing of demands in small-scale primitive systems, such as Bushmen
bands, where the number of demands are few and the members are in
constant and primary contact. Most political business can be trans-
acted during the course of other labor or at special periods of apparent
rest and relaxation.

Few systems leave the conduct of political business, including the
transmission of demands, to the general or undifferentiated member of

the social system, at least where the society extends beyond the primary group structure. In most societies with secondary institutions, the capacity for the performance of political tasks is assured by some minimal differentiation of political from other social roles. This distinction in itself provides for an increase in channels available for the communication of demands to the political authorities.

In a society in which political and other social roles are completely fused and empirically indistinguishable, each person has many other tasks to perform in addition to those of voicing, discussing, and helping to transmit demands to the authorities. As expressed in the *Federalist Papers,* in a period of commercial and agricultural dominance, there comes a time when the legislators must return to their fields. Although this is no longer literally true for the legislators, it is true for society as a whole. There is a limit, however ill-defined, to the amount of time that the society as a whole can devote to its political affairs. Where there is no specialization of political roles at all, as compared to general social roles, the capacity of a system for handling political matters is quite restricted. The need to feed, house, and clothe the members of the society imposes firm and inescapable limits on the time that can be devoted to politics.

One of the first reflections of the transition to a politically modern society is the rate of growth of specialized political institutions in which persons adopt politics as a major vocation. The emergence of specific, differentiated political roles indicates the arrival of additional channels for the performance of political tasks, including that of processing demands.

We have come to take it for granted that with the founding of new nations welded together from tribal groups, some sort of legislative and administrative apparatus should be established. But from the point of view of the persistence of the new system, one of the consequences of such specialized political institutions is the provision of facilities for dealing with a larger volume of demands, a novel phenomenon for transitional societies. Bureaucratization and professionalization of politics and administration have many effects on a political system, one of which, however, is the improvement of the system's capability for processing a greater volume of demands.

Increase in the Number of Channels: Specialization within the Political System

In addition to the differentiation of political from other social institutions, increased capacity for processing demands is also assured through the emergence of internal differentiation and specialization among the political roles themselves. The history of modern systems illustrates the part that specialization within a political system itself has played in adding to the demand-processing capabilities of a system.

For example, during the eighteenth century, the British legislature was committed to handling a large share of administrative as well as legislative demands. With the rapid advance of industrialism and the problems it brought in its train, Parliament was compelled by the nineteenth century to devise means to free itself from the resulting congestion, inefficiency, and confusion within its own organization. The channel capacity for handling demands at this higher level in the system was improved through the development of a separate administrative apparatus. Its task was to handle routine demands for action so that the time and energies of the political leaders might be reserved, among other things, for the demands associated with broader areas of novelty and change and political crises. Furthermore, the code of behavior that finally evolved for the administrative services—anonymity, impartiality, and neutrality—had the consequences of enabling the administrator to concentrate on routine demands and other matters and of sparing the politician-legislator the time that would have been consumed if the civil service had set itself up as a competitor to Parliament.

Almost every increase in internal political differentiation and specialization adds to the capacity of a system to handle a greater volume of demands. On the one hand, by rationalizing task performances, specialization increases the skill of those members through whom demands must pass and thereby increases the speed with which they can be expected to process such demands. On the other, specialization also usually means the multiplication of the number of channels available for processing demands.

Thus, the invention of special offices to handle requests (demands) for licenses on the basis of routine procedures; the continued effort to ease overburdened legislative channels through the creation of special administrative agencies to process demands in a more regularized fashion; the specialization within legislative bodies themselves in the form of standing and special committees for processing demands crystallized in bills; the increasing dependence on courts to relieve legislative institutions of certain kinds of claims that we characterize as legal; all have consequences that we can now interpret as serving to increase the channel capacity of a political system.

As is normally the case even with highly differentiated internal structures of social systems, these specialized organs usually fulfill multiple functions. Accordingly, the fact that I am here drawing attention to the effects with respect to channel capacity is not to be understood as exhausting the discussion of significant consequences that such structures may have for other parts of a political system.

The Competition among Alternative Channels

Intrasystem structural differentiation also increases the capacity of a system to handle demands to the extent that it provides the members with alternative channels through which demands may be expressed and communicated to others in the system. For example, mass media such as newspapers are known in some systems to act as a "third force" providing, among other things, an avenue for the expression of demands where other means may be more difficult or impossible to utilize. To the extent that a channel retains relative independence from control by other channels, it also helps to maximize the capacity of a system for communicating demands. It increases the variety of demands that can find an avenue for expression. In that way, a genuinely independent press, for example, would help to increase the actual number of demands that the system could process.[3]

Increase in Open Time of the Channels

In addition to the number and independence of channels, their capacity refers to the average number of man-hours the individuals, groups, or organizations of which the channel is composed devote to formulating, discussing, negotiating, and selecting demands. Some members or groups may be so over-involved in their task that they will devote all of their time to it; but most members spend only part of their waking hours on political matters, and, of these, still less on demands. Thus, at the same time as the number of channels for processing demands may be growing, it is frequently possible to increase the length of time that any single channel remains open.

This is a relatively simple point. Yet under the impact of all those factors mentioned earlier that have contributed in modern times to the rapid growth of demands, the time available to communication channels for handling demands had to be substantially increased. But for this, it is doubtful whether even the provision of new channels would have been enough to enable political systems to function at all,

---

[3] Cf. at the subsystem or parapolitical level, S. M. Lipset, M. Trow, and J. S. Coleman, *Union Democracy* (Glencoe, Illinois: Free Press, 1956), pp. 347–385.

at least with the emergence of the modern industrialized societies.

Perhaps one of the most significant ways in which modern systems have responded historically to the pressure of the increased inflow of demands has been through the professionalization of political roles. In part, as has already been indicated, this has meant the multiplication of structures for handling demands. But in part, it has also permitted the occupants of the roles to devote more of their time to political matters. In this way channels have been kept open for longer periods.

Thus, professionalization has been encouraged through the emergence of the practice of paying legislators and continuing to increase their salaries so that in an increasing number of jurisdictions, they are being freed to dedicate themselves largely to their political tasks, including the processing of demands. Many salary surrogate devices have appeared with similar consequences, as in the use of sinecures at the local level in the United States for party workers where it is impossible or politically unwise to legalize the tasks that need to be fulfilled. By unofficially providing greater time to party workers for building strength among the members of the system, this practice has incidentally served to maximize the time made available to search out and transmit demands to the authorities, among other political tasks. The establishment of administrative offices on a permanent basis and their decentralization to bring them closer to their clientele have similar effects.

Whatever the manifest motivations underlying all such innovations or the ulterior purposes at work, they have added substantially to the amount of time available for handling demands. They thereby have served to relieve the pressure that might have been occasioned by any large volume of demands.

9

Regulation of the Flow of Demands:

Reduction Processes

IN THE PRECEDING CHAPTER WE WITNESSED THE CONSEQUENCES OF IN-
sufficient channel capacity for the transmission of demands and
typical patterns of response through which systems have managed to
increase their load-bearing capacity. In this chapter I shall assume that
numerous and capacious enough channels are available to carry demands to the various parts of the system for further consideration. The
problem becomes one, not of too many demands and too few channels
but of enough channels operating so effectively that they may let too
many demands through. In this case it would not be the transmission
channels that would be overloaded but the decision-making centers
themselves. Under conditions where a system is able to process its
demands so that an excessive volume may reach the output points,
measures of various kinds must be taken to prevent input overload.

The Function of Demand Reduction

In most systems, even if the channels are well able to bear the load,
the raw demands, in the form they take when converted from wants,
seldom manage to get through unchanged to the ultimate centers
where binding decisions are made. In most systems, except perhaps in
the small primitive type, the demands will usually be subject to some
kind of pre-processing which modifies them so that they are different
than they were when first converted from wants.

Typically this has at least two consequences. One of these is that it
enables members of the system to modify the demands sufficiently so
that support for them can be mobilized and maximized or so that at
least some part of the demand can garner sufficient support to form the
basis for a binding decision.

128

But as a second consequence, the volume of demands may be substantially reduced at some point along the network and their content may be modified. If this were not a possible outcome, there would be little opportunity to regulate the flow of demands with respect to these aspects. Where the initial input of demands is heavy, as in the case of most modern and transitional societies, and especially where the channel capacity to carry the flow of demands to the authorities is more than adequate, the heavy volume would create serious difficulties for the decision-makers. They could scarcely be expected to give the demands serious and adequate consideration. Confusion or paralysis could easily result from the competition among those voicing the numerous demands, for the attention of those who have the power and the socially recognized right to deal with these demands and to decide whether to convert them into binding decisions.

It is true that the authorities might respond to such stressful conditions by increasing their structural capacity to handle any possible increase in demand load. Every legislative branch of government and every administrative service, today as in the past, has expanded its structural capacity to cope with the increasing burdens that modern industrialization, mass populations, and proliferation of independent political systems have imposed on them. But as we shall see, these problems with regard to the processing of demands have occurred in face of the fact that modern systems have adopted a considerable variety of methods for reducing the demand input load. If difficulties still do occur, it takes little stretching of the imagination to estimate the disorganization among the authorities that would develop if all raw and unprocessed demands appeared for consideration as possible outputs.

The closest approximation to such a condition appeared from time to time during the Third and Fourth Republics in France. A good share of the responsibility for the crisis form of government in France, at that time, has been attributed to the fact that insufficient pre-processing of demands had taken place. The result was that a vast number of demands fed almost directly into the legislature and helped to clog the decision-making procedures in that body. Insufficient negotiations and compromises, that is, modification in content and reduction in numbers prior to the legislative stage, repeatedly imposed an excessive burden on the representatives, one that periodically ended in the virtual inability to act at all.

Few systems could persist if all raw demands, those initially put into a system, proceeded directly, without modification, to the authorities, the output points. As we shall soon see, this applies to non-democratic as well as to democratic systems even though the nature of most modern non-democratic systems has made research with respect to such matters less accessible.

Reduction through Collection and Combination

In a conceptually meaningful sense, the aggregate of demands seeking the attention of the authorities in a system may be compared to a crowd of people trying to force their way through a door at one time. If those who controlled admission wished to do so and also had the ability, all or some of those seeking entry might be turned aside. In the case of demands this is equally possible; some demands may be neglected, ignored, or rejected out of hand and these will require no further attention with respect to their contribution to input overload.

But for those who are not turned away and are still seeking admission, one alternative would be to build a few new doors. We have already examined the analog of this in a political system as the development of new channels. Another alternative would be to keep the door open for longer hours if possible; a comparable measure with regard to demands is the lengthening of the processing time in the channels.

But if none of these responses were available or effective, efforts could be made to organize the crowd either in order to assure that all persons get through at some time, even if they have to come through in clusters rather than individually, or to allow admission to some as representatives of the remainder. Similar kinds of procedures are available in political systems in order to prevent a breakdown from the clogging and chaos that would ensue if all demands pressed for the attention of the authorities at one time. These ordering and clustering procedures I shall call the collection and combination of demands.

Collection of Demands

Reduction of raw demands may be brought about in two different ways. The number of demands due to the frequency of occurrence of the same demand may be lowered. For example, if each time a person favoring unemployment insurance legislation communicated his demand in a direct, unmediated form to the authorities, the volume with which the decision-makers would have to deal would be enormous. Reduction of the frequency of identical or very similar demands can be accomplished through their collection or pooling into one demand that is supported by many members. In this event, instead of the authorities being confronted by an endless number of requests for action on unemployment insurance, it would be faced with only a few requests, from some trade union organizations, let us say, but with the indication that the demand has the support of a large number of members. If the individuals who voiced this demand were to have them collected by a trade union of which they were members, in place of the many separately voiced demands, there would appear only the one demand supported by a large number of members. *Collection* of almost identical demands in this way represents one important kind of reduction.

Combination of Demands

A second type appears, however, through which different demands relating to the same general area or subject matter may be negotiated and combined into a common position. This can then be used as the basis of some issue. Many different demands for hospital care, payment of medical bills in chronic illnesses, provision of medical services, personal catastrophe insurance, security in old age, and the like, may be merged into a single demand or appeal for a general health insurance program. In a case such as this, it has not been a matter of gathering support for a single demand but rather of incorporating a host of varying demands into a single one. In this way the addition that variety of demands might make to the volume entering a system may be substantially reduced. We may designate this as the reduction of demands through their *combination* or amalgamation.

Illustrations of Collection and Combination

To some extent the reduction of demands through collecting and combining, synthesizing or fusing them into fewer units is constantly under way in all political systems. The moment that one person presumes to speak for or represent the expressed wants of two or more others, he has probably violated the integrity of each demand, taken singly, in order to be able to present them as one set of demands. When the lobbyist acting for an interest group indicates that his clients seek improved tariff and trade protection, it is unlikely that the program his group has worked out represents more than a compromise among divergent points of view held by the constituent firms. Although all may agree with the program, thereby adopting it as their demand, the demands out of which it was composed would in most instances differ more or less from the final outcome.

Similarly when a leader presents the presumed views of his followers, whether he is a member of a primitive, traditional, or modern political system, the demands so articulated will be understood to summarize or summate the demands of his followers. If these demands had been stated separately by each follower, probably no two would have been exactly alike. In this way the function of political leadership, among other things, is to reduce the volume of demands and modify their content as they move along through the system.

Many farmers may seek some means for maintaining prices for agricultural products at a level they consider equitable. Farm organizations may work out statements of policies they would like to see adopted which represent compromises among their membership. Key farm legislators and administrative agencies will, in turn, rework these policies and propose alternatives that are themselves further compromises among the programs advocated by numerous agricultural and other groups. The varied and numerous proposals are in this way gradually being reduced to workable sets of alternatives until at some point, a combined set of demands is finally accepted or rejected.

A classic illustration of the way in which many demands are collected and synthesized may be found in developing systems today. There the rising aspirations for a higher standard of living, increased social responsibility for disease and employment, rapid economic development, and the eradication of the evils of urban concentration of population, are all combined at some point into the call for national independence. The grievances, hatreds, and fluid energies of vast aggregates of members are brought to a focus on a single overarching demand that is interpreted, perhaps falsely, to embody and transcend, at least temporarily, all other demands. The political crisis of independence creates a major objective that for the moment obliterates other related varieties. In thereby incorporating many grievances into a single one, it is this one that is given priority; the others must await its fulfillment before they can be treated as demands in their own right.

Reduction of this kind is constantly taking place in most political systems. Except in the small, primary group types, seldom does the single demand of a single individual, representing his own idiosyncratic want, find its way directly to the decision-making centers. On occasion, of course, this is possible, as when a legislature undertakes to pass a law granting a divorce upon request, still the practice in a few political systems; or when some special circumstance, such as an emergency, permits an unprocessed demand to be presented for action by the decision-makers. But in the normal course of events the raw demands of a number of persons will be collected, combined, and consolidated into a single set of demands and this, in turn, may be modified many times before it reaches the output stage.

Reduction through Intrasystem Gatekeeping

Reduction through collection and combination occurs continuously as a result of the normal operation of various channels in the demand network. These modes of reduction are linked particularly to the activities of intrasystem gatekeepers and they may be accepted as virtually inherent types of response to potential overload, so universally do they appear.

In the preceding chapters, I have discussed the way in which gatekeepers help to regulate the input of demands through their impact on the conversion of wants at the boundary of the system. But gatekeeping activity is not confined to this moment alone. In fact, structurally identical gatekeepers are to be found at numerous points clearly inside the system itself. Shortly it will even appear that the identical members, groups, and organizations that at times initiate demands will also at some subsequent stage be in a position to reduce the same demands through collecting or combining them with others. The fact that these gatekeepers may stand across the flow channels at numerous points puts them in a strategic position for performing collecting and combinative actions that affect the number and content of demands as they are processed through the system. Indeed, this constitutes a vital part of the pre-processing through which demands are put before they even reach the point of being entertained as possible outputs at the hands of the authorities.

To appreciate the role that intrasystem gatekeepers play in a system's reduction response, we must return to Diagram 3 in Chapter 5. There I had outlined a set of channels that represent the logical alternatives available to a demand as it courses through any system. With respect to these, we have had an opportunity to discuss only what happens at the boundary, at the beginning of any of the varied channels depicted there. For the first time we are now in a position to follow a demand as it makes its way through a system toward the authorities and to describe what may happen to it at different moments of time.

The Location of Gatekeepers

Since I have been attempting only a systematic analysis of processes rather than of structures, here, as elsewhere in the discussion of the flow paths, I am more concerned about the temporal phasing of various activities or events than about the structural paths along which a demand may flow. It would be perfectly feasible to trace out, analytically, various communication structures in a political system and to follow a demand as it moves through these structures. In this event we would have to be particularly interested in who speaks to whom about what and the determinants of these relationships.

But it is important to keep in mind that our present analysis delves into problems related particularly to the nature of processes taking place rather than to the form in which they take place, at least to the extent to which the discussion of structure can ever be divorced from process. My central concern is to identify, describe, and interpret the systemic functions of processes. At the moment our attention will be directed to the time order in which various parts of the reduction processes occur.

The immediate significance of this caveat is that we shall now find that different structures, such as gatekeepers, can appear at different moments in the sequence of activities through which demands are reduced, once they have begun to flow through the system. On a diagram, this would look as though such structures appeared at two or more places at the same time, that is, at various reduction points. But this is an artifact of diagrams, not necessarily a fact of reality. The diagrammatic representation would have to be interpreted to mean only that a given structure, such as an interest group as a gatekeeper, may be activated at different times with respect to the reduction of demands. It may act on a set of demands in one way or another depending upon the moment in the flow of the demands that the interest group becomes concerned with them.

If we now reconsider the arrows on Diagram 3 in Chapter 5, we can see that they really represent points in the flow of time, hence flow charts, rather than physical locations in a system of behavior. In this interpretation, we can appreciate how it will be possible for a gatekeeper, such as a trade union, at points R on the flow paths, to be "present" across a channel not only at the beginning of a demand, during the want conversion phase, but also subsequently at various moments in time as the demand undergoes further reduction in which the same union takes a hand.

Unreduced Demands

Although reduction activities constitute a typical kind of regulative response in systems, some demands are able to escape them entirely. As

I indicated when Diagram 3 was first presented, the lack of reduction symbols in channels S and T points up the fact that some demands, once they have gained admission to the system, may escape further regulation. In the one case, the demands do not require reduction since they expire before progressing very far along the communication channels. In the other, they are transported to the authorities before any regulation can take place.

With respect to the first kind of demand, represented by flow path S, the demand may continue to be bruited about as a possible course of action for government. But ultimately it is unable to collect sufficient support from those who count in the system. It is neglected, postponed indefinitely, or it dies a natural death. Most popular demands, at least in a democratic order, probably wither on the vine in this way. Indeed, many are probably voiced without any intention by the advocate to pursue them further, beyond their mere statement, and without any serious expectation that they will be adopted by others. They serve their purposes when they have allowed their articulator the pleasure or catharsis of complaining and criticizing. Even in dictatorial systems, undoubtedly there is a far greater proportion of suggestions for political action that are informally raised for discussion among the elite than in fact ever become a serious focus for policy. Failure to strike a responsive chord among the influential members of a system is one of the major ways in which demands are quickly reduced in volume although it would not be analytically helpful to consider this a regulative device.

In the second case mentioned, however—flow path T—demands are equally free from regulation. These we may call uncontested demands; they advance directly to the decision centers in the system without the intervention of any reduction mechanisms. This is typically what happens with those demands that have a high order of priority due to emergency conditions. It also applies when a demand has such widespread support among the influential members of a system that they are virtually irresistible.

The Functions of Intrasystem Gatekeeping: A Model

Aside from these two kinds of situations, demands will all be exposed to the possibility of regulation of the type I have called collection and combination, at points represented on Diagram 3 by the letter R next to a pyramid. This symbol indicates that at some point in time after a demand has been converted from a want, it encounters further gatekeeping activity which in one way or another succeeds in reducing or modifying the demands involved. Our focus, therefore, must shift from gatekeeping at the boundary to the same process that, by definition, lies within the system itself. We must now look at the way in which this kind of process manages to shrink the number of demands or modify their content.

Where the gatekeepers decrease the demands through neglect, omission, or outright rejection, they thereby contribute to the probability that these demands will disappear from the political scene. But for the remaining demands, it is of course the gatekeepers themselves, through the support that they tender the demands, who help to keep them alive and coursing through the system to the points of output. But in the process, they may also act upon the demands in such a fashion that, as the demands move closer to the point of possible implementation as binding decisions, they constantly become smaller in number although at the same time more comprehensive in scope. That is to say, if we were to construct a model of a first approximation of what tends to happen to demands as they undergo successive stages of reduction, regardless of the kind of political system, we would be forced to put it in the shape of a pyramid. A large number of demands gradually is reduced to a few but, in the process of reduction, these few may incorporate some or all of the content of many of the demands that had been eliminated as independent units.

Let us see what this model would look like and test its plausibility later by comparing it briefly in passing with at least a commonly accepted, if somewhat ideal, stereotypical account of demand reduction in the British political system. In the model, at the base would lie many demands being voiced by the politically relevant members of the system, insofar as they are permitted to do so and the culture induces it. The members who are relevant may include all, many, or few of those in the system.

The demands may then flow in one of two basic directions. They may diffuse outward to all members of the system without the intervention of intermediaries. In small systems, such as those composed wholly of a face-to-face group, this is entirely probable and possible. But aside from this type of system, analytically and empirically it is more probable that the demands will flow to intermediary concentration points. These are the gatekeepers who in traditional systems may appear as notables, aristocratic families, age-sets, and the like. In modern societies they take such structural form as opinion leaders, interest groups, legislators, mass media, political leaders, or parties. Among gatekeepers such as these, some of the demands may fail to find any support at all; through indifference or decisive negative action, this percentage of demands will die out. The gates are closed to them.

But gatekeeping involves more than just the opening and closing of communication channels through whatever power the gatekeepers possess. It includes as well the performance of those operations on demands that I have been calling collection and combination. Demands will frequently be assembled, fused, synthesized, or in some way reformulated so that they are different after they have been further transmitted by the gatekeepers than they were upon reception. How different they are and in what ways will depend upon the characteristics of the gatekeepers, the norms by which they operate and the goals they adopt as criteria of selection.[1]

But there is no reason why the demands need be communicated by the first gatekeepers directly to the authorities, their expected terminal point. We may conceive of the single points marked R on the flow paths U and W on Diagram 3, as really consisting of many possible gatekeepers. Demands may pass through many hands to be combined and modified numerous times before they reach the output centers, if they ever do get that far. In each case new and different gatekeepers are responsible for additional sorting out and reformulation until some few issues have been identified or defined and, thereby, an agenda developed, one that may be used by the authorities for helping them to perform their tasks. In effect, the political agenda is under continuous development as a result of these sorting, winnowing and reducing activities on the part of the gatekeepers in a system.

The authorities themselves also participate in the processes of gatekeeping and, thereby, in the reduction of demands, as well as in the production of outputs. It is axiomatic today that structures perform multiple functions. Hence we cannot allow ourselves to be deceived by the name of the structure—such as that of authorities or government —into believing that thereby we have excluded from that structure activities other than those denoted by the name. Governmental or authoritative structures not only produce authoritative outputs: they also participate in the processes of gatekeeping insofar as legislators, administrators, or executives help to collect or combine demands as they move toward the decision point.

---

[1] Of course, where the gatekeeper is a group of members, the resources available to the group, its organization and its internal power relationships will also be determinative of the kinds of demands that it initiates, adopts, or reformulates and passes along. A partial theory of interest groups, for example, would seek to develop an analytic structure for understanding the part that such groups play in processing demands, both in generating them and regulating their volume and flow.

An Empirical Approximation to the Model

But regardless of who helps to decrease the volume of demands, we can appreciate how the pattern of reduction in a system tends to assume a pyramidal shape if we turn from an analytic model to compare it cursorily with what we may now designate as demand reduction structures and processes in some empirical system. For this purpose I shall consider the British system, or at least the stereotype that has grown up about its operation. In this system there is a greater tendency than in most other modern democratic systems for the structures that contribute to demand reduction to be related to one another in such a way that, in effect, a modest if not sharply defined division of labor prevails. Each type of political structure tends to collect and combine demands at increasingly higher and more inclusive levels.

For example, a relatively ineffective member of the system may express his wants by writing to newspapers, his representatives, or simply complaining to a friend. If he happens to belong to an organization such as an interest group or if such an organization senses his felt needs, it may act so as to combine the overlapping demands and wants of a large aggregate of members. Thereby the organization will have fused similar demands into a common and relatively integrated set of demands. We recognize this by giving it a name, such as the "program" or objectives of the interest group. If we wish, we might describe this as the creation of a limited consensus among an aggregate of persons, limited because in the normal course of events, in the British system, such organizations are only limited purpose associations rather than comprehensive communal units as, say, an Indian linguistic-religious-geographical group.

At the next level, a higher order consensus is typically created through the structure of the political party, at least with regard to those demands that are seen as relevant to political campaigns. A British political party will endeavor, where necessary or opportune, to incorporate into its program demands taken directly from what it perceives members of the system to be seeking or needing. In addition, by its very structure and function in the political system, it will seek to embody in its platform those demands already incorporated in the less inclusive demands of interest groups. Where, as in the British system, there is a relatively clear differentiation between parties and interest groups with regard to the level at which they perform their combining activities, parties will have a later and more inclusive voice. They help to regulate the volume of demands as well as their content at a later stage. In much the same way, we can interpret the actions of Parliament and the Cabinet, components of the authorities, as combining the pre-processed party demands at a still more inclusive level.

In its stylized form, therefore, the infinite number of popular demands in the British system is sharply reduced to a relatively smaller volume by interest groups; these are then further combined by parties; and in the legislature and executive they are still further winnowed out into an agenda from which policies are formed. In practice, of course, not even the British system in its most idealized version quite achieves this neat correspondence of structure and function. Certainly in other democratic systems, such as the American, it is quite customary for the legislature to offer many more alternative sets of demands in a particular area than may be proposed by the major political parties. Weak party structures help to ease the way for direct access to legislators. They lead to much reduction through the combination of demands that takes place in the legislature itself. As we know, this level of reduction is more frequently performed in the British system by political parties. On the average, therefore, demands get closer to the output stage in the American system with much less processing than in Britain. But in neither of these systems do the structural means for pre-processing demands throw upon the authorities the primary or sole responsibility for working out major kinds of consensus from a welter of raw demands.

In those systems where little preparatory reduction is attempted through combining demands, and all is concentrated in one major effort, an exceedingly heavy burden is imposed upon the final decision-making centers. Although this was not exactly the situation during the Third and Fourth Republics in France, nevertheless, as I suggested before, France came close enough to this state of affairs to experience grave difficulties in processing demands. Parties and interest groups were so intertwined as virtually to eliminate an important pre-processing stage.

In part, deep and almost irreconcilable differences in the content of demands were to blame. But mere quantity of demands played a role as well. Additional institutions for seeking out preliminary partial settlement might have made some contribution to the reduction of demands. Not that a mere institutional innovation could have "solved" the recurring crises. But we are not called upon to explore other consequential factors; it is enough to note the possible independent contributory effect of an excessive volume of demands.

I have been speaking about representative systems where, because of popular involvement in the political processes, the volume of demands is considerable. Systems such as these have had to devise structures for handling demands of high proportions. Interest groups, parties, legislatures, as well as political and public opinion leaders, and the like, perform this task. But in those systems in which a restricted elite possesses a monopoly over the input of demands, as in various totalitarian regimes, and where whatever popular demands that may be permitted are carefully guided into channels controlled by the elite, volume of demands need not present a major problem. Even though the USSR is a major industrial nation, the Supreme Soviet typically needs to meet only a few weeks a year, so sheltered is it from any influx of demands. There is no danger of demand overload at this point, at least as long as the generation and flow of demands does not get out of hand. The only real problem would be the way in which demands are handled at the level of the elite itself. Here, as I have already noted, reduction of demands undoubtedly occurs even though, by the nature of the case, access to empirical data may be difficult.

Reduction through Issue Formulation

The Functions of Issues

Before even demands that have already been collected and combined, can be processed into outputs, there must be some way for the politically relevant members to focus sharply on some of the demands requiring their attention. At any moment, where the volume of demands exceeds a few, only some of the total number can come under active consideration or can be expected to be treated as the basis for decision. Of necessity, these will be the demands that have become the subject of greatest controversy and, following standard usage, I shall call them *issues.*

In most systems, especially modern ones—but, for reasons that will gradually appear, not excluding others—there are a large number of demands that reflect problems requiring attention at any one time. The members of a system do not and cannot deal with all of them at once. Some method for discriminating and selecting among the problems is required. This is the fundamental task of issue formulation. It reduces demands to a more restricted number on which attention can be centered.

Of all the demands pressing to get through to the point of decision, only some will make it. The emergence of issues reduces the number to which attention needs to be given, establishes some priorities among the whole range of demands waiting to be acted upon, and thereby helps to reduce the pressure of the volume seeking consideration as serious alternatives for policy. In this sense, although it may not initially reduce the absolute level of demands in the system, it does cut down the load that the members have to deal with at any specific time. Some demands are set aside for the moment; they do not make the grade as issues. In being set aside, however, as we shall see, they may be neglected and may fail later to win any further attention; thereby a drop in the absolute level of demands may also ensue.

The process through which demands become converted into issues will therefore serve as a means for easing possible overload on the system. It may do this in one of two different ways. In the first place, as flow path labeled V on Diagram 3 indicates, some demands bypass any prior reduction and may be directly converted into issues. A widespread outcry for universal, free higher education, as a means of coping with the revolution in automation, might become an issue without further pre-processing or combination with other demands. It might then continue to be an issue, without resolution, for a considerable time and ultimately wither away, as indicated by the broken line on flow path V, or it might be entertained as a possible basis for immediate decision. In this event, the issue would serve to reduce the demand load, not by actually eliminating any other demands, but by taking precedence over others that have not reached the status of issues.

If a demand never becomes an issue, unless it is one of those few that move directly to the decision stage as indicated by flow path T, it may have to wait so long for serious treatment as a demand that its timeliness disappears, or the time for action passes, or those who have voiced and promoted it lose interest. In one or another of these ways, the priorities established in favor of some demands, through the fact that they become transformed into issues, help to displace and ultimately reduce the number of other demands confronting the members of a system.

But in the second place, as flow path W indicates, some issues may embrace a number of demands. The formulation of an issue may be possible as a result of a number of demands having been combined and synthesized as the converging channels suggest and these combined demands may then become the issue. The demands for social services, foreign aid, and financial assistance to education may, for some members of a system, raise as a central issue the intrusion of "creeping socialism" in government, an issue that has been formulated in the United States in the last several decades. The controversy over this topic sums up differences that members may have over a broad range of demands and, in that way, this single condensed issue reduces the number of discrete demands that have to be treated separately. As we shall see in a moment, it funnels all discussion into an orientation issue, a discussion of who, on grounds of ideological predisposition, is the best member or which is the best party to take a position of leadership among the authorities. What might otherwise have remained a long list of independent items on the agenda for discussion as issues becomes congealed into a dispute as to who can best be trusted with the job of governing.

The Meaning of Issues

As has just been intimated, to understand the way in which a system may preserve itself from demand input overload, we need to cast the meaning of issues in somewhat broad terms. We can begin by following the voting studies and define issues as "statements that allege differences between the contending parties or candidates" [2] and that have become matters of dispute among them. Such disputed matters form political issues because they are viewed as realistic alternatives from which a selection will probably be made with respect to the outputs of the system.

But from the point of view of the reduction processes in a system, we must carefully distinguish two major kinds of issues: decisional and orientational. Decisional issues deal with the substantive content of possible alternatives for decision and action. From among these it is anticipated that the decision-makers will probably make some binding selection. Orientation issues refer to differences with regard to the qualities of a contender for an office: which persons or parties are best, more experienced, honest, capable, representative, and the like, depending upon the criteria of evaluation.[3]

The fact that a person votes blindly for a party or is dazzled by the appeal of a political leader and as a result is indifferent to the content issues involved in a choice, does not thereby confirm that the party follower or the personal devotee is refusing to take a position on the substance of a controversy. In effect, and we are interested in the

---

[2] B. R. Berelson, P. F. Lazarsfeld, and W. N. McPhee, *Voting* (Chicago: University of Chicago Press, 1954), p. 182.

[3] In Burma, Pye points out, issues typically revolve around personalities rather than decisional issues. L. W. Pye, *op. cit.*, pp. 16–17.

realities and not only convenient categories of analysis, such a person is taking a stand on an issue. But the issue here is whether the party or leader with which he identifies is the one that is best suited through competence, ideological posture, trustworthiness, or any other criterion, to undertake the responsibilities of governing.

In this interpretation, votes flowing in a democratic system from party identification or loyalty to a candidate constitute stands on an issue. Party and leader incorporate substantive points of view on the decisional, content issues of the day, at least as they reflect orientations to these issues. A vote for the party ticket or for an individual leader, at a minimum carries the meaning that the voter sees this organization or individual as possessing an orientation that will lead to what he considers to be an appropriate way of dealing with decisional issues, current or future. He is entrusting to others the task of working out the details when in office.

In the context of our discussion, when an individual entrusts the task of settling the day-to-day problems of policy formation to others, he is subordinating the multitude of his demands to the one issue of who is to be the custodian of the government for the succeeding period. For the volume of demands flowing through the system, this subordination has the positive consequence of summating numerous different demands into the one issue: Shall the particular party or leader be entrusted with disposing of a multitude of what are, at times, vaguely felt needs and, at others, quite articulately held demands? Even when a person declares blindly in favor of a party or places his unstinting confidence in a leader, decisional issues or campaign "issues" in the substantive or policy sense may become less important temporarily. The matter in controversy for such a person is whether the leader or party has the general qualities he considers necessary to do the general job of running the country. Decisional issues are heavily discounted, for the moment, in favor of this orientational one alone.

If we consider as issues those demands that become a matter of contention because they are being considered as the basis for implementation in the immediate future, how are we to distinguish them from other demands present in a system? A demand that has not become transformed into an issue will fall into a residual category; it is one that is simply not a matter of immediate controversy among the relevant members of the system as a realistic alternative for policymaking. This does not mean that the members of a system will have no other differences with regard to their demands than those manifesting themselves as issues. Nor does the existence of issues mean that other demands cannot be discussed through whatever channels for political communication exist.

For example, members may differ with regard to the desirability of positive measures to preserve national parks or for the provision of social security from the cradle to the grave. In the newspapers and journals, on radio and television, such matters may even be discussed. But as long as the demand is debated primarily for educational purposes and not in preparation for doing something about it in a formal way—as in a campaign or within inner party circles in a dictatorial system—it remains a demand, one or more stages removed from an issue. Since the primary index of the issue status of a demand depends upon the degree of involvement of the relevant members of a system in its discussion and the extent to which the matter is being considered for possible authoritative action, empirically some cases of issues may be hard to distinguish from demands under discussion. But in principle the distinction is unambiguous.

If my focus were on control over the processes through which demands become converted into outputs, I would be compelled to raise additional questions, at this point, as central ones. Those individual or groups of members who, in fact, are prominent in regulating the conversion of demands to issues, who are gatekeepers over issues and thereby help establish priorities among demands seeking attention, or who are able to control the gatekeepers, are in critical positions of control or power in a system. Voting research and community power studies have shed considerable light on the characteristics of those who typically are able to sponsor issues and on the conditions under which such issues will be able to arouse or enlist the interest of the general membership in a democratic society.

But in failing to recognize issue formulation as a means of enabling a system to handle large numbers of demands, such studies have typically neglected to appreciate the full systemic significance of varying structures through which control over issues may be exercised. Control over the sponsorship of issues is an important predictor of the distribution of power within a system. But regardless of where the control may lie, in general system terms the varying methods of control stand as variable structures through which a system may be able to avoid stress flowing from demand overload. In this way the study of issues is raised to a high level of generality. Its significance extends beyond the single, although highly important question, of where power lies in a system or why members vote as they do—a subject for partial theory—to the problem of how any system manages to persist under demand conditions that may threaten to drive its essential variables beyond their critical range.

The Locus of Issue Conversion

The reduction of demands through their incorporation into issues is not an activity that need always be conducted with the participation of the general membership in a system. The fact that research with regard to issues has largely been confined to the campaign type and of necessity, therefore, to democratic systems, might unwittingly leave the impression that, by their nature, issues take shape only when popular participation is in some way possible. But this is only an accident of the fact that issues in democratic systems lend themselves to easier investigation, by the nature of the case. The truth is that *popular issues* are probably far less numerous and, therefore, a less frequently used mechanism for reducing demands than other modes of issue conversion, even in a democracy.

In practice, in democratic systems there are numerous issues that take shape and are acted upon by only a select few, except that in the conventional terminology of research we are less apt to identify as such, those issues that do not lead to popular involvement. But if all reduction of demands through issue conversion had to depend exclusively on popular issues, it is doubtful whether this mechanism of reduction would loom very large in the repertoire of a democratic system.

It is well-known that only a limited range of subject matters lend themselves to popular campaign dispute, or to popular discussion in the intervals between electoral campaigns. Such demands usually are of a type that can be readily dramatized, that enlist a broad and diversified interest among the membership, and that are not too technical. Lack of general popular appeal or excessive complexity will prevent a set of demands from being collected or combined into a popular issue. Yet, in spite of their inability to cast many demands with such content into popular issues, the authorities would find it virtually impossible to deal with each separate demand in a general area without first reducing the many alternatives to a manageable few, for consideration and decision.

The result is that even in the most democratic systems, many issues are raised and discussed in much smaller groups. In many cases, what we might call *administrative issues* are composed of demands that take shape in administrative organizations or come under consideration there. Public officials may be concerned with technical problems that few others are competent to deal with, much less to become interested in. We have already seen that demands may initially be put into a system by any group, including administrators. Here we see that the same group may even process sets of demands into issues. Under certain circumstances, the demands may not even become real legislative issues, as, for example, if they are introduced during the waning days of a legislative session and can be hurried along, without discussion, under the pressure of time.

Other demands may be reduced largely in the confines of the legislative bodies in a system and, therefore, may be designated as *legislative issues*. They may arise as a product of differences that occur among legislators themselves or between the executive and legislature. Other issues may be even more restricted in character and yet serve equally well for reducing demands that might otherwise add to the load of the authorities. Some issues may involve only select individuals, such as the members of a legislative committee or the advisers surrounding a chief executive. A resolution of the issue there may kill it and make it difficult or impossible to raise elsewhere as a serious basis for policy. Alternatively, it may succeed in condensing a number of demands into a single major issue for further consideration by others.

Such more limited loci within which issues may be raised are virtually neglected in the discussion of issues for democratic systems; yet they constitute vital variants of issue conversion as a general mechanism through which the demand load on a system may be reduced to manageable proportions. Of course, what distinguishes the non-popular character of such purely administrative or legislative issues from the leadership issues in non-democratic systems is that, under the rules of democratic regimes, it is always possible for issues raised anywhere to be brought out into the open for public discussion. Private issues of these kinds can always be transformed into public ones. Yet the realities of political life and the limited range of issues that can be appropriately dramatized, at least under modern conditions of literacy and public concern, offer no guarantee that efforts to bring private issues into the glare of publicity will succeed. Nevertheless, the availability of the opportunity to attempt to do so acts as a restraint on the kinds of issues that are privately raised and, not so incidentally, also limits the way the issues are resolved.

The Universality of Issue Conversion as a Reduction Mechanism

Although for transparent reasons, issue research has concentrated on democratic systems, everything that has been said about the function of issues applies, with appropriate modifications for differences in regimes, to non-democratic systems as well. Whether a system is constitutional but unrepresentative, dictatorial, totalitarian, or one-party "democratic," some method is necessary for coping with possible demand overload, other than regulation of want conversion or availability of channels. The absence of popular involvement will naturally be quite material to the kind of demands that are embodied in issues. But it will not eliminate issue conversion as a reduction mechanism in non-democratic systems.

However few the politically relevant or influential members of a non-democratic system may be, not everyone can play an equal role in the actual making of binding decisions. Some allocation of authority of necessity takes place in all but the smallest systems. And those who are excluded from among the actual authorities but who count in the system, will put in demands with regard to possible policies and will be called upon to lend their support in favor of various issues. The authorities do not operate in a power vacuum; and in being subject to the stress and strains of alternative proposals, they are exposed to alternative sets of demands out of which policy alternatives may be selected.

As in other systems, issues of two kinds present themselves in non-democratic systems. Some are decisional issues that collect or combine numerous discontents into a few sets of demands. In the Soviet Union, in recent years, issues internal to the bureaucracy but sending small shoots into the membership have concerned the relative merits of emphasis on consumer or producer goods, a hard or soft line toward the West, accommodation with communist China, or a continued independent leadership. Although these issues have been primarily located in the bureaucracy, they do reverberate through broader segments of the membership.

Other issues are orientational. They revolve around differences with regard to the general competence of the given leadership to conduct the affairs of state in harmony with the values and demands of the supporting members. In the Soviet Union, this has taken the form of a major fissuring issue around the desirability of a Stalinized or post-Stalin kind of leadership. In these issues, the membership as a whole is less likely to be involved since they touch the main nerves of the power system. But popular sentiment is not totally without some pressure.

The mere fact that detailed consideration of such controversies as a species of issues has not commanded the attention of empirical research workers ought not to be allowed to conceal from us their true character. In spite of the many potent mechanisms available to non-democratic systems to cut down the number of demands entering the system or moving along the political communication channels, the capacity of such systems to persist is certainly enhanced by the operation of the additional demand reducing mechanism that we have been identifying as issue conversion, however restricted membership involvement in them may be.

We can sum up this discussion of issues by saying that they take shape in all systems and that, as a major consequence, their presence contributes significantly to the reduction of the demand input load. Furthermore, without issues, there would be little opportunity for bringing an unmanageable number of demands into some orderly arrangement for consideration by the authorities. And here, as in the case of all other mechanisms viewed as a response to potential stress, there is no reason why issue formulation, together with all other demand reducing mechanisms, should always succeed in preventing the authorities from being inundated with a disorderly flood of demands. It is only one of a number of devices, as we have seen, and if the others operate so as to leave a system confronted with excessive input overload, issues by themselves may be unable to reduce enough demands so as to shield the authorities. Undoubtedly, the avoidance of stress would require the compensatory operation, in some integrated, consistent pattern, of all the kinds of regulative responses with which we have been dealing, so that the failure of no one of these central mechanisms need defeat the consequences of all the others.

In this chapter and in the preceding ones, we have been approaching demands as a major link between a political system and its environment. It has been in the capacity of the members of a system to handle the problems of excessive volume of demands and their time-consuming content, another aspect of volume, that we have found a major threat to the persistence of a system to lie. As the flow of wants increases, due to changes in some aspect of a system's environment, increasing burdens are placed upon the members of the system to reduce the number that are converted to wants. If efforts to this end are not possible or if they prove inadequate in reducing the load that the system must process, the burden for doing so is transferred to intrasystem structures. The capacity to cope with possible stress will depend upon the number, variety, and load-bearing capacities of demand channels and on the gatekeepers through whom demands are pooled or combined into overarching programs and policies, or telescoped into controversial issues.

But however successful a system may be in coping with the stress that might otherwise have been occasioned by a continuous influx of demands, this achievement alone would not assure the continuance of the system as a set of processes for converting wants into outputs. There is at least one other major input, support; fluctuations in it may have fatal consequences for the persistence of political systems.

For the students of politics as well as for the participants, support is an input the effects of which have traditionally been much more visible and salient than demands. Yet, as we now turn to support, two preliminary points must constantly be borne in mind. Although it has received an extraordinary amount of attention—in the literature on power and on voting behavior, to cite only two sources—most of this has been directed to only a limited aspect. In many ways this aspect has not always been the most interesting one, at least from the theoretical point of view of the basic capacities of systems to adapt and survive as systems of behavior.

Furthermore, the fact that support has been the object of universal concern testifies to the importance that students of politics have obviously attached to it. That it is a central phenomenon and analytically equally so, I would be the last to deny. Nevertheless, the concentration on support, especially as a base of political power, ought not to be allowed to continue to distract us from other major aspects contributing to the operation of political systems. It is easy to forget or gloss over the fact that however rich our understanding of the function of support, it can tell us only part of the story. To complete it, we must constantly bear in mind the complementary parts played by demands and outputs.

I have, of course, set this as the major task of this macroscopic analysis: to put each of the three central variables—demands, support, and outputs—in a balanced perspective. By analyzing their separate functions and tracing out their interdependence, we should be able to illuminate with a different and new light the way in which political systems perform their major task of converting inputs into authoritative allocations.

Part Three

The Input of Support

I O

Support as an Input of Systems

A POLITICAL SYSTEM MAY BE DESCRIBED IN ANY ONE OF A NUMBER OF ways depending upon the particular kind of emphasis we wish to give to it. For reasons elaborated elsewhere,[1] at the most general level it is highly useful to depict a political system as a set of interactions through which valued things are authoritatively allocated for a society. But in addition to this formulation, a political system may be viewed as a means for resolving differences or as a set of interactions through which demands are processed into outputs. From another perspective, it is a means through which the resources and energies of society are mobilized and oriented to the pursuit of goals. In the last sense, the description is particularly helpful in highlighting the need for marshaling the support of the members if the system is to be able to act at all. The function of support will constitute the focus of this section of my analysis.

Not that any one of these alternative interpretations may be said to be correct and the others false. Each cuts through the functions of a political system in slightly different ways and each is equally compatible and consistent with what I have indicated to be the most general interpretation. It is just a matter of what aspect of a system we find most useful to emphasize at the moment.

To this point I have been considering how the members establish the direction in which a system ought to move. When members convert wants to demands, in effect they are asserting that they would like to push the system as a whole, through the energies and resources at the disposal of the authorities, toward the goals expressed or implied in these demands. In emphasizing the demand aspect, I have been holding constant such factors as the energies of the members. I shall now reverse the procedure and temporarily neutralize the effect of demands or objectives and inquire into the function fulfilled by the support

[1] D. Easton, *The Political System*, chapter 5 and *A Framework for Political Analysis*, chapter IV.

that members may be called upon to put into a system at various levels.

The focus of the analysis, however, will continue to center in the same kinds of questions about a system as have already been posed with regard to demands. What kind of disturbances are there that may impose stress on the capacity of a system to marshal the support of its members behind its activities? Without the support of at least its politically relevant members,[2] the authorities would encounter severe difficulties in processing demands through to outputs or implementing decisions already taken. Where systems have persisted in the face of such stress, how have they been able to cope with the threatened loss of support?

The Significance of Support

As I indicated in Chapter 2 when first describing some characteristics of a systems analysis, there are many varied inputs going into a system. Out of these, for reasons already stated, demands were selected. We may now ask why it is useful and necessary to select for special consideration this second kind of input that I am calling support.

Support as a Summary Variable

As in the case of demands, we can begin with the fact that numerous events occur in the environment of a political system, as well as within it, that traditionally have been considered as sources of disturbance.

---

[2] The concept "politically relevant" members is adapted from a similar use by K. W. Deutsch, S. A. Burrell, et al., *The Political Community and the North Atlantic Area* (Princeton: Princeton University Press, 1957). I shall use it here to refer to those members of a system who can be said to count or whose attitudes need to be taken into consideration in the processing of demands. This use carefully sidesteps the important question of why some members have more influence than others. It relieves us of the need to specify either precisely or generally who the influential members in a system may be. These are all crucial matters, but at our level of analysis, they can be left moot. The reader is free to determine for himself who the relevant members are in any situation. All that needs to be remembered is that when I speak of the members of a system, unless the context indicates otherwise, I

The members of the system come into contact with a new culture that changes their perceived wants and expectations. New technologies modify the structure of the economy or speed the growth of population with its attendant problems. A new religion spreads and brings with it new ideals and patterns of behavior and projects new leaders into the political system. Every significant development in society has its related effects upon a political system.

As we have already seen with regard to demands, one of the ways of organizing an analysis of the consequences that are thereby communicated to a political system is to trace through their impact on demands, especially with respect to the variety and volume flowing into a system. But this focuses on only one class of effects. Environmental disturbances may help to shape not only what the members want, but the sentiments they display toward the political system as a whole, its institutions and leaders.

Where changes in the economy, for example, have led to fundamental shifts in the basis of power within a social structure, the prevailing political system could not continue unchanged. The old authorities will be seen as unresponsive to the wants and needs of the new social groups with their new-found power. In time, the newly emergent groups begin to lose confidence not only in the authorities but in the old institutions themselves within the matrix of which the authorities have asserted their control. At the same time, if changing social conditions provide some free-floating human resources that can be mobilized behind the discontented new leadership, the conditions are ripe for an assault upon the old system.

In effect, this generalizes the experience of many new systems as they have emerged from old ones.[3] It reflects, for example, the pattern of political change in early modern Europe. In the process of industrialization, the old feudal aristocracy was displaced by a discontented middle class. Out of this emerging class, competing leaderships arose that sought to rally behind them persons hitherto politically inaccessible because they were geographically widely dispersed, bound to the soil, and immobilized in a network of feudal obligations. But out of the slow processes of industrialization, there sprang up a new kind of peasantry and a new urban working class, both freed from feudal ties.

shall be referring to only that segment that research would indicate to be politically relevant at the given time and place.

[3] See for example, S. N. Eisenstadt, *The Political Systems of Empires* (New York: Free Press of Glencoe, 1963), chapter 12.

This transformation of social relationships from status to contract not only gave birth to a new pool of free labor but opened up a new reservoir of manpower that could be freely mobilized for political purposes. And what is true of early modern Europe applies with equal force to developing nations today, if we make due allowances for the special effects of colonialism and of the tribal conditions that still prevail among indigenous populations.[4]

If we are to understand how political change comes about under these circumstances, it is not enough, for example, simply to associate industrialization with transformations in the political system. We must be able to probe deeply so that we can identify the processes through which the various changes concealed in the idea of industrialization are conveyed to the political system itself. If we were to stop with the *ad hoc* analytic tools currently available, we would have to trace out individual effects as they move from the environment to a system and, in one way or another, weigh and balance their collective impact on the system. But if the task of theory is to simplify, unify, and improve our tools of analysis, it is apparent that, as in the case of demands, here too we have in the concept "inputs" an integrative device for summarizing a whole host of parametric changes. But in this case, the input that would be shaped by the vast variety of disturbances in the environment can be identified as support. That is to say, it is possible to follow these environmental influences through in a unified and systematic way if we search out the impact that they have upon the one variable, namely, support, that members are willing to extend to the political system.

Thus, in speaking of the input of support, we are able to bring the extremely varied external conditions to a focus on a single question: what influences have they upon fluctuations in support? Support becomes the major summary variable linking a system to its environment. It gives us a unified and simple vocabulary for referring to a kind of transaction between a system and its environment, in addition to that of demands. We shall see in the immediately succeeding chapters, that, simultaneously, it also offers us a relatively simplified tool for analyzing a second major source of stress on a system. We shall be able to speak of stress due to the decline of support below a minimal level.

[4] See K. W. Deutsch, "Social Mobilization and Political Development," 55 *American Political Science Review* (1961) 493–514.

Support as an Explanatory Variable

The significance of support for the persistence of a system does not hinge, however, upon our acceptance of this summary or linking function. Quite independently of this and even if we could neglect this aspect, we would still be forced to entertain support as a variable of major import. Without it we would not be able to understand another kind of stress to which all systems are exposed.

Fluctuations in support may stress a system in one or all of three different ways. First, without support for some of the authorities, at least, demands could not be processed into outputs. Only the smallest, least differentiated system could handle its demands if each time a decision had to be made, a new set of rulers arose and if each output requiring implementation gave rise to a different set of administrators. Most systems require some relatively stable set of *authorities*. .

Second, without support it would be impossible to assure some kind of stability in the rules and structures through the use of which demands are converted into outputs, an aspect that will be designated as the *regime*. And third, support is vital in order to maintain minimal cohesion within a membership, an aspect of a system that I shall identify later as its *political community*. These three systemic consequences of the input of support will provide us with a framework for its analysis. Our inquiry into support will be directed toward the way in which solidarity around these three foci or *political objects*—the authorities, regime and political community—may be stressed and buttressed. These constitute the domain of support.

The Domain of Support

Let us look at these objects of political solidarity a little more closely, although a very detailed examination will have to wait until a later point. If demands are to be processed into binding decisions, regardless of whose demands they are, it is not enough that support be collected behind them so as to impress the authorities with the need to adopt them as a basis for decisions. Basically, a large proportion of political research has been devoted to just this matter. Studies of voting behavior, interest groups, parties, and legislative analysis have all sought to reveal the way in which support is distributed, shifted, and mobilized behind varying demands (issues) or behind personalities and leadership groups seeking positions of authority. But if the authorities are to be able to make decisions, to get them accepted as binding, and to put them into effect without the extensive use of coercion, solidarity must be developed not only around some set of authorities themselves, but around the major aspects of the system within which the authorities operate.

Regardless of the kind of system we may have under consideration, its ability to process demands will depend upon the politically influential members being ready and able to support two other levels or objects of a system: first, the unity of the group of members who constitute the system; and second, some kind of structures and rules through which authoritative decisions are made and actions taken. These I have described as the political community and regime respectively. Their properties will be fully delineated in later chapters.

To put these functions of support in negative form, I shall seek to show that the decline in the inflow of support below a minimal point will threaten to detach members from one or another of these three central objects or levels of political solidarity, the authorities, regime or political community. Thereby it will serve to stress the system. Disturbances which disillusion the politically relevant members with one or all of the levels so that the system is unable to provide any set of authorities at all for processing decisions, or to develop agreement on a regime, or even to hold together a cooperating group of members, must lead to the complete collapse of the system.

Our task will now be to inquire into what is meant by this support, the absence of which can prove so disastrous to the political system. What is the exact nature of the objects or levels to which support must be directed if the system is to persist? How do the environmental disturbances and internal conditions conduce to the stressful decline in support? Finally, what kinds of responses are typically found in systems that have succeeded in coping with the stress so induced?

These questions foreshadow the objectives of the discussion in the succeeding chapters. In the present one, I shall seek only to lay the groundwork by analyzing the meaning to be attributed to the concept "support." Since I shall be referring to the minimal level of support necessary for persistence of the political objects, it will also be important here to examine various dimensions of support that are implicitly included in any metrical statement relating to it.

Meaning of Support

We can say that *A* supports *B* either when *A* acts on behalf of *B* or when he orients himself favorably toward *B*. *B* may be a person or group; it may be a goal, idea, or institution. I shall designate supportive *actions* as overt support and supportive *attitudes* or sentiments as covert support.

Overt Support

The external actions of a person may contribute to the promotion of goals, ideas, institutions, actions, or persons. This is overt support since it consists of observable behavior. We may support goals or ideals by literally fighting for them or by merely espousing them, an institution by verbally defending it, the actions of others by joining them, and persons by voting for them or acting on their behalf. All these kinds of observable behavior fall into the category of overt support.

More generally, we may defend a decision by the courts of the land, vote for a political candidate, pay taxes willingly, or voluntarily join the armed forces. We may engage in riots against the government, refuse to pay taxes, resist authority at every turn, join forces with a separatist movement, migrate to another country, or participate in a revolution against the existing regime. Unless such behavior is being pursued under duress, we may infer from the overt behavior that some degree of support for the object involved is present or absent as the case may be. Here we need say nothing about the state of mind of the member. We are concerned only with the observable forms of the behavior. Regardless of how a member may say he feels about an object, if the objective consequences of his actions are such as to lend aid and comfort or to oppose and undermine, he has extended or withheld support.

Intention need not necessarily or constantly accompany this kind of supportive behavior. It is quite possible that others may perceive an act as supportive even though in fact the actor may not have intended it as such. A member of a system may be quite hostile to the government and all other aspects of the system and yet pay his taxes, to that degree extending support to the system, however low the amount. Alternatively, we may vote for one candidate, not to support him but simply as a measure of protest against some other candidate. Yet the vote can be interpreted as an expression of some degree of support, however slight.

Intention is certainly important especially from the point of view of what we can expect by way of future behavior. In this sense, the absence of any desire to support the candidate for whom a vote was cast would be an index of a very low level of support in the instance just cited. Differences between intention and consequence are relevant for estimating the degree of support implied in the behavior and expectations regarding its continuance. It is perhaps more significant from the point of view of measuring the support than for its definition or the identification of its presence or absence.

Covert Support

Supportive behavior may involve more than externally observable actions alone. A person may possess a supportive frame of mind with respect to others or to some object. If we wish, we may call this an internal form of behavior, an orientation that takes the shape of a set of attitudes or predispositions or a readiness to act on behalf of someone or something else.

If a person votes for a candidate of a party once, we may say that he has supported the party at that time. But if consistently over the years, come what may he has always voted for the party, we may infer from his behavior a frame of mind that we call party loyalty. When we characterize a person as being patriotic, dedicated to a cause, infused with a sense of duty, in effect we are attributing to him a state of mind that programs him, as it were, to respond favorably to the particular objects, under most circumstances. What such phrases share is their reference to an imputed state of feelings that will have a high probability of displaying themselves through supportive or hostile actions.[5] Where the actions fail to measure up to imputed attitudes or where, through other tests, it is discovered that attitudes are inconsistent with observed behavior, we may assume either that the observer has made an error in judgment or that changes have taken place.

[5] It is to this aspect that A. Downs, *op. cit.*, was, in effect, calling attention in his effort to distinguish between a consensus of views and a consensus of intensities. The former identifies agreement with respect to demands, in our conceptualization; the latter, the sharing of equally intensive supportive feelings with respect to these demands.

In many cases, the ability to detect accurately the existence of covert support, or supportive states of mind, is far more important than its actual expression in overt behavior. The members of a system may not be called upon to demonstrate their affection for their leaders or for the particular constitutional order, at least on a day-to-day basis. But the continuing activities of the leaders or authorities may well be based on the premise that if necessary, the members can be roused in visible and active defense of one or another aspect of the system. In those systems where leadership cannot anticipate and rely upon the unquestioning support of the membership, the extent to which the human or even material resources of the system can be committed is seriously curtailed. Special measures may need to be taken to increase the input of support, as we shall see when we come to discuss the typical methods for responding to a decline in support for a system.

Measurement of Support

Whether our knowledge of support is derived from observed external actions or imputed internal attitudes, this in itself does not give us sufficient initial information about the various dimensions of support to be able to develop an analysis with respect to the way in which its fluctuations may stress a system. In fact, the very formulation of this statement emphasizes the importance and necessity of being able to make some kind of quantitative assertions about support.

The Need for Measurement

If we are to be able to analyze the ways in which support might contribute to the persistence of a system or stress upon it, we need to be able to do more than establish its presence or absence, whether the support be covert or overt. It becomes critical to adopt as our point of departure the assumption that it is possible to estimate varying degrees of support, even if crudely. Only under this condition would it be sensible to continue to talk about whether or not a system has enough support to enable it to persist as a way of making authoritative decisions for a society.

This does not mean that I am called upon, in a theoretical analysis such as this, to consider the problems involved in the measurement of support as an empirical phenomenon. The task of refining concepts and theoretical propositions for direct empirical application—operationalizing them—is a vital yet separate enterprise, one that falls outside the macroscopic level of analysis under way here. We are spared the need to pause to deal with the onerous and complex technical aspects involved.

But if, in discussing the fluctuations in support as a source of stress on a system, it is necessary to assume that support is in some way quantifiable empirically, this gives rise to certain prior theoretical problems. It leads to the need to clarify the various dimensions of support which would have to be taken into account if any satisfactory minimal measure at all is to be attained. It has become evident by this time that I shall be referring to support at least in impressionistic ordinal terms. We shall find it necessary, therefore, to know something about the elements relating to support that are involved even in this simple statement that there is relatively more or less support available to any of the objects in a system.

Indicators of Support

That support is considered to be a measurable phenomenon ought to provoke little argument. We constantly treat it as such in everyday ordinary usage. We habitually refer to varying measures of support when we speak of a leader who has succeeded in winning the approval of a group or of a policy that has failed for want of sufficient backing. We may attribute the collapse of a regime, such as the Weimar Republic, in part to the loss of popular confidence in it, or the secession of a national minority from a system, to the inability to hold its loyalty to the existing community. In making familiar assertions such as these, we imply the existence of indices through which we measure support, in ordinal if not in cardinal terms, however imprecise and impressionistic our measurement may be. The proposition that no system can persist without a minimal level of support should at least be acceptable within the same frame of reference.

If we accept the validity of this common usage, the only question remaining is what kind of indicators do we typically adopt, at least implicitly. Since I have already suggested that types of support may be divided into two distinctive categories, we would expect it to be necessary to look for different kinds of indicators, some that would help us detect and estimate covert and others, overt manifestations of support.

As measures of overt support, a variety of activities are typically taken into account: the numbers belonging to organizations; the regularity with which citizens or subjects perform their obligations; manifestations of open hostility such as breaches of the law, riots, or revolutions; and expressions of preferences for other systems through emigration or separatist activities. Hence the ratio of deviance to conformity as measured by violations of laws, the prevalence of violence, the size of dissident movements, or the amount of money spent for security, would provide individual indices of support. Although critical measurement problems would exist with regard to the construction of a single overall index or to a decision favoring the division of indicators into a variety of independent measures, the illustration of possible types does help to provide a concrete image of the kinds of overt activities from which the level of support might be inferred.

Most of these measures refer to past or current supportive activities of members. But to determine the probable future behavior, it becomes important to be able to make inferences, from observable actions or otherwise, about the state of mind of the members toward basic political objects.

Like all attitudes, covert support might be measured on an ordinal scale ranging from low to high. At the high end of the continuum we would place members who are so intensively supportive in their attitudes that they virtually obliterate themselves as independently acting persons. They would substitute the needs, ideals, and standards of the supported object for their own. Here we might locate members motivated by blind faith, unquestioning loyalty, or uncritical patriotism. At the low end of the continuum we would find those whose support is extremely negative, those who feel the deepest hostility to a system and are most decisively disengaged.

If we call the high end of the continuum positive support, those on the other end could be said to display negative support, as indicated in Diagram 4. Somewhere at the midpoint in the range between these

High or positive support	Passive acceptance, acquiescence, or indifference	Low or negative support

←——————————————————————————————→

Increasing support   Decreasing support

DIAGRAM 4   SUPPORT SCALE

two ends of the scale, we would expect to find members who are indifferent to the political system. Here the input of positive support declines but has not been quite transformed into negative support (the actual withdrawal of all support or the presence of incipient feelings of hostility). The members are neither prepared to accept nor reject a system. Although terminological rigor would call upon us always to add to the idea of support, the qualifying adjectives positive or negative, this might be forcing ordinary usage too hard. Accordingly, unless the context indicates otherwise, the concept "support" will be used in a positive sense only and such synonyms as opposition, hostility, or decline of support will be used to indicate negative support.

Additional Dimensions

Even if we were able to generate adequate indices of covert and overt support and to combine them in a sensible way, this would still not yield an adequate roster of the dimensions involved in any measurement of its input into a system. As we shall see in the next chapter and as I have already hinted from time to time, such indices would fail to differentiate the various objects within the system toward which support might be directed. But since I shall be dealing with this extensively in a moment, here I need only refer to this matter briefly.

Beyond this, even if we could invent an index of support that summed up the total input for the aggregate of members in a system, this would not necessarily inform us of the degree of stress to which a system might be subjected. From the point of view of our interest in the persistence of a system, knowledge of the total quantity of support in the system would not in itself be too helpful. Its weakness would stem from the fact that although it told us something about the total reservoir of support, insofar as it failed to differentiate the support in accordance with certain criteria, we would still be ignorant of the effect of this support on the persistence of the system.

To clarify this aspect of the problem, we would need information about such dimensions as the number of members involved in putting in positive or negative support, the intensity of their sentiments, their capacities for putting their sentiments into effect, the nature of the distribution of such effective support among the members, and the implications of any unequal distribution of support. Even if support were precisely measurable in absolute units, comparable to feet or pounds, unless we could take into account factors such as those just mentioned, we could not establish the impact of any level of support on the political system. The relevant dimensions of support, even at our general theoretical level, must therefore include much more than just scalable attitudes or countable overt actions. Let us look at these in turn.

Objects of Support

As the next chapters will show, it is impossible to speak meaningfully of support for a system as a whole, at least at the outset. It is too undifferentiated an idea. If support were thought about in this way, undifferentiated as to objects, a measure of system support would have to take the form of a composite index summing the inputs for each of three fundamental political objects, the authorities, regime, and political community. The consequences of the input would need to be specified for each of these objects and the net effect on the system as a whole established, if necessary or desirable. This would present us with an enormously complex empirical task.

Fortunately, as it will turn out in the conceptualization to be presented, it will be enough for us to be able to take into account the degree of support for each of the three levels separately or in specific combinations. Hence, after the analysis in the following chapters I shall no longer find it either useful or necessary to continue to speak of support for the system as a whole, a formulation that has hitherto been helpful as an introductory first approximation in the analysis of support.

The Scope of Support

Support is a function not only of actions or intensities of feelings, pro or con, but of the number of members who hold these feelings. That is to say, the total input of support for a political object is a measure of the intensity of individual feelings and behavior together with the number of individuals involved and this is not a simple summing procedure. A few persons, each of whom feels deeply about a political object, may in fact be putting in less support as a group than many others who individually appear apathetic in comparison but whose lesser feelings may collectively be far more significant for the system. The converse is equally true and, empirically, perhaps more frequent. The degree of support on the part of most members of a system taken collectively may be so low that the active, fervent feelings of a few may be far more important than the casual sentiment of the many even if they are positively supportive.

As I have expressed it elsewhere

. . . under certain circumstances very few members need to support a system at any level. The members might be dull and apathetic, indifferent to the general operations of the system, its progress or decisions. In a loosely connected system such as India has had, this might well be the state of mind of by far the largest segment of the membership. Either in fact they have not been affected by national decisions or they have not perceived that they were so affected. They may have little sense of identification with the present regime and government and yet . . . the system may be able to act on the basis of the support offered by the known three per cent of the Western-oriented politicians and intellectuals who are politically active. In other words, we can have a small minority putting in quantitatively sufficient supportive energy to keep the system going.[6]

The Effectiveness of the Support

Intensity of feelings and the numbers associated with them are insufficient to serve as reliable indicators of the impact of the support or hostility being directed to a political object. The critical factor is always the potential or effectiveness of the support. Many members may support a regime or community intensely, at least at the verbal level or even through such spontaneous action as the display of flags, singing of patriotic songs, and participation in other kinds of positive rituals. But they may be able to do little about their feelings, genuine though they may be, because they lack organization, resources, or skills to take whatever action may be necessary to defend the object of their support or undermine the object of their antagonisms. Input of support needs to be measured by its potential effectiveness.

Thus, knowledge of the intensity of feelings and their frequency in a population needs to be balanced and tempered by information concerning the power of the members who are involved. This is an intrinsic component of any measure of the input of support. Equal expres-

[6] D. Easton, "An Approach to the Analysis of Political Systems," p. 394.

sions of supportive attitudes cannot automatically be given equal weight with respect to their consequences for the persistence of a system. A few powerful members, such as an active political elite, a military cadre, or an organized intelligentsia, may be able to make their positive or negative support count for more than high levels of support from unorganized millions. From the point of view of the persistence or change of a system, we need to be able to specify the effective instrumental power of a group as an integral part of any estimate of its supportive input.

For example, it was possible for the Habsburgs to maintain the input of support to their multinational Empire for centuries because strategically effective social groups and classes provided support for the community. As one historian has remarked, "the sense of community developed under a system of absolutism, radiating from the crown, had penetrated only the carriers of the empire idea—the army and to a point the civil service, nobility, religious and economic affiliations and institutions—and not the people as a whole, though undoubtedly fringe sections of every social class in varying degrees." [7]

Haas has indicated that for European integration—incipient input of support for a European political community—a small active political elite from participating nations may be the relevant and effective source of support.

The emphasis on elites in the study of integration derives its justification from the bureaucratized nature of European organizations of long standing, in which basic decisions are made by the leadership over the opposition and usually over the indifference of the general membership. This gives the relevant elites a manipulative role which is of course used to place the organization in question on record for or against a proposed measure of integration.[8]

The Will toward Supportive Action

Even knowledge of the power base with which the input of support operates need not decisively indicate the extent to which supportive attitudes will induce supportive behavior. There must be a willingness to put one's attitudes and power to work.

It is well known that attitudes function in an economy quite differ-

[7] R. A. Kann, *The Habsburg Empire: A Study in Integration and Disintegration* (New York: Praeger, 1957), p. 30.

[8] E. B. Haas, *The Uniting of Europe* (Stanford: Stanford University Press), pp. 16–17.

ent from that of overt behavior. Whether we feel supportive sentiments toward a political object depends upon those deeper, underlying attitudes that give structure to our whole range of relevant preferences. We may call this the internal psychic economy. Whether we can afford to display these positive or negative supportive attitudes in overt actions will depend on the social benefits we may expect or upon the social costs we are willing to incur in order to defend a political object, such as penalties from formal legal sanctions or informal pressures stemming from the social disapproval of others. This forms the external or behavioral economy.

Members may agree in support of political objects in the abstract but differ markedly in what they are willing to give up in their behavioral economy to see their ends achieved. As has been pointed out, "the fact seems to be, judging from many poll results, that a majority of Germans hold firmly to these foreign policy objectives [such as the reunification of Eastern and Western Germany] in the abstract, but would be unwilling to fight for any of them." [9] Hence, when we refer to support, it is to the input of effective support, those attitudes which members are ready and able to express in overt and therefore telling behavior.

Support as a Net Outcome

Finally, what has been said up to this point may well be misleading in its oversimplification. It leaves the indefensible impression that a member is capable of behaving only in one direction at a time, either of putting in support for an object or acting to undermine it; or it may seem to imply that the sentiments held by a member must always be completely and unambiguously supportive or hostile. In fact, a member is able to favor and disapprove of the same object at the same time, or at least different aspects of it. This is especially true of a political system which, as I have intimated, we shall have to break down into a number of different basic parts; and each of these will have various aspects.

In practice we can expect that a member may and normally will hold conflicting attitudes at one and the same time about different components of the community, regime, or authorities. Some norms of a regime, for example, he may favor strongly, such as those of political tolerance, majority rule, and minority rights. Others, he may oppose

[9] K. W. Deutsch and L. J. Edinger, *Germany Rejoins the Powers* (Stanford: Stanford University Press, 1959), pp. 25–27.

strongly. A member also need not be consistent and may engage in contradictory kinds of activities, some of which support the objects in a system and others of which are antagonistic to them.

Thus we cannot assume that all attitudes and behavior of a member at any moment of time move consistently in one direction, supportive or antagonistic; and that even if they do, this means that they must be uniformly in favor or opposed to all the major political objects. When we speak of the input of support, we must bear in mind that the reference is to the net balance of support, opposition, and indifference of a member or group. Similarly, when speaking of all members collectively, we can be referring only to the presumed sum of the net balance for each member or group severally considered.

In summary, if we are to discuss the input of support even at this theoretical level, it is essential to recognize that it appears in the form of both sentiments and behavior and that it is less useful to interpret it as being extended to some undifferentiated system than to certain basic aspects, shortly to be detailed as the three major "political objects" in a system. If we are to speak intelligibly about some minimal support, even though we cannot identify what this minimum may be except to recognize its presence, it is essential to know what kinds of variables would need to be taken into account to obtain an ordinal measure of support. We have seen that we would have to balance the number of members supporting and opposing a system, their power position, the intensity of their feelings in these respects, their capacity to express these feelings in action, and their readiness to do so under the circumstances. Finally, any summation of support would also weigh simultaneous positive and negative feelings and actions entertained by a member or group in order to ascertain the net consequences with respect to the level of support being extended to each of the political objects.

It scarcely needs to be pointed out that empirically this is a large order, one that would require considerable ingenuity to execute adequately. It would be convenient indeed to be able to avoid or postpone all inquiry into support and we could do so if the only consideration in theoretical analysis were that of empirical preparedness to deal with the matters that theory raises. Although theory cannot neglect empirical possibilities entirely or even largely, nevertheless it would be unfaithful to its own objectives if it did not frankly face up to the requirements of a satisfactory political analysis and pursue these ends even when the technical means for the implied research have yet to be devised. Just as computer technology has today provided empirical research workers with techniques that in the social sciences have already outrun the theoretical capacity of these disciplines to utilize the machines fully, so at times theory itself may out-distance the current capabilities of empirical technology. In each case, efforts of the one to catch up to the other are not only unavoidable; they are an essential ingredient of scientific progress.

I I

Objects of Support:
The Political Community

MANY A SYSTEM MANAGES TO PERSIST IN THE FACE OF FAR-REACHING and intensive conflict. Deep cleavages with respect to party preferences, candidate choice and issue determination occur but they need not even shake its foundations much less dislodge the system entirely from its basic structure or practices. But from what has already been said, it is at once clear that we can no longer find it acceptable even to pose the problem of systemic persistence or change in this way. It is quite inappropriate to continue to speak about a system as though it were an undifferentiated whole that must change or persist as a total unit. To do so would be to perpetuate an ambiguity which, it is true, we have had to tolerate to this point in the analysis. But this was just in order finally to be able to demonstrate its presence and clear the obscurities away.

The Basic Political Objects

If we are to understand the function of support, we must begin by clearly recognizing that a system consists of numerous subsystems and aspects, some of which are more important and some less so from the point of view of support. Those that are fundamental, in the light of the perspectives of the mode of analysis being developed here, we could not entirely avoid during the preceding discussion although we were able to gloss over them lightly. But this is no longer possible. The task now is to conceptualize the various components of a system in such a way that we may handle economically the problems arising from possible stress due to the decline of support below a minimal level.

What elements of a system are most relevant to its capacity to persist in the face of a threatened loss of support? The search for answers to this question will lead us to identify and categorize those aspects of a system with respect to which support may vary independently and with respect to which fluctuations in the level of support may stimulate stress in different ways. These in turn may provoke differential coping responses on the part of the members of a system.

The relevant aspects of the system I have already identified as three basic political objects: the authorities, regime, and political community. Now, however, I shall develop these objects more fully so that we may see exactly what aspects of a system are involved in them. Thereafter, I shall indicate the kinds of responses through which systems have typically sought to inculcate and reinforce supportive attitudes and behavior to maintain minimal levels of input.

Change of a system will turn out to mean change of one or another of these objects and only where all objects change simultaneously can we consider that the former system has totally disappeared. Conversely, a system may persist *in toto* or only with respect to one of its basic objects. It will also become apparent that modification in one or another of the objects may represent a fundamental way through which systems are able to cope with stress from the environment and to keep some kind of political system in operation for the particular society.

Alternative Uses of the Concept "Community"

In speaking of the persistence of a political system, it is impossible not to imply at the very least that the members of the system show some minimal readiness or ability to continue working together to solve their political problems. Otherwise there could be no expectation of compliance with any authoritative allocation of values. This notion lies at the heart of that aspect of a system that I have been calling its political community and which will now be explored in detail for the first time.

To avoid any misunderstanding about the meaning of this concept, much more than a word or two needs to be said about its use by others. Although the idea "political community" itself rarely appears, the concept "community" is probably about as overworked a term as any that occurs in both the lay and professional lexicons. In lay terms, as well as in much professional discourse, it frequently appears as an ideological tool, a "practical concept" [1] intended to arouse and

[1] "By a practical concept I mean a concept whose primary function is to guide action, direct and redirect attitudes, and to state commitments of one sort or an-

strengthen the affective bonds of a member for the political system or the society of which he is part.[2] But if we confine our scrutiny for the moment to the idea of *political* community, this immediately shrinks to a mere handful the number of cases in which it is used, at least in a technical or scholarly sense.

Two recent and well-developed applications of the concept, in the work of Deutsch and Haas, bear special attention as an aid in clarifying the implications of the special meaning that will be adopted in this analysis. Although the use by these authors falls into the general area of international relations, this in itself need not interfere with its relevance for our purposes. From my point of view, an international system is just another system at a different level of organization. But in all other respects it is amenable to investigation through the same conceptual apparatus that is being developed in this volume with respect to what we normally call domestic political systems.[3]

Definition of the Concept by Deutsch

Unfortunately, as the concept "political community" has been employed in the international sphere, it cannot be conveniently adopted for the identification of that aspect of a political system which we must isolate for an understanding of the effects of the input of support. In the work of Deutsch, for example, two different but related meanings appear, each of which were certainly appropriate for the specific context in which they were employed but neither of which is quite suitable for the more general theoretical analysis under way here.

In one piece of research, Deutsch finds it advantageous for the specific purposes of seeking to create indices for the measurement of the growth of a community, to adopt an approximation of the classic distinction between community and society prevalent in sociological and anthropological literature. He describes a society as "a group of individuals connected by an intense division of labor and separated from

other. A practical concept is contrasted to a theoretical concept, which is used to refer to and to describe various kinds of objects." J. Ladd, "The Concept of Community: A Logical Analysis," in C. J. Friedrich (ed.), *Community* (New York: Liberal Arts Press, 1959), pp. 269–293, at p. 270.

[2] For a recent survey of the meaning of the concept "community" and research relating to it see G. W. Blackwell, "Community Analysis" in R. Young, *Approaches to the Study of Politics* (Evanston, Illinois: Northwestern University Press, 1958), pp. 305–317.

[3] As D. Singer has pointed out, one needs only to keep his level of analysis straight. See "International Conflict: Three Levels of Analysis," 12 *World Politics* (1960) 453–461; and "The Level of Analysis Problem in International Relations," 14 *World Politics* (1961) 77–92.

other societies by a marked drop in this intensity." [4] Community, on the other hand, he sees as "people who have learned to communicate with each other and to understand each other well beyond the mere interchange of goods and services." [5] By this he refers largely to the cultural integration of a people, culture consisting of those symbols, ideas, and artifacts transmitted from generation to generation. Since the focus of the work in which these concepts are defined is on communication, the utility of this kind of distinction is transparent.

In another work, however, where the emphasis of Deutsch's research on integration spreads to include aspects of political life other than communication, a considerably different, even though related concept appears. The generalized notion "community" now becomes more specific. It is transformed into the specific idea of political community. However, in pouring more concentrated political content into the concept, one might have expected that the term would have become somewhat narrowed in its meaning. But, in fact, in one sense it is broadened even further. It no longer seems to refer just to those components of social life that are communicable across the generations—that is, culture—and to interacting persons as they engage in the process of communicating it. The meaning of political community is now extended in a way that converts it if not into a synonym for, at least into an approximation of what I have been calling a political system.

Thus Deutsch describes a political community as "a community of social interaction supplemented by both enforcement and compliance." In this sense, it is a community of persons in which common or "coordinated facilities for the making of decisions and the enforcement of commands are supplemented by habits of compliance which are sufficiently widespread and predictable to make successful enforcement in the remaining cases of noncompliance probable at an economically and culturally feasible cost." [6] And this definition is repeated in subsequent works so that it seems to have achieved some stability.[7]

One cannot cavil with this use of course. It is a forthright statement of a possible meaning for the concept and a meaningful one in that it is directed toward understanding a central problem: the way in which groups of people gradually link together, particularly internationally,

[4] *Nationalism and Social Communication* (New York: Technology Press of Massachusetts Institute of Technology and Wiley, 1953), p. 61.

[5] *Ibid.*, p. 65.

[6] K. W. Deutsch, *Political Community at the International Level* (Garden City, New York: Doubleday, 1954), p. 16.

[7] "We are dealing here with political communities. These we regard as social groups with a process of political communication, some machinery for enforcement, and some popular habits of compliance." K. W. Deutsch, S. A. Burrell, et al., *op. cit.*, p. 5.

to form units that are able to solve their problems peacefully, either in a unitary or in a federated system. But from our point of view, the reason Deutsch finds it helpful to select a meaning for political community that makes it equivalent to what I have been calling a political system is that in fact he is seeking to understand the processes underlying the initial formation of societies and political systems associated with them. Yet, since we are not in need of a special concept for this purpose but do seek one that will point up only one aspect of a political system to which members typically extend support, the definition of the concept as proposed by Deutsch will not serve our purposes.

Definition of the Concept by Haas

Haas presents us with a second case in which the concept appears in a carefully delineated context. Haas adopts the term to describe a condition in the relationship among political groups such that "specific groups and individuals show more loyalty to their central political institutions than to any other political authority, in a specific period of time and in a definable geographic space." It is a condition "towards which the process of 'political integration' is supposed to lead." [8]

If we disregard the author's intention to formulate an ideal or model political unit, a norm against which other coalescing groups en route might be measured, his description of a political community comes very close to Deutsch's second usage. In fact, the specifications by Haas tend to fuse the idea of political community with those of a *modern* political system and therefore to restrict it somewhat more narrowly than in Deutsch's usage. Since he views "loyalty to their central political institutions" as a key ingredient, it signifies that the acceptance of a single superior set of authorities as the significant variable constitutes the most important variable in the emergence of a common political life. Even more so than in the case of Deutsch, he is apparently seeking to describe, not the communal aspect of a geographically based group but the total set of political relationships in which members may engage, which I have been calling a political system.

The Dual Implications of Political Community as a Concept

It appears that in at least these two cases, where the concept "political community" is introduced as a carefully and deliberately selected tool of analysis, it tends to be employed in a way that makes it a

[8] E. B. Haas, *op. cit.*, p. 5.

synonym of some kind for political system. It is important to recognize this because I now wish to give the term an alternative content, if only because in "political system" we already have a concept for the most inclusive set of interactions that can be called political. I wish to reserve "political community" for the special purpose of identifying only one particular aspect of a political system, as one of a number of basic political objects toward which support may be extended or from which it may be withdrawn.

This new way of looking at this concept will not estrange it completely from the implications it already bears for Deutsch and Haas. It is not accidental that they and others have seized upon the concept "political community" to help understand the phenomenon through which previously independent or separate groups coalesce into one political system. The peculiar value of the concept is that it conveys the latent notion that, underlying the functioning of all systems, there must be some cohesive cement—a sense or feeling of community amongst the members. Unless such sentiment emerges, the political system itself may never take shape or if it does, it may not survive. Whether it is defined as a bond created through common traditions built up in the communication processes within and across generations or as ties created out of loyalty to a common set of central institutions, in each case the emphasis is upon the essential ingredient of affective solidarity for the existence of something that resembles what I have been calling a political system.

It is understandable that those concerned with the conditions under which a peaceful international system might arise should temporarily, at least, isolate the community aspect of political life and elevate it to the point where it threatens to become the sole or dominant aspect. To common sense it is not immediately evident that new political formations are likely to take shape and achieve long-range stability either without the prior growth of community-like sentiments or their subsequent emergence. Feelings of community with one's fellows are so noticeable an ingredient in domestic political systems that it can easily lead the investigator, searching for the function that communal sentiments play, to substitute the communal aspects of political life, at least temporarily, for the whole.

To capture and retain the contribution that the idea of political community has for an understanding of the functioning of political systems, it will be necessary to break it down into the implications inherent in it. In the first place, it contains the suggestion that a group of persons are for one reason or another joined together in a common political enterprise. If this idea were not implicit, there would be little reason for turning to the idea of a community at all. Community suggests cooperation of some sort. In the second place, it also implies that the way in which the common enterprise is conducted may vary with respect to the degree of cohesion or sense of community the members feel. A community is usually something more than just an aggregate. It is a group that may be bound by the subtleties of sentiment.

The first implied notion I shall characterize as the *political community*. It represents an object toward which support may or may not flow. The second, I shall identify as a sentiment to be called the *sense of community*. This will represent a measure of the extent of support for the political community and will only be a possible characteristic of a political community, not an essential part of the meaning of the term. I shall examine each notion in turn.

The Political Community: Definition

This concept, as I shall now use it, will refer to that aspect of a political system that consists of its members seen as a group of persons bound together by a political division of labor. The existence of a political system must include a plurality of political relationships through which the individual members are linked to each other and through which the political objectives of the system are pursued, however limited they may be.[9] In confining the idea of political community in this way, I do so in order to focus not on the form or structure of political processes but rather on the group of members who are drawn together by the fact that they participate in a common structure and set of processes, however tight or loose the ties may be.

For the moment it does not matter whether the members form a community in the sociological sense of a group of members who have a sense of community or a set of common traditions. The members of a political system who are participating in a common political community may well have different cultures and traditions or they may be entirely separate nationalities. The cultural and psychological distance among these component plural groups may well be increasing rather than declining.

Participation in a common division of political labor need not un-

[9] Cf.: "A human community is a body of people sharing in common activities and bound by multiple relationships in such a way that the aims of any individual can be achieved only by participation in actions with others." R. Firth, *Elements of Social Organization* (London: Watts, 1951), p. 41.

der all circumstances conduce to strengthening the sentiments of mutual identification; witness the comments already quoted with regard to the Habsburg Empire. It was never able to develop potent psychological bonds among its many nationalities to underpin the support coming from the loyal administrative services and other selected groups. But regardless of the degree of cohesion among the members of the system, as long as they are part of the same political system, they cannot escape sharing in or being linked by a common division of political labor. This forms the structural connection among the members of the system that gives minimal linkage to political activities that might otherwise be isolated or independent.

A member of a system will be said to extend support to his political community insofar as he stands ready to act on behalf of maintaining some structure through which he and others may play their part in the making of binding decisions or is favorably oriented towards its perpetuation, whatever form it may take from time to time and however insignificant the role of the average member may be in the division. A group of people who come together to draw up some kind of constitution to regulate their political relationship—as in the case of the thirteen colonies in America—thereby indicate their intention to share a division of political labor. The particular structure of the relationship may change, the members of the system may be ranked, subdivided and rearranged politically so that the structural patterns are fundamentally altered. But as long as the members continue to evince an attachment to the overall group in which the changing interrelationships prevail and through which demands in a system are processed, they will be supporting the existence of the same and continuing community.

From the point of view of the existence of the political community, the extent of the sharing in the division of labor is immaterial. At the one extreme, we might conceivably find a system in which each member has an explicit and highly active role in the regulation of conflicting demands or the authoritative allocation of values. Every adult may be expected to show some interest in politics, participate at least to the extent of casting a vote and discussing the issues. At the other pole, it will be enough if a person sees his role as one of complete passivity and acceptance of the absolute authority of others over him. In this case, the member's part in the division of political labor is entirely that of owing a duty to accept his subordinate status in political life.

But if a person could not locate himself anywhere in the political division of labor in a system, was not able to relate himself to anything else that occurred in the system, even to the extent of feeling it was his obligation to obey a superior or abide by some vaguely apprehended tradition, one of two conditions might exist. Either he would not be part of the system or his ties to the political community would be in imminent danger of being severed. To avoid any ambiguity as to who is or is not a part of this division of labor, each system provides criteria of membership through territorial presence, legal definition, blood, subjection, kinship, or the like.

Systemic and Community Changes

Not all changes in a political system need affect the political community. This is why there will always be residual ambiguity if we describe a political system as having changed and yet fail to specify the basic objects with regard to which the change has occurred. Authorities typically come and go, regimes or constitutional orders may change. In both cases the community may remain quite stable. If we take metropolitan France alone as an example, in its community aspects it has experienced little change since the French Revolution aside from minor fluctuations at its geographic boundaries. But this is not equally the case for France's regimes which have undergone innumerable drastic transformations. Governmental changes, if not at the administrative, at least at the leadership level, have been too numerous to count easily.

But political communities are capable of changing. This occurs at moments when the membership undergoes some internal subdivision indicating that whole groups have withdrawn their support from the pre-existing division of political labor. The American Civil War, like any political fission, illustrates concretely what occurs with the cessation of the input of support. The war itself offered evidence that the members of the American political system could or would no longer contribute together to the prior division of political labor through which binding decisions had been made for the society. Their attachment to the most inclusive group in and through which the tasks necessary for the processing of demands to authoritative outputs were performed, was destroyed.

It was no longer a question in the United States of whether the South would support one or another alternative government, or whether it could envision its demands being satisfied through the normal procedures of the regime. The issue turned on whether the members could conceive of themselves continuing as a group that was part of and subject to the same set of processes for arriving at political decisions and taking political action. Support for such a group, which shared a division of political labor, had temporarily crumbled.

In principle, in addition to the kind of subdivision sparked by civil strife, a political community may lose its support, and thereby be destroyed, in several typical ways. Through emigration, if permitted, individuals may withdraw from a political community. If the trend is sufficiently pronounced as in the case of an informal but large-scale separatist movement, it could well affect the size, composition, and structure of the political community. The longing of some 60,000 members of the Ras Tafari sect in Jamaica to return to Nigeria or Ethiopia indicates the consequences of disillusionment with the benefits to be gained from continued participation in the Jamaican political community. In effect the poorest and most alienated blacks are saying not only that they dislike the authorities and regime of the whites and browns, but that they no longer have any feeling left for contributing by their presence to a common political structure with the whites and browns. They are choosing to share their labors, in resolving political differences, with the Nigerians or Ethiopians, the regime and governmental forms being left open-ended.

Perhaps the most decisive indicator of the withdrawal of support from a political community consists of group separation. By collective action a subgroup may hive off to join some pre-existing political community, in this way transferring support from one shared division of political labor to another, or to found an entirely new political system. In some systems, it is possible for such hiving off to take place without the type of regime itself being seriously influenced. In the case of many traditional tribal systems in Africa it was the accepted and ethically unrestricted custom for members of a lineage segment to break away from the parent stem in order to found a new chiefdom or kingdom under a purposefully selected leader.[10] The new system might retain the identical kind of regime that prevailed in the old system of which it had been part but out of which two new societies and political communities had been created.

Levels of Political Communities

Loss of support may therefore lead to different kinds of ruptures in the political community. But lest it appear that only those political

[10] See the reference to this kind of separation in my essay, "Political Anthropology" in B. J. Siegel, *Biennial Review of Anthropology 1959* (Stanford: Stanford University Press, 1959), pp. 210–262.

units we call nation-states and some disappearing tribal political systems display community aspects or that nationalism is the one significant ideological expression of support for a political community, we need to generalize our discussion more clearly. As I have indicated elsewhere,[11] political systems may be identified at different levels of inclusiveness, from the parapolitical system of a voluntary organization to a municipality, province or state, national unit, and various kinds of international systems.

Some systems are independent of others in the sense that one cannot be included as a subsystem of the other. The United States and France represent such mutually exclusive systems. Some nest within others; that is to say, a given system may be alternately viewed as a separate system coordinate with others at the same level of analysis—two national units, for example—or as a subsystem of a supra-system of which it is part, as the United States is a subsystem of an international political system such as NATO or the United Nations.

In like manner, we can visualize an extensive nesting relationship beginning with a small municipality, say in the United States. It will be included in an ascending order of more comprehensive political systems, and each lower system in the hierarchy will be a unit in the higher one and, therefore, a subsystem of it. The municipality will be a subsystem within a township perhaps, the latter will constitute a subsystem in the political system of the county, this, in turn, a subsystem within a state and the state a subsystem within the national unit and so on up to the most comprehensive international political system. Whether we choose to view any of these systems as subsystems of a broader system or as systems coordinate with others at the same level will depend solely on the level of analysis being undertaken.

This conception has immediate relevance for the identification of political communities. It follows that just as the scope of a political system will vary with the systems level, so will the scope of the political community. It is just an aspect of the system to which we may be referring. We may range from the local to the broad international community. For a person to say that he is a Parisian, a Frenchman, and a European indicates three different levels of political community to which he simultaneously adheres. Each of these communities stands at a different systems level, with each lower community nesting within its next higher supra-system. In every case, however, we find a different division of labor for the fulfilment of political processes at that level.

If we broaden our systems to include NATO and the United Nations in ascending order, it may appear that the more inclusive the

[11] *A Framework for Political Analysis*, chapters II–IV.

group to whose division of labor we are referring, the lower must be the degree of political cohesion or integration. In those we have specified, this may well be the case. But there is no necessary connection between the level of analysis and the degree of cohesion. We may find tightly or loosely knit communities at all system levels; in principle all political communities, including those at the same systems level, may differ with respect to cohesion. Just as the European community may be low in integration compared to one of its subunits, each of the coordinate subunits will usually differ from the other along the same dimension.

But aside from the matter of its integration, from whatever level of systems we select our political unit, we can distinguish each one from the other through the fact that it will display a different, even if at times overlapping, division of labor for the negotiation and regulation of political problems. The most inclusive group at the given systems level to which a particular structure applies constitutes the political community at that level.

It is clear that, in its theoretical status, political community is an analytic concept. It refers not to the total human being as such or even all of his political interactions but to an aspect of his political behavior. We are looking at him as he is related to others as a member of a group that shares a political structure, however much or little any member may be emotionally attached to the group for the fulfillment of his political purposes. We can appreciate, therefore, how a person may be able to offer support to two or more communities simultaneously. Different causes may trigger his input or withholding of support with regard to the various communities toward which he may be oriented. For example, he may withdraw his support from NATO or the United Nations, if he is at all oriented toward either one, and yet increase his input to the French political community. Indeed, at the present juncture, it is Gaullist policy to require just that.

Society, Community, and Political Community

In describing the political community as an object of attachment in this way, I have abandoned the classic sociological conceptual distinction between society and community.[12] In that view, society describes the instrumental or associative aspects of a group. It draws attention to the formal ties among the members, those that link them through the

[12] For the classical distinctions, see the well-known discussions by Ferdinand Tönnies and Max Weber. For recent commentaries, see C. J. Friedrich (ed.), *op. cit.*

need to live and work together and to exchange goods and services. Community, on the other hand, is a concept that identifies the affective aspects of group relationships, those resting on personal and informal bonds and expressed through shared feelings, values, and knowledge or all cultural symbols that reflect and contribute to sentiments of solidarity. In Weberian terms, a community exists when there are actions that are "oriented to the feelings of the actors that they belong together." [13]

In order to separate clearly my use of the concept "political community" from the meaning such as this, typically attributed to it for other purposes, I shall refer to the sociological use as the *social* community in contrast with my concern with the *political* community. The differences implied in these two conceptions of the term "community," I shall explore in a moment. But it is clear now that, however helpful it may be, for purposes of general social analysis, to differentiate between society and community—or what I am calling social community—for our analysis of political life this kind of dichotomy holds little value. Nor does it make much sense, solely for the sake of keeping a uniform vocabulary, to try to force ourselves to develop an exact parallel with respect to the political system.

If we did, we would want to be able to distinguish what we might call a political society from a political community: the formal political relationships from the informal solidary bonds. It is true, the creation of such conceptual categories would not present an insurmountable hurdle, if it were necessary or useful to do so. But if we are to treat the canon of simplicity in analysis seriously, we would lose little and gain much in clarity if we find it possible to retain only one term, that of political community. This can incorporate what for other purposes and in other areas of analysis we might find necessary to divide into the societal and communal aspects of a group.

A simplified conceptualization has much to commend it. It will permit us to distinguish unambiguously between the political division of labor as an object of support, which I shall continue to call the political community, and the strength of feelings associated with this attachment, which I shall designate as the *sense or feelings* of community. This sense of community or these feelings of mutual identification will offer a possible measure of attachment to the political community.

It is important to bear in mind this distinction now being made between the political community and the sense of community. The latter is a dimension of the former, the affective aspect. It may or may

[13] H. H. Gerth and C. W. Mills (eds.), *From Max Weber: Essays in Sociology* (New York: Oxford University Press, 1946), p. 183.

not be present; and when present, it may appear in different degrees. It will reflect the varying cohesiveness of the political community. This is decisively different from the juxtaposition of society and (social) community in sociological literature. In that context, the concept "community" refers not to a *quality* of a common set of relationships but to a *different* set of relationships entirely. Each set must exist in every social group.

In the meaning with which I am using the term "political community" as against "a sense of community," the group that shares a political division of labor may or may not have developed a sense of community. Hence, a feeling of community need not always be present, and if it is, this sense may appear in varying degrees. Although, as we shall see, the utter and total absence of a sense of community may not be a frequent phenomenon, it is in principle possible. In this conceptualization, therefore, we shall always be able to keep clearly in mind the difference between the existence of a group with a common division of labor—the political community—and the degree of solidarity, if any, that it may possess— its sense of community. These feelings of community will indicate the extent to which the members support the continuation of the existing division of political labor, that is, of the existing political community.

The Sense of Political Community

Sense of Social Community versus Sense of Political Community

What is this sense of political community which will form an indicator of the degree of cohesion in the division of political labor and thereby one measure of attachment for the political community? To clarify its meaning and appreciate its significance, the first point to note is that it does not represent the same thing as the sense of community often referred to with respect to the social community. If we speak about society at large, the idea of a sense of community is frequently used almost as a synonym for the feelings of solidarity already incorporated in the concept "(social) community" itself. As the affect involved in the idea of social community, a sense of community may be described in Deutsch's terms to be "much more than simply verbal attachment to any number of similar or identical values. Rather it [is] a matter of mutual sympathy and loyalties; of 'we-feeling,' trust, and consideration; of at least partial identification in terms of self-images and interests; of ability to predict each other's behavior and ability to act in accordance with that prediction. In short, it [is] a matter of perpetual attention, communication, perception of needs, and responsiveness." [14]

This describes the communal sentiment of people generally with regard to working and living together in a society to fulfill all their individual and social needs. It is an indication of the cohesiveness of *society*, what has already been identified as the social community. But as in the rest of our analysis, we are concerned only with the political aspect of society and here it is represented in the political community —that aspect of a group of persons as represented in those acts through which they contribute to a common political division of labor. The we-feeling or sense of community which indicates political cohesion of a group of persons, regardless of the kind of regime they have or may develop, consists of the feeling of belonging together as a group which, because it shares a political structure, also shares a political fate. Regardless of the dissimilarities of customs, religion, socio-economic status, nationality, and the like, to the extent that there is a *feeling* of political community, the members will possess mutual sympathy and loyalty with respect to their participation in a common political unit.

It is a mutual identification that may be expressed in many ways. We are the men of a great chief; we are subjects of the king; we are the citizens of this democracy. Often to say that we are Americans, British, Jamaicans, is to point less to the social and cultural differences than to the political bonds that unite a group of persons, even though the nonpolitical overtones are never entirely removed. At least in modern societies, especially where cultural diversity prevails, national identification does have a strong political coloring, of necessity. Nevertheless, in every society the common political structure shared by the members tends to create minimal affective political bonds and it is to these that the concept "sense of political community" will be applied.

The Level of Communal Affect

As has already been implied, this approach does not compel us to postulate that before a political system can exist or even if it is to persist, a sense of political community must first rise to some specified level. Although we may adopt the degree of mutual identification as one kind of measure of the input of support for the political community, it is conceivable that for considerable periods of time, the sense of political community may be low or non-existent. Support may be de-

[14] K. W. Deutsch, S. A. Burrell, et al., *op. cit.*, p. 129.

rived through means other than mutual feelings of belonging together. Not only is this conceivable; there is ample evidence to demonstrate the relative independence for considerable periods of time of political communities from the feelings of community among the members. It is possible for a political structure to bind a group together before feelings of mutual identification have emerged.

We may go further. Frequently the imposition of a common division of political labor has itself made possible the slow growth of sentiments of political solidarity; this reverses normal expectations of the significance of sentiments of solidarity as a pre-condition for the emergence of a political community. A political community may precede and become a condition for the growth of a sense of community.

This has been the experience on the part of most systems that have been brought into being through force, in part or in whole. In the early modern European period, the princes or absolute monarchs drew a geographic area into a political unity through force, frequently before any sense of belonging together had begun to emerge. Only slowly thereafter, through vigorous policies on the part of the political elite, was it possible to merge the members, who were compelled to support the existing political community, into a relatively homogeneous political unit with a high sense of political solidarity. Initially, support had to be generated through coercion, fear of sanctions, or the seduction of material rewards; subsequently these could be supplanted or reinforced by a continuing sense of belonging together.

Coercion may be only one of the sources of support for a political community. In other cases, especially where a group has come together voluntarily, the hard fact of participating collectively may help to arouse and sustain interest in and support for the new political community. A point such as this has been made with regard to the possible development of a more cohesive European political system. It has been suggested that the entrenchment of the habit of working together in a political division of labor sometimes derives less from the pre-recognition of common political interests and traditions than from the convergence of divergent but complementary aims. This is what has been found at the international level and which underlies much so-called functional thinking about the sources of a world or European community.[15] As persons are able to work out their specific problems successfully, the common political institutions through which differences are negotiated and regulated will help draw them together. Transnational institutions may help build up support for supranational ones.

To generalize this idea, we may say that the prior acceptance of a

15 E. B. Haas, *op. cit.*

participation in a division of political labor will help to generate and strengthen other kinds of bonds. Members develop vested interest in the mutual advantages of the ongoing pattern of relationships. In other words, instrumental ties and aims may well keep a group working together while affective bonds have a chance to mature.

But if a sense of community fails to emerge and deepen over time, as a source of support, it may leave a system extremely vulnerable to stress. The collapse of the Austro-Hungarian Empire under the blows of military defeat is a good example. Prior to the nineteenth century, the Habsburg monarchy survived for centuries. Yet traditional particularistic sentiments of the multiple constituent nationalities flourished, varied social, cultural, and economic practices made unity impossible, and large segments of the membership were constantly on the verge of open rupture. Here, coercion and material rewards plus inertia were effective ways of inducing the external trappings of minimal participation in and support for the division of labor necessary to enable the political system to function.[16] But in the long run, the input of support was insufficient to hold the political community together as a unified political system when it came under the stress of military defeat.

The Austro-Hungarian imperial system illustrates both the success and ultimate failure of structural integration under conditions in which strong affective solidarity is absent. A sense of political community is relevant, not to the possibility of a political community but to its duration under stress, a point to which we shall return when we come to consider possible responses to low inputs of support.

To some extent today, developing systems too have taken shape with low feelings of mutual responsiveness on the part of the participating tribal or other plural groups and although a common political structure may exist, an increase in the level of support will have to wait upon the slow stimulation of a sense of political community. But its present absence or low level does not indicate that the input of support for the political community is below the minimal level necessary for its persistence, even though undoubtedly without a gradual increase in feelings of political solidarity it is not likely that the community could endure.

The idea that it is possible to participate in a division of political labor in developing systems, even before the growth of sentiments of political solidarity, is supported by some students of developing systems in Africa. "Whereas in homogeneous societies," writes M. G.

[16] R. A. Kann, *op. cit.*, p. 111.

Smith, "it is a society which constitutes law, in plural societies such as those of Africa, there is evidence that law may serve to constitute society. Thus law both derives from, and may establish society. In the first case the social milieu is typically homogeneous, ethnically and culturally, and the basis of society is primarily consensual. In this situation, law may express organic institutional relations. In the second, or plural case, the social milieu is heterogeneous in cultural and ethnic constitution and coercive in base, and the law which seeks to constitute it and serves to regulate is essentially sectional. In the culturally homogeneous society, the state—that is, the central political institutions—like law, are derivative, expressive, and secondary structures. In the evolution of plural units, the state pre-exists society, and provides the legal framework within which the new society may or may not emerge." [17]

The differences in terminology ought not be allowed to conceal the relevance of the ideas being advanced in this quotation. It confirms the point that structural participation or instrumental ties under some conditions may precede the growth of sentiments of solidarity in society. With the necessary changes in concepts, the same ordering of events could be said to apply to the political community or group participating in a common division of political labor and the underlying supportive sentiments which may exist in varying degrees.

It is quite possible, therefore, that in the formation of new societies and associated political systems, a sense of belonging together politically may normally follow rather than precede the emergence of a political community. If this is so, there could be little doubt that a political community is phenomenally independent, at least in its initiation, from the feelings of solidarity that are usually considered to be a major precondition.

By fusing the politically relevant components of the sociological concepts of society and community into a single concept, "political community," we have succeeded in identifying and defining one of the major components of a political system. The idea of persistence and change of a political system will make sense only if the context indicates whether or not the reference is to the political community. Systems may change in many ways but where there is a decline of support below a certain level for the political community, there the system will be threatened with stress.

By adopting the concept "sense of community" to identify the affec-

[17] M. G. Smith, "The Sociological Framework of Law" in H. and L. Kuper (eds.), *The Development and Adaptation of Legal Systems in Africa*, forthcoming.

tive, cultural aspects of the political community, we have been able to devise an analytic approach that provides us with a major indicator of support for the political community. It is true, under certain conditions, the virtual absence of such feelings need not in itself prove that the political community lacks the minimal support necessary to avoid stressing the essential variables. Nevertheless, since over the long run it is unlikely that many systems could persist without the development of a rather high sense of political community, or withstand severe crises, it does represent a significant measure of support.

The criterion by which political community has been selected as one central focus of support has been the probability that loss of support for it would prevent the system from continuing to process demands through to binding outputs. Using the same criterion, we shall now be able to identify the regime as a second major component of a system, no less significant than the political community for a full appreciation of stress due to loss of support and responses related to it.

I 2

Objects of Support: The Regime

I N REFERRING TO THE PERSISTENCE OR CHANGE OF A POLITICAL SYSTEM
we may have in mind something quite different from the political
community. The German political community had remained relatively intact after the first World War and in 1933. Yet no one could
doubt that in both periods the system underwent fundamental
changes when it shifted from the monarchy to the Weimar Republic in
the first case, and from this Republic to the Nazi order in the second.

The political community that is Great Britain has experienced some
limited modifications in the last century and a half, if we set aside the
colonial empire and its vicissitudes. But in that period, Britian witnessed the introduction of the party system, many new rights for individuals and groups, popular suffrage, and a host of other clear constitutional changes of a kind that on any grounds may be considered fundamental in character.

In the case of France, since 1789 there has been a succession of such
changes. "Uncertain of legitimacy, discontent with their institutions,
the French question the form of the state each time the nation faces
danger . . . Too many citizens or functionaries adjust their obedience
to today's Government according to their anticipations of tomorrow's
regime." [1] As a group conducting its political affairs in common, the
metropolitan French have maintained their community relatively intact since the Revolution. But even though democratic constitutions in
France have revealed an amazing capacity for re-asserting themselves
in the face of repeated assaults, the French political order has displayed greater instability than that of most other modern democracies.

This distinction between what is often called the constitutional order and what I have named the political community has been familiar
to students of politics from time immemorial. But its theoretical implications for the persistence of systems in the face of change need to
be spelled out. Following an old tradition, I shall call this object of
support the regime.

[1] R. Aron, *New York Times*, Magazine Section, December 3, 1961, "Can De Gaulle
End the Ordeal," p. 28.

The Function of the Regime

If the members of a system consistently failed to support some kind of regime, this lack of support would drive the essential variables beyond their critical range and would thereby prevent a system from operating. It is this potential outcome associated with the regime that compels us to characterize it as a second fundamental component of a system.

The need for a regime stems from an elemental fact about human organization, however uncomplex it may be. Even if members of a group displayed the strongest feelings of mutual identification in a political community, they would still be left with the task of establishing some regularized method for ordering their political relationships. Ultimately, for the outputs to be accepted as binding, the members would need to accept some basic procedures and rules relating to the means through which controversy over demands was to be regulated and work out some ends that would at least broadly and generally guide the search for such settlements.

The alternative would be for the rules and aims of political interaction in a system to be largely random and indeterminate. In that event, members of the system would have to argue about day-to-day actions and decisions at the same time as they questioned the fundamental assumptions about the way in which these daily differences should be settled or about the validity of the procedures that determined who was to have the major power and responsibility for negotiating differences and establishing authoritative or binding outcomes. They would argue about how to go about doing things that they want to get done as well as about the things themselves; matters of basic procedure as well as substance would be intermingled.

Many new political systems today are confronted with this very situation, especially where the retiring imperial power has failed to make adequate provision for at least a structure of authority, as in the Congo since its separation from Belgium. In the crises provoked by simultaneous dispute over two levels of a system, what I shall call the regime and the day-to-day policies, there lies a major source of failure in any effort to create a new society or political system.[2] If at least the

[2] E. C. Banfield, *Government Project* (Glencoe, Illinois: Free Press, 1951) describes a similar confounding of levels in efforts to create a small political subsystem in the United States and clearly reveals its disastrous results for the social unit involved.

primary issues at the regime level were not resolved in some way, in due course it could not help but lead to the downfall of the existing system.

Even a small social club finds it necessary to lay down some ground rules to order discussion and help validate the outcome. Where a group is larger, it cannot undertake the political tasks directly itself but must place responsibility and power in the hands of others. It becomes even more urgent to stabilize the processes through which these others are to be selected and to assure, with some high degree of probability, that their decisions and actions will be accepted as valid. The other side of the coin is that the members of a political system as a whole also need some regularized expectations about what is required of them, whose decisions they are to accept as authoritative, under what conditions, and with regard to what matters.

The regime represents relatively stable expectations, depending on the system and its state of change, with regard to the range of matters that can be handled politically, the rules or norms governing the way these matters are processed, and the position of those through whom binding action may be taken on these matters. Within this range, the politically relevant members are less likely to challenge the authority and validity of settlements arrived at, even though they may of course question the wisdom.

What this means is that every system needs to develop a set of formal or operating constraints that are generally accepted, through quiescent indifference or positive consensus, by rulers and ruled alike and that give at least broad indications of what are or are not permissible goals, practices, and structures in the system. Whether the limits are broad or narrow, relatively changing or constant, the same for all or specific to various social groups or individual members, they do set up expectations about who is to wield power, the limits within which it is to be used, who are expected to comply, and the conditions under which these obligations arise.[3]

Not every system need be successful in stabilizing such a set of constraints on behavior; nor need it always be clear in any system as to

[3] This is *not* the same as establishing criteria of legitimacy. As we shall see when we come to discuss legitimacy, some few types of systems are able to survive without it. It cannot be part of what is necessary in all regimes, although empirically a belief in legitimacy is found in most. Furthermore, the extent to which members believe that decisions or authorities are legitimate will fluctuate and a system may have to rely almost exclusively on force or fear, at least for limited times. Hence such a belief could not be part of the regime. Rather, as we shall see, it is a possible and empirically a highly probable response to prevent a lowering of the level of support.

what the culture has placed in this special category of expectations. Within a system, ambiguities over what is included as fundamental to the political relationships and what is accidental or relatively unimportant form the growing edges of political change. The existence of this indeterminate boundary indicates that past practices may be undergoing challenge and that new areas of consensus or acquiescent indifference with regard to what are considered basic relationships are being carved out. But aside from considerations of change, if a system is to avoid turmoil or near chaos, the basic ways for processing demands into outputs and the broad limits within which these outputs may fall, must be stabilized. As we shall see, this is one of the primary conditions that will prevent even deep and passionate conflict over day-to-day outputs from shattering a system.

The Components of the Regime

The regime as sets of constraints on political interaction in all systems may be broken down into three components: values (goals and principles), norms, and structure of authority. The values serve as broad limits with regard to what can be taken for granted in the guidance of day-to-day policy without violating deep feelings of important segments of the community. The norms specify the kinds of procedures that are expected and acceptable in the processing and implementation of demands. The structures of authority designate the formal and informal patterns in which power is distributed and organized with regard to the authoritative making and implementing of decisions—the roles and their relationships through which authority is distributed and exercised. The goals, norms, and structure of authority both limit and validate political actions and in this way provide what tends to become a context for political interactions. This context changes more slowly than other kinds of political relationships.

To avoid any misapprehension about the referents of the concept "regime," we need to take note of the fact that it includes more than what in political science we usually call a constitution, at least in the formal sense. A written code offers a first approximation to the values, rules, and structures that constrain the ways of processing demands and circumscribe the nature of the outputs. The regime also includes, however, those parts of the established expectations in political life that may seldom be envisaged as part of a constitution, formal or informal, written or customary, even in a highly legal system. The regime refers to the general matrix of regularized expectations within the limits of which political actions are usually considered authoritative, regardless of how or where these expectations may be expressed.

Although, in the process of our analysis, it may at times appear that a regime in this sense is static, we well know in political research that regimes and their components adapt continuously to changing conditions. Where they fail to do so, fictions develop to cope with change or violent eruptions may modify or destroy them dramatically. A specific regime at any moment in time will be the product of the accommodation among the pressures for new goals, rules, or structures stimulated by social change and the limitations imposed by existing conventions and practices.

In suggesting that no system can order its relationships or conduct its political business without support being extended to some kind of regime, this means that the support must underlie each of the components. If the regime represents the overall object of support at this level of a system, values, norms, and structure will be sub-objects to which support must be extended or withheld. We can thus probe more deeply into the meaning of support for the regime by exploring each component separately.

Regime Values and Principles

Every regime consists, in part, of a broadly defined underlying set of political values and principles, articulated or implicit, which impose constraints on the purposes for which the energies and resources of the system may be committed. They may be incorporated in ideologies and doctrines or they may be inarticulately assumed in political practices. A full and accurate picture of the operative regime values [4] could be obtained only by balancing practice against verbal expressions.

We are familiar with the considerable variety of values underlying political systems. The ideological symbols that express political values show vast differences and reflect greatly divergent ways of life among systems at any one moment of time or historically considered. Freedom as against slavery or coercion, social equality as compared to fixed status, individual political responsibility in contrast with acceptance of the wisdom of political authority, maximization of popular participation in place of rule by a restricted elite, racial superiority rather than equality signalize deep value cleavages among political systems.

---

[4] For the concept "operative ideals" see A. D. Lindsay, *op. cit.*, p. 37. We shall return to this subject in chapter 19.

Underlying principles such as divine right, popular consent, the will of the Volk, the general will, social contract, or dictatorship of the proletariat express conflicting premises to guide action in varying political systems. In recent years, in response to the special situation flowing from the colonial era in world history, new systems, striving for economic and social development, have generated new political value premises in the form of developmental ideologies. In these, democratic values are, at times, reduced to a secondary and instrumental position. In general, the very nomenclature used to classify systems—democratic, communist, authoritarian, traditional and transitional, modernizing autocratic and the like—highlights differences in the value premises of such systems.

The Function of Regime Values

Could a system persist without some minimal agreement, or at least acquiescence, among the politically relevant members about the broad values within the context of which outputs would be acceptable? The suggestion here is that if the outputs of a system could be of any kind at all, the politically relevant members would soon lose confidence with regard to the probable range of decisions that might be made or in the authorities themselves. The members would constantly be alerted to a two-level problem. If any specific issue were at stake, they would need to take a position on it. But at the same time, if the antagonists over the specific issue could operate on any value assumptions at all, they might also be involved in a much deeper struggle over fundamental orientations. Each issue would be transformed into a deep cleavage about a whole way of life, a condition that occurs typically in those systems in which the value premises are in fact in process of significant change.

Although any system in process of fundamental change could be conveniently used to illustrate this point, the developing nations today offer innumerable examples. In these systems, as the basic value orientations of the colonial powers and the indigenous groups seeking independence have come into open conflict, even the smallest political issue almost immediately tends to become converted, in part, into the broader issue of the kind of regime and its basic orientations. In the last analysis, there is only one issue, prior to the elimination of the colonial power: independence. Once independence has been obtained, the multiplicity of individual issues that it has concealed is immediately revealed in the variety of problems that the new regime must face.

For limited periods a system may be able to tolerate such fundamental cleavage. As Britain shifted in the last few decades toward a social welfare economy, it quickly became apparent that if everything that the Labor Party undertook might be completely undone by the Conservatives, life would become intolerable. The supporters of neither party would be able to trust the other to operate within a minimally acceptable range of alternatives. With the relatively rapid shift of each party program toward the other, however, a value framework quickly developed that enabled all members of the system to have some minimal confidence that regardless of which party obtained power, the same basic expectations would remain inviolate. This took the form of general acceptance of the value of a vaguely defined welfare state.

If a middle road had not been found and support for it had not been developed, each pendular shift in policy could only have served to aggravate the political cleavages. Although undoubtedly other mechanisms could have come into operation to preserve some kind of regime, the existing one might well have succumbed. If such other mechanisms were to fail, however, it is doubtful whether any political system could survive long under the oscillation between polar extremes in value orientations on the part of different segments of the politically relevant members. They would exhaust themselves in seeking to settle the prior question of the assumptions that ought to underlie policy and would have little opportunity to deal with the immediate issues of the day.

Plausibility of Value Consensus

But how plausible is it to assume that we can ever speak about *the* basic values of a system? Perhaps we can never validly speak of the values and principles supported by any group of persons, much less by the enormous aggregate frequently composing a political system. May it not be a snare and delusion to go about searching for the impossible?

The argument may be and has been raised that not even small organizations, let alone such vast aggregates as political systems in modern mass societies, can be said to have common values. We can identify and isolate specific objectives which groups pursue if they have a way of speaking as groups. But when we come to the presumed common values underlying these objectives, this position would hold, they dissolve before our eyes. Individual members of the group interpret them in such diverse ways that we must get completely bogged down in a complex morass of varying perceptions, goals, and purposes.

For example, who can say whether the purposes of a trade union are to raise wages, improve conditions of labor, share control over industry, regulate leisure time, increase productivity, recreate the bases of society, or any combination of these? Whose purposes are to be taken as representative of the trade union—those of the leadership, observers of the union movement, implications of a series of decisions by the executive or membership conventions, an articulate subgroup in the membership? All that can be said is that different persons inside or outside the group attribute basically or marginally different values and goals to the group.

When applied to the regime of a political system, there is certainly some credibility to this point of view, especially as the scale of the system increases. Not all members of a system can be expected to support the identical set of political values, at least so long as we do not push our search for values to such high levels of abstractions that no reasonable person in a given culture would be likely to disagree with them. There will usually be subsets of members who will even interpret the same goal symbols quite differently. Freedom does not bear the same content for all persons. We can expect to find members who apparently hold the same political ideals but who place substantially different emphases and priorities upon their constituent parts. This is especially true among the most articulate interpreters—the intelligentsia—who are notoriously unable to achieve consensus or unified support for an identical set of values. Furthermore, we will usually find subsets of members who espouse values at considerable variance from those of the rest of the system. In any empirical test of the nature and distribution of political values, we might end up with demographic clusters each of which had somewhat distinctive views of what the fundamental values of the regime are and should be.

Values as a Framework of Contingent Constraints

Yet, however great the internal variations in perception and preferences with regard to the value premises of a system may be, several things do stand out. In the first place, the actual specification of the degree of consensus with regard to political values is an empirical rather than a theoretical matter and is one that has never been fully faced up to, much less resolved through testing whole systems. We really do not know the extent to which fundamental political values are shared, if at all, by large segments of a political community, or the intensity of attachment to them.

In the second place, even in the face of this lack of reliable knowl-edge, it does seem to make sense to say that different systems orient themselves favorably to different kinds of political values and princi-ples. The underlying values of authoritarian Spain and democratic Britain could not be confused in any important way. Implicit here is the idea that, in any system, there are certain dominant political val-ues that give tone and direction for political practices, norms, and structural arrangements.

The conditions under which some political values instead of others become dominant for a system is a moot question. Perhaps they need only to be adopted by the most powerful members or groups in the system or conform to the general cultural conventions of the society. What is obvious is that not all members need to share all of a system's goal orientations. There may be many variant subsets of goals held by non-effective members of a system. These may remain dormant subval-ues in the system without great validating potency, but ready to emerge if the conditions should prove propitious. The political goals and values of minorities in the United States, say, supporting fascist, communist, black nationalist, theocratic, or racist ideologies represent such non-dominant belief systems. It seems reasonable to assume that systems will vary with respect to the degree of value consensus they display and the level of generality at which it appears, and that the group whose values do dominate, will also vary from a minority to a much larger number.

But we may assume that in most systems some values will appear as dominant. Yet the implication here need not be that the members of the system do in fact, relentlessly or unambiguously, pursue the goals implicit in the regime values. Nor does this approach suggest that there need always be a conscious, well-articulated, or popularly sup-ported impulse to fulfil these values. What is suggested, rather, is that insofar as the politically effective members of a system lend their sup-port to the expression and elaboration of such values and they are not openly rejected by other members in the system, they will form limits within which the day-to-day policies will be expected to con-fine themselves.

Values may be of greater interest for the outer, even if ill-defined limits they impose upon political action than for the specific objectives they dictate or the universal consensus they command. It is for this reason that vastly divergent concrete policies may be pursued by gov-ernments without violating the underlying dominant value premises, even assuming that all members were sufficiently wise and well enough informed to be able to see the relationship between the objectives of governments and the values of the regime.

What then is the way in which political values may confine the actions of the authorities in a system, if only broadly? Part of their function derives from the very fact that they may lie dormant most of the time, serving as the silent assumptions of behavior rather than as articulate ideologies. In this role, their peculiar part is that of watchdog, as it were, ready to spring into action in self-defense. In moments of crisis or under pressure, they may be activated as one of the major sources for mobilizing support in the pursuit of specific objectives. At such a point, the measure of support for the regime values in question are empirically tested, their meaning is amplified or clarified, their content is reinforced, modified, or rejected. *Ex post facto* at least, it would be intelligible to report that certain political values received varying measures of support.[5] As an example, during the McCarthy period in the United States, the challenge to the underlying values of political tolerance and freedom implicit in this movement stirred a response that included a renewed evocation of the traditions of legality, tolerance, and individual freedom of thought and expression, and an attempt to re-interpret the meaning of loyalty as a value.

The kind of limits defined by regime values is further brought out by the way in which they infuse and help to shape the content of other parts of the regime, such as the operating norms or the structure of authority. For example, with the appearance of a new elite that seeks to move a system in fundamentally different directions, whether through pacific or violent means, new ideologies typically arise as the basis for mobilizing support behind the new elite. These values give birth to new visions for the future and normally incorporate new goals together with revised structural arrangements for the regime. The

---

[5] In part, the support for regime values has been indirectly studied in American voting research. The distinction drawn by some research workers between style and position issues or between ideological as compared to "contingent needs" kinds of issues points this up. It draws attention to the conflict between specific objectives of material interests as against the less tangible but nonetheless real issues over the fundamental assumptions about the kind of political life to be led in the U.S. Style or ideology touch upon what we have been calling the regime and refer, therefore, to regime issues. They rouse the members of the system with respect to the broader values characterizing political life. As we might expect, voting and related studies show that not all persons are equally interested in style issues nor can they be equally roused to action by them. Insofar as some subsets of persons are ideologically more sensitive than others, we might suspect that they will be more important in defining and reformulating the fundamental value assumptions of the regime in any system. See B. R. Berelson, P. F. Lazarsfeld and W. N. McPhee, *op. cit.*, chapter 9; S. M. Lipset, M. Trow and J. S. Coleman, *op. cit.*, chapter 15. There is a rich storehouse of material dealing with the underlying psychodynamics of support for the regime, in R. E. Lane, *Political Ideology* (New York: Free Press of Glencoe, 1962), especially chapter 5 and pp. 173–176.

overthrow of the *ancien régime* by the French Revolution and of the Tsarist regime by the October Revolution each led to fundamental transformations not only in the political values of the respective systems but in the structure of the regime. The new values could not tolerate the old structural frame; they could not be pursued even broadly under the old forms.

We may conclude that even if we cannot describe the members of a system as sharing a set of political values or being committed to a common set of political principles, at least we can say that the politically dominant values do impose some broad constraints upon the actions that can be taken and even upon the structure of the regime itself. In this way, they provide a minimal, relatively stable context for a membership within which all political life may be pursued. To that extent it frees the interest and energies of the politically relevant members for attention to the ongoing daily tasks involved in converting wants to binding outputs.

Regime Norms

A second major component of a regime consists of its norms or what may variously be called its operating rules and the rules of the game. In most general terms, these norms specify the way in which members of a system are expected to behave in political life: how they are to go about putting in demands, helping to process them into outputs, and influencing their implementation. These are the ground rules for participating in all aspects of the political process.

Unless the politically relevant members extended minimal support to such norms, they would have to devise separate *ad hoc* rules for arranging the way in which they were to proceed in resolving each difference. If dispute about these occurred, as might appear more rather than less likely, little time and energy could be left for dealing with the substance of their differences other than those related to the procedures to be used. How things are to get done needs to be stabilized to some minimal extent. This is just a way of stating that there must be some rules of the game that are supported at least by those members who are influential enough to count in the given type of system.

When we speak of the rules of the game, we might think exclusively of those that are embodied in formal documents such as written constitutions or legal codes. In fact, norms consist of two separable kinds of expectations: customary and legal. Both kinds help to provide a framework of order for political interaction; without them turmoil or chaos could scarcely be avoided.

Customary or Effective Norms

These are the general conceptions about right and wrong ways of behaving in political life that have never acquired the kind of binding quality or sanctions that convert them into legal rules. Nevertheless, they are the effective operating rules that have become so firmly entrenched in a system that any violation would provoke informal reactive sanctions of varying grades of severity.

By way of illustration, in most democratic systems the members expect to be able to act through political parties and interest groups, and to be able to enter into the political market place with relative ease. They come to tolerate the fact that others will seek to win the favor of the authorities and to expect equal toleration from these others. All members also expect to be able to gain the attention and consideration of the authorities, that is, that the authorities will be responsive.

Some norms are incidental in a democracy; others are central to pervasive conceptions of what democracy entails. For example, although spirited debate of political issues is permissible and expected, there is nevertheless also some anticipated outer limit on virulence and accusations. Beyond this, members feel the disputants have gone too far and have failed to recognize that regardless of who the victor is, they must do nothing that is so divisive as to prevent the contenders from continuing to live together in a common system.

This norm of temperance and tolerance in dispute is intimately bound up with the additional basic premise that the members must be prepared to negotiate and compromise. Since today's loser in an electoral campaign or policy has an opportunity to become tomorrow's victor, differences do not have to be fought out to the knife, unlike those systems in which the winner takes all. The loser is expected to accept defeat gracefully and typically, to behave in such a way—as through a statement acknowledging defeat and encouraging support of the winning candidate—that the unity of the system is maintained and the solidarity of the members around the winner is encouraged for the sake of the persistence of the system.

In many ways, customary norms such as these that are not converted into laws or constitutional codes, form a vital normative understructure for democratic systems. So vital are they, that if there they were to be eroded, this could easily bring the whole formal, legal structure top-pling down. This is one of the reasons why the cry of "twenty years of treason" raised against one of the political parties during the McCarthy period in the United States could be viewed as perhaps the most dangerous of all accusations. Regardless of who is the victor in a campaign, one cannot live with a traitorous party; it left the implica-tion that all hope of compromise might be lost and therein lay a formidable threat to the regime.

All systems, and not democratic ones alone, are characterized by such customary norms that constitute the matrix within which the legal norms themselves are able to operate. In totalitarian systems, for example, one rule of the game is that the winner takes all. When it becomes apparent that although the loser need not share in the fruits of victory, at least he is no longer under threat of being destroyed or exiled, the regime can be said to have experienced a remarkable modi-fication. In the Soviet Union, when, after the death of Stalin, succes-sion of new leaders was conducted without the physical elimination of the incumbents, there was general recognition that a fundamental norm of the system had been altered. The question arose as to the extent to which other effective norms relating to greater freedom of speech and organization might not be affected in due course.

Legal or Formal Norms

Aside from these effectively operating rules which are part of the actual customs of the system, many of the expectations with regard to the way in which political relationships ought to be ordered may take on a formal status. They represent formal prescriptions, practical or ideal, that provide for such rules of the game as due process of law, freedom for all to vote, freedom of speech and association, restriction of participation to a single party or to a restricted group, or inherit-ance of the major office of authority.

In part, such ideals may be expressed in the customs of the system and are closely associated with or molded by the general ideals that we have already discussed as part of the regime. But in part, insofar as they have attained a formal status, they may be embodied in legal rules. These rules may be so central to the system that they are in-cluded in such basic documents as its constitution, written or other-wise; or they may be written in legal codes and judicial decisions. But at other times, as in primitive systems, they may merely be customary rules that have acquired the status of law. That is to say, all of these rules are formal in the sense that their violation is expected to arouse those special public sanctions that can be called legal, however we may define law.

As legal rules, they differ from customary norms not only in their formality but also in the probability that they may not reflect the effective operating code of the system, although the extent to which they diverge will always be an empirical matter. The disparity between the legal norms with regard to the political and economic position of the Negro in the United States in the past century and the actual practices testifies eloquently to this. The actual expectations we would have to classify under the customary rules of the game; they are as intrinsic a part of the regime as the legal norms that specify the formal conditions of participation in the political life of the system.

It is clear that as conceptualized here, a regime embraces considerably more than is usually associated with the term. In addition to the usual legal rules, it includes a vast body of cultural expectations about how members ought to behave in a system even though these may never become part of a constitution or even be considered as representative of the underlying constitutional principles and legal codes. In fact, they may even violate or diverge fundamentally from the formally avowed principles. But to omit them would be to neglect a basic part of those expectations that help to order political relationships and, thereby, to determine the procedures through which demands become processed into binding outputs.

The Function of Regime Norms

If we were concerned with problems of classifying political systems according to their regimes, we would have to devote some time to specifying the norms, both customary and legal, associated with each regime. No classification would be complete without taking into account normative differences in rules of behavior. But the question to which this analysis has been addressing itself is quite different. Could a system persist at all if it did not win minimal support for some set of rules regardless of their content, to regulate the relationships among its members?

In the case of norms we are faced with a situation somewhat different from that of values. Values limit the range of alternative goals that a system might pursue or even norms to which it might adhere. The limit is important, even if it is broad and ill-defined. It provides the politically relevant members with some end points beyond which they can expect the decisions and specific outputs will not go. At least this is so with respect to the actual political values that underlie a system.

In the case of norms, the situation is in part similar. The formal norms, as prescriptions of what ought to be, either serve to limit the range of variations possible in the effective norms or may possibly, at some future time, act as a sanction or a kind of leverage to force practice into conformity with ideals. Even if a system suppressed freedom of speech, as long as its formal constitution asserts a belief in such freedom, its regime is importantly different from one in which the formal rules severely restrict it. At least in the former system the constitutionalized ideals may at some point be used as a weapon to compel changes in practice, an opportunity that is closed to a system that does not even recognize freedom as an ideal.

But if the formal norms may at times serve to impose some possible limits on the range of effective operating rules in a system, the effective norms play another vital function in a system. They provide one of the conditions necessary for a system to convert demands into binding outputs. If the members could look forward to no stable rules at all or, as recently, in the former Belgian Congo, the politically relevant members had to engage in constant dispute with respect to which rule, if any, to invoke, conflict would be compounded. Members would be arguing about what they wanted at the same time as they sought to settle the rules according to which they would seek to resolve their differences over what they want, a two-level dispute that would leave a system floundering in shifting sands. In other words, for any system to persist at all, the politically relevant members, or at least a significant proportion of them, would have to support some set of ground rules. These, both formal and effective, I shall consider to be part of a regime.

Regime Structure

The regime structure represents the third and last major component for which support must be present if the regime is to persist over time. Even though in this volume I am not directly concerned with structural factors, nevertheless where they do appear as critical elements in the primary processes of systems, I shall not avoid discussing them.

The Authority Roles

It is patent that demands could not be negotiated through to outputs without a variety of structural means. Several things are necessary and these can be summed up as decisions, compliance, and implementation. First, the system must provide a way for making decisions. Second, it must be able to obtain the commitment of the relevant members of the system for the adoption and attainment of these objectives or neutralize those who might be opposed. Third, it needs to provide the continuing energy to put the decisions into effect and to supervise their implementation. The dynamic character of a political system resides in the fact that it is the kind of system through which human and physical resources can be committed in the pursuit of specific objectives and general ends. This is equally the case whether the system is a dictatorship, in which only the acquiescence or agreement of a few is involved, or a direct democracy, in which the continuing direct participation of all is required.

Theoretically it would be possible to envision a condition in which each decision was made and implemented by means uniquely extemporized for the occasion. In practice, the kind of commitments involved compels every system to provide some members to care for the day-to-day activities related to the making and execution of decisions. Even in the smallest group, we can expect to find that the power and responsibility of caring for recurring matters as well as crises tend to reside in the hands of the few.

This organizational concentration of power has long been recognized as axiomatic wherever a group seeks to act. Usually the reason for drawing attention to this tendency for power to gravitate to a minority has been to demonstrate the impossibility of avoiding control by the few or the difficulties of implementing Rousseauan notions of popular democracy.[6] But since we are not primarily engaged in an ethical critique or in the development of a normative theory, for us the important implication of this fact is that it provides the basis for the emergence in all systems, from the smallest to the largest, of a minimal division of political labor. Through it some members, either formally or informally, acquire the special powers and responsibilities of attending to the daily tasks involved in the conversion of wants into demands. This is so even in the smallest Bushman bands which may not exceed fifty members; a headman, sometimes in the form of an

[6] For the tendency toward oligarchy see the well known writings of Robert Michels, Gaetano Mosca, and Vilfredo Pareto.

infant and its regent, will emerge. At the very least, an informal opinion leader can be expected to give direction and energy to a group.

This specialization of labor enables some recognized few to take the initiative or to help in other ways to bring about some adjustment or accommodation in conflicting demands and to implement any settlement where necessary. In some systems, these roles may be formally specified in an organizational chart or written, in part at least, into a constitutional or legal code; in others, they may appear as informally developed patterns of leadership. But in each type or combination of them, in effect, the day-to-day control and responsibility for processing demands is undertaken through more or less stable sets of roles which tend to be complementary and which, as a set, are distinguishably different from other roles in the total political structure.

Again, theoretically we could envision a situation in which even though such structural means for fulfilling this special responsibility were available, the occupants of the roles might need to justify each act as it occurs. But empirically it is difficult if not impossible to discover such a system. Most frequently, some roles will have been endowed with some authority or will have acquired it through success or tradition, so as to facilitate the ready acceptance of binding decisions. Usually the authority is not exclusively associated with the individual person, aside from the case of the leader who arises at moments of political crisis—a special condition when the pattern of authority may be in the immediate throes of political change.

But usually, where regularized patterns of behavior have emerged, the authority attaches to the role itself, rather than to the individual alone. It is in part because of this that the paramount tribal chief, the monarch of a state, the legislators and chief executive of a modern democracy, are all able to perform their special tasks in the process of converting wants to outputs. This capacity derives from the expectation on their side and the reciprocal expectations of others that, within the perimeters of the roles, the actions of the authorities will be accepted as compelling. The probability will be high that others will normally comply.

These roles I shall refer to as the roles of political authorities. The roles themselves need to be distinguished from their occupants. The roles consist of regularized patterns of behavior and expectations about the way in which the occupants of particular positions in society will behave and of how others ought to behave toward them. The occupants are the particular individuals who, at the moment, happen to be acting in these roles. At this point in our discussion, it is the roles themselves rather than the occupants that I shall consider the third component of a regime toward which support might be directed. In the next chapter when we deal with the last of the major objects of support,[7] I shall return to the occupants, whom I shall call simply the authorities.

The Power of the Authority Roles

In varying degrees, quite distinctive expectations are associated with and thereby help to define the authority roles in all political systems. First, the roles are expected to equip their incumbents with special powers, formal or otherwise, to care for the day-to-day problems of making binding decisions for a society and implementing them. Second, to these roles are often attached a moral responsibility for undertaking such action. And third, in all systems, the members anticipate that in the normal course of events compliance with decisions and actions taken through these roles will be forthcoming. The occupants of these roles have the special capacity, formally granted or implicitly acquired, to direct, order or command, and in many systems, although not all, to compel. Hence the power associated with these roles consists of authority.

Authority is not the only kind of power that may be available to occupants of these roles even though it is probably the most economical in terms of energy and resources.[8] Authority is a special power relationship based on the expectation that if A sends a message to B—which may be called a wish, suggestion, regulation, law, command, order, or the like—B will adopt it as the premise of his own behavior. B may question the wisdom of the message; he may even seek to cast doubt on the capacity of the particular occupant of the authority role, or of any occupant, to expect compliance. But as long as the probability is high that, under the circumstances B will comply, he is subject to the authority of another. This lies at the heart of the authority role.

There may be many reasons why obedience or compliance is forthcoming. Members of a system may accept a decision out of fear, expe-

---

[7] For a most useful discussion of empirical ways of differentiating among position, role, and occupants see N. Gross, W. S. Mason and A. W. McEachern, *Explorations in Role Analysis* (New York: Wiley, 1958) and the literature cited there.

[8] The reasons for this and a complete discussion of types of power are discussed in D. Easton, *A Theoretical Approach to Authority* and in "The Perception of Authority and Political Change" in C. J. Friedrich (ed.), *Authority* (Cambridge: Harvard University Press, 1958), pp. 170–196. See also J. S. Adams and A. K. Romney, "A Functional Analysis of Authority," 66 *Psychological Review* (1959) 234–251 and my remarks in Chapter 24.

diency, habit, or lethargy. But typically, in political systems, at least in those in which the political authorities are not being fundamentally challenged, the capacity of the authorities to rule is closely connected to the presence of an ingrained belief, usually transmitted across the generations in the socialization processes, that the occupants of the political authority roles have a right to command and the other members of the system a duty to obey. The major source of power for these roles resides in the prevalence of the conviction of their legitimacy.

This does not exclude the possibility and probability that the occupants of authority roles will have other important sources of power to backstop and supplement the kind derived from a belief in their legitimacy, especially when at times this belief is in danger of disappearing. They may seek to persuade, force and manipulate through means that do not involve orders or commands. But without the additional capacity provided by the widespread belief in or acceptance of their legitimacy, except for two categories of systems to be mentioned in the discussion of legitimacy in Chapter 18, it is doubtful whether any system could assure support for its authority roles.[9]

But the power that the authorities acquire by virtue of their occupancy of these roles brings with it certain corresponding limitations. The power of authority is itself confined, with varying degrees of success, by expectations held by the general members of the system with regard to the way in which authority ought to be used.[10] The general members of the system usually come to expect that the authorities will accept the moral responsibility for undertaking to make and implement binding decisions, as defined by the culture. Such cultural expectations serve as restraints on the occupants of authority roles, in highly absolutist regimes as well as in democratic ones, even though

[9] My classification of power relationships, in the articles cited in the previous footnote, views the ability to command as one of a number of types. It may be exercised legitimately or illegitimately. If a thief orders you, at the point of a gun, to yield your wallet and you obey him, he has the ability to command you. He therefore can be said to have authority over you even though, because you would challenge its legitimacy, you consider it coercive. Coercion, however, is just another way of identifying illegitimate authority. I am aware, of course, that this diverges from ordinary usage. Authority is usually applied only to situations in which there is a belief in the legitimacy of the orders or commands. For reasons explained in the articles cited, I join others in considering that it is more useful to broaden the term to cover all command-obedience relationships, discriminating further in each case by reference to the reasons why the exercise of the power of authority is effective. This is clearly a matter of definition but it has important theoretical as well as empirical implications.

[10] This has been designated as the area of acceptance by H. Simon, *Administrative Behavior* (New York: Macmillan, 1957, 2nd ed.), p. 133.

the limitations on authority may be much less restrictive in the case of non-democratic systems.

Nor are these cultural expectations with regard to the way in which authority is to be used purely moral. Depending upon the nature of the system, varying kinds of empirical sanctions may be activated if the authorities fail to take their responsibilities seriously or go beyond what are considered reasonable bounds. Not the least of these takes the form of smoldering discontent among the general membership. Marie Antoinette's quip, upon being informed that the people had no bread, "let them eat cake," although worn and hackneyed through repetition, is nonetheless still unsurpassed in epitomizing the loss of any real sense of moral responsibility for attending to the day-to-day problems of governing. Revolution became the last sanction for enforcing conformity with the general expectations of the responsibilities that go with the authority roles.

The Structure of the Authority Roles

To this point the analysis has left the impression that support is directed to authority roles as a mere aggregate or set of isolated individual units. But it is transparent that these roles are not randomly distributed or unrelated. They will stand in some determinate order to each other and to the excluded set of all the non-authority political roles in the system.

The particular structuring of the relationships among the authority roles will both reflect and condition the way in which power is distributed and used in the system. The rights and duties assigned to each role and the extent to which each limits or reinforces the power of the other helps to determine who has what authority and how it is used. Thus, even though the separation of power in the United States no longer stands for what it did in the past, it still plays a fundamental part in the structuring of the relationships among the various authority roles as contrasted with the concentration and fusion of power that we find in the British parliamentary system.

But comparison of different structures of authority would take us further afield than is necessary for the kind of analysis under way here. The point in raising the matter of the structure of authority roles now is that support is extended not only to single roles in the system as such but to the whole pattern or system of authority roles. A person may support the Presidency or the Supreme Court in the United States as constellations of roles regardless of who the incumbents may be. But he may also be very positively or negatively disposed to the whole structure, the "system of government." By this would be meant the overall way in which authority is organized and used. Normally, when I shall discuss support for the regime or the structure of authority as a component, I shall have in mind the whole structure on the assumption that attitudes toward any one part can be taken into account through the average attitude to all parts.

The Authority Structure and the General Power Structure

In limiting this third component of the regime to the structure of authority, we ought not to draw the inference that the regime includes the whole power structure in the system. In every political system there are vital non-authority roles through which political activities are performed. The relative influence of the authority and non-authority roles over the processes through which wants are converted to binding outputs will depend upon the particular circumstances. The authority roles may range from mere ciphers or epiphenomena to the dominant forces in the system. Typically, the authority roles bear with them some influence over the conversion processes in a system. Popular as it has become to look underneath the formal structure of authority, to locate what is called the real sources of political power, normally the authorities themselves will wield some real power, whether they are visible in a formal and well-defined structure or whether they constitute a purely informal set of roles fused with other roles, as in many small traditional systems.[11]

In the processing of demands and, as we shall also see, in the generation of support, the roles of opinion leaders, interest groups, and influentials of all sorts together with a vast complex of interpersonal relationships constitute the components of the general political structure through which power may be wielded. But these are not included in the regime. They are not part of the structure of authority even though at times some of these roles may be so incorporated; and usually they are all of some political significance to the extent that they are ultimately able to influence the authorities.

[11] However much modern group and voting behavior orientation has seemed to anesthetize research to the inherent power potential in the formal structure of authority, when Floyd Hunter in his ground-breaking *Community Power Structure* (Chapel Hill: University of North Carolina Press, 1953) dared to neglect examining the influence of members of the municipal government as a group with some independent power, he was quickly taken to task for his omission. Recent over-emphasis of informal behavior has tended to obscure formal structure and status as a real source of power.

Thus with respect to the input of support for the regime, minimal attachment to some kind of structure of authority will be essential, if the system is to persist. Otherwise the system clearly could not maintain the minimal organization to rally and commit, on any kind of continuing basis, the human and other resources of the system. The authority roles not only help to knit the members of a system together structurally; they also are able to give direction to collective actions when taken in the name of the system.

Persistence of a system as a means for converting wants to binding decisions will depend in part, therefore, upon the capacity of the system to stimulate enough support so as to maintain some kind of viable regime. Without values, norms and structures of authority as broad and relatively stable limits (at least of a kind that can be activated and vitalized in moments of need or crisis) it is doubtful whether sufficient minimal order would prevail so as to enable the members to devote their time and energies to the tasks involved in processing demands through to outputs. If the politically relevant members are to be able to rally and commit human and other resources to the attainment of the specific ends involved in political outputs, they must be prepared to share an understanding of the range of matters that are subject to political action. They must also be willing to support rules through which differences may be negotiated and settled as well as structures through which the initiative and responsibilities may be taken. These are what we have identified as the regime of a political system.

I3

Objects of Support: The Authorities

I F NO SYSTEM IS ABLE TO PERSIST WITHOUT ASSURING ITSELF OF A MINI-
mal flow of support toward the regime, including the structure of
authorities, there is equally little likelihood that a system could survive if it failed to support occupants for these authority roles. These
occupants I shall call the authorities. In practice, we frequently identify them as the government of a country or group but there is need
for a term with a broader scope than that implied in the concept
"government."

The Concept "Authorities"

The occupants of the authority roles need to be clearly distinguished from the roles themselves, which I have already discussed. The
presidency, prime ministership, or legislator are offices or highly formal
roles that may endure for generations, even centuries, whereas the
incumbents patently will change periodically. It we use the concept
"authorities" to identify these occupants, generically it can be said to
include members of a system who conform to the following criteria.
They must engage in the daily affairs of a political system; they must
be recognized by most members of the system as having the responsibility for these matters; and their actions must be accepted as binding
most of the time by most of the members as long as they act within the
limits of their roles.

Specifically, we refer to such occupants of authority roles as elders,
paramount chiefs, executives, legislators, judges, administrators, coun-
cilors, monarchs, and the like. At times, they may be occupants of
highly differentiated roles as in modern political systems; but in many
less specialized societies particularly, the occupants may not perform in
a specifically political role. It may be difficult to distinguish the gardener of a clan who has important ritualistic and ceremonial functions
from his role as the major political aid to the chief. But we may
disregard the degree of role differentiation that exists and, therefore,

the ease or difficulty with which the occupants of authority roles may be identified empirically. In the case of undifferentiated social roles through which political activities are conducted, the same occupants who act as the authorities will also play the part of religious, ritual, social, or other leaders simultaneously.

The authorities, as defined here, may be divided into two strata or they may be ranged on a continuum of which the strata represent alternative ends. At one end of the continuum, we would place those authorities who have acquired the primary responsibility for making decisions at the most inclusive level in the system and hold the broadest discretion in doing so. At the other end we would find those occupants whose range of discretion is considerably less and the scope of whose authorities is considerably narrower. The continuum would include within its range the President of a modern system at the one extreme and a postman or agricultural agent at the other; or the headman of a primitive band and an informal friend or henchman who helps him in exercising his informal authority.

If we break the continuum into two parts, based on greater or lesser degrees of discretion and scope of authority, in effect we would be dividing the occupants of authority into two strata. This helps us to appreciate the range of positions in a system that may be included in the category of authorities and with respect to whom we shall be speaking about the input of support. In a hierarchically organized political system, one stratum would be nominally superior to the other although in actual practice, as in France during the Third and Fourth Republics and to some extent in all modern political systems, the lower stratum may at times unobtrusively dominate or sharply delimit the authority of the upper one through a variety of subtle means.

In the United States, for example, something approximating these two strata can be identified in what we call the administration, on the one hand, which includes all elected officials at the national level and their immediate appointed executives and on the other hand, the public service. In Great Britain, these strata are distinguished as the government in contrast to the civil service. At times we generically refer to them as the official elite as against the administrative staff, to use Weber's term. The judicial branch in modern systems tends to stand somewhere in between these two strata depending upon the kind of powers that it exerts in the system. But regardless of the kind of strata that do exist, and their interrelationships in terms of dominance or subordination, their importance to us, conceptually, is that all types of occupants are included within the concept "authorities" as it will be used here. Even though in an organizational or structural analysis or for certain kinds of ethically oriented inquiries, it would be vital to elaborate and make use of the differentiation in strata among authorities, for our immediate purposes this distinction and other intra-structural differences among the authorities of a system may be glossed over.

The Power of the Authorities

At first glance, the reader might suspect that in adopting authorities as a central concept, I am unwittingly exposing myself to the danger of slipping back into the arid legalistic formalism prominent at the turn of this century. Conceivably, this might indeed be the case if I were to insist only upon legally defined roles as constituting the structure of political life. It would compel us to conclude that the legally selected occupants are always dominant in the decision-making process or that they alone are decisive in influencing the conversion processes. But such legal structural formalism is not in the least intended here.

In the first place, as I have just indicated with respect to primitive and other traditional systems, even if there is no legal specification of these special authority roles and they are imbedded in diffuse and general roles of the society, they would still meet our requirements. In the second place, and more significantly, the fact that I am here referring to the authorities, members who occupy a special place in the structure through which values are politically allocated in a system, does not thereby imply that I have described the whole political structure or that the authorities need be the most influential members in the system. In fact, from the contrast already developed between the structure of authority and power structures, it should be clear that a parallel distinction needs to be made between the authorities and the occupants of other political roles.

Unfortunately, in political research we have no convenient term for distinguishing the authorities from all other members in the system. Marx's ruling class as against the ruled, Pareto's elite, Mosca's political class and Michels' oligarchy versus masses are transparently not satisfactory for this purpose. They classify members of a system according to the power they hold whereas here we wish to point up the difference between those who are occupants of authority roles as against the occupants of all other roles. But however we might classify members in a systematic structural analysis of political systems, this much can be said here and has also been implied in all of the preceding discussion:

the authorities need not be co-extensive with the politically relevant members.

The influence of the occupants of the authority roles in the conversion of demands into outputs will depend upon the specific relationships between them and all other members in a system. Although a position of authority in a system may well be the source of an independent base of power and alerts the observer to look for it, nevertheless on occasion, as in some dictatorial systems today, the authorities may be virtually devoid of all influence. I introduced such a caveat before, when speaking about the authority roles, but it can bear repetition if only to clear away any of the musty legalistic cobwebs from the nineteenth century that may still cling to authorities as a concept.

Yet we cannot lose sight of the fact that normally, formal authorities are more than a powerless façade. Even in dictatorial systems that create a fraudulent front through democratic constitutions, the mere existence of such a formal although ineffective organization provides a set of symbols to which dissident movements may at times attach themselves. At such moments, the apparently powerless structure may be elevated to a position of effective authority. And the fact that the politically relevant members of the system find it necessary to build such a façade is an indication of the need for authorities, if only as one channel of regularized communication with the membership of the system as a whole. It is inescapable unless the relevant members wish to govern by coercion alone; in this case the diseconomies of such a mode of regulation would soon assert themselves and force upon them the need to provide for some authority roles.

The Function of Political Authorities

If a system is to be able to deal with its daily affairs of converting demands into binding outputs, it is not enough for the members to support the political community and the regime. It is true, support for the structure of authority or for a given system of government as we often phrase it—as for a democracy or for the authority of a royal clan in a dominant lineage—would assure the perpetuation of the basic rules and structures through which demands might be processed. But it would not provide for any members of the system to conduct this business. Support for a pattern of relationships that we call a system of government or regime is quite different from support for a given set of occupants for the roles of which the regime is composed.

If it were not so obvious, this requirement for the persistence of a system probably would have been expressly recognized and built into political analysis long before this. But the fact is that because it is intuitively so well-known and taken for granted, however critical the theoretical implications, they have been lost from sight. Every system, we know, must be prepared to support some members who will be ready, willing, and able to pay some degree of special attention to seeing to it that differences are settled or handled in some way that is acceptable, to the politically relevant members at least. Alternatively, those specific members who occupy authority roles must be able to mobilize enough support for themselves if they are to have the power to formulate and implement their decisions.

This does not mean that they need to be the most influential members in the system; they can perform their tasks of governing as long as they have the support, or acquiescence at least, of those who are the most powerful. But if the members of a system are unable to provide enough support for some set of authorities who can assume responsibility for the daily affairs of the system and provide initiative and direction in identifying problems and taking some steps toward their resolution, the system must collapse, for want of leadership as we might say. And it would not be a matter of the lack of "good" leadership but of support for any leadership at all.

The vital part played by support for the actual incumbents is brought out more prominently if we look at the negative condition. If the members lose confidence in the ability of any authorities at all to cope with the problems of the day, the effect on support to other levels of the system may be very serious, at least for the persistence of that kind of system. But if no authorities are seen as being equal to the tasks of managing the affairs of state and confidence in any set of authorities or any government is completely undermined—historically a most unusual but possible condition—the result is that no set of persons will be able to mobilize enough support behind them to make and put into effect the necessary day-to-day decisions. Clearly, the system would become paralyzed; it would lose its capacity to act as a collectivity.

Normally, to be sure, this outcome is avoided through the introduction of forcible compliance, a special kind of response that meets the loss of support by generating new support through coercion. But if for one reason or another, the conditions do not permit any authorities to control enough means of violence to use coercion effectively, then no government may be possible.

It may appear that this is an unlikely eventuality and although theoretically interesting, empirically void. But the fact is that if there is any point in the history of political systems when the stability or persistence of a system in all its aspects may be brought to the danger point, it is precisely as a result of a failure to muster sufficient support for any set of authorities.

Walter Bagehot, in his remarkably precocious letters from France during the turmoil preceding the rise of Louis Napoleon to imperial power, was apprehensive that this was about to happen there. Fearing the collapse of the whole society, he felt impelled to support any government, or regime for that matter, even if established by the sword, for the achievement of order at the very least.[1]

Indeed, in most revolutionary situations, it is this very fear, that inability to agree on a set of authorities might destroy the system as an entity, that may well be a strong motive for inducing the acceptance of compromises that fall far short of what any of the contending groups might have desired. There may come a point of attrition in civil strife when exhaustion and devastation create a situation in which order may be preferred above all else. This is just another way of saying that the inability to marshal support behind a set of authorities may be seen as a distinctive threat to the whole system.[2]

The Existing Empirical Base

Strangely enough, even though the input of support for the occupants of authority roles has been largely ignored for theoretical purposes in American political research, empirically the components of support underlying any specific government have received an overwhelming amount of attention. A major focus of research has been on the upper levels of the authorities, the political leadership. Concentration of research on this aspect of the authorities has been quite disproportionate to the needs of a rounded theory of political systems as interpreted here. Most attention has been devoted to support at the level of the authorities.

This direction of political research in the United States needs little documentation. Interest group inquiry has sought to reveal the sources of strength or power of governmental leaders and their competitors and to establish the variety of influences, and therefore of positive or

[1] Mrs. R. Barrington, *Works and Life of Walter Bagehot* (London: Longmans, Green, 1915), in volume 1, the "Seven Letters on the French Coup d'État."

[2] See the discussion by Leon Trotsky, in his *History of the Russian Revolution*, of the brief period of dual power during the Russian Revolution and the intolerable situation thereby created for the political system.

negative supportive behavior, that help to shape decisions and their implementation. The immense literature on political parties explores their effectiveness as instruments for organizing support behind candidates and occupants of authority roles and as vehicles for reflecting the demands of the members of the system and thereby helping to shape the kinds of policies that authorities pursue. Legislative and administrative studies and explorations of public opinion are normally concerned with the way in which, or the degree to which, popular and group values are transformed into public policies by the various political groups and structures. The reactive effect this has upon the relationship between members of the system and the government reflects a broad and general support analysis at the authority level.

The voting studies take their place in the same tradition, although they still suffer somewhat from the fact that whatever theoretical relevance was initially implied in them derived largely from the origins of this research in social psychology.[3] Until recently, it was social psychologists who provided the major inspiration for research in voting behavior. Their preoccupation was to widen the range of subject matter through which they could continue to enrich their understanding of the way in which individuals arrive at decisions. Since the vote represented a well-defined decisional unit in a context normally not explored by social psychology, it was a bold and inventive step to move into the political field. But in doing so, the social psychologists brought with them their own implicit conceptual apparatus and it has been only recently that political science has shown signs of escaping from this theoretical context and striking out on its own.

In the process, however, political science has not formally reconsidered as yet the theoretical context in which such studies might be made; rather, it has simply assimilated its research to the prevailing currents in political research as a whole. Hence voting studies, even those with a stronger political bias than formerly, have turned their attention to the determinants of support for leaders who compete for governmental office. From these have emerged the independent and interrelated effects, on the mobilization of support, of such variables as the personality of leaders, the nature of the issues, and identification with party, primary groups and other units.

This overemphasis on the sources of support for the authorities in such a stable system as the United States is quite understandable. There is little policy need to underscore the characteristics of this

[3] I refer to this briefly in D. Easton and R. D. Hess, "Youth and the Political System," in S. M. Lipset and L. Lowenthal, *Culture and Social Character* (New York: Free Press of Glencoe, 1961), pp. 226–251, especially pp. 231–234.

stability in the regime and community by inquiring into its determinants. From a theoretical point of view, however, the sources of persistence and change may well stand at the head of any list of research priorities. Certainly, if the emergence of the new nations in the last decade has done nothing else, it has thrown a new and intense light on the part that regime and community levels play in the persistence and change of systems.

But even if we restrict our remarks to the level of support under consideration in this chapter, that extended to the authorities, the extensive empirical research at this level has been a product less of theoretical intention than of preoccupation with practical concerns. There is an urgent theoretical need to build this research into a broader analytical context. In doing so here, I am suggesting that it can be best interpreted as the study of one level of support, namely, for the occupants of authority roles. It is therefore largely relevant to only one of three major aspects of a political system.

The authorities are the last of the three aspects of a system that are contained in the very notion of political system itself. The persistence and change of a system henceforth will be understood in this differentiated sense, to apply to one or all of these aspects.

Now that we have analyzed the objects toward which support in a system may be directed—the political community, regime, and authorities—we must turn to a discussion of those conditions that may lead to the imposition of stress. Thereafter, as in the case of our study of the input of demands, we shall be in a position to analyze the variety of typical responses through which systems may seek to cope with disturbances of the input of support for any or all of these objects.

14

Stress Through the Erosion of Support

NOW THAT I HAVE COMPLETED AN EXAMINATION OF THE MEANING OF support and of the various political objects to which it may be directed, we can return to the analytic problem that led us along this path. I have hypothesized that the persistence of a political system hinges not only on an appropriate regulation of the inflow of demands but on a second major condition, the maintenance of a minimal level of attachment for each of the three identified political objects. Where the input of support falls below this minimum, the persistence of any kind of system will be endangered. A system will finally succumb unless it adopts measures to cope with the stress.

This very general and relatively simple proposition will serve to organize our further discussion of support. We shall want to know something first, about the conditions that lead to a reduction of attachment to the major political objects and later, about the way in which systems typically have sought to anticipate or meet these disturbances.

The plausibility of this hypothesis that relates stress to the input of support will not hang upon our success in pointing to any system that has in fact collapsed due to support failure, any more than we found such exemplification necessary with respect to demands. Yet in the latter case, the fact that we conceived of stress as potential at least rather than necessarily actual, did help to improve our understanding of the various kinds of processes related to the conversion of demands. We shall find a comparable situation for disturbances of the input of support. Even if we could point to no system that utterly disappeared due to the decline of attachment to one or another of the political objects, it would still be instructive analytically to attempt to understand the typical ways in which systems have prevented this, by their responses to a declining flow of support.

As compared with our discussion of demands, however, we are in a much better empirical position here. At least general types of systems, such as absolute European monarchies, democracies, or dictatorships, have unmistakably failed as support for them has atrophied. Even though new political objects usually rise out of the ashes of the old, the transformation can be traced ultimately to the reduction in attachment to one or another of the pre-existing political objects. But even if, as I have said, we could never prove that a system collapsed, beyond revival, due to loss of support, even if it is only a speculative outcome that never materializes, it would still remain as a useful theoretical construct. It would enable us to work out the nature of the responses whose timeliness prevents utter destruction.

The special utility of the kind of systems analysis ordering our thinking is that, through the adoption of the idea of inputs, it permits us to link what happens outside a system to what happens inside it. These represent intervening or summary variables that link different kinds of disturbances to a system. Like demands, support is a link of this sort. Our mode of analysis directs us to pose the following question: What kinds of parametric (and in many instances, internal) conditions so interact with a system as to produce significant fluctuations in the flow of support toward any of the three objects, such that the level may threaten to drop below an undefined but determinable minimum?

It will shortly become evident that the search for these conditions will lead us to a discussion of social diversity and its impact on the evolution of political cleavages. But before embarking on a discussion of cleavage as one major source of a decline in the input of support, and therefore of possible stress for a system, it will be necessary to prepare the ground a little further by pursuing the implications of the idea of loss of support as a cause of stress. At first glance, it looks like a perfectly straightforward idea. But upon closer examination, there will emerge a number of ambiguities that require clarification.

Decline in Support—Its Meaning

Relative Loss

When can we say that a political object has suffered a reduction in support? In the first place, when we speak of support as being so inadequate for any of the political objects as to threaten the essential variables of the system, this need not mean that the support has declined to the point where each or any one of the objects has lost all support. We could scarcely expect that the collective attachment expressed by the politically relevant members would drop to zero; and on a scale measuring support, we have seen, zero would represent absolute hostility. Indeed, some few members at least, and if civil wars are an adequate indicator, often very many, can be expected to find their predispositions or interests linked to an existing set of authorities, regime, or community. But the fact that support does not vanish even if the object itself disappears need not create theoretical trouble. We may assume that there is a minimal point below which a system is unable to maintain itself. It is anticipation of this relative rather than total loss of support that will lead to activation of special coping mechanisms. We may take it for granted that some members will always favor the objects of a system.

The Significant Support

In the second place, as already indicated in discussing the measurement of support,[1] its level will always be related to the input of the politically relevant members of a system. Relevant applies only to those members of a system who count, those who share in the effective power of the system. They may be few or many; they may fluctuate within systems over time and certainly their general properties differ across systems. Research on small communities, in the ordinary sense of this word, clearly demonstrates the intrinsic difficulties in constructing the conceptual and technical tools for laying bare the roots of power and the boundaries of influence groups even in relatively small political subsystems. If we encounter so many barriers in the way of identifying and describing the politically relevant members of these subsystems, we can scarcely expect that the task will be made any easier if we turn to the more inclusive systems. Fortunately, for our purposes we can set these difficulties aside as a second order matter; it is feasible and useful to talk of the politically relevant members even though they may be presently indeterminate, as long as we believe that in principle they are empirically discoverable groups.

Minimal Level as a Threshold

In the third place, even if adequacy of support is interpreted as an indeterminate but determinable minimal amount, it is not without its continued ambiguities. At given moments in history, even if we had measures of support, it might turn out that we could not be certain when the minimal point had been reached. We are frequently confronted with recalcitrant situations in research that defy analysis in black and white terms. We may not know whether we do or do not

[1] Chapter 10, footnote 2.

have minimal support since it may fluctuate rapidly around a neighborhood of bare adequacy. In many historical circumstances, for extended periods of time it is virtually impossible to forecast the outcome with respect to the survival or change of an existing political object.

This condition is not just a matter of inadequate predictive tools. Rather, the political struggle may be such that the outcome is in a constant state of balance or indeterminacy. At times, as in the Congo since independence and in France during the Algerian crisis, we would have been hard put to predict the kind of political order or community that would emerge and become stabilized. Between the two World Wars, there was considerable doubt as to whether the regime in the USSR could overcome at least the crisis of succession in leadership. In regimes the support base of which is fickle or disguised by circumstances, adequacy of input may fluctuate from day to day. In primitive systems, internal feuds may be protracted over many years, keeping the political system tottering on the edge of an abyss.

Minimal support would not appear always to be a specific condition that occurs at a point in time or on a scale dividing viability from collapse. It may represent, rather, a critical range within which a system or its objects may roam. Instead of an all or none situation, it may better be described as a broad threshold, a limbo in which a system may linger for a considerable time.

Empirically this conceptualization would seem to be plausible. Research indicates this to be the situation for the integration of communities, a condition that we might describe as the presence of sufficient support to stabilize a political community. "Somewhat contrary to our expectations, however," one set of authors conclude, "some of our cases [such as the Habsburg Empire, the American states to 1865, the Swiss cantons from the 13th to 19th centuries] taught us that integration may involve a fairly broad zone of transition rather than a narrow threshold; that states might cross and recross this threshold or zone of transition several times in their relations with each other; and that they might spend generations wavering uncertainly within it. . . . Not only the approach toward integration, but the very act of crossing the integration threshold, have turned out to be much lengthier and more uncertain processes than had been expected." [2]

What this points up is that we ought not to conceive of the authorities, regime, or community as either receiving or failing to receive adequate support, even though to avoid circumlocutions I may well write as though this were the case. Zones of transition probably inter-

[2] K. W. Deutsch, S. A. Burrell, et al., *op. cit.*, p. 33 and p. 35.

vene in most cases and during them, the input of support may be radically altered for better or worse from the point of view of survival of the object. But even though this is true, at some point, even if it can be established only *ex post facto,* when the decline in support leads to the abandonment of the political object, support will have decisively fallen below its minimal level.

Decline and Fall

In the fourth place, we may return to a point touched upon in Chapter 10 but which needs to be recalled now in a new context. Decline in support will stress a system but the decline alone need not lead to its fall. Even though the flow of support for an object were to slow to a mere trickle, this need not automatically bring about the abandonment of that object in favor of another.

It is true, at times in history, the withdrawal of support has been so sudden or widespread that a system has been left in utter chaos; or, as in the case of some developing systems today in Africa, insufficient support has been forthcoming during a transition period so that it is extremely difficult to keep a government in power, a constitution alive, and a community together. But where pre-existing systems of some stability are threatened with loss of support, unless a counter-elite or organized groups are available and ready to give direction and impulse to the disaffected, the *status quo* can survive for long periods. Apathy, inertia or inadequate leadership have accounted for the persistence of political objects in many systems when the level of support is astonishingly low. Presumably this would be an indication that the politically relevant groups have not moved beyond the point of indifference on our support continuum. If they have shifted to outright antagonism—negative support—it would suggest that their morale, commitment, or resources may be such as to vitiate any will to act or to undermine their capacity to do so. But in the normal course of events, manifest antagonism would be the prelude to positive action of some kind.

Regardless of how we might specifically account for the existence of low support input, on the one hand and reluctance or inability to shift attachment to a new political object on the other, the main point is that erosion of support needs to be viewed only as a threat to the system. When support begins to slip away visibly, this is a danger signal to those who remain attached to the political objects and will typically trigger responses to prevent the support from falling too low.

Decline and Response

Finally, before we enter into a discussion of the factors that help to corrode support for the objects of a system and thereby bring stress down upon it, we must remain alert to the fact that a system need not respond in a mechanical and supine way to threats to its survival. Since it is composed of reflective human beings, it is capable of evaluating what is happening and of taking evasive actions. Through outputs, time delays, ingenuity in response, command over a repertoire of tactics available in the political culture, awareness of relevant political events, inducements to act, and the like, a system may set in motion counter-forces to neutralize those ongoing processes that threaten the support level or even to reverse the trend.

We shall return to the response possibilities. But I mention them here because, as I proceed to discuss certain conditions that influence the inflow of support, using the order of presentation adopted in the case of demands, I shall for the moment follow these out to their logical conclusion as though no response were forthcoming. I shall hold the responses in abeyance so that we may better understand the inherent nature of the tendencies that may play upon and undermine the level of support.

The Mediation of Support

Mediation through Groups and Leadership

I have been discussing the erosion of support as though members related themselves directly to political objects and, therefore, as though their sentiments toward them were a function of their immediate attitudes. This may well be true for many individuals and under many circumstances. But the probability is high that attachment to a political object will also be mediated through subgroups to which a member belongs and from which he takes his political cues, whether cognitive or affective.

Although it is not likely that a member is entirely devoid of direct attachment to each of the three political objects, these feelings may be supplemented by the support or hostility independently generated through membership in groups. As far as the individual himself is concerned, he may be quite indifferent to the political object. Yet his adherence to a group would mean that to the extent he was persuaded to go along with attitudes and behavior of the group or that his presence contributed to its perceived strength, he would thereby be contributing some part of his own support or opposition as it is mediated through the group.

We might expect, therefore, that where group membership in a system is possible and where groups play some part in the political processes, each member may be advancing or withholding support directly, on an individual basis or indirectly through the availability of his support to a group. Thus, as a citizen of a modern political system, a member may feel strong ties to its regime; as a member of a subgroup in the system, these ties may be reinforced or undermined as the case may be. As a "man of the Shah of Iran," a member of this system may consider himself bound to the Shah as the political authority and symbol of the regime; as a member of a kinship or village unit with strong dissident leanings, his energies may be used by the leadership of a group in an antithetical direction.[3] The cross-pressure to which the individual member, caught in these circumstances, would be exposed, would undoubtedly have important implications for the influence of the group in action. But the fact would remain that both the direct and mediated kinds need to be independently considered in any estimate of the rise or decline of support.

To illustrate the role of mediated support further, historically it has been dramatically operative in the large blocks of ethnic groups that only now are becoming politically assimilated into the United States. In an earlier period, and to some considerable extent even today, where an ethnic group, such as the Polish, Italian, German, Czech, or Ukrainian, has not spoken English as the dominant language in the system, and has felt culturally estranged, a leadership has regularly emerged to act as brokers between its own group and the broader political system.

This was an especially critical phenomenon in the United States during the first few decades of this century. Walled off from intimate communication with the broader society, through linguistic and cultural barriers, ethnic groups gave birth to native political leaders who seized the opportunity to guide or control the flow of support toward competitors for office in the system at large. These ethnic leaders, some in public office themselves, others, bosses beyond the public eye, served as brokers of support who helped the minorities to define their situation with respect to the world beyond the pale. Where minorities felt little personal involvement in that world, the brokers had a relatively free hand to commit the support of their group and to trade it

[3] See L. Binder, *op. cit.*

off for whatever advantages they may have sought. In some cases, these brokers would themselves have to work through intermediaries in a support chain. The support of the ethnic group might be marketable only through a political party; the latter, in turn, would mediate between the ethnic minority and the figures of authority in the general system.

The kinds of intermediaries between one of the three political objects and the membership of a system are legion. They will depend upon the particular social and political structure that has grown up. But in each case, the capacity of the group to give direction to the support which its membership represents will depend upon the extent to which it is able to win the loyalty of its own adherents in the face of competition from other groups.

The Network of Support Ties among Elites

To put the matter at its most general level, it is not necessary, if a political system is to persist, for support to move directly from the membership in the aggregate to the political objects. Conditions may make possible extensive chains of support in which units are linked to units through intermediate leaders who can command or commit a following. At times erosion need occur, therefore, only at the leadership level, to be effective.

For example, in highly stratified political systems, various social and political classes may communicate with each other only indirectly for the most part, intermediate elites acting as communication links and focal points of support. The membership of the whole system may have only vague feelings of belonging to the system but they may have strong attachments to the subunits of which they are part. Yet this low input of support from the ordinary members of the system may not pose any threat if each intermediary leadership itself evinces strong attachments to the next higher level of leadership.

Indirect or mediated support of this kind occurred in its classic form during the period of late feudalism in Europe as centralized monarchical absolutism began to take shape. In the contests between the powerful monarchs and the old feudal lords, the stage was finally reached, as in France and England, where the lords and barons were driven by circumstance and necessity to lend increasing support to their kings. Although in the relevant historical periods in each country, the serfs and sub-lords were developing a sense of national community, the low literacy level, the lack of media of communication, and the rural dispersion of the population tended to leave the basic lines of political attachment in the hierarchical form they had taken during the full blossoming of feudalism. As long as the local dignitaries and notables could count on the support of the peasants and burghers they could commit it on behalf of the next higher ranks of nobility. These, in turn, were able to build in pyramid fashion upon the fealty or support of the subordinate orders and so on up to the pinnacle of authority in the monarchy. The critical efforts of the monarch to bypass the chain of intermediaries and to obtain direct and independently controlled access to the reservoirs of support, if not of the mass of the population at least of the middle classes, constitute the familiar central theme in the political history of feudalism as it slowly disappeared.[4]

In an entirely different historical context, the same general considerations with respect to mediated support apply to loosely knit political systems such as confederations or newly developing political units in which the problems of integration have not been solved. In the Congo today, for example, the input of support from the general membership in this amorphous system is directed toward the leadership of tribal groups or regional authorities. In part, the availability of support depends upon the direction in which the leadership of these component units moves, although those striving for a national focus for support also seek to circumvent the local and plural leadership by appealing directly to the general membership through symbols and structures of unity.

In the international sphere, it has been surmised that the growth of a European political community may depend less upon the emergence, at the outset, of a sense of common identity among the people of various nations than upon elites in different economic and political sectors working together for specific, functional ends. "The emphasis upon elites in the study of integration derives its justification from the bureaucratized nature of European organizations of long standing, in which basic decisions are made by the leadership, sometimes over the opposition and usually over the indifference of the general membership. This gives the relevant elites a manipulative role which is of course used to place the organization in question on record for or against a proposed measure of integration." [5]

It is quite conceivable that the initial and major bonds among the relevant political systems of Europe, if a European political community, in our sense, finally succeeds in emerging, will depend upon the

[4] A particularly helpful political analysis of this and related periods occurs in S. N. Eisenstadt, *op. cit.*, chapter 12.

[5] E. B. Haas, *op. cit.*, 16–17.

leadership rather than the general members of all cooperating national political units. A possible sequence would be simple to identify. Each unit would be tied to an emerging European political community through the fact first, that the leadership of each unit has such sentiments; second, that the followers in each unit identify closely with their elite; and third, that support from the followers will continue to be available even if the policies of the leadership lead to the subordination of each political system to a European suprasystem. In due course, however, we might anticipate that the continuation of a new political community might depend upon nurturing some direct bonds between the general members as individuals and the new political community. But this opens up a response problem linked to output and socialization to which I shall later return.

Erosion of support may therefore occur through a complex network of relationships among elites rather than as a result of the individual direct withdrawal of support by members in a system. In this way, we once again see that the support of all members may not be necessary for the persistence of a political object or its change. In many important instances, the support only of an influential few, interlocked through the system, need be taken into account, at least as long as these few are perceived to command the support of many others or to be able to assure their acquiescence.

We can now see that the identification of erosion in support is not a simple matter; it is a complex phenomenon. Not that our discussion resolves these complexities in any sense. But complexity is not a thing-in-itself. It is a function both of the object observed and the means available for observation. To the extent that in this chapter we have been able to extricate the elements that constitute what we may consider to be a decline in support, we have clarified at least one half of the equation. As usual, the other half, the one that entails the construction of methods and techniques for obtaining valid test data, is a separate enterprise logically following the conceptualizing that we are undertaking here and outside of our frame of reference. But with this understanding of the elements woven into the conception "insufficient support," we can now proceed to discuss various sources out of which such stress might arise.

15

Cleavage as a Source of Stress

NUMEROUS CONDITIONS CONTRIBUTE TO THE DECLINE OF SUPPORT. A large part of them may be summed up under one category: output failure.

Much more will be said about outputs in later chapters, but here a few preliminary and anticipatory remarks will be in order. For the moment I shall adopt a rough and ready definition of outputs as those decisions and actions performed by the authorities in a system. What the authorities do or fail to do will play no small part in helping to strengthen or undermine the support that members extend to the various objects in the system. In this chapter, I shall seek to show that as a result of a basic condition in a system, to be described as political cleavage, the authorities may find themselves unable to provide adequate outputs. Cleavage will therefore emerge as a possible major source of stress on the system.

Output Failure

Its Meaning

Since the failure of the authorities to produce adequate outputs is postulated as a major possible determinant of a decline in the input of support, our first task is to clarify the meaning to be attributed to this idea. Output failure will be said to occur under any one of the following circumstances. First, it arises when the authorities fail to take any action to meet the demands of the relevant members of a system. This will result in an imbalance between demands and outputs; that is, between what members have indicated they would like to see done and what the authorities are in fact able or willing to do.

Second, even if members have put in no specific demands about a matter, output failure may still occur. This is the case when the authorities fail to take action that anticipates conditions which may later arise and to which relevant members of the system might then object.

It becomes output failure if the members blame the authorities for not having had the foresight or wisdom to have prepared for such an eventuality. Whether or not such an accusation is justified is immaterial. As we shall later see,[1] the effect on support is in considerable part not a matter of who, in fact, is to blame but whom the members of the system perceive as culpable. The fact that Hoover was not primarily responsible for the Great Depression is of importance; but from the point of view of the input of support it was more significant that a large proportion of the American membership saw him as the person to blame.

Third, the authorities may take action of an important nature that they interpret as a response to demands. But the outputs may in fact be considered by the affected members as quite inappropriate for the conditions or incompatible with their demands. In that event the failure has not been in the quantity but in the quality of the outputs. The probability is that the outputs would encounter more hostility than support and in that way add to any shortage of support.

Clearly, output will always be relative in character: relative to the number and kinds of demands as well as to the number of members in the system voicing these demands. At what point in the failure to meet demands, support will decline, constitutes an empirical matter. But theoretically, we need to recognize that at some point this will occur.

Its Effects

A further basic assumption here will be that if a system is unable to meet a minimal number of demands of most of the relevant members with some minimal frequency, it will be impossible to prevent these members from developing feelings of deep discontent. Initially, the discontent might be directed toward the authorities. But if, where possible, these are changed and especially if this happens again and again, and still little improvement in outputs occur, it will be impossible to prevent the dissatisfaction from shifting toward the regime and even the political community. I continue to assume, as usual, a most unlikely condition: that actions are not taken in the system to compensate for the failure of outputs.

History amply testifies to the plausibility of this kind of progression of the effects of output failure. Many pacific and certainly most revolutionary transformations in regime or political community have occurred in this manner. They are preceded by repeated if not exhaustive efforts to eliminate present discontents by first appealing to

[1] Chapter 22.

the existing authorities for remedial action. Especially is this true where authorities occupy their positions ascriptively or by coercion and, accordingly, cannot easily be removed or changed. But frequently, even where the authorities have undergone periodic changes, as each set in turn proves unable to stem the tide of discontent, at some point, the relevant members will feel they have reached the end of the road as far as waiting and compromise are concerned. Unable to obtain their objectives by influencing the authorities, they are likely to feel the need to turn to more drastic measures in the form of efforts to modify the regime fundamentally or even to break up the community.

Most socio-political revolutions fit into this pattern as do even less traumatic and dramatic efforts to modify constitutional arrangements. They reflect persistent and recalcitrant output failure, at least as so perceived by the relevant members in the system. As I have pointed out in the preceding chapter, however, whether the loss of support resulting from output failure leads to the destruction of a system or its transformation will depend on a number of other contingencies as well. It is a necessary but not always sufficient condition.

The importance of outputs as one major variable contributing to the decline of support is demonstrated further, if such additional evidence is required, that to the extent that outputs are perceived or felt to meet demands, present or anticipated, they will thereby go a long way toward relieving any stress due to other conditions. Outputs themselves may frequently represent a vital kind of positive response to stress arising out of the erosion of support due to other causes and I shall treat them in just this way later, under the category of specific support.[2] We shall therefore need to attend here only to the possible effects of output failure and postpone consideration of the positive consequences of output success in meeting demands.

Its Causes

What conduces to the outcome that I have described as output failure? The causes are varied and numerous; the task will be to devise a conceptually economical way of handling this multiplicity.

Output failure may be a product of the qualities of the authorities themselves—their human fallibility, their lack of wisdom, of skill in governing or of responsiveness to the members—or to the shortage of the necessary resources. I shall return more systematically to these aspects of output failure in connection with a broader set of response processes with which they are interwoven. This will be in Part Five

[2] Ibid.

which will be devoted exclusively to consideration of outputs as a basic type of positive response in a system and the various ways in which the processes associated with them, such as feedback, shape the input of support. But in this chapter I shall focus on an entirely different set of parametric and related internal conditions which, through their impact on outputs, help to rob the various political objects of the support that members are willing or able to extend.

Major tendencies to output failure will be set in motion as a result of the degree of internal dissension and conflict to be found among the members of the system. Cleavages may so divide the relevant members that they find themselves unable to cooperate, negotiate, or compromise their differences even to the minimal extent necessary so as to discover some kind of acceptable output resolution. And cleavages give rise to other difficulties that compound these effects on support. Since cleavage will be interpreted as a central condition in inducing output failure and undermining support in other ways, it is to the basic consequences of cleavage that we must turn if we are to understand those conditions to which a system must be able to respond if it is to avoid or cope with stress in some way.

The Meaning of Cleavage

Social Diversity

In current political research, cleavage proves to be an ambiguous term. In political sociology particularly, it often appears with the paired opposite, consensus, especially in the context of voting and opinion studies and inquiries into the conditions of democracy. In either context, it is at times used in a way that leaves the impression that it has only one dimension: agreement or disagreement in opinions or attitudes. These are often expressed in the form of votes or other means of choice or of underlying opinions accessible through opinion polls of various sorts.

In this context, to say that a population is characterized by cleavages is to indicate that there is considerable diversity in points of view. Typically, the cleavages or differences in attitudes, opinions and preferences are described and explained with regard to such demographic variables as occupation, socio-economic status, region, religion, ethnicity, or race or such political variables as party identification, issue orientation, leadership appeal. We may speak of the cleavages between liberals and conservatives, isolationists and internationalists, Democrats and Republicans, and the like and relate these points of view to conflict over demands. In identifying such categories of differences, we obtain a description of the fragmentation of political opinions and attitudes over such issues as government intervention, the role of the army, church and state, or foreign policy. In relating these to demographic and other variables, we establish relationships from which hypotheses might be derived to explain the diversity and distribution of these points of view.

Those engaged in opinion research have frequently tended to take it for granted that disagreements in points of view reflect underlying conflict in a population or at least strongly predispose those holding the diverse opinions to enter into controversy with respect to them. The assumption is that disagreement in views corresponds to opposition of groups.

However, critics of opinion polls have pointed out that such research is more likely to yield more information about the range and variety of points of view, that is, about social diversity, than about the way in which the holders of these opinions will actually behave in the midst of active political controversy. We learn more about the nature of the differences in opinions or demands than about the kinds of active conflict in which groups will engage. Knowing just the distribution and types of opinions tells us little about the organization of members holding these views, the likelihood of actions based on them, the strength of each group, or its influence on various parts of the political process. Description of diversity in opinions or demands offers only a half completed picture of the possible cleavages in a political system.

Group Conflict

When we turn away from the sociological literature to that in political science, we find that cleavage is more frequently interpreted to mean divisions among groups with reference to the way in which they act in the political process. Concern usually focuses on the way in which groups, such as interest groups or parties, conflict in their efforts to influence the making and execution of policies at all levels of government. The frequently expressed fear in this literature that cleavages may destroy a society, especially a democratic one in which the rules permit their proliferation, does not stem from apprehension over the excessive diversity of opinions on public policy. Rather, it is instilled by the image of large and powerful interest groups and parties engaged in titanic battles over issues and the immense barriers in the way of negotiating compromises among these leviathans.

This is a substantially different approach from that of searching for cleavages viewed as diversity in opinions. The political interpretation of cleavage certainly accepts as a necessary and prior task the description and understanding of the alignment of the members in a system on different sides of a point of view or issue. But it does more than that; it points up the disagreements. It sharpens our perception and understanding of what is involved in the number of members who are actually or potentially opposed to each other and in competition with respect to the use of their influence. It highlights the struggle for power over policy.

This has led research away from the study of opinion cleavage alone, in the sense of social diversity, toward what is often called the study of political institutions. From this perspective, the subjects of importance are to be found in the sources of strength of contending groups—the determinants of cohesion, techniques of control and influence, patterns of group relationships, interaction between the formal structure of authority and interest groups, and the origin and change of such groups.[3]

Social Diversity and Political Cleavage

It is evident that research about cleavage among groups that may offer or withdraw support in a system, can lead into two different although intimately related paths. On the one hand, it may center in an interest on mere diversity of opinions and attitudes or cultural patterns: who thinks what about what subjects? How do religions, customs or languages differ? This provides knowledge of the basis of differences around which conflict has turned or may develop. On the other hand, it may lead to inquiry into the nature of the patterns of conflict that revolve around these differences. As a concept, cleavage therefore refers to these two different dimensions: diversity of opinions, attitudes, or culture and conflict among potential support groups.

Analytically, we may choose to view these dimensions as two sides of the same coin. Groups that act against each other are apt to have different points of view; and groups that disagree over objectives, outlooks, or demands are apt to fight about them. In the concepts being developed here, what this means is that cleavage refers to diversity in demands or their parameters on the one hand, and to group antag-

[3] D. B. Truman, *The Governmental Process* (New York: Knopf, 1951).

onisms with respect to the support extended to demands or leaders on the other. Not that we usually have demand differences without some conflict over them or that we can ever have conflict without some differences in demands. For every demand there is at least one member, its advocate, who stands behind it ready to act in its favor, if only to articulate it. For every member ready to act politically, there is some demand toward which his actions are oriented.

We can conclude, therefore, that cleavages may be defined either as differences in attitudes, opinions and ways of life or as conflict among groups. We may distinguish these as social diversity, or attitude cleavage, and political cleavage respectively. Unless the context indicates otherwise, I shall adopt a unified meaning so that the single word "cleavage" will henceforth embrace both types of divisions. What is clear is that potential stress on support for the political objects will derive both from the predispositions toward conflict implicit in the presence of social diversity because it breeds different attitudes, opinions and, therefore, demands; and from the more easily identifiable stress due to actively expressed conflicts among support groups.

The Consequences of Cleavages

Although I am emphasizing the stressful tendencies of cleavage in this unified meaning, I would not want this understood as implying that diversity and active conflict among groups must work in one direction only. Neither social diversity nor political cleavage is a synonym for disunity. They represent conditions that may also help to integrate a system. We need, therefore, to distinguish clearly and to bear constantly in mind the way in which diversity and cleavage may also promote support for a system.

Positive Supportive Consequences

The opportunity provided members to express conflicting points of view or to align themselves in contending support groups so as to influence the processing of demands may contribute to the unity and persistence of a system. Where the regime norms permit the free expression of diverse views, it is plausible to assume that, aside from any other consideration, it has a cathartic effect for the relationships of the members. In enabling them to vent their grievances and hostilities, it frees the air for the task of negotiating and compromising differences. Furthermore, where demands are genuinely negotiable among members of the system, it may involve more than just agreeing that each gets some of the available values. The attainment of compromises suggests that members have learned to formulate their demands in such a way that others perceive that they too may benefit from them. In fact, in those systems where the regime rules call for a readiness to negotiate differences, such as any constitutional order, democratic or otherwise, demands are usually presented in non-particular terms so as to broaden their appeal. Even if in fact they are designed to serve the special interest of a narrow part of the membership, the demand itself will usually be broadened, so that it may be interpreted as furthering the "general interest" or the welfare of the nation or the people. Under conditions such as these, either where the expression of demands provides for a genuine sense of participation or where conflicting demands are expanded in order to include benefits for more than just those who are actively seeking them, the cleavages should serve to build confidence and support in the various objects in the system, even though this may not be their only effect.[4]

But conversely, in systems where members expect to be able to participate politically, dictatorial insistence upon restrictions on the venting of grievances could be expected, in the long run, to breed disaffection. Of course, to say that cleavage in demands under such circumstances tends in a given direction is not to argue that the anticipated outcome will in fact occur. As always, counter-tendencies may be set in motion by other circumstances, including deliberate efforts on the part of the authorities, that thwart whatever supportive or contrary consequences that are set in motion.

If the free expression of diversity in demands operates in a supportive way, a system may be bolstered even more effectively if, in addition, it permits freedom to mobilize support behind one's demands or to join others of like mind in order to impress a point of

[4] G. McT. Kahin, G. Pauker, and L. Pye, "Comparative Politics in Non-Western Countries," 49 *American Political Science Review* (1955) 1022–1041, at p. 1034 where a similar point is made. The problems raised by cleavage in a political system and varying methods for coping with it form the central theme of M. Weiner's study of India, *The Politics of Scarcity*. He suggests that "one must also remember some mitigating elements in the demands of [plural] groups. In the political sphere . . . the very multiplication of caste, tribal, religious, and other ethnic associations within a particular state increases the possibility that politicians are less likely to build their careers by seeking to satisfy only one group. Equity becomes politically feasible in a society of many associations. And if an increase in occupational diversification takes place within ethnic communities, primordial loyalties to one's own caste or tribe are likely to be overloaded with other loyalties, with the very likely consequence that the intensity of political demands will be reduced" (p. 232).

view on the authorities. Social diversity and attendant attitudinal differences may lead to the verbal expression of differences. But talk may also be reinforced with tangible action, thereby fulfilling the promise implicit in freedom to discuss differences.

Evidence from research on small subsystems, such as trade unions, indicates that the presence of a legitimate internal opposition favors greater loyalty than the imposition of dictatorial rule.[5] If what is true for the smaller group may be extended to the broader political system, we would assume that it is valid to say that social diversity and political cleavage, under conditions of freedom of discussion and organization, contribute to the persistence of the political objects and under conditions of suppression work in the opposite direction.

Furthermore, many kinds of differences as well as cleavages may be complementary, compatible, or at least neutral with respect to each other. If different groups expressing conflicting demands have something to offer each other in the way of a trade for mutual support, any centrifugal forces set up by group cleavages may be avoided or mitigated. This suggests that differences alone need not mean stressful conflict if they are not competitive or mutually exclusive.[6]

Complementary but diverse attitudes or demands may even draw members together in support of all aspects of a system. At the legislative level, log-rolling is a well-known manifestation of the way in which groups may go even further than the achievement of a mere accommodation of objectives. They are able to combine forces to their mutual advantage. To the extent that such cooperation is possible, cleavage need not create dissatisfaction with a system and undermine support for its objects.

Hence, tendencies arising out of diversity and cleavage will contribute to the input of support for a system and need to be balanced against the opposite effects that they also induce. But even though cleavage may have such positive consequences, this is not to suggest that any system could maintain a sufficient input of support without creating conditions that lead to some degree of consensus. A system that was rent by cleavages and in which the members could agree on little else than to disagree, would seem to have little likelihood of surviving.

[5] S. M. Lipset, M. Trow, and J. S. Coleman, *op. cit.* For additional discussion of positive effects see L. A. Coser, *The Functions of Social Conflict* (Glencoe, Illinois: Free Press, 1956), especially chapters 4 and 7, and M. Gluckman, *Custom and Conflict in Africa* (Glencoe, Illinois: Free Press, 1955).

[6] K. W. Deutsch, S. A. Burrell, et al., *op. cit.*, p. 90.

If this is so, the reader might well ask: Can we afford to neglect the opposite of cleavage, consensus, if we wish to understand the bases of stress?

To answer this, however, we need to look at what is contained in the idea of consensus itself. On the one hand, it certainly refers to a condition opposite to that of social diversity. It suggests agreement or unity in culture, opinions, attitudes and, flowing from them, demands. Just as social diversity basically describes a state of the social environment in which a system exists, so social unity or agreement refers to that environment in its polar condition. But on the other hand, comparable to the dual use to which the concept "cleavage" is put, consensus also bears within it connotations about the political system itself. Reference to political consensus suggests what we might now designate as the antithesis to political cleavage or conflict among groups; that is to say, it implies political harmony or unity in action. This gives us two sets of paired opposites: social diversity and social unity or agreement; political cleavage and political harmony or unity. These ideas are all included within the normal terms, cleavage and consensus.

Thus, the question of why I do not choose to examine the bases of consensus becomes one of asking why I do not consider it theoretically important to explore the supportive consequences of social unity as it creates conditions of political harmony. The answer is simple. Given the perspectives of my mode of analysis, there is little reason to do so. To the extent that, because of basic social unity, the members are in agreement on what ought to be done and on how to go about it, there would be no schisms in the political system to stand in the way of outputs. Output failure would not be likely to occur, at least on these kinds of grounds, and there would be no diminution of support. Since consensus, in the dual sense of social agreement and political harmony, creates no stress, it does not command our attention.

However, this is true from one point of view only, namely, while we are considering the sources of stress. But when we turn to the kind of responses through which systems are able to cope with the stress occasioned by cleavage of any kind, indirectly we shall be dealing with measures through which systems seek to build support through the creation of conditions of agreement and harmony. My approach to consensus, therefore, will not follow the path typically taken in political sociology which has sought to correlate social conditions with various indices of consensus. Rather, since my mode of systems analysis typically insists upon a dynamic approach, it will lead us to inquire into the kinds of coping mechanisms utilized by systems in their constructive efforts to modify the effects of cleavage. Among these responses will appear those that seek to strengthen social as well as political consensus among the members.

Negative Supportive Consequences

What are the consequences of cleavage that lead, not to an increase in support, but to its decline? As I indicated at the outset, a major way of summing up this effect is by noting that cleavage ultimately leads to output failure; this in turn contributes to discontent with each of the political objects, if it persists for a long enough period of time and is not countered by other measures. But how does cleavage contribute to the degree of output failure? For this there are at least three explanations.

In the first place, by definition, cleavage spells diversity in points of view. It means as well that competing groups of members, organized or not, are to be found aligned behind one or another of these points of view. Regardless of the positive effects, even under conditions of free discussion and organization, the mere fact of such differences in outlooks and in organization must interfere with the extent to which the members of a political system are able to achieve compromises and to cooperate with regard to any objectives. Except under some very special conditions of complementarity in aims, each group or aggregate that differs with the other is competing for a share of the limited values in any system. Any increase in the degree of cleavage can be expected to aggravate the difficulties in the way of obtaining a settlement over outputs.

But what do we mean when we say that cleavages in demands and support reduce the capacity of the members of the system to negotiate and compromise their differences? This lies at the heart of its consequences for the input of support. In order to process a demand through to an output, the political leadership requires the support, or at least the acquiescence, of important segments of the politically relevant members. In a democratic system, we are accustomed to hear of the need for a give-and-take attitude in order to find a compromise solution. But we often forget that in totalitarian and dictatorial systems compromise is also normally necessary, although the politically relevant groups within which the compromising takes place are restricted in number and scope to the leadership itself. Even in single-man dictatorships, as at the pinnacle of Stalin's power, Napoleon's rule or Hitler's domination, it is a crude oversimplification of history to assume that these men, powerful as they were, could manipulate vast nations at will, except perhaps for moments of extreme crisis.

Whatever means they used, ranging from terror to manipulation and exhortation, effective combinations of support groups had to be welded together among those who counted in the system.

If the leadership in all systems must depend upon marshaling support from among the politically relevant members, the greater the cleavages among these, the greater the obstacle the leadership must encounter in obtaining working combinations and coalitions of these groups. Cleavage introduces rigidities into the coalition structure available for promoting and processing any proposed output.

If the tendencies thus implicit in cleavages were allowed to run their course without hindrance, if a system had no way of responding to regulate the conflict occasioned by internal divisions—a hypothetical situation difficult to conceive and impossible to detect in any empirical system—the Hobbesian war of all against all would undoubtedly be the only outcome. Paralyzing, unnegotiable schisms would prevail. The probability of processing demands through to outputs satisfactory to the relevant members would quickly dwindle away.

It is not a speculative condition worth dwelling on or arguing about since all systems provide some minimal means for avoiding it; otherwise they would never have been able to survive even briefly. But what it does point up is that even though cleavage may have positive consequences under specified conditions, there, too, the disintegrative forces are at work. No system, whether it provides for the open expression of divisions of groups and opinions or whether it seeks to suppress them, is able to escape the difficulties in reconciling differences. As Lipset has put it in a volume devoted to the discussion of consensus and cleavage in democracies alone, "inherent in all democratic systems [and I would add, in any system where cleavage among the politically relevant members manages to express itself] is the constant threat that the group conflicts which are democracy's lifeblood may solidify to the point where they threaten to disintegrate the society."[7]

But, in the second place, not only do cleavages hamper the negotiation of coalitions based on possible resolutions of disagreements among groups. In addition, the hostilities engendered among the various groups may leave such scars over time that finally the participating members, profoundly dissatisfied with their total situation, may find themselves unable to accept a common regime or political community. Their expectations about the future may be so colored by past frustrations that they may find it impossible to agree on any set of occupants for the authority roles, or on the ground rules for continuing to

[7] S. M. Lipset, *Political Man* (Garden City, New York: Doubleday, 1960), p. 83.

discuss differences. They may even become disinclined to continue to share the same division of labor as a single political community.

This is a result somewhat different from just output failure. It involves a history of unhappy experiences with the existing political arrangements that finally convinces the members that the real trouble lies in the system as it is presently structured. It colors their future expectations to such an extent that the aggrieved members lose all sense of shared identity with essential parts of the system.

Finally, cleavages add to the centrifugal forces in a system by virtue of the fact that the groups involved, through their very presence, offer points of emotional attachment that seriously compete with the basic political objects for the loyalty of members. The particularistic orientations that group loyalties encourage offer an alternative that siphons support away from the system itself. This assumes that bitterness and discontent have already been aroused by output failures or by the recurrent trials and tribulations in seeking to work out what are at best unhappy compromises. In thus taking shelter within the plural groups to seek their basic satisfactions there, members will tend to aggravate an already divisive situation. Communal groupings and encapsulated minorities demonstrate just this kind of pull on the support of members in a system.[8]

In these various ways cleavage may swell the dissatisfaction that the politically relevant members feel with respect to outputs. It would be of prime importance to analyze the kinds of external and internal conditions that usually contribute to political cleavage in the strict sense. Undoubtedly in such a partial theory of political cleavage and harmony, the role of varied demands and the social structure of society—its variety of groups and sub-cultures and the degree of interpenetration or overlapping membership—would loom large. But from the point of view of a general theory, we may assume the presence in

---

[8] Cf. with the comments of M. Weiner, *op. cit.*, p. 231, about India: "The problem of governmental responsiveness as opposed to governmental authoritarianism leads us appropriately to an exploration of the actual threats to the political system that are posed by community associations. Intense identification with one's community to the exclusion of a sense of national identification and a concern for the national interest could be an inhibiting factor in India's modernization. The adoption of the regional language through the school system and the colleges could decrease mobility of both individuals and ideas. Pressures for the employment of members of particular castes or linguistic groups, or for the exclusion of those who come from other states, could decrease efficiency in administration, in the colleges, and in private employment. And the pressure of a number of ethnic minorities for the creation of separate states could, and does, continue to inject conflict, violence, and political instability into a number of states."

all societies of conditions of social diversity that aggravate political cleavage. They are of the very nature of the social structure. The central task of general theory is to explore those means to which political systems have typically resorted in an effort to cope with cleavage-induced stress, whatever the sources of this cleavage may be. Not that the coping mechanisms will be unrelated to the pre-existing or continuing social conditions of cleavage. But insofar as they are, the relationship will become sufficiently apparent from our discussion.

Part Four

Responses to Stress on Support

16

Structural Regulation of Support

SOME EROSION OF SUPPORT IS INEVITABLE IN ALL SYSTEMS; CLEAVAGE among collectivities and accompanying output failure could not be entirely avoided. In all systems, sharp conflict in competition for scarce social and economic values represent a normal aspect of political interaction. If we accept this assumption, we may infer that without some provision to compensate for the dissatisfaction with outputs or to regulate the relationships among actually or potentially conflicting groups, a system would be open to the constant and ultimate danger of disorder or chaos. How is this avoided? What varied means or responses typically prevent such forces from coming to a head? Answers to these questions will engage our attention in the following chapters.

Regulation of Support: Introduction

The Responding Agents

Before we can proceed to speak about the different types of response, some preliminary questions must be raised with respect to responses as such, regardless of type. When we say a system responds in a given way, just who are we to assume does the responding?

These will vary considerably depending upon the system and the time. A response may take the form of deliberate and calculated actions on the part of a political leadership or some segment of the authorities to meet the conditions conducing to the stress. In this event the response will be quite specific; segments of the political elite will be the sensitive responding points. But a response may also be more diffuse and diversified; it may appear as individual and isolated reactions on the part of the members severally considered. In the aggregate, their actions may lead to a new set of circumstances that can be designated as a generalized response in the system.

Thus, some part of the authorities may take action to allay the dissatisfactions occasioned by an economic depression before uncontrollable discontent with the regime sets in. Alternatively or simultaneously, ordinary members may be reacting in the aggregate by calling for a new regime in which the political authorities will be more responsive to the needs of the membership. In the one case, we would be focusing on the specific response of the leadership and in the other, on the general response of members at large. It is vital to bear in mind this distinction between producers of the response since it is easy to forget that responses need not imply activities only on the part of the leadership or authorities.

The Direction of Effects

The response may vary with regard to the direction of the effects. It may serve to increase the level of support available to one or another of the political objects; in this event it is negative in nature since it seeks to nullify the unfavorable consequences of the antecedent conditions.[1] The objective is to reinforce ties to the existing regime.

But the response may also be positive in that it moves in the same direction as the initial disturbance and thereby contributes even further to the erosion of support. No effort is made to offset the initial consequences; rather, they are deliberately aggravated or pushed further in their initial direction until support swings to a new object, such as a new regime.

These represent two different responses to the same set of conditions. They indicate the way in which responses may vary in the direction of their effects; they may serve to support or destroy one of the political objects. Where responses operate in both directions simultaneously we shall be concerned with the net effect.

The Timing of Responses

Timing of the response may be vital, whether the objective is to maintain support or to shift it to a new object. However appropriate the response may be formally, unless the action taken is timely, it may be insufficient to attain the desired result. A system must have the institutions or other means to sense when the input of support threatens to decline below a threshold level. This is at least the first step.

In addition it must have a means to trigger or delay action so that whatever response is taken is appropriate in terms of timing.[2] A politi-

---

[1] I am here using the terms "positive" and "negative" as they typically occur in the literature on feedback. Positive feedback reinforces the consequences of a given stimulus. Negative feedback serves to reduce or destroy these consequences.

[2] In Part Five we shall inquire more fully into this aspect.

cal leadership has frequently distinguished itself by its intuitive capacity to sense the appropriate moment for obtaining maximal results from any action. Regulation of support therefore involves sensing and activating structures and processes which respond with the appropriate alacrity or delay.

Finally, although I have spoken of timing as though it involved a once and only action, in fact it normally consists of a process continuing over a period of time, possibly even extending over generations. A regulative response may consist of a set of actions and reactions in a continuous flow of adjustments to changing conditions.

Basic Types of Responses

The processes through which systems seek to maintain a minimal level of support for the political objects do not vary randomly among all systems. It is possible to identify typical kinds of responses to stress on support. In part, I shall show, they are geared to the direct reduction in cleavages through what will be called *structural changes,* especially in the regime. In part, they are designed to build up a reservoir of support upon which a system may draw credit in times when things are going badly from the point of view of providing satisfactions for the members of the system. This I shall examine under the heading of *diffuse support.* In further part, the responses may offer passing rewards for the support of some set of authorities without necessarily intending to add to the contentment with the regime or community. But support for the latter two objects may emerge as an added dividend. This kind of response, I shall describe as outputs; they will breed *specific support.* Each of these types of responses will engage our attention in turn: structural or regime modifications, in the present chapter; the stimulation of diffuse support in the remainder of this Part and, in Part Five as a whole, the production of specific support through outputs.

Homogenization

One of the major ways in which a system may respond to stress from the kind of cleavage brought about by intense social diversity is through efforts to encourage homogenization of the membership—the reduction or elimination of religious, linguistic, or other cultural differences among groups. To do this, the response may be of a sort that seeks to modify the regime rules (norms) in a number of ways.

Where a system is able to provide, compatible with other rules of its regime, for a gradual program of fusing cultures, although this may not be expected to lead to utter homogeneity, it can bring about some shrinkage in the gap among divergent groups.

But history has shown that such efforts at blending groups have normally proved unsuccessful as a source of marshaling support for the objects of a system. They tend to generate the opposite effect, leading to a secondary response on the part of the system in the form of coercion so as to bolster support. Extended periods of time alone, involving complicated and diffuse processes of assimilation, probably feasible only under conditions of loose political ties as in the case of early Britain or France, may bring about some measure of cultural uniformity and integration.

Indeed, recent research suggests that deliberate efforts to draw members of a system more closely together through measures of assimilation may be the least effective way of achieving an integrated system. Resistance is more than likely to meet those outputs that are calculated to blend groups through the development of a common language and shared mass media, the growth of similar values as represented, for example, in the attempt to win acceptance for similar national idols and ideals, and the introduction of uniform educational curricula and practices. Greater success may be attained through steps that conduce to the development of a deeper sense of mutual awareness and responsiveness among encapsulated cultural units.[3] In systems of multiple nationalities, if the relevant members feel that each group recognizes, respects, and is willing to consider seriously the major needs and demands of others, the probability of eliciting support for a common community is increased. I shall return to this idea later, in connection with the stimulation of support for the political community specifically.

Expressive Structures

Even if we leave this as a moot point, the fact is that a general kind of response adopted to maintain an adequate input of support for the community and regime itself, under conditions of multiple, rivalrous cultural units, has consisted of so structuring the regime that each group or grouping obtains institutional recognition in the political sphere and self-expression as a unit. Cooperation is encouraged by the

[3] K. W. Deutsch, S. A. Burrell, et al., op. cit., pp. 56–58 and pp. 129–133.

creation of mutual benefits to be derived by each of the participants to such an arrangement.

Although policies in the direction of homogenization may also be continued, the major hope of avoiding stress may lie in attempting to incorporate and manage rather than to eliminate the diversity of cultures. Typically, to this end the general structural response in a regime has been the introduction of some form of federal or confederal system. Through it, relatively self-contained cultural-linguistic-religious units retain a degree of control over their own continued identity. It may be that such overall structural arrangements also help to instill and fortify the feelings of mutual awareness and responsiveness already mentioned.

To some extent, every multinational society that does not rely exclusively on coercion as a response must construct regimes that permit the persistence of cultural diversity while allowing for some measure of political integration. The more complex a society is economically and socially, however, and therefore the more interdependent its parts, the less likely will it be that the political cleavages set in motion by cultural variations, if they are embodied in well-defined, cohesive and sizeable groups, can be handled largely through the regime. Under those conditions, inventive genius has seldom measured up to the task of developing norms and structures able to keep a political community together, that is, to hold support at a minimal level. The centrifugal tendencies of what, in our day, we call nationality, have in many cases been too powerful to be kept enchained by a regime, however appropriate it has appeared to be.[4]

If political systems divided by conflicting cultural groups had to rely largely or exclusively on the existence of a loose political structure to knit the community together, there is little likelihood that such cleavages could be contained and regulated. As in all other responses to be examined, alone probably no one of them would be effective. In combination of different sorts, they may have a chance to overcome tendencies that reduce support.

Representative Structures as a Response

The differences among diverse groups may be shielded from aggravation by building into the system additional expressive structural means that give the groups an opportunity to attempt to resolve their

[4] Cf. the quickening inadequacy today of the Canadian federal structure for reducing friction between Quebec and the rest of Canada.

differences, if at all possible, under acceptable ground rules. A major device for this purpose is to be found in all kinds of representative structures, including those typical of but not exclusively confined to democratic regimes. It is a response that seeks less to mute the differences or blend groups than to provide avenues for negotiation and reconciliation.

The Stress-Reducing Function of Representation

Representation can easily be overlooked as a response that helps to bring divided groups together even where other means are weak or inoperative. It may well be, as the constant success of representative democracy in reasserting itself in France testifies, that without the integrative character of representative institutions, the divisive forces in France might have won out. In spite of the immobilism reflected in and reinforced by the special-interest, encapsulated parties, France has returned to the representative system time and again—in each of the first four Republics—and is currently balking at the ineffective operation of these institutions in the Fifth one. The contribution of the appeal of representation as a means for expressing and accommodating differences has still to be evaluated as a dynamic structural force in the resiliency that the French democratic system has shown in the face of paralyzing cleavages over the last century and a half.

As a possible response to cleavages, representative structures in their many forms operate so as to enable groups to obtain access to the centers of authority in the system. Either the recruitment processes permit elites from the groups to occupy some of the authority roles; or the members of the group obtain some kind of sanctions, such as the popular vote, over those who do occupy these roles. The rise of middle class groups in the feudal and absolutist political systems of Europe led to just these kinds of adaptation in the existing regimes. These are vital and obvious functions of representative structures.

But representation does more than modify the elite recruitment patterns or means of control. It provides those who are affiliated with groups an opportunity to meet each other in a common forum so as to undertake negotiations to discover the exact nature of their differences, the degree of flexibility of each other's positions, and the extent to which reconciliation of points of view and demands is feasible. This lies at the heart of political interaction as demands move to conversion into outputs. It is a process no less typical of dictatorial than of democratic systems, of non-literate or traditional than of modern ones. These varying systems differ, not because of the presence or complete absence of representative structures, but by virtue of the scope of the representation—who is represented?—and of control over the representatives, whether it is effective, virtual (in Burke's sense), spurious, or non-existent.

There need be no reason to believe in advance that any given substantive issue must lend itself to settlement. In some cases, regardless of the means used, the cleavages may be so wide and acrimonious as to be beyond repair. Nevertheless, effective political expression for a demand, through the processes of representation, at least provides the satisfaction that an opportunity has been presented for trying to bridge the gap among differences. We may not be able to argue convincingly that the conflict among differences in demands must always recede in proportion to the availability of means for giving effective political expression to these differences. Yet the confrontation, however informal, does offer an opportunity to iron out disagreements. The simple assumption is that communication is more likely to yield a working arrangement among contenders than isolation. At the level of international systems, this belief has been a driving motivation behind support for the United Nations as part of the regime structure.

Variant Forms of Representative Structures

If we are to attribute a cleavage-reducing quality to representation, we must be prepared to interpret representation in a very broad sense. To confine it exclusively to popular representation in legislatures, as we find it in systems using popular electoral processes, would be to restrict this kind of cleavage response to simply one manifestation of representative structures. It is of course a central one from the point of view of democratic political values. Yet if we are to continue to adopt a broad theoretical and analytic posture, we must recognize that many systems, whether democratic or not, offer some avenues of representation to groups and groupings.[5] In fact, without means for some self-expression in such highly differentiated structures as modern bureaucratic systems, it is doubtful whether the political authorities would be able to obtain the kind of knowledge they need in order to govern; or whether the participating groups would not finally arrive at the point where they were at loggerheads with each other. The system would probably be driven back upon coercion exclusively, if it was to maintain some semblance of integration.

[5] For the differences between groups and groupings, see D. Easton, *The Political System*, p. 185 ff.

Representative processes are usually associated with direct and recognized participation by selected individuals who are linked with given groups or groupings in the system. We can ignore the various problems involved in developing a partial theory of representation such as the nature of the ties between a representative and the members to whom he is linked. Whether he is their advocate, a creative and reflective leader, a mere mouthpiece for his constituents, or a combination of these and other roles need not concern us.[6] But formally recognized representation has assumed a variety of shapes ranging from representative legislatures, to special functional bodies in which groups have formal membership, such as economic councils today or guild councils at an earlier time, to executive bodies such as cabinets or ruling councils in which various regions and points of view may be explicitly represented. At the formal level, we can expect many new kinds of structures to arise in the future, without foreseeable limit, especially when we consider the experimental mood that prevails in the political systems of today's developing nations.

But informal responses have equally important effects on cleavages, even though analysis is apt to ignore or neglect them. In many systems informal responses also serve to permit confrontations of contending groups and points of view, often in a politically less visible setting. Informally groups and groupings may succeed in penetrating administrative structures and thereby they may be able to obtain representation for their views at effective points in the political system. At times the process may also be formalized so that certain groups have a right to representation although here I shall speak particularly of the informal aspects.[7]

Even in systems that provide representation based on general popular suffrage, competition and conflict among groups lead to the search for every possible avenue for bringing demands to bear upon the formulation and execution of decisions. The selection of administrative personnel to reflect the political points of view of groupings—say, of a particular ethnic or religious composition—or of specific occupational groups is a well-recognized way of coping with the general competition and cleavage over influence on outputs. Hence we find the familiar claim that criteria of recruitment to administrative positions

[6] In J. C. Wahlke, H. Eulau, *et al.*, *The Legislative System* (New York: Wiley, 1962), we have a major effort in the direction of developing a partial theory about representation.

[7] The informal aspects are dramatically set forth in J. D. Kingsley, *Representative Bureaucracy* (Yellow Springs, Ohio: Antioch Press, 1944).

and subtle controls in the selection procedures may easily tend to favor one or another set of members in the system, aggravating any pre-existing cleavages through the feeling on the part of others that these members have obtained a definite advantage in the informal representative processes.

In Britain, for example, changes in the selection procedures for the upper administrative levels in recent years was a concession to those who argued that the upper classes had been favored by the existing arrangements, geared as they were to the qualities of graduates from Oxford and Cambridge. The modifications in recruitment criteria to permit the admission of others can be viewed as an adjustment in the representative mechanism and not just as a purely administrative measure. It reflected the fact that cleavage had spread from struggle over control of the legislature and executive to the desire for a greater measure of influence over administration, a core area of power in all bureaucratic societies. The presence of informal representation from divided groups and groupings can be expected to help allay the anxieties that their points of view will be overlooked in the day-to-day business of administration and bolster general supportive attitudes.

Perhaps we can better appreciate the importance of informal representation for support stress if we look at what may happen in its absence. If a significant political group were systematically excluded from some kind of recognition in the administrative structure, we would expect this normally to lead to an exacerbation of differences between it and groups with which it was in competition and which did find a place in administration. In multinational systems, for example, ethnic or other component groups frequently have their antipathies raised to a high pitch, as in the case of French-Canada, by a realization that they have not been given what they consider to be their fair share of administrative posts. Confrontation of contending groups and points of view at additional levels in a political system, in its net effects, may help to reduce cleavages just as it tends to in the case of representative institutions formally designated as such, even though the specific processes are quite different.

Once we recognize that representation is not a function exclusively of formal structures designed for that purpose, we are able to identify another kind of structural response to cleavage. In general, norms permitting the permeation of the political structure by conflicting points of view in the society can be interpreted as an effort to cope with cleavage. This even sheds some additional light on the way in which non-democratic systems, at least in a bureaucratic society, cope with cleavage, a matter which such systems can no more escape than can democracies.

In the USSR, for example, informal "representation" constitutes a major effective mechanism through which political cleavage can be channeled and possibly brought under some kind of regulation compatible with the persistence of the system. Coercive institutions and the Party help to reduce diversity of outlook, to be sure, and they stand as major devices of high priority and effectiveness. But the permeation of the administrative institutions, enormous and pervasive as they must be in a communist society, by diverse points of view, converts these institutions into an informal forum in which the contending groups in society can express themselves, within the limits permitted by the leadership and regime.

This informal even though undoubtedly imperfect mirroring of social cleavages helps to explain the real utility found within the USSR for representative bodies at various levels in the system, from the village to the system as a whole. As we know, these declared representative organs have become converted largely into administrative organizations. Although as such, they violate Western conceptions of the functions of popular representative bodies, this administrative function does not entirely choke off competing points of view within the limits of discussion set by the system. If we assume the need and desire to minimize the use of coercion, we can appreciate why there should be a ready acceptance of the transformation of what are nominally popular representative institutions into largely administrative bodies. Since effective popular participation in policy-making cannot take place, the development and acceptance of the administrative activities of these organs offer a medium through which efforts can be made among groups and groupings to achieve acceptable rapprochements at a point in the political process that counts. In a system with the diversity of the USSR, neither Party nor coercion alone or together could be expected to ward off the stress inherent in the vast variety of latent political cleavages that inhabit the system, except perhaps at an extraordinary outlay of energy.

The Intersection of Political Structures

Parties in Democratic Systems

A further structural mechanism for coping with cleavage stress is to be found in positive action that invites the overlapping of groups and groupings.[8] For example, in systems where the regime permits party competition for the control of political office, the structure of the parties may develop in such a way as to encourage maximum inclusiveness. In recent decades the literature of political science has dealt extensively with the cleavage-reducing potential of the coalition as compared to the single-interest party so frequently found in multiparty political systems. Where each party restricts its appeal to only a limited class of members, cleavage is reinforced; where the parties seek to embrace the widest mixture of groups and individuals, as in two or three party systems, the political divisions are softened. In such instances the parties are able to draw together a variety of groups and thereby bring about some prior reconciliation of points of view.

Research has also suggested that electoral rules are responses available, at least for such competitive parties, for reinforcing the divisive or integrative consequences of party formations. The single member constituency, we suspect, encourages more inclusive points of view among representatives, whereas proportional representation and its variants offer incentives for the promotion of single and therefore divisive interests.

Parties in Non-Democratic Systems

But even in those systems in which competitive parties are not compatible with the general orientations of the regime, as in those types where there is a self-perpetuating leadership, organized groups need not be entirely forbidden or destroyed. In fact, especially under conditions of modern bureaucratic society, totalitarianism itself cannot undertake the organization of the normal range of necessary economic and social activities without the emergence of many and varied social groups and groupings. Unless we are to assume complete homogenization or atomization of a population, a theoretical limit but not a practical possibility, cleavages associated with such groups must therefore emerge, however inarticulate, guarded, or circumspect the antagonisms may be.

What mechanisms for regulating inescapable cleavages in such systems are there available? The most obvious one is the response that

[8] For the consequences of overlapping membership toward muting cleavages, see D. Truman, *op. cit.*, p. 510 ff; G. Simmel, *The Web of Group-Affiliations*, trans. R. Bendix (Glencoe, Illinois: Free Press, 1955); T. Parsons, " 'Voting' and the Equilibrium of the American Political System" in E. Burdick and A. J. Brodbeck (eds.), *American Voting Behavior* (Glencoe, Illinois: Free Press, 1959), pp. 80–120; R. E. Lane, *Political Life*, chapter 14; and E. E. Schattschneider, *Party Government* (New York: Rinehart, 1942) *ad hoc*.

takes the form of suppressing all groups except those either sanctioned specifically by the dominant leadership or tamed if they do arise. But if group formations and variety of views from different groupings formed around such foci as specific interests, socio-economic status, ethnicity, or regionalism cannot be eliminated, safeguards must be devised to prevent them from getting out of hand. Otherwise they may ultimately lead to disaffection from the regime, and the latter, in turn, is often indissolubly linked with a specific set of authorities, and possibly the community. This is particularly necessary in systems that forbid the formation of competitive parties as a basic means for integrating varying points of view into a form that can be mobilized for varying purposes.

As in democratic regimes, however, a major mechanism for regulating cleavage continues to be the political party. This conclusion will enable us to appreciate a vital aspect of the role of parties in nondemocratic political systems in mass, industrialized societies.

In part, parties have long been understood as a means for direct control to prevent disaffection due to output failure. They act as a policing mechanism. But in part, they are also a response to the danger of destructive cleavages that might otherwise occur among groups and groupings, such as in the USSR for example, among the peasants and urban workers, unskilled, skilled and professional vocations, and the intelligentsia and professional politicians. To keep the groups in check and to prevent the emergence of conflict among them that might endanger the survival of the given regime, supervisory or tutelary organizations, such as a political party, may be interpreted as a specific mechanism.

In the USSR, the Party is itself composite in character, drawing its membership from broad strata of the population. It also follows a calculated policy of seeding strategic social groups with party members. Multiple or overlapping membership of a limited sort is deliberately attempted by interlocking party members with membership in other groups. In this way, an effort is made to avert the growth of significantly diverging points of view among organizations and groups.

It it true, as I have already indicated, the presence of party members in various social and economic groups in a totalitarian system is evidence of the existence of an internal intelligence apparatus to aid in the application of sanctions, formal or informal, so as to compel conformity with established policies. But we cannot accept this as the only aspect of the integrative party,[9] a recent phenomenon as a system

[9] S. Neumann, "Towards a Comparative Study of Political Parties" in S. Neumann (ed.), *Modern Political Parties* (Chicago: University of Chicago Press, 1956), pp. 395–424, at pp. 404 ff.

response. It also performs the more general function of helping informally to shape attitudes and views while they are in process of formation. In this way, any tendencies of groups with different life-expectations to go off in sharply different directions and, thereby, to enhance inter-group tensions, may be impeded.

We may conclude that through deliberate policy, some commingling of strategic groups may be encouraged. As a response, it has the consequence of inhibiting fissiparous tendencies inherent in the group structure that is characteristic of any mass society.

Modifications in Regime Norms

In addition to responses that affect the basic structure of a regime, various kinds of responses involving the manipulation or changes of other aspects of the regime contribute to the alleviation of the effects of cleavage on the input of support. Although these are numerous and varied, only one type will be examined here; I shall return to others under the category of diffuse support in the following chapter. The response to be discussed here is only associated with the structure of the regime in that it takes the form of changes in existing norms.

The Function of Norms in Meeting Stress

Every system has a host of cultural norms regulating the way in which political disputes are to be conducted. Attitudes toward the use of violent instead of pacific means, sometimes considered to be matters of political style, are in reality matters of substance. Norms under which members may feel encouraged or at least not strongly inhibited from adopting violence in the form of riots, mass demonstrations, assassination, or military coups in the search for the settlement of differences, leave scars and smoldering frustrations and resentment that may aggravate rather than modify pre-existing cleavages.

Norms may also shape the severity of disputes in other ways. Where they specify pacific means for reconciling differences, the norms may incorporate the ideal that disputes should be conducted in terms such that the participants never forget that they must continue to live together as continuing members of a common political system long after a particular difference is past and forgotten. One ought not to go too far in condemning one's opponents. In some systems, such as dictatorial types, since defeat in basic issues may mean separation from the system physically through execution or exile, only the norms of self-interest and self-preservation limit the severity of dispute. But in other systems, if the members are to retain unity in the face of cleavage, they cannot permit conflict to be conducted in such a way that irremediable damage is done to political relationships.

Thus, as mentioned in Chapter 12, during the McCarthy period in the United States, when it appeared that one of the political parties was being accused of "twenty years of treason" during its long domination of the executive, a general revulsion to the nature of the accusation passed through many politically articulate sections of the system. This quick reaction served as a social sanction to bring those who were levying the accusation back within the range of permissible political debate. To do otherwise would have been to run the risk that wounds would have been opened that could not have been easily healed for generations. Norms may regulate debate over issues to prevent the cleavages from being reinforced and brought to a point of doing permanent damage to the cohesion of the system.

The Depoliticizing Norms

Since I intend only to illustrate the function of norms as responses muting cleavages, the part that they play may best be illuminated by considering that subclass of norms that helps to depoliticize political issues. Empirically, no system seems to forego the opportunity to use this mechanism and without it, probably no system could begin to handle the strains occasioned by cleavages due to issue conflict.

If each political controversy terminated completely upon the adoption of some output in relation to it and no residue of hostility were left behind among the participants, the effects of issue conflict in cleavages would be much less than they are. If no decision, once made, were ever challenged, resisted or raised again for new consideration, the issue would be completely deprived of further importance for cleavage. Each participant would start from the beginning, as it were, with regard to each new issue. Issues would simply smolder, flare up, and finally die away into a cold ash.

But this represents a limiting case that never occurs in reality. The fact is that the controversy surrounding an issue may leave a deposit of bitter hostility among the participants. This may be considered its historical effect. We come to recognize the political opinions of members of the system by virtue of the position they have taken on past political issues. On the basis of this experience, we come to expect that certain members will typically take a given position on any new issues. Identifying labels of conservative, liberal, authoritarian, libertarian, isolationist and the like indicate our expectations. Especially with regard to political leaders who have been called upon publicly to take sides on issues, there is an opportunity to estimate their future behavior. Thus, even if each issue arose and disappeared immediately as a matter in conflict, after a decision had been achieved, through its historical effect it would help to shape the form of the cleavages in society.

But even if we make allowance for the scars and residues left by history, many issues refuse to disappear even after some kind of decision has been made. They are often kept alive for many years, if not for generations, overflowing from one period to the next. As we know, this overflow effect has contributed significantly to cleavages in France. The alignments around the interpretation of the French Revolution, the role of the church in public life and education, and the nature of popular participation in politics have persisted for a century and a half. Each decision seems to be less effective in resolving differences than in laying the ground for new and equally controversial disagreements.

The result is that as each issue persists in one form or another, it often tends to mingle with others to form the basis of an accumulated mixture of issues. By adding fuel to the fires still smoldering from past controversies, it helps to reinforce, or intensify and polarize any existing cleavages. The alignments of parties in France have taken this character in a pronounced way. But parties in every system, by their very nature, represent a classic case of the intermingling of the scars of past conflicts, the hostilities of present differences, and the carry-over from past unsettled issues. The fact that they can build programs with some stability, and envelop themselves in ideologies with some degree of consistency indicates the presence of an overflow effect from past controversies as a factor in perpetuating cleavages. Even a limited combination of current and past unresolved issues helps to maximize the number of groups to which a party can turn for support and often to intensify the support of those already in the party.

Systems will, of course, differ with respect to the degree to which their failure to extinguish past issues contribute to current differences. But let me now make an assumption opposite to the one I used to initiate this discussion. There I speculated on the results of assuming that all issues died away immediately after they had been considered by the authorities and acted upon positively or negatively, in whole or in part. If we now consider what would happen if parties and other groups managed to keep all issues alive, regardless of the steps taken to resolve them, we can appreciate the need for all systems to make provision for taking some issues out of the arena of controversy.

If no issue could be withdrawn, the overflow effect could lead to a combining of issues of such an explosive character that the resulting cleavages could not help but destroy a system. This possible outcome would not stem only from the presence of an excessive number and variety of issues. It would also arise from the alignment of antagonistic support groups implicit in the notion of cleavage. In this speculative case of issue immortality, the stress of excessive numbers and variety of issues would link up with the stress from the increasing hostility among support groups.[10]

Types of Depoliticizing Responses

It appears that if a system is to take some steps to prevent issues from perpetuating themselves indefinitely and agglutinating around support groups, some means must be adopted for depriving issues of political value. Systems have developed a number of different kinds of responses.

In the first place, it has been suggested that sometimes there is a tacit agreement among the politically relevant strata to withdraw from the arena of political importance any disputed matter that might remain after some major conflict.[11] Normally this response might be expected to occur only after considerable conflict has already been generated about an issue and the strains so occasioned have been recognized as highly dangerous to the regime or community. Alterna-

---

[10] Of course, I make the further assumption that each issue would not call up a new and unique combination of forces behind it. Rather there would be a tendency, as there is at least in those systems with political parties or factions within single parties, for positions on issues to correspond to existing group divisions. This assumption is entirely reasonable since existing groups will seek to take advantage of each old and each new issue, as a means of extending the base of its support among the members of the system.

[11] ". . . the gradual depoliticization of the continuing difference between Protestant and Catholic religious values in the course of the eighteenth century furnished an essential precondition for the successful amalgamation of Germany and Switzerland, respectively, in the course of the following century. Examples of a partial depoliticization of conflicting values include the partial depoliticization of the slavery issue in the United States between 1775 and 1819, and of the race problem after 1876. Similarly, Germany saw a reduction in the political relevance of the liberal-conservative cleavage after 1866 with the emergence of the National Liberal Party. A similar reduction of political relevance occurred in regard to the conflict of Scottish Presbyterianism with the Episcopal Church in England and Scotland after 1690, and in the further abatement of the Protestant-Catholic issue in Switzerland after the mid-eighteenth century, and further after 1848." K. W. Deutsch, S. A. Burrell, et al., op. cit., pp. 46–47.

tively, in anticipation, a struggle of this sort might be aborted before it even starts, by agreeing to consider it outside of politics.

Such withdrawal from political contention assumes that the politically relevant members are able to adopt or accept as a norm the idea that it is inappropriate or politically unacceptable to throw the relevant issues into the arena for dispute. But where, in advance, these members have been able to establish some constraints on the introduction of issues, they may be able to incorporate norms explicitly into the formal or informal constitution of the regime. The norms thereby acquire the status not of an implicit understanding but of a political settlement and indicate in advance a serious intent to exclude the particular area from political dispute. This is a second kind of response leading toward the withdrawal of issues from political life.

Constitutions that forbid governments from trespassing on certain areas such as religion or freedom of speech, that establish official languages, or provide for the procedures in selecting and rejecting political authorities, thereby help to depoliticize these matters. Not that any agreed-upon constitutional restraints on the use of power are forever locked in some drawer labeled "not for political use." But being in that drawer, either they are in fact less accessible or it is evidence that the members of the system prefer to put them outside the realm of day-to-day controversy.

To lie outside the normal framework of political dispute, a subject matter does not have to be included within what is recognized by the members of the system as a constitution. I refer here to the fact that in all systems, whether dictatorial or democratic, modern or traditional, literate or non-literate, the political culture of a system excludes many areas from debate. We can call these the fundamental assumptions or inarticulate premises, usually politically sensitive subjects. However we identify them, some constraints exist upon all persons, the political authorities as well as ordinary members, which inhibit them from injecting some subjects into the political process. The existence of such implicit or explicit prohibitions and taboos against politicizing problems serves to restrict the range of subjects that can add to the issue cleavages.

The two kinds of responses I have been talking about—tacit agreements and incorporation into constitutional restraints—act in a way so as to prevent, if possible, the sparking of a cleavage-inducing issue. There is a third kind of response that takes an existing controversy, removes it from the open political arena, and siphons it through special channels in a system so that the effects of the cleavage are controlled. This consists of the processes of adjudication. In modern society, what we call legal settlements may be viewed as a universal response to the stress inherent in political cleavages. It has long been recognized as a means, not for eliminating conflict but for regulating it so that it is less likely to create unnecessary stress on the political system.

The norms that govern the resort to adjudication serve to reduce the stress of cleavage through the fact that they establish regularized expectations about the way in which differences of the kind the system declares to be appropriate for this process, will be settled. In part, the degree of stress inherent in a dispute is a function of the indeterminacy of the results. The maximum stress is occasioned by disputes settled or regulated through the use of violence. There, the outcome is unpredictable except insofar as the relative command over physical forces by the participants is known. Somewhat less uncertainty is obtained where the matters in dispute can be negotiated within a settled context of procedures that we call the legislative processes. In both cases, whether it is that of violence or legislation, the ability to shape the outcome depends in large part on the effective support one can mobilize on one's behalf. The nature of the process conduces to the development and aggravation of cleavages, even if in different degrees. From the smallest non-literate system to the most developed modern society, the resolution of disputes in these two ways leads to the alignment of members of the system on different sides of the issues. Cleavage is assumed and, in part, encouraged by these processes for settling differences.

Adjudicative processes provide presumed or known and accepted rules under which differences can be adjusted and, thereby, they may whittle conflict down to a minimum. Even though adjudication may require the formal alignment of members on different sides, and, in fact, it has often been compared to a stylized but pacific jousting match, the degree of cleavage is confined to the actual participants. In many judicial systems those who may feel affected by the ultimate outcome tend to be excluded, unless they can demonstrate a very special interest. Hence this procedure helps to confine a dispute, to prevent it from spreading and infecting other members. It thereby helps to reduce the degree of cleavage that might otherwise be generated if either violence or legislative methods had been adopted as a mode for seeking settlement.

Furthermore, adoption of judicial processes implies the antecedent acceptance of the idea that an established rule does or must exist for the settlement of the issue, that it has some degree of commonly recognized equity and justice about it, that it has the sanction of the community behind it, and that it ought to be obeyed. Without such assumptions, a process of judicial settlement could not prevail. The submission of disputes to judicial settlement predisposes the disputants to accept the settlement and, therefore, to limit the duration of the cleavage. Not that appeals may not be made from the judicial processes to the field of legislation or violence, a mark of the failure of judicial processes in reducing cleavage. By regularizing the process of adjusting difference, expectations with regard to the outcome are stabilized, and if, in addition, sentiments of justice and equity are associated with the rules applied, the degree of discontent attached to a judicial resolution of a conflict is minimized.[12]

The response through judicial processes to withdraw issues, at least partly, from intense political dispute, must not be confused with the existence of any structures that we may identify as courts or judicial systems. Frequently, under the guise of judicial structures we may find processes that show a greater resemblance to the negotiation of differences than to the application of settled, accepted or presumed rules. In part this caveat applies to the settlements obtained in the courts of bureaucratic societies. But it is especially true of many traditional systems where institutions have been lightly misnamed as judicial. An inspection of the *Judicial Process Among the Barotse of Northern Rhodesia*,[13] for example, reveals that the chief's court would be best characterized not as a judicial body but as an undifferentiated compound of judicial, legislative, and administrative actions. Hence, as we would expect, the members of the system align themselves in political array with the parties to the dispute and the cleavage reducing consequences of the Barotse court, which are considerable, cannot all be traced to judicial processes alone.

As I have been describing political life, judicial processes form a significant part of it and are not non-political in character. As we shall see, they are also one of the means through which a system manufac-

[12] Judicial decisions of the Supreme Court in the United States might seem to dispute this interpretation since they have regularly served as the focal point for the alignment of hostile groups. In some cases, as recently with respect to racial integration, they have even sparked new manifestations of old cleavages. But we have only to think of the severity of conflicts that might have arisen, if the resolution of racial cleavages were left entirely in the hands of the normal legislative or other political processes, to realize the ultimate tendency, even in this case, of judicial processes to moderate the cleavages. Nor does this interpretation mean that judicial processes need never aggravate differences. We can speak only of average tendencies, not of all possible outcomes in individual instances.

[13] M. Gluckman (Manchester: Manchester University Press, 1955), especially p. 17.

tures outputs. In a strict sense, therefore, since judicial decisions will be seen to be outputs, we cannot characterize judicial processes as a device for entirely depoliticizing political issues. But I deal with this matter here because judicial processes do weaken the capacity of issues to broaden cleavages. These processes confine issues within narrowly restricted boundaries by deliberately limiting the number of participants who may be aligned on either side and by formalizing the procedures. Especially by controlling the form for expressing cleavages, a major step is taken on the road to withdrawing them from the major stress-creating arenas of conflict. If, in the outcome, judicial processes do not completely depoliticize issues, they at least denature them sufficiently so as to reduce their stress potential.

In summary, through the way it structures its regime, a range of alternatives is available to a system from which it may select means for ameliorating the stress occasioned by cleavages among groups and groupings. It thereby helps to maintain the input of support at a minimal level. Groups may be entirely suppressed and the society atomized, a limiting kind of tactic. But even here initial conflict in outlook would continue to occur because of occupational, religious, regional, educational, or other kinds of differences, although they might not be able to express themselves openly. Efforts may be made to homogenize society by blending or erasing religious, linguistic, or other kinds of cultural differences.

But at the other extreme, diversity may be accepted for what it is and mechanisms devised to allow for its expression, but in a context that moderates the stress of conflict. Systems may respond by structuring their regime so as to permit maximal expression for cultural variations through a federal type system, rules may be included to depoliticize or denature issues, and norms may encourage overlapping group membership. Through representative structures, broadly conceived, varied and effective avenues may be provided for groups to express and negotiate their differences so that no group feels entirely excluded from a part in the effective political process. In these ways, structural and norm-oriented, a system may seek to respond to cleavage so as to prevent the sources of support for the political objects from diminishing or evaporating entirely.

17

The Generation of Diffuse Support

NO SYSTEM COULD RELY EXCLUSIVELY ON DIRECT MEASURES, SUCH AS those of modifying the structure and norms of the regime, as devices to alleviate cleavage or to compensate for output failure. However careful, facilitative, and powerful the authorities of a regime were, however successful efforts might be in regulating cleavage, there could be little expectation of ever coming close to erasing all conflicting differences. Some dissensus and political cleavage must always prevail.[1]

Fortunately whether or not, through structural changes of the kind dealt with in the last chapter, efforts to compensate for the dangers inherent in political cleavages could alone ever prove adequate to permit the persistence of any system is a theoretical point we do not have to consider further. Empirically, we can point to no system that relies exclusively on such mechanisms. In every system two other general categories of responses are constantly available to maintain a minimal level of support for the various political objects. I shall identify these as specific and diffuse support. Here, aside from a few introductory remarks about specific support, I shall confine my discussion to diffuse support; in Part Five, under the heading of outputs, I shall work out in full the details with respect to specific support.

Outputs and Specific Support

Implicit in what I have already said about outputs is the idea that, in part, support for any of the political objects will, in the long run, depend upon the members being persuaded that outputs are in fact meeting their demands or that they can be expected to do so within some reasonable time. Output failure can be said to occur when members feel that outputs are not likely to do so. When we come to discuss

[1] L. A. Coser, *op. cit.;* R. Dahrendorf, *Class and Class Conflict in Industrial Society* (Stanford: Stanford University Press, 1959); and M. Gluckman, *Custom and Conflict in Africa* (Glencoe, Illinois: Free Press, 1955).

outputs in detail, I shall take up this theme again and explore its many implications. But what is of importance here is that, at times, the input of support may flow as a consequence from some specific satisfactions obtained from the system with respect to a demand that the members make, can be expected to make, or that is made on their behalf. Where support is in this way a *quid pro quo* for the fulfillment of demands, I shall call it specific support.

For example, a trade union seeks a higher minimum wage and persuades the legislature to approve of it. Elderly members and those responsible for them seek publicly controlled programs of medical care. Farmers appeal for a more generous underpinning of the prices for their produce and obtain laws to that effect. A manufacturer argues for and wins a higher tariff for his goods. Here the gratifications can all be related specifically to the outputs. Even in the case of what the economists call indivisible benefits—such as the satisfactions obtained from knowing that the country is well defended, that the authorities are working toward a peaceful world, that the various public services are well attended to, or that the monetary and other resources are being frugally spent—the linkage between the outputs or actions of the authorities on the one side, and the response of the members on the other is, in principle at least, sufficiently close so as to be able to trace out the effects of the one on the other. In the eyes of the members, there is some connection between their wants or demands and the activities of the authorities.

Indeed, much of polling and opinion research has been devoted to testing the nature of the response on the part of members of a system to the policies and practices, both included in outputs, of the authorities. There is already well imbedded within the empirical literature the conceptualization that underlies the notion of support as a specific response to actions taken by authorities. In summary, then, although there will undoubtedly be marginal and penumbral cases empirically difficult to distinguish from diffuse support, wherever the input of support can be closely associated with the satisfactions obtained from specific classes of output, I shall designate it as specific support.[2]

[2] Previously, in "An Approach to the Analysis of Political Systems," I had adopted Talcott Parsons' term, "contingent support"—see his article, "Some Highlights of the General Theory of Action" in R. Young, *Approaches to the Study of Politics* (Evanston, Illinois: Northwestern University Press, 1958), pp. 282–304—to describe this relationship between outputs and support. But since all support has large degrees of contingency associated with it, it seems more precise and informative to use my present terminology which distinguishes support given for returns instead of support offered because of affective ties to an object in and of itself.

The Insufficiency of Specific Support

Against the stimulation of specific support as a response related to the persistence of a system, we know from history that members of a system have proved able to tolerate long periods of frustration in the satisfaction of their wants without support falling below the minimal level and passing over the threshold into stress. Indeed, no regime or community could gain general acceptance and no set of authorities could expect to hold power if they had to depend exclusively or even largely on outputs to generate support as a return for specific and identifiable benefits. Other means of adaptation to stress are necessary.

Postponement of Benefits

If a system were forced back on specific support alone, responses to encourage its growth might often prove futile. It is not always feasible to balance outputs against demands so that the wants of most politically relevant members are met most of the time. All systems require of individual members, groups and often of whole generations that they sacrifice present goods for future rewards. Frequently it is transparent to all that present actions can benefit only future generations. In effect, a system asks its members to subordinate present known wants to future uncertain rewards for unknown descendants.

If it were not that, as members of political systems, we are all so accustomed to accepting the validity of such "sacrifices," we might well consider it an extremely doubtful matter as to whether we could expect people to postpone their present demands for tenuous future gains for remote others. Yet in the face of the apparent impracticality of such an imposition, whole ideologies of sacrifice, implicit in Marxism and in the varied less structured belief systems of developing countries, are able to thrive on the prospect they hold out of delaying material gains to the future generations.

Partial Satisfaction of Demands

Even if the postponement of benefits were not at stake, since scarcity or lack of resources is as much a political as an economic fact, at any moment some members of a system are asked to subordinate the complete fulfillment of their demands for the sake of at least the partial fulfillment of the demands put in by others. Even powerful minorities may feel impelled to exercise considerable restraint in the face of circumstances under which they might have the technical capacity to assert their demands more strongly and fully. This need not be a matter of giving up present gains for future generations; nor does it even involve the delay of present rewards in favor of future greater benefits for oneself. Normally, members of a system are willing to give up all hope of fully satisfying their own demands so that others may obtain partial fulfillment of theirs.

In short, whatever the reason, all members are in part frustrated in the realization of their political demands. All experience output failure with respect to themselves, at least in some degree. To paraphrase an aphorism, you can satisfy some of the politically relevant members some of the time, but not all of them all of the time.

However painfully obvious this is once it is stated, it needs formulation because it is only too easily and typically neglected as a theoretical component. Without taking these facts into account, we cannot adequately understand the various ways in which systems are driven to cope with the potential loss of support inherent in this kind of stress situation. If a system had to rely exclusively on specific support, a kind elicited as a return for the perceived benefits to be gained from specific outputs, it is doubtful whether any system could persist.

Time Lag

Finally, modern systems in particular differ from traditional ones with respect to matching outputs to demands. For traditional systems, the time lag between outputs of authorities and evidence of their effects on demands was much shorter. For many kinds of decisions, the members could expect to see the results of outputs while the authorities continued to occupy their roles. The fact that the occupancy of positions of authority was of longer duration, due to the ascribed rather than achieved nature of these roles, made this linkage of outputs to actions of authorities quite possible. If need be, to reinforce support among the politically relevant members, the authorities could stand on their record, as it were, for the results of their actions could be evaluated through the personal experiences of these members.

In the case of modern systems, however, the situation has changed radically. With the need for long-range planning and the greater technicality and complexity of problems handled by the authorities, considerable time lags intervene between output and results as they affect the wants of the relevant members. As the matter has been put with respect to organizations in modern societies, the authorities are more likely to be "judged on results determined by [their] predecessors and [to] make decisions that will affect primarily [their] successors." [3] In Part Five I shall reconsider the problems raised by this time lag. But here it helps to underscore another reason why it would prove difficult, at least in modern structurally complex systems, to rely largely on outputs to stimulate the input of support.

The Validation of Compromise

Why should members of a political system be willing to advance support for the political objects even under circumstances where they have to give up any hope of satisfying many vital immediate or even future demands, and especially where they are embroiled in deep cleavages with respect to the division of a system's limited resources? For those members who are politically weak or powerless, we can appreciate that they have no alternative. But if we confine our attention to those members of a system who are politically relevant and of some substantial influence, that is, who count in the system for whatever reason, the question still remains.

Expediency

One good reason might be that out of self-interest or expediency, it pays to do so. Acceptance of compromise may be forced upon a group, not because it desires the outcome, but because of the combinations and coalitions arrayed against it. Under the relationship of competing power groups in a system, some members may consider themselves fortunate to be able to influence outputs in any significant way.

Equilibrium theories of democracy, for example, have been based on this very kind of reasoning. Every output or policy arrangement has been described as the outcome of a parallelogram of forces or as an equilibrium of competing groups so that each group, where competition for power is freely permitted, has a share in the influence on the outcome that is proportionate to the power of the group.[4] Acceptance of the output appears, in this conceptualization, as a product of the assumption that the process through which the equilibrium is achieved allocates to each participant precisely that proportion of the social values that he can get in the light of the relative power position he holds in the system.

[3] W. Forrester, *op. cit.*, p. 8.
[4] See *The Political System*, chapter XI.

The viability of an equilibrium is explained through the fact that the participants are compelled to accept it. If they sought to upset the allocation based upon an equilibrium of forces, lacking the means to do so, their actions would prove ineffectual. If indeed they were able to get more favorable results, *ipso facto* we would have proof that the presumed equilibrium was not a genuine one; nature had not run its course.

The inherent Candide-like and circular nature of this reasoning is apparent. But however inadequate it may be as a method for analyzing political processes, it does point up the fact that outputs are in part accepted because in the struggle over them, the contenders may have no alternative.

Generalized Attachment to Political Objects

But more than equilibrium is involved in compelling acceptance of less than members may think they are in all equity entitled to in the way of outputs. Members may be willing to accept the validity of an outcome because of their prevailing attachment to the regime as such, that is, to the procedures and arrangements through which demands are negotiated and compromised. And the peculiar characteristic of this attachment is that it is not conditional upon specific returns at any moment. Unless the outputs run violently contrary to established expectations for considerable periods of time, the probability is that the members would prefer to accept them than to endanger the whole regime, or community for that matter.

This is not to say that a highly rational process is actually at work in the minds of members of a system. Positive and diffuse sentiments of this sort toward the political objects are probably instilled at an early stage in the maturation process of the individual.[5] But it does assert that in every system, part of the readiness to tolerate outputs that are perceived to run contrary to one's wants and demands, flows from a general or diffuse attachment to regime and community. It is a sentiment usually already present in the mature members of the system.

Political self-restraint is undoubtedly to some extent a function of the equilibrium attained through competing power groups.[6] It also

[5] For some discussion of these processes, see D. Easton and R. D. Hess, "Youth and the Political System"; "The Child's Political World" 6 *Midwest Journal of Political Science* (1962) 229–246; and "The Child's Changing Image of the President," 24 *Public Opinion Quarterly* (1960) 632–644.

[6] G. Mosca, *The Ruling Class* (New York: McGraw-Hill, 1939), ed. A. Livingston, chapter 5; C. J. Friedrich, *Constitutional Government and Democracy* (New York: Ginn, 1950), 2nd edition, chapter 7.

reflects the positive benefits associated with any specific set of outputs. But the acceptability of outputs that fall far short of what is sought cannot be fully accounted for unless we take into consideration the diffuse support or broad political good will that a system generates through various means over the years. It is the strong bonds of loyalty to the objects of a system as ends in themselves that also serve to regulate conflict attendant on cleavage and help to keep it within bounds consistent with the persistence of a system.[7]

Diffuse Support

This analysis enables us to identify diffuse or unconditional attachment as a second type of support. As we have seen, specific support flows from the favorable attitudes and predisposition stimulated by outputs that are perceived by members to meet their demands as they arise or in anticipation. The specific rewards help to compensate for any dissatisfactions at failing to have all demands met. But simultaneously, members are capable of directing *diffuse* support toward the objects of a system. This forms a reservoir of favorable attitudes or good will that helps members to accept or tolerate outputs to which they are opposed or the effect of which they see as damaging to their wants.

Except in the long run, diffuse support is independent of the effects of daily outputs. It consists of a reserve of support that enables a system to weather the many storms when outputs cannot be balanced off against inputs of demands. It is a kind of support that a system does not have to buy with more or less direct benefits for the obligations and responsibilities the member incurs. If we wish, the outputs here may be considered psychic or symbolic and in this sense, they may offer the individual immediate benefits strong enough to stimulate a supportive response. Members may get satisfaction, for example, from the promise of future greatness for their system and even some gratification from being made to feel an important part of a larger historic process that calls for present restraint on behalf of future benefits for the political system, an object with which they come to identify in and

[7] H. Guetzkow, in *Multiple Loyalties* (Princeton: Princeton University, Center for Research on World Political Institutions, 1955) shows that the underlying psychological mechanism is composed of three elements: (1) loyalty as a subconscious autonomous need; (2) the need for self-avoidance, that is, to lose oneself in an object of support; and (3) a conscious belief in a group or other object as an end in itself. See also S. N. Eisenstadt, *op. cit.*, who distinguishes ascriptive or unconditional support from achieved or free-floating support.

for itself. They may feel such contentment with their life situation that they generalize this feeling to include the political system itself in all its aspects.[8] It would be misleading, however, to equate these kinds of diffuse benefits with rewards deriving from outputs that satisfy specific demands here and now, as for a tariff, minimum wage, high economic growth rate, or publicly financed medical care.

At its highest level of input, although from the point of view of an ethic of rationality, not necessarily in its most admirable form, the reservoir of diffuse support might be fed by a feeling of blind loyalty to the authorities, regime or community. Such unquestioning loyalty reflects a kind of attachment for which specific benefits are not expected except for the psychic satisfactions of identification with or subordination to a higher cause or object. If we assume that most kinds of patriotism reflect some degree of deep attachment, such attitudes enable a system to violate the expectations of its members with considerable impunity. If excessive and noisy patriotism is a poor symbol of true support, at least the notion of la patrie, in its finest sense, identifies the presence of powerful ties to the political community for itself alone rather than for what the individual expects to derive from it, ties that only persistent failure in outputs would be likely to sever.

But regardless of the many names we have for the sentiments that define diffuse support, its one major characteristic is that since it is an attachment to a political object for its own sake, it constitutes a store of political good will. As such, it taps deep political sentiments and is not easily depleted through disappointment with outputs.

[8] ". . . a person may have a set of experiences in a society that, while not really relevant to the political order, nevertheless create for him a *general* sense of satisfaction that leads him to accept and endorse the political system of his society. This is a little like the 'halo effect' in judging persons; if a teacher likes a child's manners, she will see him as brighter and handsomer than she otherwise would. Thus if a person likes the opportunities for education and self-advancement in a society, he may tend to like everything about that society. It is, too, a little like the process of stimulus generalization; if a person, say, responds favorably to a monetary reward, and this is reinforced, he may respond favorably to other rewards that can be seen as having monetary value. Partly it is that the causes of social phenomena are so obscure that any institutions that are associated in one's mind with a satisfactory situation may be thought to have some causal relationship to that situation. In any event, the satisfactions the men of Eastport receive from certain aspects of career and family do seem, by some one or all of these processes, to generalize to the political and social order in which their careers come to fruition and their families have their existence." R. E. Lane, *Political Ideology*, pp. 91–92.

General Types of Responses to Stress

Recognition that support consists of two fundamentally different types clarifies important distinctions in the function of varying kinds of responses for the stimulation of support. We may now reinterpret structural changes, of the kind discussed in the last chapter, as manifestations of efforts to arouse a greater measure of specific satisfactions with a system. But even more importantly, it draws our attention to three broad classes of responses open to a system, and all systems can be expected to resort to them at one time or another and probably simultaneously in varying proportions. These responses are outputs, coercion, and the stimulation of good will.

Outputs

As we have seen, few political systems can be expected to offer sufficient *quid pro quo* for the input of support. Yet, if the danger signals go up and it is recognized that discontent with the regime or community is increasing, the first, easiest, and most direct response which may be taken to cope with the situation is to make some effort to improve the adequacy of the outputs. We can expect that direct satisfaction for demands will at least generate specific support; and the longer such satisfactions are felt, the more likely it is that a higher level of political good will can develop. If members continuously perceive that their demands are being met on a day-to-day basis, their loyalty to all objects can naturally be expected to increase.

As we have seen, a response of this sort is not always possible. Certainly under conditions of changing political systems, at most one can hold out the hope that the new system will be better than the old. But as in the case of modern colonial and social revolutions, the disorganization attendant on the change-over, the exhaustion of resources occasioned by the struggle for independence or social change, the instability of the new patterns of political rule, all contribute to the probability of a low ratio of outputs to related demands. Broader means must be found to mobilize support behind some set of rulers, the order within which they operate, and the community they have helped to draw together.

This applies equally to more stable, modern systems. Even though they may be able to rely somewhat more extensively on a continuous flow of satisfactory outputs to stimulate diffuse support over the long run, they too must look to other ways of mobilizing favorable sentiments behind the objects of the system. The stress of day-to-day conflict and cleavage or the possibility of a serious drain on the resources of the system forces this alternative upon it.

Coercion

Although it may not be customary to do so, we may view coercion as another possible kind of response to a decline in support. It represents a special response through outputs that may succeed in generating specific support. The effect of coercion is to offer specific negative rewards or unfavorable sanctions for failure to comply. Members may not be willing to offer their support voluntarily, but under the threat of force they may be led to engage in activities, the objective consequences of which reflect at least a low level of support.

To pay taxes, serve in the armed forces, and carry out other political tasks under coercion indicates some degree of objective support, however small. It certainly indicates more support than in the case of persons who refuse to engage in these actions and accept the sanctions imposed for failure to conform. To some extent all systems rely on coercion as a temporary or episodic adjunct to other means of sustaining the inflow of support. But it is doubtful whether a system could endure through force alone and no system has ever sought to do so.

Nevertheless, setting aside the vital moral issues involved, force as a response to stress may be an effective stop-gap at periods when the input of support is low and falling and it may help to prevent it from evaporating entirely. It at least may be expected to reduce the spread of negative support or opposition to the authorities. If through it the authorities have weathered a particular storm, they may thereby gain sufficient time to try a variety of other responses in the expectation of increasing the reserve of specific or diffuse support sufficiently to eliminate the need of coercion as an important ingredient in the regime. But because of the obvious diseconomies in the use of coercion for maintaining a minimal level of support for a system, authorities typically seek to displace it by voluntary and willing attachment based upon belief and conviction.

Good Will

Finally, a major means for meeting stress is to seek to accumulate a high level of political good will or diffuse support. Typically, we shall find that there are three major subtypes of responses through which such support may itself be nurtured. Support that is not directly linked to specific material rewards and satisfactions or coercion (negative rewards) may be generated through responses of the following types: first, those that seek to instill a deep sense of legitimacy in the members for the regime as a whole and for individuals who act on behalf of it; second, those that invoke symbols of the common interest; and third, those that promote and strengthen the degree to which members identify with the political community.

These are three interrelated but at least analytically separable, complex sets of responses the outcomes of which tend to strengthen the diffuse emotional attachment toward political objects. Alternatively, any drop in the level of this support reservoir will flow from parametric or internal conditions that wear away at the sense of a system's legitimacy, at acceptance of the idea of a common interest, or at the members' identification with the community. With these responses operating ineffectually, a system would be thrown back on outputs or coercion as a major means of bolstering support. Yet, as we have seen, outputs cannot help but provide a weak reed upon which a system might rest its full weight and coercion tends to impose excessive costs, social as well as financial.

Because in most systems, these three classes of means for nurturing diffuse support play so central and typical a part as responses to possible stress, I shall devote the following several chapters to their exploration. We shall then be in a position to return to outputs and analyze their role in holding support at a critical level.

18

Diffuse Support for Authorities and Regime:

The Belief in Legitimacy

THE INCULCATION OF A SENSE OF LEGITIMACY IS PROBABLY THE SINGLE most effective device for regulating the flow of diffuse support in favor both of the authorities and of the regime. A member may be willing to obey the authorities and conform to the requirements of the regime for many different reasons. But the most stable support will derive from the conviction on the part of the member that it is right and proper for him to accept and obey the authorities and to abide by the requirements of the regime. It reflects the fact that in some vague or explicit way he sees these objects as conforming to his own moral principles, his own sense of what is right and proper in the political sphere.

The strength of support implicit in this attitude derives from the fact that it is not contingent on specific inducements or rewards of any kind, except in the very long run. On a day-to-day basis, if there is a strong inner conviction of the moral validity of the authorities or regime, support may persist even in the face of repeated deprivations attributed to the outputs of the authorities or their failure to act.

The Need for Legitimacy

How extensive must the feelings of legitimacy be if they are to serve as a basis of support for the authorities and regime? Could a system survive without such sentiments?

If we recall the overwhelming attention paid to problems of political obligation in traditional political philosophy, we might be inclined to conclude that no system could endure, at least for very long, without the presence of some moderate belief in its legitimacy. The fact is that this would not be easy to demonstrate on theoretical or even empirical grounds; I shall shortly adduce evidence to indicate that if, as has been my custom, we broaden our sample of political systems to include those outside the Western world, we shall find at least two types for which this is not correct.

Nevertheless, it cannot and need not be denied that most political systems, especially those composed of large numbers of persons, have found it helpful and perhaps even necessary to create and strengthen such convictions with respect to authorities and regime. At least for those systems we might ask: why has there been this need or tendency to rely on a belief in legitimacy?

Answers have been offered frequently in the history of political thought, more usually perhaps from an ethical point of view, but on occasion in descriptive terms as well. But it is important for us to explore some of the reasons why the whole idea of legitimacy has played so central a part in reflections on political life even though in empirically-oriented perspectives, it has received surprisingly little attention.

If a system is to convert inputs into outputs, it must provide means for committing the resources of the system to the attainment of goals and to rallying the energies of the members for the associated tasks. In most systems, as the occasion demands it, the authorities rely to some extent on persuasion, appeals to self-interest or tradition, or on force to obtain acceptance of or acquiescence in their outputs and the structures through which they are produced. But in most systems, the effectiveness of outputs cannot be left either exclusively or largely to chance, the accident of coincidence of interest between system goals and individual goals, or the diseconomies and indeterminacy of force. Especially in the case of large-scale systems, it is important to stabilize the relationships between those who are responsible for the day-to-day activities in the name of the system, that is, the authorities, and the general membership. If the constant threat of living on a precipice of disorder is to be avoided, at the minimum the authorities require some assurance that within the limits set forth in the political system, limits that I have been calling the regime, they can expect regularly to obtain compliance with respect to the adoption and implementation of outputs and the performance of necessary tasks. The belief in the legitimacy of the authorities and regime provides such a stable connection.

Regardless of what the members may feel about the wisdom of the actions of authorities, obedience may flow from some rudimentary convictions about the appropriateness of the political order of things. One simply ought to obey the authorities and abide by the basic political rules; no alternative is conceivable since it is the right thing to do. They are legitimate.

It might be argued that this state of mind must flow from the conviction on the part of members that order and established procedures are better than chaos. They would prefer to obey an unwelcome law rather than to destroy the basis of all order. But it is highly doubtful that members of a system empirically entertain so rational an interpretation or motivation. Rather, they are imperceptibly socialized into a belief in the legitimacy of an order, at least in older systems, and the sentiment is continuously reinforced among mature members through means that we shall later mention. In newly developing systems, before a new generation can be socialized into ethically approved habits of compliance, self-interest and notable personalities as models may be additional decisive sources.

If there were no unquestioned propensity to accept or acquiesce in outputs, no authorities could ever commit themselves or the members of the system except through a process of continuing referenda or force. But with a belief in their legitimacy, the authorities can rest assured that if their activities fall within a definable range, they can obtain at least the acquiescence of other members and at best, their enthusiastic cooperation. Alternatively, if neither is forthcoming, the whole weight of the system can be brought to bear on recalcitrant members, as in the use of force or, in many systems, through less formal but nonetheless equally compelling sanctions.

But insofar as there is the belief, however inarticulate, that the authorities and the order within which they operate is right and proper, this implies a predisposition to accept the outputs regularly as authoritative or binding. Simultaneously, since it also indicates general acceptance or approval, it expresses diffuse support for the objects toward which the approval is directed. Regardless of how it may be stirred into existence and kept at an adequate level, it forms a belief in its own right that attaches a member to the objects of a system.[1]

---

[1] Cf.: "The political consensus that was evolved in these societies did not focus on the principal common symbols alone. The trend was toward differentiating the basic legitimation of the rulers (kings, etc.) from their concrete policies and the policies of the various government organs. This trend's manifestations were the distinctions made between the norms regulating basic loyalty to the ruler and the norms pertaining to attitudes about different concrete policies, and the shifting interrelations among various social groups and between them and the rulers.

"Although the first type of norms and values was usually very traditional and ascriptive, the other was far more flexible and given to change. Much of the political struggle was focused on the concrete definitions and derivations of the latter types." S. N. Eisenstadt, *op. cit.*, p. 305.

The Universality of a Belief in Legitimacy

To what extent do systems require a belief in legitimacy if they are to maintain an appropriate level of support? If we were to take into consideration only the experiences of the major political systems of the world and those that have passed beyond the kinship stage of social organization, we might be inclined to conclude that a belief in legitimacy is necessary for the maintenance of support, at least for political systems that persist for any appreciable length of time. This conviction among scholars has been so pervasive that it helps to account for the reason why authority has typically been described as a power relationship that exists only where there is a belief in the legitimacy of those who exercise the power.[2]

As we have already seen, it is possible to take a much broader interpretation of the basis upon which authority rests. Sentiments other than legitimacy may account for the willingness or readiness to obey others. If we now seriously take into account non-literate systems, we find that among them there is at least one type in which observers

[2] Cf.: "The rule is: those who wield power must establish their right to do so. This is not a pious wish, or a peculiarly democratic canon, but a general political necessity. Every ruling group that presumes to gather prerogatives for itself, or to inflict deprivations on others, must identify itself with a principle acceptable to the community as justification for the exercise of power. Such doctrinal tenets are known as principles of legitimacy. Their function is to establish authority as distinct from naked power. A rule is based on authority when most of those who are supposed to obey do so willingly and need not be coerced." P. Selznick, *The Organizational Weapon* (New York: McGraw-Hill, 1952), p. 242.

Weber recognizes the possibility of orders based on tradition or expediency rather than legitimacy but does little with the idea. It has usually been entirely ignored by others. Thus Weber argues that "in concrete cases, the orientation of action to an order involves a wide variety of motives. But the circumstance that along with the other sources of conformity the order is also held by at least part of the actors to define a model or to be binding, naturally increases the probability that action will in fact conform to it, often to a very considerable degree. An order which is adhered to from motives of pure expediency is generally much less stable than one upheld on a purely customary basis through the fact that the corresponding behavior has become habitual. The latter is much the most common type of subjective attitude. But even this type of order is in turn much less stable than an order which enjoys the prestige of being considered binding, or, as it may be expressed, of 'legitimacy.' The transitions between orientation to an order from motives of tradition or of expediency on the one hand to the case where on the other a belief in its legitimacy is involved, are naturally empirically gradual." T. Parsons (ed.), *Max Weber: The Theory of Social and Economic Organization* (New York: Oxford University Press, 1947), pp. 114–115.

of these societies have found that belief in the legitimacy of those who wield political power does not exist; or if it does, it is quite ineffectual in sustaining the power of the authorities. It turns out that the isolation of legitimacy as a necessary source of political power has been an artifact of the range of systems under scrutiny.

Furthermore, if we continue to extend our conceptualization to include the international system as a system analytically coordinate with all domestic systems and, therefore, a significant part of the sample of systems to which we can turn for an understanding of systems in general, we shall confirm what we are able to learn from some types of non-literate systems. It enables us to conclude that although legitimacy is a major source of diffuse support in most systems we know about, this is certainly not the case in all. In these two classes of exceptions, the absence of this belief need not constitute a danger or threat of stress for the system.

Legitimacy in Segmentary Lineage Systems

As I have been suggesting at various points in our discussion, it is quite possible to conceptualize authority relationships in such a way that we can see their presence even in the absence of a belief in the legitimacy of those who wield political power. The members may accept the authorities, not because they believe them to be right and proper but because it is necessary or expedient to do so. Persons in positions of political leadership and administration may be able to get others to carry out their intention simply because on grounds of custom, expediency, self-interest, or fear it pays the others to do so.

This is the very situation that prevails in segmentary lineage systems, those that anthropologists have inappropriately named stateless political systems.[3] At the level of the tribe or groups of clans, the political system so formed does not support a stable set of persons who rule in any formal sense. Rather, as disputes or matters of common concern arise among the clans, or as other occasions demand, gatherings are held among the elders for purposes of ironing out differences. Disputes may last for years; some may be settled at once. But in any case, whatever the consensus or dominant view, the implementation of the "decision"—an artificial term for what is often an extended series

[3] See A. W. Southall, *Alur Society* (Cambridge: Heffer, 1953), p. 241 ff.; M. Fortes and E. E. Evans-Pritchard, *African Political Systems* (New York: Oxford University Press, 1940), the Introduction, pp. 1–24, and especially the easily neglected Preface by A. R. Radcliffe-Brown; and for a general discussion and further bibliography, D. Easton, "Political Anthropology" in B. J. Siegel, *Biennial Review of Anthropology 1959*.

of adjustments among conflicting lineage segments—cannot rely upon any belief on the part of the members that the actions of the elders are morally binding on all the clans and their subunits. On the contrary, a settlement can be effective or authoritative, even though not legitimate, only if the participants consider it expedient and useful or traditional to abide by it.[4] It is not felt to be morally binding in and of itself or because it is right and proper to abide by the product of a particular process or of a special set of members.

As we might expect, the absence of strong feelings about the legitimacy of the authorities has important consequences for the degree to which diffuse support is available in such systems. In those systems in which the actions of the authorities are considered legitimate, a centralized, hierarchical organization of power is possible. The authorities are able to commit the system's resources, human and otherwise, to the pursuit of goals adopted in the name of system. There is a reservoir of diffuse support available to enable a set of authorities to persist, often for very extended periods of time, in the face of decisions and actions perceived as unpalatable to most or all members of the system.

In systems composed of segmentary lineages, where a major means of soliciting support for the ill-defined authority figures, the elders, depends upon each lineage or clan segment persuading itself of the wisdom of the course of action decided by the elders from a number of clans, support needs to be constantly renewed with each decision and its attendant actions. In the case of segmentary lineage systems, self-interest and expediency, without reinforcement by sentiments of legitimacy, often seem to be adequate for the task of obtaining compliance with the outputs of the informal authorities and of maintaining a system intact. We must remember, however, that the cleavages in such systems are typically muted by ideologies such as ancestral cults and by the close web of social relationships built around affinal ties among the lineages, cross-cutting age-sets in many tribes, and geographical prox-

---

[4] It is absolutely vital to distinguish between tradition as a basis for legitimacy and tradition as the direct reasons for accepting the actions of the authorities as binding. (1) In the case of tradition as the basis of legitimacy, the authorities are viewed as right and proper occupants of their roles. This flows from a prior belief that those who exercise authority according to the traditions of the system ought to be obeyed. (2) But where tradition is directly a basis for accepting the authorities as binding, there need be no belief that it is right and proper to do so or that it is morally compelling. It may be merely a matter of custom and this inertia makes it probable that the actions of the authorities will be accepted as binding on the members. Weber was probably seeking to explore this distinction in two little understood, apparently conflicting passages, the one quoted in footnote 3 of this chapter and one appearing in T. Parsons (ed.), *op. cit.*, pp. 126–127.

imity. Adjustments of differences under the pressure of expediency is not the only reason that keeps such political systems from falling apart.

It appears that although most systems of historical interest have hitherto turned to the encouragement of a deep and abiding belief in legitimacy as a major response to weld the members together behind some set of authorities, we are able to discover some types of systems in which this kind of mechanism plays a negligible, if any, role. Mobilization of support for a set of authorities or a regime must be sought in other areas, such as the rewards received in return for conformity with the decisions or the satisfaction engendered by the actions of the authorities in effectively meeting the wants of the members. Under some circumstances it is possible for support to be entirely specific, a return for rewards obtained, and the system will be able to persist. Stimulation of a belief in legitimacy is just one kind of response to potential stress but not the only or necessary one under all conditions.

Legitimacy in International Political Systems

We may think that segmentary lineage systems are unique with respect to their reliance on expediency or custom as the major bases for the acceptance of outputs as binding. It is true, as we have seen, to some extent all systems will depend upon a satisfactory relationship between outputs and the input of demands. But in international society, there is another large and politically significant class of systems in which such expediency provides the major basis for the acceptance of outputs as binding.

For this purpose, I shall view international society as including analytically and empirically isolable political systems, composed of all or some defined portion of those systems we call domestic systems. No student of international affairs needs to be persuaded of the extent to which decisions and actions performed by international systems rely for their acceptance upon accord with the perceived self-interest of the participating members. Not that international systems are entirely devoid of practices and even some structures, such as the League of Nations, the International Court, the United Nations, and various functional organizations that receive some of their support from at least an incipient sense of legitimacy. In some small degree at least, it is considered right and proper that decisions taken through the appropriate structures and procedures should be accepted as authoritative.

Needless to say, the impact of a sense of legitimacy is still extremely low. Furthermore, the proportion of actions taken through authoritative decisions is also extremely low. And even with regard to this small number, expediency and a sense of mutual benefits provide the solid ground upon which decisions may be accepted as binding. But what these illustrations from segmentary and international systems do demonstrate is the following. Under appropriate conditions, where any decisions at all are adopted as binding, support for the authorities, however few and undifferentiated they may be, need not be regulated by the inculcation of a sense of legitimacy.

The Relative Function of Legitimacy

One may take exception to this line of analysis and maintain that a set of relationships in which the presumed authorities have little power to command and obtain obedience, as we find in segmentary and international systems, and in which each output depends upon the cooperation of component subsystems such as clans, lineages or nations, ought not to be included as political systems. One may wish to define political systems in terms of the presence of a sense of legitimacy that provides a strong moral basis for the acceptance of procedures for processing demands into outputs.

The interpretation being presented here has a different point of departure.[5] Any set of relationships through which values are authoritatively allocated for a society, whether it is a so-called domestic society or an international society, is identified as a political system. Furthermore, we do not need to ask in advance what the grounds of compliance with the decisions of the authorities are. Whether the basis of acceptance is legitimacy, fear of force, habit, or expediency is irrelevant. In practice, as I have sought to show, we can expect every system to employ a combination of these and other measures as well, to improve the probability that outputs will be accepted as binding. The particular mixture will vary from system to system and time to time within any one system.

The nature of the mixture used to induce support for the authorities and regime will without question be highly significant in the eyes of the members of the system. But the fact that they are favored or abhorred, in itself does not detract from the existence of a political system. Nor ought we to allow it to conceal from us the grounds alternative to legitimacy on which support may be induced for a system, depending upon its type.

Having said this much about the possibility of some systems maintaining themselves without a high level of diffuse support, we must

[5] For a full elaboration, see *The Political System*, chapter V.

remind ourselves, however, that even in the international systems there have been repeated efforts over the centuries to create a support reserve firmly imbedded in a sense of legitimacy for some international authorities or regime. Major types of systems may have been able to persist without authorities strongly grounded in feelings of legitimacy among the members. But under most conditions, we might suspect, there is a pressure to stabilize political relationships through diffusion of sentiments of legitimacy. Aside from any other consideration, where acceptance of outputs as binding must depend upon force, the social costs are high; where they depend largely and continuously upon expediency, the unavoidable indeterminancy of the effectiveness of each output can be indefinitely tolerated only by systems in which the pace of life is slow, change is infrequent, and the functional interdependence weak.

The Objects and Types of Legitimacy

But where legitimacy is a central mechanism for infusing members with positive attitudes, to what objects will the members ascribe such legitimacy? Traditionally, the quality of legitimacy has been applied to the power of political authorities, such as an elite, an administrative staff, or the whole undifferentiated set of persons through whom authority in a system is exercised.[6] But once we seek to identify precisely the objects toward which sentiments of legitimacy may be directed in a system, we quickly discover that more than the authorities, as persons, are involved. Legitimacy is also a quality that is ascribed to the norms and structure of a regime.

This duality in objects which are described as legitimate is, of course, frequently implicit in any analysis of the ideas of legitimacy. But it is not usually built into a theoretical analysis of its functions in a system. I shall do so here by seeking to distinguish between two types of legitimacy in accordance with the objects toward which they are directed. We shall be able to classify legitimacy into the kind that supports a regime as against the kind that supports the specific occupants of authority roles.

But legitimacy may not only be classified according to the object to

---

[6] I am of course aware of the possibility and probability that different segments of the authorities may rely upon different bases for their own legitimation. S. N. Eisenstadt, *op. cit.*, p. 159, has also shown this to be the case. But this need not be built into our analysis; it would complicate the presentation and would add little to our fundamental understanding of the place of legitimacy in diffuse support.

which it adheres. If we are to appreciate how it serves as a response mechanism to stress on one or the other of these objects, we shall also find it important to know the origins of this sentiment. Support mobilized on behalf of the authorities and regimes may derive from several different sources: from underlying ideological principles, from attachment to the structure and norms of the regime as such, or from devotion to the actual authorities themselves because of their personal qualities.

These will constitute three variable sources of legitimacy—ideological, structural, or personal—which may characterize support to any of the two objects, as indicated in Table 3. Examination of these three types of legitimacy in relation to the two objects will illuminate the ways in which they help to determine differential types of response mechanisms that a system may adopt to avoid being endangered by stress. Support may be bolstered by encouraging feelings of ideological, structural or personal legitimacy, depending on whether the object is the regime or the authorities.

TABLE 3   TYPES OF LEGITIMACY

| Sources of Legitimacy | Objects of Legitimacy | |
	Regime	Authorities
	Ideological Legitimacy	
Ideology	Moral convictions about validity of regime	Moral convictions about validity of incumbents of authority roles
	Structural Legitimacy	
Structure	Independent belief in validity of the structure and norms	Overflow from belief in structure to the incumbents of the authority roles
	Personal Legitimacy	
Personal Qualities	Overflow from belief in the validity of the incumbents of authority roles to the authority roles (structure and norms of regime) themselves	Independent belief in validity of authorities because of their personal qualities

For most systems, it is clear that if they are threatened with stress due to a decline in sentiments of legitimacy, any efforts to understand the nature of the responses will have to take two things into consideration: the objects with respect to which legitimacy is declining and the kind of legitimacy that is on the wane.

For the objects, loss of support may mean that the members are losing confidence in the authorities but not in the regime; or in the regime alone and yet with the hope that they can maintain the authorities relatively intact. An event such as this takes place when the leaders come to power under one regime and seek to change it while they continue to hold power, as in the case of De Gaulle in May, 1958. It may also mean that the members have turned away from both the authorities and the regime, as in the case of most social revolutions. To understand the nature of the responses in a system for bolstering feelings of legitimacy as a broad base of support, it clearly matters very much which of these combinations is occurring.

The identification of three different sources of legitimacy also bears certain transparent implications for the stimulation of diffuse support. Under the usual conception of legitimacy as a belief in the right of authorities to rule and members to obey, within the limits of the legitimating principles, the major stimulus for the input of diffuse support would arise from efforts to reinforce such ideological convictions among the membership. But recognition of the other sources from which such beliefs may spring adds to the repertoire of responses available to any system. To appreciate the consequences of this typology of legitimacy, I shall examine each kind as a possible way of encouraging the input of diffuse support.

19

Sources of Legitimacy

HOW DOES A SYSTEM MANAGE TO BUILD UP A RESERVOIR OF FREELY available support? I shall argue in this chapter that the sources that feed and fortify sentiments of legitimacy can also be interpreted as devices through which the members of a system may seek to arouse or maintain a minimal level of support. Those very conditions that give rise to feelings of legitimacy or sustain them can be used by a system to prevent the level from dropping to a critical point.

Ideological Sources of Legitimacy

As I have described the regime in Chapter 12, it embodies three distinct aspects: the roles through which power in a system is organized and distributed; the stable expectations about or the norms for the use of this power; and the values and principles that form the broad limits of outputs and infuse all areas of political interaction. The identification of a regime already presupposes the existence of ideologies or belief systems in all political systems.

In analyzing the ideological aspect previously, we were not concerned with its possible impact on sentiments of legitimacy; in fact, this idea was deliberately excluded since it was not relevant to the definition of a regime. Here, however, it is appropriate to draw attention to the part that the values and principles play with regard to legitimacy. Not only do they serve as a body of constraints within the limits of which the authorities are expected to act, as we have seen. They also provide a context within which the authorities as well as the political structure and related norms may themselves be tested for their legitimacy.

Components of Regime Values

To appreciate the function that the regime goals and principles play as legitimating responses, we must recognize that they consist of two politically significant parts. In the first place, however varied or consensual they are, included within the regime goals and principles are what we may call the *operating values* of the system.[1] They refer to those political ends, purposes, and preferences of all the members of the system, including of course the leadership as well, as related to the system as a whole. But since they are operating values, they would consist of those goals and principles that can be inferred from behavior. They are implicit in the actions of the members of the system. The kind of political structure and norms actually introduced, the kinds of policies pursued, would enable us to infer the nature of the implicit values at least. In some cases, these values may be quite explicit since the accord between declared intention or desire and political practice may be very close or identical. But articulation of the values is not necessary to discover the operating ideals. The presence of such values is assumed in the frequently expressed opinion that most systems seldom live up to their expressed ideals.

But in the second place, besides the operating values, we also find articulated sets of ideals, ends, and purposes, which help the members of the system to interpret the past, explain the present, and offer a vision for the future. Thereby they describe the aims for which some members feel political power ought to be used and its limits. They may be deceptive myths about political life; they may be realistic appraisals and sincere aspirations. But they have the potential, because they are articulated as a set of ethically infused ideals, to capture the imagination. From a manipulative or instrumental point of view they may be interpreted as categories of thought to corral the energies of men; from an expressive point of view we may see them as ideals capable of rousing and inspiring men to action thought to be related to their achievement. Values of this kind, consisting of articulated ethical interpretations and principles that set forth the purposes, organization, and boundaries of political life, I shall describe by their usual name, *ideologies*.

Ideologies, therefore, are part of the principles and goals that I have already identified as a component of the regime. But they are only the articulated or verbalized part of these goals and values. We may find that, at the implicit level, the members are accepting and pursuing objectives at odds with the expressed ideology, and that the political structure strays far from prescriptions consistent with the ideology. The exact relationship between the operating values and the sought-

---

[1] See chapter 12, footnote 4.

after but only articulated goals and principles of ideology is always an empirical question.

Types of Ideologies

Not all those belief systems that are designated as ideologies need contribute to the growth or maintenance of legitimacy. Some ideological positions may be relevant only to the competition among political leaders for positions of authority in a regime, the legitimacy of which is not in doubt. Ideological conflict of this sort occurs over foreign policy in the United States, as reflected in so-called soft or hard foreign policy postures, or in the degree of economic intervention in the economy, embodied in general beliefs about free enterprise or social welfare.

Contending beliefs such as these contribute to the divisive forces in a system and thereby may indirectly affect the confidence the members may have in their authorities and regime. But they need not directly challenge or support the legitimacy of the existing political order. It may be taken for granted by all disputants. Such sets of beliefs we may call *partisan ideologies;* they serve to mobilize support for alternative contenders for political leadership or office. Only indirectly do they leave an impact on the legitimacy of the regime. Those sets of beliefs that go to the heart of the regime itself we may call *legitimating ideologies.*

In most systems we may expect that competition among partisan ideologies will appear. We might even suspect that careful inquiry would show that these kinds of more or less well-defined "policy" differences, relatively stable alternative ways of looking at political issues, turn up even in small non-literate systems. Categories of belief and conviction are too inescapable and useful a tool in power relationships to be neglected by men anywhere. Certainly enduring factions in dictatorial or totalitarian systems represent at least embryonic partisan ideological positions. But even though these are probably not avoidable, in the case of legitimating ideologies there is no need to assume that we will find competition among them in all or most systems. There is indeed a tendency in most systems, even those in which tolerance and freedom of speech themselves are prized, to discourage and, in many instances, to bar at least those ideologies that would challenge the existing regime and its principles.

The Objects of Legitimating Ideologies

The Authorities

As I indicated earlier, the acceptance of the actions of the authorities and of one's role in a system may depend on any number of factors. But most frequently, and especially in those systems displaying a high degree of stability, the power of the authorities and of the regime both depend upon continuing validation through some set of values, a legitimating ideology. We may describe these as ethical principles that justify the way power is organized, used, and limited and that define the broad responsibilities expected of the participants in the particular political relationships.

In traditional political theory, with its hortatory and prescriptive overtones, they have been called the proper principles of obligation. In descriptive terms, we may identify them as the felt bases or grounds of obligation, the standards by which basic political arrangements and practices are tested and validated. Belief in the rightness of these values or principles and in the compatibility of a regime and its authorities with them, constitutes a major source of motivation for support of these objects.

Thus, with respect to the authorities, political stability is related to the feeling on the part of the members of the system that they, the authorities, have the moral right to rule. It accounts for the phenomonon in political systems—almost but not quite universal—that information if sent by certain individuals and according to expected procedures carries with it a quality of "oughtness," a moral imperative. Power is thereby asserted or, if it exists on other grounds as well, it is thereby clothed in the principle of legitimacy. It indicates an ethical predisposition to accept the actions of the authorities within recognized or determinable limits.

It is important to stress a point that I made earlier. The authority relationship, as defined, forms a sub-type of power, a kind that may quite conceivably be effective even though it is not based upon accepted right. The authorities consist of those persons who have the capacity to order others. This is all that is involved. Empirically, there is a high degree of probability that their commands or directions will be accepted by others as the basis of their behavior. Once such a relationship has been identified, the question as to why such authority is accepted as binding raises a second and different question. Members may comply for many different reasons.[2] A belief in legitimacy is one and only one among numerous motives for compliance. Because it flows from ethical conviction or a feeling of obligation, it necessarily reflects a high level of positive affect moving from the members of the system to the authorities.

The Regime

In thus drawing attention to the part that ideology plays in legitimating the authorities, there is little with which to cavil. This is a familiar point that can virtually be taken for granted. But this is not equally the case for understanding the impact of ideology on the structural and normative aspects of a regime. Typically, we have become so accustomed to referring to legitimacy in relationship to the authorities that we are apt to forget an equally vital consideration. One of the most stable sources of support for a regime originates in sentiments of legitimacy that may be directed toward it.

The structure of a regime and its norms may themselves quite independently be validated as right and proper by the same ideological principles that apply to the authorities. Elliptically, we usually speak of the divine right of kings, hereditary rule, consent through popular participation, government by tradition or by the wise, and other principles, as bases of obligation to authorities. But what this glosses over or neglects entirely is the likelihood that the very patterns in which the authorities are organized—the structure and norms governing the use of their power—will themselves also acquire validity from these same ideological principles. The stability of attachment felt by the members for these aspects of the regime will in significant part be a function of the degree of legitimacy they associate, through their values, with the regime itself, over and above any similar sentiments they may be led to develop with respect to the authorities directly.

The Mobilizing Potential of Ideologies

Ideologies as Responses

The capacity of legitimating ideologies to mobilize diffuse support will vary with two factors: their perceived relationship to performance and their appeal on broader psychological grounds. About perform-

---

[2] See earlier discussion in chapter 12 and my classification of power and authority in "The Perception of Authority and Political Change" previously cited.

ance, little needs to be said. Insofar as members perceive that the promises and goals explicitly stated or implicitly roused by an ideology, have been met, the resultant gratifications would be sufficient to assure the continued input of support. For this purpose we must assume, of course, that the members already desire to achieve the goals embodied in the belief structure. Once that condition prevails, the critical consideration becomes a matter of whether the outputs of the system are perceived to be consistent and harmonious with the expectations roused by the ideological promises and commitments.

It is quite conceivable that the perceptions and the reality diverge radically; but we shall return to the special problems that this creates when we consider outputs in detail. For present purposes it is enough to note that if the members of a system considered that their ideologically inspired expectations were being fulfilled, this would help to bind these members to the various political objects.

But the assumption we have made is not always operative. Indeed, it may beg the very question. Members may not be drawn to an ideology initially. Even before we are called upon to decide whether performances match the ideals, if an ideology is to serve as a stimulus for support its content must first be such as to appeal to the members of the system.

Among other things, an ideology purveys an image of the purposes, organization, and operation of a system in terms of which obedience to the authorities and acceptance of the regime may be considered right and proper and, therefore, morally binding. In general, the extent to which an ideology offers a means for promoting diffuse support will depend upon its success in capturing the imagination of most of the members in the system and in thereby fostering in them sentiments of legitimacy toward the authorities and regime. It is clear that ideologies will vary in their effectiveness. They represent means that can be controlled or manipulated to achieve given ends. We may, therefore, interpret them as variable responses through which efforts are made to bring the members of a system to the point of subscribing to the legitimacy of authorities and regime or sustaining that belief once it does exist.

But what conditions dictate their success or failure as a response for bolstering up support? However complex and varied these conditions may be, one thing is certainly clear. It is not likely that every belief structure has equal probability of becoming an acceptable interpretation and justification for a regime and its authorities. Some belief systems are never able to take root. Others may once have been able to infuse a system with the breath of legitimacy but have become shop-worn or have fallen into complete desuetude and disrepute. Beliefs woven around the ideas of social contract, divine right, dominium, hereditary right, virtual representation, and aristocratic responsibility are able to command little support today.

Two major factors account for the consequences of all ideologies in summoning up support. The appeal of an ideology flows, in part, from its expressive dimensions, that is, its capacity to enable its adherents to express their needs and wants. In part, it also derives from its effectiveness as an instrument of control in the hands of a leadership, that is, from the capacity of its component ideas to move men into action. Separately or in combination these two aspects of an ideology, the expressive and instrumental, determine the proba-bility of its reception.

Expressive Aspects

Expressively, the emotional roots of the appeal found in a vision of life, society and politics lie in the capacity of the belief system to establish a firm link with the motivational structure of the members in the system: to their conception and feelings about their own needs, interests and place in the political and social system or to their convic-tion that the ideology correctly or truthfully explains the real world. It may arouse in them a sense of purpose in the face of material and psychological conditions that might otherwise lead to feelings of futil-ity and utter frustration. It may provide a simple and plausible inter-pretation for a world that is otherwise complex, recalcitrant and unin-telligible, thereby appealing to a desire to know the truth about the world or to a need for a feeling of mastery over nature. It may allay anxieties and concerns roused by the apparently unpredictable turns of a rapidly changing culture and society.

Undoubtedly, the likelihood that an expressive component in an ideology will win the support of a membership will be enhanced if it can and does appeal to a prior set of predispositions such as these. But as we can see in the case of developing nations today, an ideology need not build only upon existing or past sentiments: it may be helpful in offering a new sense of direction to change that is already under way.[3] To enable a political system to cope with broad changes in its parame-ters, an ideology may constitute a response of a kind that seeks to lead the members of the system to discover new types of perceived values

[3] See P. E. Sigmund, Jr. (ed.), *The Ideologies of the Developing Nations* (New York: Praeger, 1963).

and needs so that they may be more receptive to new political goals and directions. The effectiveness of an ideology in building up a belief in the legitimacy of a new leadership may depend upon the capacity of the new sets of beliefs to identify and interpret new experiences, to give coherence and meaning to them. It may thereby be helpful in adding shape and purpose to new or modified motivations rather than in merely conforming woodenly to existing ones.

In either case, whether it gives expression to desires that already exist or whether it raises new or revised wants out of the old, by virtue of the fact that it enables members to tie their hopes and aspirations to articulated goals of some sort, it frees the energies of the members for support of a regime and its associated authorities. This need not mean that the support flows toward an existing set of political objects, of course, since the ideology may be drawing the members toward an entirely new regime and set of authorities.[4]

Instrumental Aspects

If we confined our analysis to the linkages between ideology on the one side and sentiments, attitudes and perceptions of the members of a system on the other, it would not be possible to account wholly for the effect of ideology as a response in marshaling the diffuse support provided through convictions about legitimacy. The advancement and promotion of ideological positions, especially under conditions of competition among them, is also a function of the skill of the elite, in whose hands the initiative lies, in utilizing the beliefs. The instrumental or manipulative potential of an ideology, therefore, will also help to determine its consequences for eliciting support.

The organizational ability of a leadership, its internal cohesion and compatibility as a group, its sensitivity to its following, and the competition from alternative ideologies are all relevant for the success or failure in the propagation of an ideology. But out of the whole range of ideas available to a leadership for winning and maintaining the support of a following, those must be selected which can be so formulated as to appeal to the members in a system.

This is the other side to the expressive aspect of a set of beliefs. From the point of view of the membership, an ideology reflects their

---

[4] For more general discussions of ideology, in addition to the standard works on the sociology of knowledge, see R. E. Lane, *Political Ideology* (New York: The Free Press of Glencoe, 1962); D. C. McClelland, *The Achieving Society* (New York: Van Nostrand, 1961); and D. Bell, *The End of Ideology* (Glencoe, Illinois: Free Press, 1960).

hopes and aspirations; but the same ideas from the perspectives of the leadership, present a means for harnessing the energies of the members for particular goals as defined by the leadership. They represent instruments of control rather than vehicles for self-expression.

If, for every system at a given time and place, the members could appropriate one and only one set of beliefs, there would be no special problem in understanding the manipulative or instrumental aspect of an ideology. The leadership would have no choice. But however prepared a membership may be psychologically for the reception of a new ideology as the result of its disillusionment with existing ones, it is entirely unlikely that one and only one set of beliefs might be adopted. It is more probable that a membership will be open to the persuasion of a number of alternative ideological positions. The potential of such belief systems for winning the support of a membership will vary with the nature and appeal of the ideological categories. The decisive factor will be the skill of a leadership in inventing and interpreting a set of values for the politically relevant membership and defining its relationship to their presumed needs and motivations.

We can thus see that the consequences of an ideology for building up diffuse support in the form of a belief in the legitimacy of a regime can be traced to two factors. How we distinguish them depends upon the stance we take. From the position of the membership itself, the effectiveness of an ideology flows from the fact that it offers them fulfillment for their hopes and aspirations as human beings. From the point of view of the leadership among the authorities, the ideology provides it with categories of thought for manipulating the support of the members in a direction interpreted by the leaders themselves as appropriate.[5]

[5] Although I have been speaking as though in any system there is one and only one articulated ideological position that serves to nourish diffuse support, the number and variety of interpretations may be considerable. We have already seen this to be so with regard to regime norms and values in general and we may therefore anticipate that it is equally true for that part of the regime values I am designating as ideology. Thus in the United States there is wide variety in the interpretations of the principles and values underlying the regime. Certainly this is true at the scholarly level where no two persons are able to agree on the nature of American democratic values and wide discrepancies exist even in the interpretation of the principles underlying the Constitution.

If we carry this to the popular level, there is little reason to believe that members of the system perceive the ideals, procedures and norms of the regime even in broadly similar terms. We may find modest convergence of views on some broad norms, such as popular participation, and on some vague notions about the political structure. But it is certainly open to serious question as to whether, in the membership as a whole, such structural concepts as Congress, the office of the President, or the bureaucracy convey images that can be described as identical or necessarily

Structural Sources of Legitimacy

In part, the principles that motivate members of a system to accept their authorities as legitimate can also be expected to contribute to the validation of the structure and norms of the regime, as I have already suggested. But regardless of how a belief in the legitimacy of the regime arises, once it has become an established fact, it will produce independent effects as it concerns the acceptability of the authorities.

If the members are convinced of the legitimacy of the regime, those authorities who come to power through that regime would thereby find that this legitimacy has clearly rubbed off on them. The degree of legitimacy attaching to the authorities will vary with the extent to which they are perceived to occupy valid roles in the political structure, to have been selected in accordance with the norms of the regime, and to wield their power in the manner prescribed by these norms and

very similar. It is a moot question as to whether the political objects about which we customarily presume consensus in the United States are even perceived, let alone interpreted, in similar terms. Proof of ideological consensus is still an expectation, hardly a fact.

If this is so, when we view legitimating ideologies as a source of diffuse support for a regime, we do not need to imply that a system must rely only on one belief structure for the same membership, to perform this function at a given moment. It is not a matter of exploring *the* belief structure of the members, but the varied sets of beliefs. This is entirely aside from any substantial conflicts in ideologies about the general nature of the regime and authorities. Here it is solely a question of a relatively stable system in which there is a continuing effort to maintain diffuse support through typical ideological means. Even under such conditions, I am suggesting, there is probably a greater range and variety of ideological positions, that can serve as responses, than we might have expected from the emphasis usually given to the need for consensus as a condition of survival for a system.

If we adopt the theoretical orientation that variety in ideological perspectives, probably within some determinate but unspecified range of variation, is not inimical to the persistence of a regime and, indeed, that different perceptions of the nature of the same regime need not be destructive of its support, it does pose some important questions. From the point of view of the persistence of a regime, we would need to know what degree of inconsistency or dissensus is permissible among alternative legitimating ideologies. We might also wish to inquire into the range of variation in the interpretation of an ideology by a membership of a system that sees itself as subscribing to one and the same set of legitimating beliefs. It is said that individuals differ about the degree to which they can tolerate ambiguity; it is entirely likely that under the varying conditions of stability, crisis, or change, the members in a political system will manage to tolerate different measures of ambiguity about their perceptions of the nature of their regime and the ideological positions they adopt in support of it.

by the regime goals. If they are seen to meet these requirements, if, as we would say for a legal system, for example, they were selected for offices authorized by law and by means of legally accepted procedures, this would be enough to confirm the legitimacy of their authority.

Legitimacy is acquired in this way, however, not only in bureaucratic legal systems but in all political systems, even non-literate, structurally relatively undifferentiated ones. Every system has roles through which authority is wielded and some rules governing the use and exercise of this political power. The fact of occupying these roles and of abiding by the rules applying to them will normally in and of itself place the seal of moral approval upon the authorities.[6] We may therefore call this basis of validation, *structural legitimacy*. The validity of the authority stems from the acceptance of the legitimacy of the role a member holds in the structure of authority and his conformity with the norms defining rights and obligations of that position.

The Independent Effect of Structure

Some evidence of the effectiveness of the institutionalized structures and practices as independent validating factors can be seen in systems that are undergoing great and sudden political changes, as in the case of revolutions. In those instances where the revolution has been carried to the point where dual power exists for some period of time, before the outcome of the conflict has been assured, it is not at all to be taken for granted that the authorities will be obeyed. They may have to "prove" their authority, that is, that they ought to be obeyed. To do so, they may appeal to the fact that they represent constituted authority and thereby seek to bring into play the independent validating power of the traditional structure and norms; or they may assert that, regardless of whether they conform to established structural arrangements and practices, they represent a new order of things which, in accordance with new ideological principles, is right in itself. Here the legitimating capability of the ongoing structures and norms are pitted against new principles that have not yet been incorporated into a new regime.

It is true, the old regime acquires its legitimating capacity from the fact that it reflects and is associated with the principles of the old

[6] I am assuming that there is no general conflict over the validity of the authority roles and related norms. I am also taking it for granted that legitimacy in the given system is an effective means for generating support for the authorities. As we know, there are some exceptions to the first assumption and, as we have seen, there are at least two general classes of systems in which legitimacy need not be a significant source of support for the rulers.

order. But I am suggesting that if the pre-existing order has been more than an ephemeral event, there is a strong tendency for the members to develop attachments to the structure and norms of the regime itself, quite independently of the underlying moral principles to which they also subscribe. Of course, these legitimating principles operate in the same direction; but the point here is that they are not alone.

For example, a particular structural arrangement and its norms may in time become invested with a special sanctity. In the United States there are particularly deep feelings against tampering with the Constitution in any important structural or normative sense. Indeed, quite irreverently it is often described as a sacred and consequently virtually untouchable cow. The prevalence in the United States of a strong belief in "constitutionalism" reflects this separable consequence of regime structure and norms.

In contrast with this, it has proved much easier in other systems, such as France, to undertake basic readjustments in the structure of authority. The independent legitimating impact of this part of the regime is apparently much more potent in the United States than in some other systems. The corollary is that to establish an act or policy as a direct consequence of the constitutional arrangements is a much more persuasive argument in its favor in the United States, than, say, in France.

Unless we recognize this independent effect we would find it difficult to explain adequately the simple fact that two systems, in which the underlying *principles* of legitimacy are quite similar, may have substantially different rules to determine whether the authorities are holding and wielding their power legitimately. In a democratic system such as the United States, the occupants of political office lose their aura of legitimacy if it can be shown that they have come to power in violation of the Constitution or the laws derivative from it. But in other democratic systems, such as Great Britain, the legitimacy of their authorities are not in the least determined by the rules that prevail in the United States. Validity of authority there depends upon conformity with other kinds of regime norms.

Yet, underlying both systems are certain very similar ethical principles about popular participation, limits on the use of power, and the rights and duties of citizens and authorities. These principles lend the color of legitimacy to their quite different ways of organizing political life. It is possible to make the apparently inconsistent statement that the principles of legitimacy in these two systems are the same and yet different. But this presents much less of a paradox than we might at first think. They are the same, or very similar, in fundamental underlying moral principles, validating different kinds of regimes; they are different in the kind of regime norms and structures to which the authorities must conform if they in turn are to be considered legitimate.

The Stimulation of Structural Legitimacy

Regardless of the varied motives for believing in the legitimacy of a regime, the fact of such a belief in itself constitutes grounds upon which day-to-day authorities may be considered legitimate. This is what is meant by the statement that structural legitimacy has independent effect. Under those conditions in which the existing structure and norms are accepted over time, they will be effective to some important degree in contributing to the legitimacy of persons who operate within them.

Hence, any measures taken to invest the authorities with greater validity because of their conformity with the regime will serve to increase the input of diffuse support on their behalf. The ritual surrounding the accession to offices of authority, the emphasis on constitutionalism in some systems, the repeated urgings to conform to law and traditions, the symbols of authority in their various forms are empirically well-known mechanisms through which a system will strive to build up the validity of those who occupy positions in the structure of the regime. Where the regime itself is not a subject of conflict or is not in doubt, the whole weight of the culture and the processes of political socialization serve to reinforce the conviction that only those authorities who occupy their roles according to the recognized rules, laws or conventions merit the support of the members. The attachment will be expected to flow to such members in authority because of their conformity with the requirements of the regime.[7]

[7] Structural legitimacy as a type of legitimacy immediately brings to mind the much used and much abused classification by Max Weber. However instructive Weber's ideas may be for pointing up the various dimensions of a belief in legitimacy, they nevertheless have several shortcomings that seriously limit their potential for the study of political life.

(1) It is difficult, if not impossible, to fit comfortably into Weber's scheme, such age old principles of obligation as consent, divine right, social contract, the right of the wise, or the rights of a religious elite. These seem to be largely ignored by Weber and yet they have served as central validating principles in the history of Western political thought. They would fall under my category of ideological legitimating sources.

(2) Weber does not clearly identify the two objects to which legitimacy applies—

The Personal Basis of Legitimacy

Whether or not the authorities in a system will be considered right and proper may depend not on their conformity to an accepted regime but upon the extent to which the members see the occupants of authority roles as personally, in their behavior and symbolism, worthy of

the authorities and the regime. His bases of legitimacy are oriented largely to the authorities and the inadequacy of this limitation should now be apparent.

(3) One of his bases, the legal-rational, is a very mixed category. Although it has been of enormous value in helping us to understand the nature of bureaucracy, it is of dubious value for a fundamental analysis of legitimacy. The legal-rational concept is interesting, however, because even though it is far too narrow for understanding the very source of legitimacy that Weber may have been struggling to uncover, it does skirt a broader conception of legitimacy.

Weber describes the legal-rational basis of legitimacy as a "belief in the 'legality' of patterns of normative rules and commands." (T. Parsons (ed.), *op. cit.,* p. 328.) As we can see from this definition, two separable objects of legitimacy are included: first, the norms as part of the regime ("the 'legality' of patterns of normative rules") as well as the occupants of authority roles ("those elevated to authority"). What we find intermingled here are, in my terms, ideological and structural types of sources of legitimacy. But because they are so undifferentiated conceptually, the potency of legal-rational as a category of analysis is seriously impaired. It provides us only with a single instance of what is in reality a much broader class, that of ideological legitimacy.

Thus if we look at what is included in Weber's definition of the legal-rational basis of legitimacy, we can see that the "belief in legality" is an ideological component, equivalent in theoretical status, perhaps, to such other components as a belief in traditionalism, social contract, rule by consent of the governed or by divine right. But Weber does not go quite so far.

But the second part of this description, the "right of those elevated to authority under such rules to issue commands" may mean one of two things. It may be proposing that the authorities are also legitimated by the same ideological premises; and it just barely hints that a belief in the validity of the "patterns of normative rules" in itself is enough to legitimate the authorities, regardless for the moment of why these normative rules may be accepted.

In this sense, Weber just manages to touch on structural legitimacy as a source of support. If he had extricated this conception for separate analysis, it would have enabled him to pay more systematic attention to the many ideological principles alternative to the two he does identify: the traditional and the legal-rational. At the same time it would have enabled him to recognize and elevate attachment to regime norms and structures as a separate analytic element. It would have revealed to us the considerably greater complexities involved in an analysis of the sources and objects of legitimacy than Weber's relatively simple threefold classification permits. The fact that Weber's categories have been widely adopted by students of developing political systems should not be allowed to obscure from us the very ambiguities that would be revealed by a careful analysis of the uses to which Weber's categories have been put.

moral approval. To explore the varied psychological processes involved in this kind of relationship between the authorities and members of a system would require a different level of analysis. But whether they are displacement, identification, substitution, rational choice, the effects of charisma and personal magnetism, demagoguery or genuine appeal, the resultant belief among members of the system that it is right and proper to accept the position and actions of the authorities as binding, will be the basis upon which support rests.

In a relationship of this kind, where the behavior and personalities of the occupants of authority roles are of dominating importance, it is possible for the authorities to violate the norms and prescribed procedures of the regime and to ignore its regular structural arrangements. They may break away from existing roles and create new ones for the occasion, as happens constantly where regimes change. Yet, if the members see the new authorities as personally trustworthy, concerned, or called to lead, in Weberian terms, the legitimacy of the authorities is not to be denied. Hence, we may designate this as *personal legitimacy*. As a source of support it will flow from the estimate of the personal merit and worth of the authorities rather than only from the validity of their position in the system or their compatibility with the ideological premises of the members.

Personal Legitimacy and Charisma

The implications of this category of analysis are of considerable significance for the kind of responses it enables us to identify as available to a system for building up diffuse support. To begin with, personal legitimacy refers to much more than is included in Max Weber's conception of charisma, one of the basic grounds on which, for him, a belief in legitimacy is established or reinforced. As he described it, charisma meant a very narrowly delimited relationship between leader and followers, one in which the leader feels a genuine sense of calling and in which the followers submit because of their convictions about the exemplary character of the leader. Charisma, Weber wrote, rests "on devotion to the specific and exceptional sanctity, heroism or exemplary character of an individual person, and of the normative patterns or order revealed or ordained by him." [8]

But these qualities in leaders and followers represent only one kind of charisma, frequently found, to be sure, in those instances in which leaders are able to command large followings for considerable periods

[8] T. Parsons (ed.), *op. cit.*, p. 328.

of time. Yet we know that many powerful leaders display what might be called a spurious charisma.[9] They are able to manipulate large numbers of followers precisely because they can appear to be what in fact they are not. Lacking a genuine sense of calling and dedication to a cause, they scarcely fall into Weber's type; or if one considers his ideal type to be, not a class of concrete objects but only a trait found in many different empirical objects, they do not even share charisma as a quality. If we were to insist upon using Weber's conception of charisma to identify what it is, in leaders of this manipulative kind, that gives them their legitimating potency, we could not avoid vulgarizing and denaturing it.

This has very frequently been the case in recent research, to be sure, and it may well be too late to insist upon a purist usage of the concept. But if we do wish to continue to reserve the concept for the specific purposes for which Weber invented it, we cannot conceive of the effect of leadership as always being purely charismatic in character. There is a large class of leaders who, regardless of any inner conviction of being called or outer recognition as such by followers, manage to build up a belief in their legitimacy. Even where fraudulent, leaders are able to win the allegiance of large aggregates through the emotional, magnetic appeal of their fabricated public image. But genuine or spurious, it does represent a personal element underlying the creation of sentiments of legitimacy. All political leadership, and not the charismatic type alone, if it is effective in winning support at all, carries with it this legitimating potential; hence the concept personal legitimacy covers a broader range of leadership phenomena than charisma, in Weber's original sense, and includes the latter.

The Transferability of Sentiments of Legitimacy: Changing Systems

Another consequence of personal legitimacy flows from the fact that, regardless of the genuineness of its charisma, it helps in the transfer of legitimating sentiments from one regime and its authorities to another and to the stabilization of attachments once the transfer has taken place.[10] The experience of mass societies confirms that at least large

[9] J. F. Wolpert, "Towards a Sociology of Authority" in A. W. Gouldner (ed.), *Studies in Leadership* (New York: Harper, 1950), pp. 679–701.

[10] This assumes the transferability of sentiments from persons to norms, structures and goals. Most research on developing systems at least implicitly adopts this assumption. See, for an illustration, D. Apter, *The Gold Coast in Transition* (Princeton, New Jersey: Princeton University, 1955).

aggregates of members do not usually respond to ideas and ideologies in and of themselves. To collect and focus the support of large numbers of members and to link their feelings to other objects requires some way of concretizing their attachments. Typically, this has been achieved in part by the emergence of vigorous and trusted leaders who, the members and followers are led to believe, in some way embody the ideals and stand for the promise of their fulfillment. They are the personal bridges acting as ties to the new norms and structures of authority.

Max Weber's stress on the charisma of leaders and his preoccupation with the administrative staffs of corporate groups unnecessarily and restrictively diverted attention from the ranks of leaders other than those at the pinnacle of a set of authorities. Lower level leaders, whether part of the authority structure or not, are often able to rally their followers behind a regime. In some cases, empirically, the success of a new regime has been a matter of getting a group of prominent persons in a political system to place their stamp of approval on it. And although research has been distracted into excessive emphasis on top leadership, it is likely that wherever large aggregates of persons are involved, personal legitimizing occurs through lower echelon leaders, permeating down to the smallest groups in the political system. It is highly unlikely that in spite of the success on the part of pinnacle leaders to weld strong bonds with individual members of a system in the aggregate, this will destroy a partly supplementary and even partly independent personal legitimizing function of lesser leaders. The generation of diffuse support may be more widely distributed through a political structure than we are accustomed to believe.[11]

Whatever levels of leadership have been involved, it is indisputable that the symbolization of a new order in personal terms has been characteristic of most situations in the past where basic changes have occurred and where large groups need to be set in motion in order to achieve them. Without this personal focus for the membership of a system, it would be extremely difficult to mobilize its energies, not only for action but for commitment to and moral approval of a new regime and its authorities. Regardless of the source from which there arises the feeling that what a leadership does and recommends ought to be considered right and proper, the presence of this sentiment and belief has in itself left open the way for its transfer to the political norms and structures approved by the leadership.

[11] For some indications that this is so, see G. McT. Kahin, "Indonesia" in G. McT. Kahin, *The Major Governments of Asia* (Ithaca, New York: Cornell University Press, 1958), pp. 471–592, especially at pp. 570–571.

The Transferability of Sentiments of Legitimacy: Stable Systems

The transfer of legitimacy as a means for generating or maintaining diffuse support for a regime and its authorities is not exclusively a problem for newly founded regimes or political communities. As a response to stress, this puts the personal qualities of a leadership into too narrow a perspective. Personal affect may be as vital for attaching members to a regime and authorities in a stable system as in one that is undergoing change or some severe political crisis.

Although we may not be accustomed to conceiving of it in quite this way, old and established regimes and authority structures are constantly confronted with legitimating problems similar to those of new systems. Succeeding generations of children mature to adulthood and take their regularly expected political roles, but they are not born with a built-in instinct to accept the authorities and the regime. Nor can we anticipate that they will necessarily learn to do so if left entirely to their own devices. In any event, no system has yet left this entirely or even largely to chance. Although the responses in this area to assure the growth of diffuse support in the maturing members of the system may be quite varied, they may all be summed up by the statement that children learn to accept legitimacy—or beliefs in illegitimacy in cases where cleavages and conflicts in legitimating ideologies exist—through the processes of political socialization. The child in any system needs to be bound for the first time to the regime and its authorities through perceptions of their legitimacy.

Numerous processes and structures are brought into play to socialize a child into a political system.[12] But among them the personal aspect of authority looms large as a mechanism. It would appear from preliminary inquiry in this area that key persons in the authority structure stand as symbols which may help a child to learn to accept the legitimacy of the whole set of institutions and processes for producing outputs.[13] In the United States, for example, it has been suggested that very young children will tend to see the leading figure of authority, the President, as a person with the ideal moral and personal qualities approved of in the society. If this is so, it furnishes the very young child, before ten years of age, with a fixed point in the system to which

[12] For a full discussion, see articles cited in chapter 17, footnote 5 and the references therein.

[13] On this point, R. D. Hess and D. Easton, "The Child's Changing Image of the President."

he can direct his attention, insofar as he has any interest or concern with political institutions, and for which positive feelings may be stimulated. As we might expect, where the agencies of socialization from which the child learns, such as family or school, are hostile to the existing authorities, it is probable that he will absorb disaffective rather than supportive attitudes.

But regardless of the direction of the affect, I am proposing that the child in any stable system may find a focus in some prominent or central figure of authority—a President, chief, monarch, Prime Minister, heroic leader, or historic models—and the feelings so generated with regard to this personal embodiment of authority may then be subtly transferred to other institutions of political authority. We would not expect that this is the only mechanism at work in forming the bonds between children and their political norms and structures. But if it is likely that the personal attachment to figures of authority at an early age do diffuse outward to other more impersonal institutions of authority in the system—such as legislatures, courts, and government in general—we can discern in this process a possible source for nurturing sentiments of legitimacy in children, viewed as new members of a system. It would indicated that even in stable systems the role of personal legitimation performed by political leadership needs to be taken into account.

A final point about the role of leadership as a means for adapting to threats to the input of diffuse support, I have already intimated. The fact that leaders draw the allegiance of members of a system and may convert it into moral approval that extends beyond the leadership itself, does not mean that the activities of leadership move only in a legitimating direction. It is clear that leadership may be divisive in the support it generates; rather than building up a belief in the legitimacy of a regime and its authorities, a segment of the political leadership may be concerned with tearing it down. As we have found in other matters, what we must be concerned with is the net effect of the regulative consequences of personal legitimacy.

Omnibus Legitimating Responses

Not all responses that help to strengthen the legitimacy of a regime or its authorities utilize specifically ideological, structural, or personal sources; nor need they be directed exclusively to one or the other of the political objects. Many mechanisms have what we may call omnibus or comprehensive effects; empirically, they may simultaneously stimulate legitimacy in more than one way for all appropriate objects.

In the case of systems undergoing sharp changes, we have seen that various kinds of regulative means might be employed to foster a belief in the legitimacy of political objects. The very fact of manifest instability under conditions of rapid change would normally be expected to lead to responses calculated to keep up the level of diffuse support. But what, on purely theoretical grounds, might be less expected, is that systems free from any visible threat of stress should find it continuously necessary to attend to the renewal of sentiments of legitimacy. If this occurred only with respect to recurring new members, such as children, it would be quite understandable. But it applies as well with equal force to adults who are well-entrenched members of a system.

Indeed, this seems to be one of the major and characteristic qualities of this sentiment. It cannot be taken for granted for any class of members nor does it seem to thrive in the normal interstices of political life. Systems give the appearance of behaving on the assumption either that feelings of legitimacy cannot be readily stored or, if so, any reserve can be quickly dissipated. Special measures appear to be necessary to assure its continuing input. It may be that the pressures from cleavages and output failures, ineluctable as they are in all systems, are intuitively felt to be gnawing constantly at the bases of support. At the least, the behavior of all systems suggests that there is the fear that without constant efforts to inspire a conviction about the rightness of the regime and its authorities, members might quickly lose the feeling that there is a special "oughtness" about the outputs. Special measures are everywhere taken to insure its input—everywhere, that is to say, where legitimacy is the source of support for the objects of a system.

Broad legitimating principles and values are reinforced by subsidiary, derivative, and related norms through which the principles are implemented. In addition, constant efforts are made to associate the day-to-day authorities with the structural legitimacy of the regime itself. Just as through their personal qualities, leaders may be successful in spreading the aura of legitimacy over a regime, the appeal of an existing regime as legitimate is used to validate the actions of the particular incumbents of the authority roles.

Every system seeks to strengthen ties of legitimacy through the propagation of appropriate ideologies. Such symbolic responses are intensified through concrete expression in rituals, ceremonies and physical representations of the regime.[14] Together, on the varied and numer-

[14] For a discussion of the means used, C. E. Merriam, *Political Power* (New York: McGraw-Hill, 1934).

ous occasions when they are brought into play, they serve to bolster an aura of sanctity, respect, and reverence for the existing political institutions and to reassert the legitimacy of the incumbent authorities. Accession and installation ceremonies, display of the physical symbols of authority such as coats of arms, wands, or seals of state, favored ceremonial treatment for individuals representative of the special character of the regime, special penalties for offenses against such representative persons, displays on patriotic holidays and events, all stand as specific and variable responses that nurture diffuse support. By focusing on the major political values of the system, on the exemplary character of the incumbents of authority roles, or on their conformity to the regime, such procedures are able to contribute to the reinforcement of sentiments of legitimacy, ideological, personal, or structural, as the case may be.

The Psychological Need to Believe

The reliance on legitimacy as a source of diffuse support may have a peculiar result. So ingrained may it become in some systems, that we may suspect that it gives birth to a psychological need to find some leaders and structures in which to believe. If so, a belief in legitimacy may become an autonomous goal for the members of a system. Some students of modernizing nations have observed, in this respect, that the breakdown of a sense of obligation to the old authorities leaves attitudes of "free floating obedience." These can readily be attached to an appropriate leader who is clever enough to recognize and take advantage of such loosened attitudes. The new leaders fill the void created by the absence of objects to which these attitudes of obligation may attach themselves.[15]

We do not need to postulate that there is an innate psychological need to believe.[16] Nor do we need to conclude that persons are socialized to believe in a set of goals from which it is difficult to break them away. It may be that this does in fact occur but it is not to this phenomenon that the need to believe is related. Rather, the implication is that the early processes of socialization may develop in persons a need to believe in *some* set of validating symbols and to find strength in attachment to *some* persons and structures. If this is so, it would shed a different light on the great battles often preceding or accompanying the physical struggles over the shape of the regime; the ideo-

---

[15] G. Pauker, L. Pye and G. McT. Kahin, *op. cit.*
[16] As did Gaetano Mosca in *The Ruling Class*, chapter 5.

logical form of the struggle would be more comprehensible from the point of view of its appeal to the general members of the system.

The conclusion that every system tends to breed in its members an internalized need to believe in the legitimacy of some set of authorities and regime is not essential to our analysis. But if it were indeed true, it would just reinforce our emphasis on the role this belief plays in the production of diffuse support. Yet, as I have already suggested, at the least we can explain the growth of a belief of this kind in terms of its consequences for the solidarity behind a regime and its authorities. We may even go further. Under most conditions, it represents a requirement which, if it is not fulfilled, may find a system unable to marshal enough support or general political good will for its persistence in any form. No other source of support can assure such ready acceptance of the outputs, however much they may fly in the face of demands. Nor is there any more secure way to regulate the cleavages that appear in all systems so that they do not irreparably rend asunder the fabric of political life.

20

Diffuse Support for Authorities and Regime:

The Belief in a Common Interest

W<small>E CAN IMAGINE THAT IF MEMBERS OF A SYSTEM WERE ENTIRELY</small> unregulated in the pursuit of their demands, not a few might say to themselves: "If my wants and demands are being ignored and unfulfilled, and if in the foreseeable future I cannot anticipate that the situation will improve, why should I put my trust and confidence in the authorities or in the regime in terms of which they operate? They represent only the political forces in the system that are powerful enough to control or dominate us." In the face of such presumed but unlikely universal rationality, the rule of expediency might become the only guide to action. Perceived self-interest would dictate the extent to which a member would support a regime and its authorities.

Under special conditions, a system might be able to rely on this motive exclusively to bolster the input of support. But as we have seen, the likelihood of this is very remote. The competition for scarce resources is in most systems too divisive. We know that legitimating beliefs help to counter the centrifugal tendencies that unalloyed self-interest may have on the solidarity of the members. But ideologies of legitimacy do not stand alone; systems tend to hedge by providing a variety of means for accomplishing the same purposes. We can expect to find legitimating devices reinforced and supplemented by other means.

The Idea of a Common Interest

In many although not all systems, as an additional source of diffuse support, we usually find a belief that has quite different consequences from those I have referred to as legitimating ideologies. This is the conviction that there is something called the interest of the realm, the public, common, or national interest, the general good and public

311

welfare, or the good of the tribe, of "our people." The authorities through the regime are represented as the major spokesmen for this interest. This common interest is viewed as taking priority over local, ethnic, class, or other component interests within a society.

Regardless of the particular words used to express this notion, in part it is closely affiliated with the conception of legitimacy. In systems where the idea of a general interest is a test of policy cherished by most members, any perceived, serious, and persistent deviation from it by the authorities would certainly help to undermine belief in their legitimacy. If the feeling were to prevail that the regime itself militated against the public interest, in time continued acceptance of the regime as right and proper could not be taken for granted. But separate and apart from any possible effect on beliefs in legitimacy, the conviction that there is a general good, that it can be determined or defined, that it makes intuitive sense to use it as a guide for political action, and that the authorities through the regime ought to pursue and promote this general good, have important consequences for the solidarity of the members behind a regime and its related authorities.

For the purposes of our analysis we can set aside the age-old problem concerning the objectivity or subjectivity of the general interest. Whether or not there is an objective interest in the sense that it can be observed, reported, and verified in the same way that any empirical proposition can be discovered and confirmed is an important matter but it has little relevance here.[1] The question confronting us is of another kind. Regardless of how we interpret the idea of a common good and regardless of the particular content with which we endow it, what consequences do the belief in its existence and the prevalence of this conviction in a system have upon the input of diffuse support for the regime and its authorities?

Its Solidary Effects

Wherever the conception of a general interest actively operates, it helps to regulate or limit the disposition toward divisive behavior on the part of the politically relevant members in general. It accomplishes this basically through the fact that such a belief pushes in the direc-

---

[1] See G. Schubert, *The Public Interest* (Glencoe, Illinois: Free Press, 1960); W. A. R. Leys and C. M. Perry, *Philosophy and the Public Interest* (Chicago: Committee to Advance Original Work in Philosophy, 1959); C. J. Friedrich (ed.), *The Public Interest* (New York: Atherton, 1962); and the voluminous references included in these volumes.

tion of establishing common standards for evaluating outputs. Not that all members of a system will interpret the consequences of outputs in identical terms. But however they may perceive the results of policies or administrative acts, for example, if members assume they are all using a similar standard for judging their desirability—a shared idea of a common good—this will reduce one of the major sources of differences. This does not mean that the adoption of a political vocabulary that speaks of a general interest or common good will necessarily invest the phrase with the same content; it may conceal inextinguishable valuational differences that do in fact exist among members in conflict over policy. Nor need the adoption of a common test for evaluating policy eliminate strife; members may still use the same test but because of conflicting judgments in applying it, they may stand diametrically opposed. Nevertheless, as we shall see, this vocabulary does have possible beneficial aspects from the point of view of the input of diffuse support.

Cleavage-Increasing Consequences

Where politically relevant members cannot agree on broad objectives, a normal rather than an unusual situation, it may well appear strange to suggest that a belief in a common interest nevertheless contributes to ameliorating differences. In fact, at first glance, just the opposite seems to be the more likely outcome. In many systems, it is the hallowed custom for contenders debating the merits of demands, to formulate their several positions as a search for the public or common interest or good. Not only do the initial differences fail to disappear; through this mode of articulation they may become more sharply defined and divisive than ever.

A simple illustration demonstrates this. Controversy may entail, let us say, the continuation of a policy of foreign aid with minimal political conditions attached. By converting the dispute into a debate over whether the national or public interest demands the continuation of such aid in its various forms, the tendency is to broaden the points at issue and possibly sharpen or intensify them. In effect, this ideological formulation is saying to all politically interested or relevant members in the system that what may have appeared to be a broad but nevertheless limited issue now merits the attention of all. It concerns the welfare of all.

It may be, of course, that this kind of appeal for broader involvement in the issue falls on ears that have become immune to it as a meaningless form of political rhetoric. But where it has any effectiveness, by seeking to include greater numbers in the dispute, it would tend in the direction of aggravating rather than muting cleavages. The ideology of the common interest would thus serve to broaden and sharpen a controversy, one of the results of every effort to convert issues into ideological disputes.

Cohesive Consequences

But if we accepted this as the sole effect, we would be neglecting a significant latent consequence. The conversion of a particular controversy into a more general one over its connection with a presumed common interest also helps to promote solidarity. In effect, disputants who argue that the general interest is involved, are already implying that the members of the system do share some interests or goals and that one of the tasks is to explore their nature. Any associated dispute about the nature of this public interest usually presupposes that such an interest exists or can be uncovered. Even if it could be shown that the term "public interest" must be vacuous in any objective, substantive sense, the very belief that there is such an interest or that it is discoverable, would help to bring about some accommodation among conflicting views. It keeps the door open for the discovery of some shared principles as a basis of possible negotiation and compromise.

We can perhaps better appreciate this tendency if we envisioned a political system in which the members assumed just the opposite, that is, that there was not and could not be a general interest, however it is described. Presumably debate would be formulated exclusively in terms of what would be best for each of the participants. This does not signify that the disputants would necessarily be unable to reach agreement on outputs; self-interest might dictate a strategy of mutual accommodation. But what would be lacking is a prior conviction that a policy could be found that would transcend the demands of any particular group and yet be acceptable to all on the basis of some criterion other than particularistic wants. To the extent that this conviction is absent, it could not help but aggravate the differences. To the extent that such a belief is present, at the very least it backstops any failure of expediency and, at its level of most effective operation, it offers a positive base for compromise.

In practice, it is undoubtedly true that outputs promoted on the grounds that they serve a broader and higher interest may reflect or be designed primarily to meet the wants and demands of a narrow or limited combination of political groups. Nevertheless, regardless for the moment of this concealed effect, the ideology of a common interest does serve as a social sanction or norm to impel members to substitute for their own private or particular wants, a new or different one, that of a higher entity or ideal called the common good. It helps to orient the members of the system to the wants of others in the system and to the necessity of outputs that transcend particular demands. Insofar as members can be induced to accept an output as satisfying the common good, the failure of outputs to accord with particular demands can be more readily or willingly accepted. It can be justified and interpreted as a necessary subordination of private wants to the general good.

In thereby tempering the degree of discontent that might otherwise be stimulated by dissatisfaction with the authorities or the regime, or by the lack of a *quid pro quo* for support, the idea of a common interest helps to maintain the input of a broader, diffuse kind of support for the authorities and regime. History has confirmed this from time to time. In instances when the political leadership has proved incapable of nurturing an image of the common good, the attachment of the members to the system has been seriously impaired. As one student of the Habsburg Empire has been moved to generalize, "success in politics can be measured by two yardsticks. It may mean simply the partial fulfillment of a party program, irrespective of its merits in regard to the citizenry as a whole [what we would call specific outputs]. It may on the other hand—at least in intent—live up to absolute ethical standards in the service of the common welfare. Political leadership in the Habsburg Empire, not necessarily through any fault of its own, had limited success only when evaluated according to the first concept. It was bound to fail by the standards of more comprehensive values, which the multinational empire idea entailed." [2] It failed to generate a sense of a common welfare that all members of the system felt they should and could pursue.

The Common Good as an Internalized Norm

As this quotation further suggests, the invocation of the symbols of a higher and more general interest may operate most effectively as a social sanction for mobilizing support where this ideology, as a response, has in turn been deeply imbedded in the minds of the members. This would be particularly probable in those systems in which the culture and processes of socialization have already held out concern for the common welfare as a valued goal, "absolute ethical standards in the service of the common welfare," as it is put in the

[2] R. A. Kann, *op. cit.,* p. 134.

previous quotation. If it has been an internalized norm for political behavior, it can act as a subjective censor, a stricture on conscience that imposes restraints on the degree to which a member may pursue his own wants and demands to the jeopardy of the cohesion of the system as a whole.

But even in this event, the norm need serve less as a restriction on behavior in any inhibiting sense than as positive motivation. In subordinating his wants to the presumed common interest, the individual member may acquire alternative rewards, such as the gratifications of making a significant contribution to the greater whole of which he feels himself to be a part. He may also feel that in pursuing the common welfare he is fulfilling a goal valuable to him for its own sake.

In this way, the idea and ideal of a common interest acts to trigger psychological mechanisms which justify acceptance of outputs that might otherwise lead to extreme dissatisfaction with the authorities and even the regime. It contributes to the diffuse support underlying the regime and authorities. Unless some kind of internalized norm such as this did function in the political culture, especially in large-scale political systems, the burden on other and more formal mechanisms for generating diffuse support might become impossibly onerous.

Instrumental Structural Responses

As we might expect, the presence of an ideology of the common interest as a response to potential stress is often accompanied by specific structures through which the influence of the ideology makes itself felt. Variable structures arise to vivify it and to help enforce conformity to it. Insofar as these structures have proven effective, they help to increase the reservoir of diffuse support. A belief that there is in fact a common interest, efforts to act on its behalf, and a willingness to endure the sacrifice of one's own interest and wants in its name would all be indicators of the level of the reservoir.

Structures specific to the development and intensification of convictions about the common interest, as an ideal guiding political action, have appeared particularly in constitutional and democratic systems. In these, so-called third forces have typically emerged whose special concern it has been to invoke the image and symbols of the "community at large," or of the public interest as the goal that ought to be sought or the criterion that ought to be used to evaluate programs and policies.

Although always a part of the struggle, the self-appointed guardians of the public interest tend to give the appearance of somehow being a little above the day-to-day conflicts among parties and politicians. These guardians may appear in the form of a press or other mass medium, relatively independent, not of the power groups in society, but of the authorities. They may occur as uprooted social groups adept at communication, such as an intelligentsia and publicists, or, at times, as special groups that claim to act for the general public without any partisan axe to grind.

Empirically, it may be demonstrable that the members of any or all such groups and groupings speak for only another particular interest or combination of interests in the system. Their dedication to a presumed common good may be spurious or suspect. But as long as there is a conviction that they have no special goals other than this generalized one, or at least that it is dominant, and as long as groups do undertake the representation of a presumed general interest as their special domain and conduct themselves in a demeanor calculated to convey this impression, these conditions present a powerful combination for forcing discussion beyond the needs of any one particular set of interests or wants. They thereby help to move controversy to a level less damaging to political solidarity. The very presence of such structures implies that there is in fact a more general good in which all may share and which can be independently protected. To that extent, members of the system become more receptive to policies pursued by authorities in the name of the common good and they become less disconcerted with any imbalance between outputs and their demands.

Limitations on the Authorities

The discussion to this point has emphasized the impact that a belief in the common good has upon the readiness of the politically relevant members in general to accept something less than the full satisfaction of their demands. Thereby indirectly the regime and authorities may benefit from the good will that is created with respect to them. A second major effect, however, relates to the regime and authorities directly.

Where the possibility or perceived existence of a definable common interest becomes identified structurally with the authorities and regime, it has a chance of becoming a central source of diffuse support. In many and varied kinds of systems, there can be little doubt that members look to the authorities operating within the context of a given regime to undertake, as a prime responsibility, the articulation and defense of something called the general welfare or public good. However antique the formulation, this was a basic truth underlying the social contract political philosophies. In return for the power and position they held, the political rulers were expected to accept some moral limits to their powers, at the very least, and to take seriously their parallel responsibilities of caring for the commonweal.

Whether rulers did in fact do so is an entirely different matter, as is the question of whether the regime so organized power that rulers could comfortably ignore a presumed common interest. But what is meaningful is that at least in many ethical theories of obligation throughout the world, ideologies appear that hold the authorities, through the existing regime, responsible for attempting to meet those needs of a system identified as the public or common interest. As long as members believe not only that the authorities and the nature of the regime should lend their weight in favor of defending the common good, but that they do so in fact, this in itself is a vital stimulus for regulating the input of diffuse support.

If, for their part, the authorities rely upon the use of symbols of the common interest, especially as a sanction or incentive to induce the sacrifice of normal expectations, it becomes difficult, although not necessarily impossible, for the authorities to escape subjecting themselves to the same criteria of evaluation. The act of judging outputs by reference to the general interest imposes constraints on the political leadership in general and on the authorities in particular.

In requesting in the name of the common welfare that the membership accept less than they expect in the form of outputs, it raises the expectation that the authorities can justify their behavior and policies in terms of the same broader interest. In this way the ideology of a common good helps to create social pressures on the authorities to conduct themselves so that, at the very least, they do not take into account only the particular interest of themselves or a favored few. To this extent, where the public interest as an ideology prevails, it is likely to impose constraints on the authorities that help to bring outputs into line with some of the more inclusive needs or demands of the membership. In doing so, it will generally enhance the positive feelings that members are willing to extend to the authorities and, ultimately, to the related regime.

It would be erroneous to conclude from these remarks, however, that it is in the nature of political systems in general that they should inevitably turn to the ideology of a public interest and general welfare as a response for regulating the level of diffuse support. The fact that many ethical political theories have argued that authorities should entertain the common good, specifically defined, as an ideal, has not been successful in making it universally acceptable, even as a general ideal.[3]

In some traditional and transitional societies, for example, appeals for the authorities to consider the general good or for a regime that would impel the authorities to act in this way, would fall on deaf ears. The will of the authorities may be a sufficient justification for actions; and such authorities, as in the case of an absolute monarch, may be viewed as legitimate even though action is not taken in the name of the general welfare. In many systems, it is expected that the authorities will put their power to use for the benefit of a particular class, military bureaucracy, ethnic group, race, or other political entity within the system. Particular rather than general interest is accepted as the criterion to govern outputs.

In this atmosphere, few structural devices such as a press independent of government or non-partisan publicists are available or encouraged to interpret the nature of a possible general interest. For overcoming cleavages among groups and for building a reserve of support, such systems typically rely on means other than appeals for compliance on behalf of the general welfare. It has led students of developing areas to suggest that to relieve the pressure on other mechanisms for reducing cleavages and building up a solid reserve of uncommitted diffuse support, it may be necessary to socialize the members in such a way that the concern for a presumed general welfare becomes an inner need difficult to displace. But even though a belief in a common interest may not constrain behavior in all systems, it is typically a response through which many systems have reinforced the input of diffuse support. It is a theoretical component of support that cannot be ignored.

[3] In so far as political philosophy does seek to persuade members of a system of the existence of a verifiable objective common good, it does serve, with respect to its possible political consequences, as a response that may aid in the growth of diffuse support.

2 1

Diffuse Support for the Political Community

I HAVE BEEN RESTRICTING OUR DISCUSSION TO THE PRODUCTION OF DIFFUSE support for the regime and its associated authorities as they may respond to stress. This leaves us with the need to understand the special ways in which systems may seek to cope with stress at the level of the political community. Although hostility to and disaffection from the authorities may be the first link in a chain that ultimately leads to the dissolution of the political community, we have already seen that it is quite possible, and indeed customary, for authorities and regime to change, the community remaining quite stable. Only in some few, unusual cases, will contentment with the regime be consistent with the collapse or fragmentation of the political community.

In this chapter I propose to deal with the input of support for the political community in a separate analysis. This will permit us to trace out some of the more significant ways in which any threat to the input at this level may be typically handled. In anticipation, we may summarize these responses by saying that they take the form of regime alterations and stimulation of a sense of community. Through these means diffuse support is typically stimulated for the political community.

Modifications in the Regime as a Response

Under certain circumstances, we may expect that measures taken to maintain or create support for a regime will contribute to strengthening the growth of general political good will toward the community as well. I touched on this aspect earlier, when dealing with the relationship of structural modifications as a direct way of seeking to reduce or regulate political cleavages. Here we can pursue the matter more systematically and tie it in to other kinds of responses usually employed to generate diffuse support for the community.

It is quite apparent that the fewer complaints members have about the regular processes and institutions through which demands are converted into outputs, that is, the regime, the more encouraged they will be to feel that the group with which they share the processes and institutions ought to be maintained intact. Alternatively, where members become discontented with the outputs of a regime, they may perhaps place the blame on the authorities at first but if the outputs persist in failing to meet what are considered just expectations, or if they are at once seen as being related to the nature of the regime, the temptation presents itself for the members to seek a change in the structure and norms of the regime itself. If they should find it impossible to achieve this or to bring about the desired changes in time, as a last resort some members may be driven to question the desirability of maintaining the political community itself in its existing form. They may make efforts to shape one that includes only members who are more responsive to their wants.

Traditionally this has frequently happened, as cases of nationalist separatism or irredentism amply testify. In the United States, for example, small but vocal Negro groups have periodically sought an independent political community as a result of their failure to obtain both a regime and other non-political conditions that they have considered necessary to meet their minimal expectations. In Canada, some French-speaking Canadians have become part of a separatist movement in part due to the perceived failure of the Constitution, the B.N.A. Act, to provide for an equitable distribution of power in the Canadian political community as a whole. As in these instances, decline of support at the regime level, if it persists for a long enough period, readily spills over into the community and adversely affects attachment to it.

The obverse is equally true. Responses to cleavage and output failure that succeed in stabilizing support for the regime can be expected ultimately to touch off favorable repercussions for solidarity around the community as well. To the extent that modifications in the goals, norms, and structure of a regime manage to bring it into greater harmony with the wants and demands of the politically relevant members, this will help to strengthen their attachment to the community as well as to the regime.

We can appreciate the decisive significance of this kind of response when we recall that threats of irredentist or separatist movements within a community have frequently and typically been alleviated by changes in the political processes. As I had occasion to mention in Chapter 16, and as is well known, the introduction of federal structures may be designed to provide enough autonomy, in religious or cultural matters at least, to win the support of potentially dissident groups.

Structural changes that offer greater opportunity for vertical political mobility make possible a more active circulation of the politically relevant members and give a broader range of groups some voice in their own destinies. Such regime alterations help to nurture a sense of contentment with the political community itself; they demonstrate that the various segments of the political community are willing to give serious consideration to each other's wants. The whole group is encouraged thereby to continue sharing its political division of labor.[1]

The fact that regime changes are available does not vouch for their effectiveness, of course, in holding a community together. As in the case of all responses, their success is a matter of the actual circumstances surrounding their application.

The effect of regime changes upon the cohesion of the political community has been equally operative in the sphere of international

[1] Cf: "Yet Metternich, though quite realistic in regard to the German situation, still hoped that an Austrian empire amalgamated by force of a German administrative and cultural superstructure could still be maintained and even strengthened, in spite of the fact that the acquisition of Italian territory (the bulk of that of the Republic of Venice, 1797–1805 and 1815–1866, and Lombardy, 1815–1859) and the simultaneous permanent relinquishment of the Vorlande (the non-contiguous Habsburg possessions in southwestern Germany) again weakened this German superstructure. The national revolutions and independence movements in Europe between 1815 and 1848 and the stormy events of 1848–1849 shattered this illusion. An Austrian solution in the Great German national revolution failed in 1848. The success of Prince Felix Schwarzenberg, the new prime minister, between 1849 and 1851, proved to be merely transitory. The democratic revolution failed likewise and, closely connected with it, the national revolutions of the Austrian national groups. In an age of rising nationalism a German solution in Austria could not be accepted by the national groups in the multinational empire. The idea of a democratic federal or semi-federal solution of the question, on the other hand, was not acceptable to the old forces of absolutism. Since absolutism proved victorious in this struggle, its solution was imposed, a temporary reconstruction of what seemed on the surface to be a closely amalgamated, centralized, absolutist state with German superstructure—in other words the neo-absolutist, Austria of 1849.

"The tragic irony of this neo-absolutism, and later of the persisting absolutist tendencies, was that the system failed most in the field where it had sinned least. This regime was not particularly intolerant in nationality questions, certainly far less so than some other issues of domestic policy. It sincerely believed that a German imperial superstructure would appeal to Slavs, Magyars, Italians and Rumanians as a genuine supernational system. But even if the statesmen of the period had realized this fatal error, they could not have changed their policy, since a multinational compromise acceptable to all groups could have been concluded only on the basis of a democratic empire organization. This the regime was unwilling and unable to grant. The results, though not due entirely to this particular misconception, were the wars and defeats of 1859 and 1866. They finally shattered Metternich's old dream of a unified Austrian empire with a German superstructure." R. A. Kann, *op. cit.*, pp. 33–34.

types of systems. In imperial political communities,[2] for example, concessions to colonial systems in the way of self-government, and ultimately of responsible government, as in the British sphere, have been measures that have altered the structure and norms of the imperial regime, usually in an effort to pacify anti-colonial movements potentially disruptive of the imperial community itself. Furthermore, in the British Empire, it was historically possible to modify the old imperial regime by transforming a large part of it into the kind of loose political association that we identify as the British Commonwealth of Nations. In effect, through a revision in the structure, norms, and goals of the old imperial order—incorporated into the Statute of Westminster and subsequent specific legislation—the political community remained relatively intact in the face of threats to its solidarity that might well have been expected to dismember it.

In the same way we may interpret the reconstruction of relationships among the component units of the pre-existing French empire as an adaptive effort through regime changes to retain the support, at some minimal level, of what is left of the former imperial community. In this case the regime as well as the constituent parts of the former imperial community have been changed; but the regime modifications served to salvage support for some kind of French international system and, therefore, of a political community that is an integral part of it.

The Inadequacy of Regime Changes

In addition to the responses that involve basic revisions in the regime, other kinds of regulatory mechanisms are usually available to maintain the level of diffuse support for the political community. We would be led to search for other responses if for no other reason than the fact that, at times, members of a system may not take exception primarily to the regime and yet they may seek to hive off to form a political community of their own.

The sentiment in Scotland is a case in point. Even though greater representation in the British Parliament might help to mollify some of the nationalist sentiment, it could not satisfy it fully. The demand for recognition as a separate political entity does not hinge entirely on pressure for a new or modified regime. A vocal segment of Scots period-

---

[2] The concepts French Political Community or European Political Community are, of course, practical rather than theoretical terms and they are not to be confused with the way in which the idea "political community" is being used in this analysis.

ically seeks to establish Scotland's identity as a separate political unit for reasons other than perceived lack of responsiveness of the English to Scottish wants. Rather, it is the desire to satisfy a historic sense of national identity and independence that has led to the persistent demand for a separate political existence.

In fact, we can assume that in most movements for political independence, whether of a colonial unit, an ethnic group, or a nationality, the desire for a separate political community may be viewed as a variable partly independent of any dissatisfaction with the regime. Implicit in this is the notion that even though greater representation is offered a separatist group and even though the authorities were to become increasingly responsive, there are conditions under which ethnic, linguistic, or national groups will nonetheless continue to seek separate identity through their own political community.

Historically, this has usually occurred when the separatist group has reached the level of political consciousness and organization which links the maintenance and gratification of a sense of dignity and freedom inextricably to mastery over its own political destiny, at least insofar as this is ever possible under modern circumstances. Recognition by others and perceptions of worthiness of self are tied to the sharing of a political division of labor with those to whom one feels linked by meaningful criteria. These criteria, often made up of combinations of such factors as language, religion, common history, or race, will vary. But when a group of people come to feel that certain criteria represent politically meaningful bonds, the desire for identity as a separate political community is almost inevitable. At least, this is so in the modern international political culture that has developed.

It is quite easy to conceive of other kinds of cultures in which initial and primary control over one's fate through political separateness need not be considered an expression of dignity and social self-fulfillment. But the spread of democratic belief systems with the idea of self-determination as an integral component, interpreted, symbolized, and reinforced in Woodrow Wilson's Fourteen Points, has carried with it at least this conviction in modern international political culture.

Thus the native population of Africa has, under Western economic and political domination, sought social and political development and the outputs associated with it. But no transformation in regime is manifestly satisfactory today in the face of the perception among the political leadership—communicated as it often is, if only crudely but nonetheless effectively, to the membership—that freedom and formal political independence from white and Western rule, and the indignities associated with it, are the minimal conditions for self-fulfillment.

To argue against the separation of political communities on grounds that it does not make for economic rationality, that the members are merely trading a set of foreign masters for domestic ones, or that formal independence creates only an illusion of political autonomy, can do and has done little to impair the mobilization of forces behind the colonial revolutions. What is most frequently at stake in the developing areas is not the nature of the regime, even though this is of necessity involved, but rather the nature of the political community itself.

From this perspective it is clear that reasons other than dissatisfaction with the regime may contribute and lead to the decline of support for a political community. Hence we would expect to find kinds of responses other than modification of the regime undertaken in efforts to keep a community intact.

The Sense of Political Community

Whatever other measures that may be taken, most systems typically anticipate possible stress, due to a decline in support, by striving to arouse and nurture among its members what I have earlier called a sense of political community or of mutual political identification. To recall briefly what was said in Chapter 11, the concept "political community" refers to a group of persons who share a division of labor for the settlement of political problems. The cohesiveness of such a group, its *sense* of political community, will be reflected in the extent to which the members hold positive feelings with respect to this sharing of a political division of labor. Where their sense of community is high, we can say that they are putting in considerable support for the political community. Where it is low, the level of support deteriorates accordingly.

We saw, however, that in addition to the growth of a sense of community there are other sources from which support might derive.[3] Specific benefits attributed to cooperation in the pursuit of political objectives or submission to the threat of force and coercion may be able to maintain a sufficient level of support even if all sense of community should disappear. But as in the case of the regime itself, if a political community is to be able to weather the storms of economic and military crises, severe internal differences, or catastrophes of various sorts, it requires more than specific support flowing either from direct rewards perceived as such by the members or the compulsory support flowing from the use of coercion by the political leaders.

[3] See chapter 11.

Even if material or other specific rewards had initially inspired cohesion within a common political framework, if they should decline or in large part disappear, a political community requires some store of diffuse support ready to carry it through. Whatever we may have to say about a presumed necessity for any given source of diffuse support, empirically and typically every political community must seek to provide a broad and deep reservoir of such support upon which it might draw in times of need, if it is to persist. The degree of conflict, cleavage, and output failure compatible with the persistence of a political community is in part a function of the extent to which the system is able to generate in its members a strong sense of mutual political identification.

Although the exact way in which this works for political systems is still being investigated, some helpful suggestions are available from research with regard to the community aspects of other types of social systems. It has been shown that sentiments of this kind act as important constraints on divisive behavior. Analogously, these conclusions may well apply to the political community as well.

Thus Coleman suggests that where members of a subsystem called the "local community"—the total social life of a subregional group within the geographical boundaries of a political system—are highly involved in controversy, its divisive effects are clearly related to the degree of attachment to the community.[4] Where the members identify strongly with one another, they can tolerate intense and passionate dispute among themselves without jeopardizing the integrity of the community. In acquiring sentiments of mutual identification, it appears that the members simultaneously develop or absorb norms and constraints on behavior beneficial for the perpetutation of themselves as a cohesive group.

This does not imply that persons who have a strong sense of community identification will refrain from political controversy. Indeed, such a feeling may well inspire just the opposite behavior. Members may become intensely concerned with what happens to the community. But their involvement and conflict need not be damaging to the cohesion of the group.

On the other hand, if those who feel alienated from the community and who usually stand on the sidelines as onlookers, should become engaged in disputes, lacking the constraints imposed by strong sentiments of mutual identification with others, it becomes much easier for cleavages involving such persons to rend the community asunder.[5] Al-

[4] J. S. Coleman, *op. cit.*, especially chapter 3.
[5] *"Identification with the community itself.* The very existence of disagreement and controversy depend on involvement and identification. But when community

though Coleman theorizes about the social community and about kinds of conflicts that go beyond the realm of politics, it seems likely that his findings are equally applicable to the political community. If so, he is alluding to the underlying psychodynamics through which sentiments of mutual political identification in a community may hold the members together.

Stimulation of a Sense of Political Community: Parameters as Responses

The Impact of the Division of Political Labor

What means have typically arisen to help create and encourage feelings of mutual political identifications? In part it appears as an automatic product of existing sets of interlocking roles, groups and institutions. The complex web of communications and political relationships forms social and political ties that help to reinforce their own maintenance once they have come into existence, whatever the initial cause. We have already emphasized this in Chapter 11 when we first dealt with the idea of a sense of community.

Although any division of political labor will set in motion many cleavages and other centrifugal political forces, the facts of sharing political processes, participating in interdependent political roles, and partaking in the same communication network will in themselves contribute to perpetuating the need to do so. The growth of an administrative staff, of an orientation to the same sets of leadership cadres even if they are in partisan conflict over day-to-day policy, the assimilation of similar kinds of political techniques, styles and general knowhow within the context of a given group of people, and sensitivity to each other's cultural cues in various roles, help to predispose members of a system to seek to continue the group within which these interac-

members are highly involved with the community per se, identifying their own future with that of the community, that identification carries its own consequences as disagreement proceeds. Particularly, it appears to modify and constrain the disagreement. People who feel apart, and *unidentified*, are quickest to overstep the bounds of legitimate methods and carry the dispute into disruptive channels. When there are few or none who are identified, then there are essentially no norms to restrain the opposing sides. Conversely, if most people and organizations in the community are identified with community as a whole, then the potentially disruptive effects of the dispute are felt by all; there are conscious attempts at reconciliation . . . In effect, communities whose members are highly involved will have more controversies, and feelings will be more intense about the issues, but these controversies are likely to be carried on within ordinary democratic processes without degenerating into a 'fight to the finish.' " *Ibid.*, p. 21 (italics in the original).

tions have taken place and continue to be possible. The resulting learned patterns of political interaction and habits of communication within a group are not easily or lightly abandoned. Not that these tendencies are necessarily decisive. Pressures of output failure, severe cleavages, or feelings of oppression and exclusion may quickly override them.

But, it may be argued, interdependence created by a political division of labor just constitutes a set of consequences that accompany political existence. They can scarcely be considered responses to potential stress even in a very general sense.

It cannot be denied that there is some merit to this position. But it need not discourage us entirely from viewing the political consequences of a division of labor as responses. Members of a system or a potential political community are not ignorant of the fact that participation in some form of political interaction is relevant to strengthening the feelings of common political bonds. This is very much the source of arguments in favor of the formation of international functional organizations, for universal participation in the United Nations and, in all cases, for seeking to bring disputing and contending groups together in some kind of organization for purposes of meeting and talking together regularly. Part of the motivation for suggestions along these lines may lie in the desire to promote the ethical position that pacific settlement of differences is superior to the use of violence. But, in addition, these proposals involve the premise that the interactions themselves offer an opportunity for some sense of mutual identification to take root and grow. Whether, in fact, this does occur is not the question here. All that we need conclude is that any steps that members of a political system take to encourage such continuing interaction or to promote any conditions of political cooperation represent the use of means to regulate the level of mutual identification.

Responses through Modification of Parameters

In fact, we may go further and say that many of the variable conditions in the environment of a political system are available to the members for regulating feelings of mutual political identification. This puts a somewhat different light on recent research in international relations and new nations, for example, as it affects the parameters of political integration. In effect we may now conceive that such studies illuminate the range of alternative responses through which a sense of political community may be created or developed.

For example, the conclusions from such research on the conditions that contribute to increasing the social homogeneity of a society, may now be interpreted as possible response mechanisms for infusing the members of the political system with a deeper sense of mutual identification. Until recently the emphasis of this research has been on mechanisms that have sought to reduce diversity in society. It has been based on the premise that the more complex and differentiated the society, the wider the geographic dispersion of the members, and the broader the heterogeneity of customs, language, or religion, the greater the need for communications of all sorts to increase the positive feelings and orientation of the members toward each other.

Empirically, the validity of the premise seemed borne out by the great emphasis in new nations on the adoption of restricted common languages for official purposes, on centralized control over educational institutions and curricula, and on careful regulation of mass media. Implicit is the assumption that by manipulating these social parameters so as to increase the literacy level, improve the media of communication, encourage the compatibility of religions and the goals of the members and the uniformity of language, a broad consistency of values and general culture might be attained. Thereby identification as members of a common political unity might have the opportunity of emerging.

From more recent inquiry, however, we would be led to conclude that even though modifications of such social parameters may be helpful and necessary, they would remain quite insufficient to bring about a high sense of political community. To do so, it may be necessary to link to them other kinds of measures that increase the "mutual responsiveness" of the members and their expectations of strong future rewards as participants in a system. In addition, efforts would be required that create the perception of an equitable balance of rewards among the component units in the system, buttressed with a relatively high degree of mutual predictabilty of behavior.[6]

It is true that the deliberate creation of conditions such as these has been suggested because of their particular relevance to the developing integration of whole social entities such as societies. Yet for political systems, in our conceptualization they do constitute independent, external variables. Their manipulation in the appropriate direction through political action could be expected to generate or strengthen any sense of political community. This sentiment in turn would add to the store of diffuse support for the political community.

[6] K. W. Deutsch and S. A. Burrell, et al., op. cit., chapter 4 has a complete list and detailed discussion of them.

The Plausibility of Viewing Manipulations of Parameters as Responses

Is it valid to consider modifications in social parameters such as these, to be genuine cases of political responses rather than the result of events that occur for other reasons and that may just happen to have beneficial political consequences, anticipated or otherwise? In some cases at least, there can be little doubt about the fact that a deliberate political response is involved. The great and often continuing debates in new nations over the need for a common language or uniform educational system testify to the importance attached to the integrative potentialities clearly seen as inherent in manipulating these social parameters.

But in other cases, changes at times occur less from any deliberate act on the part of relevant political leaders than as the product of many imperceptible and often relatively unconnected individual actions. The technological innovations that made possible and led to the introduction of the mass media and other means of rapid and extensive communications in modern societies, for example, are scarcely "responses" undertaken by the members of a system specifically to meet any political conditions, stressful or otherwise. We might well question the validity, if not wisdom, of casting our net so broadly that all institutions or processes contributing to a sense of community might be interpreted as response to prevent any decline in support.

In the light of the analysis I have been using, however, it is a valid and useful interpretation to see many of these patterns of behavior as in fact political responses. To appreciate why they do constitute responses, in the first place we need to decide upon the extent to which we will consider awareness and intention behind an action as the *sine qua non* for its identification as a political response. Certainly, if for a moment we look at the individual as a personality system, we know he may respond to stimuli or seek to cope with his problems of stress without being conscious that his behavior has been triggered by any special kind of circumstances. He may even be unaware that his actions are related to the particular stimulus. Much effort in the exploration of personality is devoted to looking for the links between stimulus and subconscious response.

Society and the political system are not organisms. Yet they do consist of the interdependent actions of groups and persons and these are not performed in a vacuum. Here too, then, as in the case of the individual subjectively considered, it is likely that we can connect political behavior to the disturbances and potential threats to which, we have seen, every system by its very nature must be exposed. Regardless of the awareness or intent on the part of the relevant political members, if a plausible link between their actions and the threatened stress on support for the community can be established on the basis of existential criteria, there is no practical reason against considering such actions as political responses and much theoretical value in doing so.

But in the second place, the fact that, in some cases, members taking the action may not exhibit awareness of potential stress on support, does not in itself eliminate the probability that in many other instances, efforts to modify social parameters do flow directly from an explicit inference that it is desirable to do so. Not that the response need occur only when stress is present or imminent; it may simply take advantage of possibilities inherent in the situation.

The technological innovations of railways, airplanes or modern mass media of communication, and even of penny postage, occurred quite independently of any recognition that they would prove to be central devices for helping to create a sense of mutual political awareness. Yet governments avidly seized upon them as an obvious means for tightening the bonds of community. In the past of today's developed nations, public funds were used extensively, in one way or another, to promote the rapid expansion of the means of transportation and communication; it had implications, of course, for the economy, defense and other areas of life aside from feelings of mutuality. But the impact on integration was never lost from sight.

In the modernizing nations today, similar measures are being adopted, such as the manufacture or distribution of radio sets, to take a very simple illustration, that are not encouraged by the political elite in total disregard to their overtones as a means for unifying a people and overcoming particularistic tendencies. The mass media especially tend to be viewed as central weapons in the arsenal of authorities for building and maintaining conditions favorable for the input of diffuse support. At times, therefore, as in the case of transformations of the political structure itself, manipulation of social parameters may be interpreted as embodying political responses with significant consequences for stress, potential or real, as it relates to the input of diffuse support.

Stimulation of a Sense of Political Community: Political Variables as Responses

There are, however, other kinds of responses—directly political in nature and for that reason, at the level of theory, less open to question—that are available to the members of a system as they seek to cope with problems of change and stability. Indeed, the variety of political means that have been used historically in the constant efforts to stimulate or renew sentiments of mutual identification are legion.

Political Responses in General

The literature on nationality and nationalism has dealt exhaustively with the varied devices for stimulating a sense of cohesion. Concrete responses for the expression and reinforcement of a sense of community appear in patriotic ceremonies, the physical symbols of group identity such as totems, flags, songs, canonized heroes and, in literate societies, even in such trivial manifestations as the coloring of territorial maps. As in the case of the authorities and the regime, the processes of political socialization operate on maturing members of a system and contribute to the internalization of supportive attitudes toward the political community. Where such socialization is effective, it leaves the conviction that the perpetuation of the given division of political labor is a good in and of itself. But since responses such as these are so well known, they present no special problems for purposes of macroanalysis and we need probe no further in this direction.

However, as in the case of the regime and the authorities, there is one kind of response that is so central that we cannot pass it by without a special, if brief, comment. This has to do with the function of ideology in the generation of a high sense of community. In returning to ideology, it will incidentally permit me to round out more systematically the interpretation of the general function of ideology in mobilizing support, a subject that I have been developing intermittently as the need arose.

Ideology as a Special Response

The sense of political community may be described as a we-feeling among a group of people, not that they are just a group but that they are a political entity that works together and will likely share a common political fate and destiny. Ideology plays an important role in promoting this belief and sentiment.

To some extent, a feeling such as this will emerge as a by-product of a common history and of related shared traditions and expectations —the past experiences that the group has already undergone and which have been transmitted to each succeeding generation. To some extent it will be based upon what happens to the contemporary generation regardless of past experience. But in both instances, whether we are referring to the shared history of the members of a system or to the current collective experiences, if these factors are to have any impact on the community feelings of the members of the system and especially upon upcoming generations, they must be interpreted and codified in a form that makes them readily visible, accessible, and transmissible over the generations. Ideology performs this function for the political community.

At an earlier point, we have seen the vital part played by ideologies in stimulating diffuse support in the form of legitimation of the regime and authorities. Here we can see ideology in a different light, as a mechanism contributing to the persistence of the political community. To identify its function in stimulating diffuse support for this political object, I shall call it the communal aspect of ideology [7] in contrast with the partisan and legitimating kinds.

As responses that fortify sentiments of mutual political indentification among the members of a political system, communal ideologies will differ vastly in the content they transmit. But as it concerns their instrumental or expressive aspects, in the sense used earlier,[8] they derive their effectiveness in very much the same ways as do legitimating ideologies. Depending upon how we look at them, we may see them serving either as symbols to capture the minds of men or as expressions of the hopes, aspirations, and adaptive interpretations cherished by members of the system. Since communal ideologies do not differ in these respects from other ideologies, we need not pursue these important aspects further.

In addition, as in the case of other types, those ideologies related to the input of support for the political community may also be divisive rather than integrative. They may serve as a vehicle for expressing and intensifying cleavages in the community. Separatist or irredentist belief systems typically display the consequences of some kinds of community-oriented ideologies that seek to withdraw support from one community and transfer it to another. Depending upon the political community from whose point of view we are examining its consequences, the ideology will be integrative or divisive.

But aside from these characteristics that communal ideologies share with other types, the content of these community-directed ideologies will differ enormously. Here, therefore, as in most other instances in

---

[7] This description is not to be confused with the implications of the adjective "communal" as used with regard to non-Western kinds of social movements and groupings particularly.

[8] See chapter 19.

political systems, the function with regard to support is stable even though the mechanisms for its fulfillment, that is, their content and structure, will vary substantially.

Thus, the common ties of membership in a political system have been expressed in the form of kinship bonds traced back through common ancestors as revealed in a patronym or other group symbol, as attachment to the soil of a common geographically defined region, or in the assertion of a common nationality. The nation may be held out as the ideological symbol in terms of which the members of a system interpret their common political bonds as against the particularistic identification with tribe, village, region or class. Its potency for raising the level of otherwise uncommitted diffuse support is well enough established in the modern period to require no further elaboration. In their belief structure, members may see themselves as a "people" with a common past, destiny, and fate—a sentiment latent in the idea that "we" are French or American and that "they" are alien and outsiders. These belief systems need to be contrasted with the ideas held by members in other political systems that their primary bond stems from the fact that each has a personal obligation to a ruler or chief. Only in him, rather than in some collectivity, is the unity of the group to be expressed and maintained. Even the word community itself, used in its practical or lay meaning rather than its theoretical sense, stands as an ideological mechanism for summoning up support for the political community.

But whatever the precise content—and a partial theory of ideologies would be intensely concerned with describing and accounting for varieties of ideological content and the conditions of their effectiveness—the development of a sense of unity as a political group sharing a single division of labor with mutual political rights and obligations is not a state of mind that is taken for granted. Each system seeks in its own way, but always using some kind of communal ideology, to generate diffuse support behind the political community.

A Note on Ideologies and Diffuse Support

This analysis of communal ideology permits us to bring the discussion of support to a conclusion by rounding out what has been said about the impact of belief systems on other political objects as well. Although I am not seeking to formulate a partial theory of ideology, it will help to clarify the analysis of support if I now take stock of the way in which we have been dealing with belief systems as one of the major response mechanisms for initiating and bolstering the input of diffuse support.[9]

The Relationship between Omnibus Ideologies and the Three Analytic Types

Although our discussion has identified what have appeared to be three different types of ideologies—partisan, legitimating, and communal—in fact this way of putting the classification is somewhat misleading. Each presumed type may and normally will appear only as one aspect of a single, general ideology in which each of the other two aspects may be represented as well. For example, the ideologies of conservatism, liberalism, socialism, communism, fascism, Europeanism, democracy, or nationalism cannot be put exclusively into any one of my three categories. Each ideology constitutes a combined set of beliefs that may express orientations to all three political objects at one and the same time. Each stands as a parent ideological stem around which any one of the three types is intricately entwined. If we call the most inclusive set of ideological beliefs held by a member, his general or *omnibus ideology*, then each of the three types about which we have been speaking refers to one of the three interwoven strands or separable aspects of the omnibus ideology.

At times, any given omnibus ideology, the parent stem as it were, may be so heavily weighted with orientations to one or another aspect, that, for all intents and purposes, it is sufficient to characterize it as exclusively partisan, legitimating or communal in nature. But in the normal case, each of these represents analytic rather than necessarily concrete types of ideologies. If we wished to maintain an excessively and, therefore, cumbersome vocabulary, we would be compelled to describe our first type, not as partisan ideology but rather as "the partisan aspects of an omnibus ideology," and similarly for the other two types. To spare ourselves frequent circumlocutions such as this, I shall continue to speak of the various aspects of a general ideology or its relevant components as though they did appear as separate sets of

[9] For general discussions of ideology interesting in the light of the classification schema that I have been developing in this and earlier chapters, see Y. C. Kim, "The Functions of Political Orientations," 16 *World Politics* (1964) 205–221; I. L. Horowitz, "A Formalization of the Sociology of Knowledge," 9 *Behavioral Science* (1964) 45–55; L. Binder, *op. cit.*, especially at pp. 40 ff.; and A. S. Banks and R. B. Textor, *A Cross-Polity Survey* (Cambridge, Massachusetts: M.I.T. Press, 1963), pp. 81 ff.

beliefs. No harm will be done as long as we bear in mind the caveat that each aspect is usually found imbedded in a single set of beliefs.

Types of Ideologies

We can recapitulate very briefly the distinctive characteristics of what we now see are analytic rather than necessarily concrete types of ideologies. Partisan ideology refers to those special sets of beliefs helping to organize opinion about the kinds of day-to-day policies and practices that the political authorities ought to pursue. Relatively stable sets of alternative convictions about the nature of outputs are not confined to democratic societies, as we may be prone to believe. Even in the absence of an expressible public opinion on issues, in dictatorial systems partisan ideologies tend to take shape among factions within the elite, if only because they are useful as ways of winning the support of others in the bid for position or power. The degree of persistence and cohesion of this aspect of a general set of beliefs is always an empirical matter. It may well have vital survivalistic consequences; to be accused of constituting a permanent faction in a totalitarian system may be the beginning of a compulsory liquidation of an opposition.

Legitimating ideologies relate to those aspects of an omnibus set of beliefs that are oriented to supporting or challenging the regime and the right of the authorities to rule. They consist of those principles and values validating a structure, its norms, and occupants in terms of images of the future, interpretations of the present, and conceptions of the past. In systems where there is conflict over the legitimacy of the regime or authorities, this aspect of the belief systems is unavoidably visible. The contenders are struggling for the minds, if not of all the members of the system, at least of the politically relevant. But as we have seen, even in those systems where controversy over legitimacy does not exist, legitimating ideologies are no less inescapable, however unobtrusive they may be. They are necessary in most systems as a basis of support for the ongoing regime and its authorities in face of the inability of any system to meet all the wants of its members or heal all of the cleavages.

Finally, communal ideology emerges as it concerns the persistence or change of the political community. Within the general sets of belief prevalent in a system, we can expect to find convictions that express, as well as reinforce, the sense of political unity among the members as a group of persons sharing a common set of structures, norms, and values for political purposes.

The Interrelationship of Types

If we look at a number of omnibus ideologies in contemporary American life, we can perhaps illustrate the composite nature of these sets of beliefs and the way in which recognition of the components of each enables us to understand them better as sources of diffuse support for the political objects. Table 4 distinguishes four omnibus ideologies: radical conservatism, traditional conservatism, modern liberalism (as contrasted with the nineteenth century variety), and communism. All the ideologies taken together share at least one object of support. They do not question the perpetuation of the American political community. None of them espouses either irredentist, separatist, or fusionist views. Each continues to think of the political community as entailing those persons who today share a common set of authorities and regime, even though some of the ideologies may embody sharply divergent images of the nature of the regime and occupants of authority roles.

But with respect to other political objects, each omnibus ideology overlaps with the ideology on the rung just below it as we descend the ladder in Table 4, page 338. Thus, radical and traditional conservatism share support for many government policies such as the strengthening of states rights, opposition to government intervention in economic policy, medical care, or aid to education, and stiffening of America's posture toward the Soviet Union.

But they differ markedly over broad principles of legitimacy. Radical conservatism is predisposed, even if subtly and ambiguously, to reject popular democracy in favor of substantive principles based upon the wisdom of self-selected guardians or interpreters of the public interest. Traditional conservatism retains a belief, if not in all the processes, at least in the long established view that popular democracy is the most acceptable of all known alternatives.

Hence, from the point of view of cleavages over outputs, that is, with respect to the partisan aspects of their ideologies, radical and traditional conservatives would throw their support behind similar policies. But with respect to the acceptance of the regime and the authorities associated with it as legitimate, regardless of its stated intention, radical conservatism tends to whittle away at the prevailing moral approval of these objects. It questions what have been assumed to be the accepted premises of American democracy, such as its norms of popular participation, freedom of political thought and related restrained styles of political controversy. Radical conservatism, there-

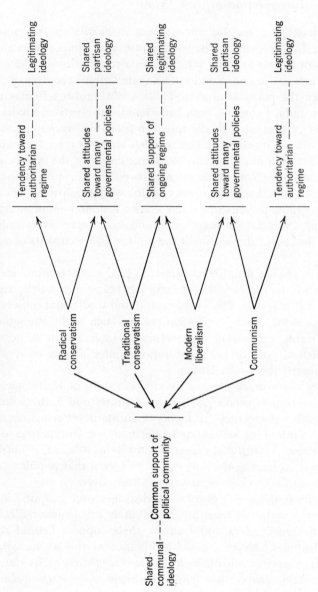

TABLE 4 OMNIBUS IDEOLOGIES AND DIFFUSE SUPPORT

fore, moves in the direction of the support of an authoritarian regime.

For the next pair of omnibus ideologies, traditional conservatism and modern liberalism, here again some components are shared and others are quite separate. As they relate to governmental policies, they are wide apart on the very outputs that draw radical and traditional conservatism together. But with respect to their support for the ongoing regime, even though there may be some differences in emphasis and interpretation, concerning the distribution of powers under the Constitution, for example, fundamentally advocates of neither ideology find fault with the ultimate goals, norms or structure of the system as it exists. Although they diverge in their partisan ideologies, they do espouse similar legitimating ideologies.

Finally, if we pair off modern liberalism and communism, they too share parts of their partisan ideologies, as with regard to the whole body of social welfare legislation. But in the area of the regime, as in the case of the radical right, regardless of their verbal statements, the advocates of communist ideologies lend their support to an authoritarian manner of organizing and implementing political power. And if we bend the ladder back on itself and draw both ends together, we can see that radical conservatism and communism may differ sharply in their support of day-to-day policies. But in their tendency to gravitate toward basically authoritarian regimes, they are not too far apart.

I am not concerned here with resolving in any sense the validity of an ideological position or, for that matter, in developing an exhaustive description of points of contact among these varying omnibus ideologies. Rather, I have been constructing categories with a view to developing a means for analyzing and understanding the place of ideologies as responses to stress, actual or potential, at each of the three levels in a system. With that in mind, it is apparent that ideologies that are usually described in undifferentiated terms, say, as conservative, liberal, or communist, when factored into their various dimensions, are revealed to have different effects at each of the three levels of a system. Any ideology may be both supportive and stressful, simultaneously, depending upon the aspect of the ideology that we may be considering at the moment.

It is clear, therefore, that the identification of the three types of ideologies—partisan, legitimating and communal—classified by the objects to which they refer, is not to be understood as asserting that they appear separately in the empirical world. It is possible for this to happen. But it is enough for our purposes that we see them solely as analytic categories, abstracted out of what may in fact be omnibus concrete ideologies in which all three types appear quite intermingled in form. But unless we carefully sort out the three types at the analytic level, it would be difficult if not impossible to clarify and appreciate the specific and different consequences that each aspect of a general ideology has for the mobilization of diffuse support in a system.

Expressive and Instrumental Consequences

To round out our recapitulation of aspects of ideologies, we must recall that the influence of omnibus ideologies on the input of support flows from the meaning they hold for the members of the system as vehicles of self-expression, that is, from their expressive side and as mechanisms of control, that is, from their instrumental side.

Thus we may interpret the partisan, legitimating, or communal aspects of an empirically undifferentiated ideology as an expression of a member's view of life, his economical way of organizing and thinking about the political world, and his way of interpreting the past or entertaining visions of the future. However inarticulate the member may in fact be and however unarticulated his ideology, for that matter, to the extent that it can be formulated by him or for him in terms intelligible to him, it offers, what for want of a more precise understanding of the psychological implications of ideologies, we may call a political meaning for his life. In this way it affects the attachment the members feel toward relevant political objects.

But the inflow of support may be a function of the relationship between the political leadership and the members as it is shaped by the prevailing omnibus ideology. For a leadership that seeks to rally members of a system to one of the political objects, ideology in all three aspects provides categories of thought through which persons may be drawn together into cohesive units available for control and manipulation. In this way it is a vital weapon in the arsenal for mobilizing support. By encouraging members to adopt the principles, purposes, and assumptions of an ideology as the premises of their behavior, a leadership may be successful in capturing the energies of the members for specific political objectives that they, the leadership, may consider desirable or necessary.[10]

[10] As we saw earlier, the instrumental effectiveness of an ideology will be related in part to its expressive adequacy. That is to say, a leadership is not entirely free to impress any or every ideology upon a membership; its appeal in expressive terms sets limits upon the range of ideologies that may be used to mobilize the support of a membership. This point is well documented, at the individual level, in R. E. Lane, *Political Ideology*.

Part Five

Outputs as Regulators
of Specific Support

2 2

The Nature of Outputs

WE HAVE MOVED A LONG WAY FROM THE INTRODUCTION OF OUR DIS-cussion of support as the second major input of political systems. In the process we have seen that it takes two major forms, diffuse and specific. Where the stress on a system threatens to reduce the level of support for one or another of the political objects, we have considered the various kinds of responses that typically emerge to enable it to cope with the stress through stimulating the input of diffuse support. Not that the system need survive or persist in its original form. Change, adaptation, self-maintenance, or redirection of efforts and goals are all equally means of coping with stress. But the important thing is that through the encouragement of diffuse support, it is possible for a society to perpetuate attachment to some set of authorities, to some regime, and to some kind of political community.

We have now come to the point where we can consider the second major kind of response by which a system, through the actions of its authorities, may seek to cope with the erosion of support. This response consists of a flow of outputs which, through their consequences, feed back into the system and may thereby add to (or subtract from) the level of support available to the political objects. Because of its direct relationship to the outputs, I have previously labeled it specific support.

Through various responses, the authorities may succeed in generating, not the diffuse attachment associated with legitimacy, dedication to a common interest, or identification with a political community, but the favorable attitudes that stem from offering the members of a system some felt or perceived returns and that accordingly appeal to their sense of self-interest. It is a form of what might be called political pump-priming.[1]

The link between outputs and the input of support is much more direct and discernible than in the case of diffuse support. Yet each kind of support will spill over to the other and influence it. Empirically,

[1] A term suggested to me by Professor Lawrence Senesh, Department of Economics, Purdue University.

343

that is to say, the prolonged encouragement emerging from specific support, as I have noted before, will be likely to lead to deep attachment to the various political objects in general. If a person feels favorably disposed toward an object for specific reasons and with sufficient frequency, he may develop an attachment to the object for its own sake alone.

Transactions Between a System and Its Environment

Delineation of the processes through which outputs arouse specific support will have to be postponed until we have had a chance to examine some general questions about the nature of the outputs themselves. The first of these involves a consideration of the general function they fulfill, in our present analysis, as transactions within a system or between the system and its environment.[2] The second will deal with a much more detailed specification of the referents of the term than our discussion has hitherto permitted or required.

To reconsider what I have already said about outputs, if we continue to look at them purely from the perspective of the internal operations of the political system, it would not be wrong to describe them as a terminal point in the intricate processes through which demands and support are converted into decisions and actions. To use the simple analogy of a manufacturing system once again, the outputs were viewed as the products forthcoming from the conversion operations performed on the mixture of items going into the system. Although this formulation is helpful and not inaccurate as far as it goes, it is by no means complete or representational.

If we stopped at this point, it would commit us to a very mechanical and misleading interpretation of the operations of political systems, as though they were simply devices for processing and reconciling differences among the relevant members of a system as reflected in the distribution of demands and support. Systems do help in the performance of this task; but they have an additional aspect which is consistent and indeed complementary with what has just been said. Recognition of this will bring sharply to the foreground our previous formulation of the nature of political life as a social system operating in an environment.

[2] For the concept transaction as applied to the outputs of complex organizations, see J. D. Thompson, "Organizations and Output Transactions," 68 *American Journal of Sociology* (1962) 309–324.

Outputs as Exchanges with the Environment

If we return to our image of a political system as an open, self-regulating, and self-transforming system, we can quickly see that the outputs frequently represent not a terminal point in an internal process but rather a transaction between the political system and its environment. It is the major way of identifying the positive contact that the system makes with its environment. Outputs are analogous in function, at the output end of a system, to demands and support on the input side.

The inputs, it will be recalled, summarize or mediate the disturbances and changes taking place in the environment. Thereby they serve as a conceptual means for simplifying our understanding of the way in which these parametric activities are transmitted to the various parts of the system. In much the same way, but this time taking the system rather than the environment as the starting point, outputs serve to conceptualize the ways in which the system acts back upon the environment and indirectly, therefore, upon itself, by modifying, at times, succeeding inputs of support and demands. For this reason there is little validity for continuing to consider the outputs as terminal points. They are, rather, part of a continuous chain of activities, soon to be identified as a feedback loop, in which inputs and outputs each directly or indirectly affect each other and together, the rest of the political system and its environment.

Indeed, a far more useful imagery conceives the system as a goal-oriented pattern of relationships through which the members are capable of adapting to their environment, using it as a source of resources, physical, financial or human, and, if necessary, transforming the system as well. It is not likely that we can find a system the members of which permit themselves to be buffeted about helplessly by events in their environment. All systems seek to adapt constructively, at least to some extent, by using, acting upon and shaping the conditions to which they are exposed. This is a major function of the outputs.

If a system were confronted with only benign conditions, inaction on the part of the members would matter little. But every system finds some inimical conditions in its environment that cannot be handled by members in their individual capacities. To prevent themselves as a social system from succumbing to the injurious effects from loss of support due to environmental and other disturbances, some action must be taken. Since another way of defining what a system does through its various parts is to identify and follow through the effects of its outputs, our present consideration of outputs will help us further in understanding ways in which systems cope with disturbances, internal as well as external in origin.

If we view outputs as the mechanism through which the authorities in a system reach out to cope with problems created by external changes as they are reflected through changing demands and support, we are led to see the outputs in their true, dynamic terms. They are not the product of the passive summation of demands, as though the role of the authorities were to add up the pros and cons in a controversy, compare one demand with another, cancel or modify one in favor of another and so forth, until, using the rules of the game in the system, they arrive at some decision or output and reconcile conflicts among relevant members.[3] If outputs had to be settled in this way alone, the alternatives for coping with a hostile environment would be severely reduced.

On the contrary, the authorities, or those politically relevant members under whose inspiration they are acting, are able to intervene positively in the course of events. They have the capacity to work constructively on the demands or issues, to recombine, reassess, assimilate or reject them. The authorities themselves may be able to sponsor entirely new demands, unthought of by other members in the system. On the basis of a complex set of operations that the authorities perform they may take the demands of others into consideration; but they may also on their own initiative establish objectives and evaluate needs in the light of present circumstances and anticipations of future resources and consequences. In voicing their own demands or ideas of what ought to be done, authorities may seek to direct or redirect the energies of the members of the system into new paths, or put to use new social groups that are emerging in the system, as in the case of developing nations today, or lay hold of resources available in the environment. This is what is meant by characterizing a political system as constructively adaptive and goal-oriented.[4] In adopting outputs, it is limited only by the variety of goals that can be invented and the conditions surrounding their implementation.

From a subjective point of view, the outputs of the authorities may appear to be directed narrowly toward maintaining themselves in

[3] This is fundamentally the approach typical of current group analysis which reaches back to A. F. Bentley's *Process of Government* for its justification.

[4] Talcott Parsons leans heavily on this conceptualization of the political function in society and although I have not found it sufficiently comprehensive to use as an exclusive approach, it does shed light on one aspect. See the references to his political writings in *A Framework for Political Analysis,* chapter I, footnote 1.

power in the face of competitors for their offices. Outputs may be viewed as an integral component in the struggle for power among politicians. Alternatively, the outputs may appear to be expressing the genuine, even rationally developed conceptions held by authorities of what would be best for the political system.[5] But regardless of the ideal self-image held by the authorities or the other clear implications that a set of outputs may have for the political fortunes of the authorities or the chances of their competitors, outputs also have consequences for persistence and change of political systems in their environments. They may help to maintain a minimal level of support for the various political objects. It is this aspect of outputs that tends to be neglected in theoretical inquiry and which lies at the heart of this part of our analysis.

Outputs as Transactions within a System

From this way of describing outputs as transactions between a system and its environment, it may appear that all outputs must take the form of boundary exchanges. But the fact is that many outputs significant in the production of specific support are also directed to objects within the political system itself. Although in general terms the location of the object of outputs is immaterial to our analysis, nevertheless we ought at least to recognize that the outputs may be oriented to matters within as well as outside the system. The concept *out*puts does not suggest that the authoritative allocation must be related to something outside the system; it refers only to the notion that the allocation emanates from or comes out of the behavior of the authorities. To speak of intrasystem outputs is therefore not even an apparent contradiction in terms.

Intrasystem outputs take two major forms. Many outputs relate exclusively to some aspect of the political system itself. Earlier we had seen that in response to support stress due to cleavages, direct regime changes typically occur as a coping mechanism. Legislative measures changing the methods for nominating and electing candidates, to use a simple example, are authoritative outputs that organize energies for purpose within the system. Insofar as the outputs are confined to the regime, by definition they must be intrasystem types.

[5] M. Weiner had described the authorities in India as possessing "images of themselves as bearers of the national policy . . ." *op. cit.*, p. 32. "From this viewpoint, government must steadfastly pursue a 'responsible' policy, which, in the economic sphere, involves allocating limited resources without regard to particularist demands so as best to achieve development goals" *Ibid.*, p. 9.

But in addition, outputs may ultimately relate to an object outside the political system. Yet in order to complete a transaction with the environment, it may be necessary to produce many preliminary intrasystem outputs. To conduct even so simple an act as to participate in a trade fair in a foreign country may require that a number of agencies from the differentiated departments dealing with foreign affairs, industry, commerce, and agriculture perform a series of actions in relationship to each other to implement and coordinate participation. The extrasystem objective is the terminal output, as it were; the prior decisions and actions contributing to the attainment of this final objective may involve a host of intermediate or sub-outputs. To the degree that such intermediate outputs concern themselves with objects within the system, they represent intrasystem outputs from political authorities that contribute toward the achievement of their terminal extrasystem objectives.

This relationship between intra- and extrasystem outputs pertains to every organization and group and is not unique to political systems alone. In fact, one of the main goals of operations research has been to learn how to regulate the flow of outputs from each subsystem so as to obtain an integrated pattern through which terminal outputs may be obtained at the least cost to the values involved.

But before we can proceed any further in examining the processes through which constructively produced outputs, whether intra- or extrasystem oriented, manage to elicit specific support as they link the system to the demands, I must for the first time fully clarify the meaning that I shall be attributing to the concept "outputs." This will be the task of the remainder of the present chapter.

General Properties of Outputs

As our analysis has proceeded, I have had frequent occasion to refer to outputs in passing. In doing so I have spoken of them in several ways: as authoritative allocations of values, as binding decisions and actions, and as transactions or exchanges between a system and its environment. These formulations all emphasize different aspects of outputs but omit others. Here I shall seek to provide a rounded and reasonably comprehensive picture of the referents embraced by the concept and the subtypes of outputs that we shall find it useful to identify. In doing so, I shall be presenting concretely the varied sources from which specific support may derive.

The Authorities as Producers of Outputs

Fundamental to the present conceptualization of outputs is the idea that they consist of a stream of activities flowing from the authorities in a system. It is the fact that they are produced by the authorities that distinguishes them as outputs. Politically powerful members may well play the tune to which the authorities dance and in this sense they effectively dominate the outputs. But without processing their own demands through the authorities, their demands would not be converted into recognized systemic outputs. Whatever the politically powerful members in fact decided to do, their decisions and actions would not have the compelling quality of authoritative allocations. In principle, their behavior would be no different from that of any other individuals in the system who may also act in ways that are relevant to the functioning of the system.

Not all political activities that have consequences for a system or even its environment are outputs. To characterize behavior as an output of a system simply because it does affect either what happens within the system or some of the parametric systems, would be to broaden the term so widely as to leave it quite ineffectual for analytic purposes. Through the concept "outputs," I am seeking to isolate those activities through which the resources and energies of the members of a system may be organized, focused and committed. It is the authorities who are at least nominally able to mobilize these energies and resources by virtue of their positions of authority, whether or not they are acting independently or as puppets in the hands of some secret and powerful cabal. That is to say, the actions of the authorities have special significance in a political system as we have already seen; they are considered to be binding upon the members of the system. We are compelled, therefore, to identify the authorities as the producers of the outputs flowing from a political system.

For at least two reasons it is necessary to emphasize the exclusive role of authorities in producing outputs. Other members of a system engage in political activities that may flow into the environment. As the result of organizing a series of large scale political strikes of workers in major industries, it may be possible to bring about disastrous consequences for an economy. Indeed, this may be the very purpose behind the strikes. Yet the politico-economic elite making the decisions involved in this behavior are not to be considered as producing political outputs in my sense of the term. Conceptually, we are able to handle the consequences of their behavior as an event that has a decided impact on the level of support, as through its aggravation or moderation of cleavages, or on the volume and variety of demands being voiced by the members of the system in general. If we conceived of such activities as outputs, the study of outputs would be equivalent to the examination of all political behavior and we would be no further ahead than when we began our analysis. Outputs are only one type of political behavior.

This brings us to the second point. Outputs are indeed a special kind of political behavior or activity because through them persons who occupy the special roles of authority in a system are able to exercise some control or direction over other members of the system. By virtue of the recognition or acceptance of their authoritative powers, the members acting in authority roles are able to commit and direct the resources and energies of other members of the system toward the attainment of goals. No society could survive without providing for such kinds of activities in at least minimal form.

Furthermore, much information necessary for producing outputs tends to converge toward the authorities. It is toward them that demands and expressions of support or hostility are directed in a political system. In all political systems they are expected to convert this information into some kind of authoritative allocations. If information about demands and support were to begin to flow toward other members in the system in a consistent and persistent pattern, this would be evidence that an unstable structure of dual power would be taking shape.[6] We would be driven to suspect that the authorities in the system would soon find themselves displaced by a new set of individuals or that civil conflict was about to break out.

In brief, outputs are activities that may have consequences for a system itself or for the environment in which the system exists. But there are many kinds of activities such as these in which individual members of a system engage, just as we have seen there are numerous inputs. From these outputs and inputs we are able to select those that have special importance in helping us to understand the way in which a system functions. What distinguishes the outputs of interest to our analysis is that they are produced by or, as we shall immediately see, they are closely associated with those who hold the positions of authority in the system and thereby set the goals toward which the energies and resources of the system may be directed. This is why I have called them authoritative allocations of values. They are central to our analysis because, as I hope to show, through them a system is able to help to determine the level of support forthcoming for its various political objects.

[6] See chapter 13, especially footnote 2.

Outcomes as Distinguished from Outputs

Outputs produced by the authorities include the binding decisions, their implementing actions and, as we shall see directly, certain associated kinds of behaviors. Such outputs may relate to the political system itself or to its environmental systems. But just as we cannot characterize all activities in which members of a political system engage as outputs of that system, so we cannot designate all the consequences that flow from what we shall settle upon as the outputs of the system, as constituent parts of these outputs. We must distinguish the outputs from their consequences or what we may call, their *outcomes*. Failure to do this would lead us to consider the infinite chain of effects that might flow from an authoritative allocation as part and parcel of that allocation. We might even be driven ultimately to consider all social behavior as part of the output of the authorities.

Let us look at some illustrations of this difference between outputs and outcomes. An output, such as a decree or a constitutional amendment, may change the structure of the regime so as to eliminate all political parties but one. This is the direct or nearest effect of the output and is to be considered part of it. The actions leading to the elimination of parties are taken under the authority of the decision and are initiated by it. The consequences or outcomes for the operation of the system, however, and for the control exercised by the members over the authorities, will be incalculable. The decision may change the course of history. Consequences so remote cannot usefully be assimilated to the initial decisions and implementing actions. Accordingly they are not to be interpreted as an integral part of the outputs.

To take another example, an administrative agency may make a decision to increase interest rates and bank reserves. These decisions are in due course communicated to the appropriate persons and rates and reserves are adjusted to the announced criteria. These are outputs of the system as initiated and implemented by an administrative agency and their proximate effects on the economy as conformity is achieved. But beyond that, as the secondary and tertiary effects of the initial administrative decisions and actions begin to make themselves felt on the economy, assuming no additional governmental intervention for the moment, the results are very closely related to prior political actions and can be designated as outcomes of these actions.

A decision is made to permit a linguistic group in India to organize into a state of its own. This is an output in the form of an authoritative decision. Even before it is implemented, rioting breaks out instigated by opponents of the scheme. This aggravates the general social tensions in the community and creates frictions that prevent cooperation in many nonpolitical areas of life. These are the outcomes of the political outputs.

In short, an output is the stone tossed into the pond and its first splash; the outcomes are the ever widening and vanishing pattern of concentric ripples. The actual decisions and implementing actions are the outputs; the consequences traceable to them, however long the discernible chain of causation, are the outcomes.

Types of Outputs

Authoritative and Associated Outputs

By the very way in which the outputs have been described, we might have expected that, produced as they are by the authorities, they would include only decisions and actions of the authorities that members of the system consider or are compelled to accept as binding. Indeed, this limiting view of outputs may seem to have been definitely implied in what we have just been discussing.

That these formal outputs must certainly be the starting point cannot be denied. Without them we have no political system and, by postulation, no society. But to confine our observations to the outputs of the authorities that are authoritative would be to narrow unnecessarily our range of interest and to neglect too cavalierly behavior that cannot sensibly be divorced from the formal outputs as sources of specific support.

Accompanying the formal outputs, very frequently, are decisions and actions that could be included as binding only if we forced the language of our analysis unmercifully. Yet their consequences may at times be such as to be virtually indistinguishable from the binding outputs with respect both to the goals of the system and to the effect on support. They are actions that are related to the binding allocations in that they occur in association with them. As part of their role, those who participate in the production of the authoritative outputs are able, as well, to engage in the production of these non-authoritative outputs.

Every system has non-authoritative or what we may call *associated* as against *authoritative* outputs. These perform a function similar to the authoritative outputs in creating or alleviating supportive stress on a system by priming the political pumps. Without the presence of persons capable of producing binding outputs, the associated kind would not be possible; but without the capacity to produce associated outputs, binding outputs alone would scarcely be able to carry the burden of meeting demands and building support, a point that will become clearer as the discussion develops.

Statements and Performances as Outputs

Both authoritative and associated outputs will typically take two forms: verbal statements and performances. At times, as our analysis has progressed, I have spoken of outputs as binding decisions, at other times, as actions. Individually, neither of these formulations is erroneous. But neither is by itself complete. Outputs appear in both modes, as verbal statements and as performances, and each mode has a number of subvariants.

It is true, in most cases a verbal output may ultimately need to be backed up with at least some token performances. It may be considered incomplete without subsequent actions to follow up the statements. The passage of a law results in verbal statements which promise that the authorities will provide certain goods or services. Unless the expected performances are fulfilled, the law may be considered insufficient as a stimulus of support. Nevertheless, at times, aside from the services actually performed, the verbal statement itself may have important consequences for support. As we shall see, the verbal mode of outputs has become increasingly prominent and essential in modern mass societies and plays a major integrating role in all large-scale political systems.

This way of classifying outputs gives us four basic types, as represented in Table 5, each of which is uniquely relevant to the development of specific support in a system. Our task in the remainder of this chapter will be to explore the prominent characteristics of each type of outputs.

TABLE 5 TYPES OF OUTPUTS

Qualities	Modes	
	Statements	Performances
Authoritative	Binding decisions, laws, decrees, regulations, orders, and judicial decisions	Binding actions
Associated	Policies, rationales, and commitments	Benefits and favors

Authoritative Outputs

Authoritative Statements

When they appear as statements, authoritative allocations take the form of verbal indications of the binding rules that are to guide the performance of tasks. They are decisions on the part of the authorities that certain actions should be or will be taken. In a legal system, they appear as laws, decrees, formal legislation, regulations, or administrative and judicial decisions. In non-legal systems, they may simply be the opinion of a council of elders or of a paramount chief, about what ought to be done under the circumstances. But whatever the specific form, they stand as authoritative outputs since they indicate that the authorities intend that activities will be undertaken to maintain or modify the distribution of some of the valued things in the given society.

Although it is true that such statements are usually prolegomena to action to be taken under their authorization or justification, nevertheless, aside from these performances, the statements themselves may act independently so as to contribute to or ameliorate stress on a system due to output failure. For example, the promised or indicated output may never occur; it may prove impossible to implement the decision, or the authorities concerned may never have seriously intended to do so. Yet the verbal output may in itself affect the attitude of the members and to obtain the input of their support, this may be sufficient.

The importance of all statements derives from the fact that persons obtain some satisfaction from symbols, as we shall see in greater detail shortly. Verbal symbols, such as those embodied in ideologies, are able to stimulate or relieve inner tensions and articulated demands. In many cases, the statement that a given situation exists, or that sometime in the distant future action will be taken, or that action is already under way may be enough, regardless of the actualities, to provide members with the gratifications they seek in the political processes or with the release from frustrations they would like to avoid. A law protecting civil liberties, even if it is not regularly or vigorously invoked and enforced, may nevertheless constitute an output capable of purchasing considerable support for the authorities or hostility (negative support) on the part of those opposing it. How far verbal expression can go in either direction is another matter. Man does not live by words alone; but they can substitute for real nourishment over considerable intervals of time.

Authoritative Performances

By implication, I have already suggested the general nature of authoritative performances. Binding decisions concerning what will or ought to be done may not be enough. Members also seek the actual goods and services implied; or the authorities expect that the goods and services required by the authoritative decisions will be forthcoming. Performances may take the form of compelling others to do something, such as to pay taxes or serve in the armed forces. Performances may involve doing things for others such as extinguishing a fire, arresting a violator of the peace, transmitting funds or food in the execution of foreign aid.

In cases such as these, the allocation of values is a direct implementation of a verbal statement of the intention to perform the actions, if the circumstances arise. Performance consists of the actions actually taken in the light of the circumstances that exist when an effort is made to implement the formal decision. The performance represents the effective as against the formal allocation of values.

But a statement of intention is not intrinsic to performance outputs and need not precede the action. The authorities may just act without forewarning or any foreshadowing of their inclinations. Whether or not there are verbal outputs that precede or accompany the performance outputs is a matter of indifference here. What we are concerned with is the effort to isolate the possible independent effect, not of what the authorities say or promise, but of what they do or have done, on the generation of specific support.

Performance outputs will assume two forms. In one, some tangible objects or facilities will be provided; in the other, some intangible services.[7] Tangibles are the stock in trade of authorities as sources for stimulating support. Money may be distributed as through the payment of unemployment insurance or public relief. Physical facilities, visible and usable, may be provided in the form of highways, power plants, dams, military hardware. In socialized societies, the authorities undertake to provide most of the major goods and facilities and

[7] Here I am indebted to an original and stimulating discussion of outputs in a forthcoming work by Bertram Gross entitled *The Managing of Organizations: The Administrative Struggle*, 2 vols. (New York, Free Press of Glencoe, 1964), especially chapters 21–23. In it, Gross distinguishes between tangible and intangible outputs of organizations. He compellingly demonstrates the considerable possibilities for measuring outputs of both kinds, a task which passes beyond our scope.

accordingly have at their disposal vast means for influencing the level of support in a negative as well as a positive direction.

But in all systems the authorities also engage in allocating intangible services such as law and order, defense, transportation, education, or medical attention. Performances such as these may be related to tangible things, their possession or use, as in the case of dams, highways, railways, or hospitals. But the ultimate satisfaction comes from the services provided through these facilities.

Intangible outputs often embrace various kinds of psychic rewards which may be distributed by the authorities and which may be even more capable of fostering support than material goods. Through outputs it has been possible to contribute to a group's sense of dignity or worth, as in cases where discrimination on the grounds of race, creed, or color has been prohibited, or where ethnic groups may be carefully included in positions of esteem among the authorities. Where outputs enable deprived groups to share in the basic values of a society, even though such groups may not be materially better off and even though improved social services may not be put at their disposal, the opportunity to participate in these values may arouse deep and enduring supportive sentiments. Although status, prestige, recognition, and social equality are states of mind that cannot be legislated into existence, outputs that help to allocate these values in a system, intangible as they are, cannot be neglected in our consideration of sources of support.

From time to time efforts have been made to describe the major kinds of general services expected of the authorities as a minimal basis for the support of a regime or the authorities. MacIver has declared that "there are certain functions that all governments always fulfill, on whatever scale, such as the police function and the administration of justice." [8] Merriam has itemized "the ends and purposes of government" to be " (i) external security, (ii) internal order, (iii) justice, (iv) general welfare, and (v) freedom." [9]

But it is doubtful whether any universal list of substantive ends could ever be constructed. Even for what to Western society appears to be so elemental and inescapable a set of services as the maintenance of law and order, it is questionable whether all systems do or must provide such services if they are to persist. In some cases, those of various tribes in southern Africa, Schapera has concluded that the only com-

---

[8] R. M. MacIver, *The Web of Government* (New York: Macmillan, 1947), p. 316.
[9] C. E. Merriam, *Systematic Politics* (Chicago: University of Chicago Press, 1945), p. 31.

mon services provided through the political system are the maintenance of territorial boundaries, resistance to external aggression, and
organization and direction of various cooperative enterprises, frequently involving the whole society.[10] But actions to assure law and
order fall outside the expected and actual range of performance of the
political or administrative apparatus. Among the Bushman groups,
self-help is the only sanction for violations of custom that has the
strength of law.

It is clear that once we widen our sample of political systems broadly
enough, we may have considerable difficulty in assigning any single list
of substantive outputs to all systems. The kind of performance outputs
provided by political systems is a function of time and place; they are
not an inherent part of political systems as such.

Associated Outputs

Associated outputs are those statements and performances that are
connected in some way with the authoritative outputs and which
could not have the consequences they do unless they were so associated. In and of themselves either these statements and performances
would prove ineffective or they would have little chance of occurring.

Associated Statements

The associated statements that I am calling outputs, we meet in the
guise, sometimes, of ideological convictions or rationales and at others,
as simple articulations of policy. In each case they derive their effectiveness for fostering or eroding support from the fact that they accompany and help to interpret or explain authoritative statements or actions. The full implications and meaning of a binding decision or set
of actions may not be apparent to the members of a system or the
allocations involved may not be appreciated in the way considered
desirable by the authorities. Whatever capacity such authoritative outputs may have to increase or discourage support may be reinforced or
counteracted as the case may be, by associated statements that succeed
in interpreting, explaining, or elaborating the implications of the outputs.

[10] "The enforcement of law and order—what MacIver calls 'the policy function
and the administration of justice'—is not, as he maintains, one of the functions
'that all governments always fulfill, on whatever scale.' " I. Schapera, *Government
and Politics in Tribal Societies* (London: Watts, 1956), p. 217.

Ideologies act in this direction by helping to mobilize specific support in the varied ways we have already examined with respect to diffuse support. In the present case, however, we are interested in the fact that the authorities will use ideological statements to interpret, justify, and explain authoritative outputs in the hope of winning the specific support of the members for the outputs. At the very least they hope to maintain support for themselves as well as for the other political objects.

For example, in developing systems, decrees restricting freedom of speech and organization may be made more palatable when the authorities link them to the need to cope with conditions permitting rapid economic growth and retaining national independence. The ideologies of nationalism and of the significance of material growth induce members to tolerate or accept such outputs more readily. The ideological statements accompany the outputs but unlike the laws limiting freedom, these statements do not represent binding allocations. Yet the ideological statements, as associated outputs, may have an enormous influence upon the way in which the authoritative outputs are received. They may make the difference between acceptance and total rejection. Not only would it be artificially restrictive to omit such associated statements as outputs capable of affecting the input of support; we would be needlessly neglecting an influential variable in doing so.

Associated statements may also appear in the form of policies. We are accustomed to thinking of policies in two senses.[11] In the one, we refer to the decision rules adopted by authorities as a guide to behavior. This is the meaning of the term when we talk about those policies that are in fact adopted by authorities as the binding operating rules. This is what we may mean when we question the wisdom of the policy of a government as incorporated into its laws on a subject. In this sense, policies would just be a term for a kind of authoritative verbal output.

But the term is also used in a second and broader sense to describe the more general intentions of the authorities of which any specific binding output might be a partial expression. As such, the statements of policies are not binding for the members. But by revealing the intentions of the authorities, they do help to interpret the meaning and direction of authoritative outputs and to this extent may encourage or discourage their acceptance by the membership.

[11] See N. D. Feld, "Political Policy and Persuasion" 2 *Conflict Resolution* (1958) 78–89, for a distinction between policies and decisions.

In the United States, we find associated outputs of this kind in the State of the Union message from the President to Congress; in Britain, in the Queen's Speech from the Throne. Policy statements are usually issued in connection with most major pieces of legislation. In all cases of policy statements, the objective may in part be that of explanation or information. But more frequently it represents an effort to persuade the members to accept an authoritative output that has been or will be produced. In this way associated statements and binding outputs become firmly interlocked. Indeed, the relationship between the two kinds of output is so close that in many legal jurisdictions, the courts have found it convenient and reasonable to examine the policy statements issued in connection with new authoritative legislative outputs in order to improve their understanding of the meaning of the legislation.

But not all associated output statements need to be so intimately related with binding outputs. In some cases, associated statements may appear in the form of proposals for authoritative decisions that are ultimately rejected. Yet they do not lose their character as a type of output that may prove influential in holding or building the support of members. In a council of elders, for example, a competitor for power may propose alternative courses for action, even if they are known to be doomed to rejection, as long as their proponent feels that the proposals may help to prove to some followers that their interests are not being neglected.

Similarly in modern legislatures, bills that are turned down or that die at some stage in the proceedings are not to be slighted as significant outputs from the system. It is true, they do not become authoritative since they fail to obtain approval. Nevertheless, in some cases spurious efforts to obtain favorable action are made through bills introduced in open anticipation of failure. The assumption is that some members of the system will gain satisfaction from knowledge that efforts were made on their behalf.

However, even where there is no special attempt to deceive and a bill is introduced out of a genuine desire and conviction about its possible acceptance, disapproval by a legislature may still have similar consequences. We have yet to find studies made of the impact that nonauthoritative verbal outputs such as these have on the level of support in a system. But we can imagine that minorities, in any area of policy, may well receive some of their gratification with the course of political events from the knowledge that in the political forum they have had a voice at least strong enough to be heard.

Associated Performances

The satisfactions coming from a political system are also intimately connected with performances which assume the form of tangible goods and intangible services associated with authoritative action and yet which do not themselves acquire any binding quality. In many instances, the growth of specific support owes as much to these associated performances as to those that are manifestly authoritative in character.

Incidental to the position that a person in authority holds, he will be able to take action that possesses a binding quality and accordingly falls into our category of authoritative outputs. But in addition, the position of authority will improve his opportunity to grant benefits, advantages, favors and facilities that stem from the range of discretion, power, special knowledge, and skills linked with his position. Through control over money, position, prestige and power itself, a person in authority may be able to regulate informally the allocation of these values so as to influence the level of specific support, both positively from those who benefit and negatively from those who may suffer.

Various motivations may lurk behind associated performances of this kind. To begin with, they need not all be self-centered or incompatible with the dominant ethics of the system. In many instances, it is true, such action may be designed to build up a following of one's own, as in the case of a legislator with his eye on the next election, or an administrator who seeks to strengthen his relationship with his clients. Typically, persons in positions of authority in all legal systems quickly become accustomed to fortifying support for themselves, with incidental consequences for the political objects, through performing numerous small and large services for individual or groups of members, services that are over and beyond the production of authoritative outputs.

For example, in representative systems, the legislator's proximity to the formulation and execution of binding decisions puts him in a strategically effective position for adding informal benefits as a bonus to his constituents in the way of outputs. Indeed, with respect to the French political system and its characteristic *immobilisme* during the Third and Fourth Republics and the virtual formal ineffectiveness of French legislators today, it is said that a major factor that has kept the system operating at even a modest level of effectiveness, has been the capacity and willingness of the legislators to perform such extra-legal services through the permanent bureaucracy. An examination of the sources of specific support for the political objects in the French system cannot neglect the role of such associated performance outputs.

But the motivation behind such outputs may also reflect a desire to do a job well, in accordance with the criteria of the occupation, out of a sense of duty under the spur of one's craft, or in dedication to the purposes of a profession. Without thought of personal advantage, the fulfillment of a task may seem to an administrator to require special favors for or help to his clients, over and above what might be formally required or even expected. Persons in positions of authority quickly become accustomed to utilizing their discretion, knowledge, and power to gain advantages otherwise not obtainable for their clients and yet which do not pass beyond law or recognized ethics.

Finally, the motivation for outputs of this kind may lie in anticipation of favors or some special reward contrary to the recognized and accepted rules of the system. Bribery and corruption are classic illustrations of this kind of associated performance outputs. But even though practices may be demonstrably illegal or merely reprehensible according to the prevailing ethical code, as long as they contribute to the services performed for members of society, we would have to include them within the category under discussion. Extended reliance on this kind of outputs as a source of specific support for political objects may well prove more effective in stressing than in maintaining a system. This would seem to be demonstrated by the extensive corruption that has accompanied the decline of numerous systems, such as the Roman Republic. But the data compel us to face up to the fact that although systems will vary enormously in the degree to which members obtain part of their gratifications through the operation of corruption, it is doubtful whether any system has been able entirely to escape such sources of specific support.[12]

[12] Compare with what M. Weiner has to say in explaining some of the consequences in India today. "(Party) machines played an important part in integrating immigrants into American life. They sponsored Americanization programs, facilitated contact between communities, and opened channels between the citizen and his government. Most important, the new, potentially revolutionary citizens were given the feeling that government was not intractable, unlike many of the European governments from which they had fled. Admittedly, much was done through a patronage system that often overlooked merit, and there was considerable corruption. But looking back to the late nineteenth centuries, it is apparent that this may have been a small price to pay for acculturating immigrants into a democratic society." op. cit., p. 71.

Indirectly, R. E. Lane in Political Ideology makes somewhat the same point. There he reports that "the laissez-faire morality of Eastport, and America in general in the twentieth century, has a special application to the matter of corruption. As we have seen, most people believe it is there, and not on a petty scale either, although mostly confined to the local and subordinate ranges of politics. But most of

As exchanges that take place between the political system and its environment, outputs appear in many forms. This makes it possible for the actions of the authorities to influence the level of support in an equally varied number of ways. Heterogeneous types of outputs conduce to heterogeneous effects. To these we shall now turn. It will lead us to scrutinize closely the processes through which outputs, precisely because of their variety, are able to stimulate or negate the input of specific support.

the men also believe that the use of governmental power to give your friends jobs, or to get contracts for firms you're interested in, is simply another method of payment, like a medical-fee system or a church tithing system. They do not see how it affects the quality or service in any serious way. And, since they think the level of temptation very high, they do not believe the degree of wickedness implied is very great. It does not affect their confidence in a responsible government; it is not, indeed, a source of great concern for them." p. 327.

23

The Feedback Loop

OUTPUTS OF THE VARIED SORTS DISCUSSED IN THE LAST CHAPTER REPRESENT transactions spanning the boundary between a system and its environment or between subsystems in the system itself. They are able to affect the persistence or change of a system through the influence they wield over the level of support. This impact on support may be either direct or derivative, as we shall see. It is direct when it meets some present or anticipated demand of the members. It is derivative when it creates conditions that prevent the occurrence of dissatisfactions at some future date. But regardless of the way in which support is generated, the fact that the varied kinds of outputs are able to contribute to an increase or decline in support and that major kinds of system disturbances and stress originate in fluctuations of support means that outputs will help to shape the destiny of a system.

But we cannot take it for granted that the mere existence of outputs will prevent support from falling below some stressful threshold. We must inquire into how this comes about. What kind of conditions determine the influence that outputs have upon support? I shall begin such an inquiry in this chapter. We shall discover that a decisive factor at work involves the kind of information that is fed back to the authorities about the nature and consequences of their decisions and actions.

Basic Assumptions

In order to begin to look at the possible independent effects of such information upon outputs and indirectly, therefore, upon support, it will be helpful to begin this discussion with four assumptions. These will temporarily and analytically eliminate variability that may be due to fluctuations in a number of factors.

1. The interrelationships of outputs, demands, and support: To the extent that a member perceives his demand as being satisfied, we may

363

make the very plausible assumption that he will be more rather than less inclined to support the various political objects.

2. Responsiveness of the authorities: The authorities are always responsive to the information they receive about the degree of support being offered by the politically relevant members and they desire to increase that support by every means at their disposal. Later I shall question this obviously unlikely condition. But here it is necessary. If the authorities were entirely indifferent to the demands of all other members in the system and attended only to their own autonomously generated demands and ideas, no problem would ever arise about seeking to relate outputs to support. Only by accident could outputs have any positive effects.

3. Competence of authorities: I shall discount entirely factors relating to the competence of authorities—what I shall later call internal resources—in pursuing their objectives effectively. I shall take it for granted that they have the necessary skill, imagination, intelligence, and organizational ability to achieve whatever goals they adopt.

4. Resources available to authorities: I shall assume that the authorities have material and social means—what I shall later characterize as external resources—in sufficient degree to meet demands and thereby to stimulate support. In later chapters, each of these assumptions will be questioned where relevant, so that we may extricate their variable influence on the behavior of the authorities in meeting support.

Information Feedback about Outputs

The Function of Information

Under the optimal conditions just specified, the objectives of the authorities will be to match outputs to demands. The effectiveness with which they succeed will be clearly and directly related to the amount and kind of information they have at their disposal about two kinds of matters. First, the information will need to describe the general state of the system and its environment. The authorities need as much relevant information as is feasible about these areas if they are to act intelligently in meeting any possible loss of support. But second, they must also have information about the effects that flow from any specific kinds of actions that they may hazard in the way of outputs. Intelligence about existing conditions in the system and its environment is not enough; the authorities must be able to evaluate the consequences of whatever behavior they have already undertaken or are in process of undertaking.

There can be no question that to expect any society to provide the authorities with even reasonably complete information in these matters would represent an impossible order. But we can understand the importance attaching to some information at least, if we glance for a moment at what we could expect to happen under the alternative extreme, that is, where there was no information at all either about the state of the system and its environment or about the effects of previous, current or proposed outputs.

Under these alternative conditions the authorities would have to work completely in the dark insofar as they desired or sought to meet demands or encourage support. For one thing, lacking relevant information about the state of the system or its environment, the authorities would not know whether the system was being menaced by a deterioration in the level of support for one or another of the political objects or whether there was trouble ahead in this respect. Only by pure chance could any actions by the authorities be relevant to stress if it should unknowingly be occurring.

Furthermore, even if we assume that from the nature and volume of demands and expressions of discontent, the authorities could infer that support was lagging or threatening to fall below the critical threshold point, if they did not have information about the effects of their outputs, the authorities would be virtually helpless to stem the tide. If they did take action of some sort, they would not know whether it was helping or hindering the flow of support. They would be unable to decide whether to continue the same kind of outputs, or modify them in some way. Even if they concluded that some change was necessary, they would have little idea about the new direction in which their outputs ought to move.

This illustration of what must happen under the extreme and unlikely condition of the total absence of information about the effect of outputs indicates the vital role that such information must play. If the authorities are to be able to gear their outputs in any way at all toward some support goal—whether it be to keep a system within its critical range or to drive it quickly beyond to its own destruction and transformation into a new type of system—a minimal condition is that they must have some information about the current state of support and the relevant consequences that flow from their outputs. Otherwise each output would be a purely random shot in the dark.

It is from as simple a requirement as this—the ability to provide for a flow of information back to the producers of outputs about the state of the system and its environment and about the effects of their own decisions and actions—that the authorities find the opportunity, although not the necessity, to settle on a course of behavior and to seek to keep to it or modify it as circumstances dictate. This does not mean that the objectives of the authorities will or must necessarily be to seek stability for their system. Historically it is not rare for some authorities to seek fundamental changes in their systems, as is indeed the case in many developing nations today. It also occurred in May, 1958 in France where de Gaulle encouraged the destruction of support for the old regime in order to transfer it to a new one.

Even if the authorities were to seek stability, the presence of such information would not assure it. It is not unusual for authorities who pursue the preservation of the *status quo* as a passionate goal, to find that through pure incompetence or lack of resources they fail. Information flowing back to the authorities about their own behavior does not compel them to use it as a basis for wise decisions. Yet without some amount of such information, no system would be able to persist in a stable world, much less in a changing one, except by chance.

The Feedback Loop

The return of information of this kind to the authorities I shall call *feedback;* the channels it follows and is intimately connected with, the *feedback loop;* the actual flow patterns and related effects, the *feedback processes.* It is by virtue of the role that information feedback plays in a system—the volume and accuracy of the information it provides, the delays in the transmission of this information, the direction in which it flows, and the behavior in the form of outputs that it inspires—that the authorities possess an essential means to mold and shape objectives in order to seek to cope with the stress inherent in the decay of support.

Strictly speaking and customarily, the concept "feedback" applies only to information. It is on the basis of the information returning to decision-makers that they are able to regulate or "correct" their behavior. But there are also other forms of behavior that are closely interwoven with or related to the returning flow of information. The reactions to the information lead to measures that seek to regulate behavior in the system, these measures act as stimuli to others so as to bring them into line, and the response of these others is then communicated back to the decision-makers to begin another control cycle, as it were.

The concept "feedback loop" is being suggested here as a way of identifying not only information that returns, but all the other actions directed toward taking advantages of this information. That is to say, feedback loop will refer to two interlocked processes: first, the regulative outputs of a system and their consequences—these represent the way in which the authorities will adjust to the situation in which they find themselves; second, the information itself that is fed back about the state of the system and the consequences flowing from whatever regulative or adjusting actions have been undertaken by the authorities. We shall see that although information feedback is a major mechanism through which stress may be handled by the authorities, it plays this function only because the authorities are also able to respond through the production of outputs. These outputs in turn have characteristic effects on demands and on support that are relevant for the input of specific support.

In brief, the feedback loop will identify a set of processes, composed of information and related outputs and their consequences, that enables a system to control and regulate the disturbances as they impress themselves on the system. If feedback—both information and responses —did not exist, the system would find itself utterly exposed to the vagaries of chance. But since it does exist in social systems, we are faced with the problem of trying to understand how it operates so that we may appreciate another way a system has at hand to cope with stress. To do this, we shall have to examine not only the feedback of information but the whole process of regulation that is inextricably woven into it.

The General Functions of Feedback

Every century or two some great seminal idea dramatically appears and spreads into the far corners of social thought, there to be shaped, adapted and molded, often beyond easy recognition, to the intellectual needs and purposes of other disciplines or fields of inquiry. Newton's underlying notions of a lawful world of matter seized the imagination of men devoted to an understanding of society; and Darwin's theory of evolution left a permanent mark on the formulation of research tasks in the social sciences. The dominant and most fertile intellectual innovation of our own age has been that of information feedback.[1]

[1] Those familiar with feedback as it appears in information models will quickly detect, in my analysis, numerous divergences and variations in conceptual formulations. One reason for this is that what information feedback models neglect of necessity—namely, the input of support and its relationship to feedback proc-

Feedback is an idea that has invaded many of the major areas of knowledge bringing with it new insights into old problems and fathering whole new generations of ideas in fields as divergent as physics and biology on the one side and social communications and aesthetics on the other. If the start of the second industrial and scientific revolution, with its dependence on self-regulating and directing machines—automation—can ultimately be traced to any single source, it must be attributed to the diffusion and deep penetration of this single insight. The same idea of feedback, adapted and selectively absorbed, is having profound significance in the transformation of our understanding of social systems. Certainly it will help us to shed new light on persistence and change of political systems.[2]

Simple Feedback

Feedback has been described as "the property of being able to adjust future conduct by past performances."[3] The kind of role that feedback plays in enabling a system to cope with its environment or to achieve its goals will vary with the kind of system under consideration. Systems do not all have the same capacity to cope with their environment. The responses of which they are capable will range from total absence of any responsive capacity at all, as in the case of a stone that is struck by a sledge hammer, to responses open to a system that can actively engage in coping with any stress from its environment and that can creatively mold itself and its environment to whatever purposes it may choose. We may place systems along a continuum according to the variety or limitations of their responses to stress. But wherever a system might fall along this continuum, we shall see that the presence of feedback loops to channel information to the source of decision and action plays a vital role in providing the stimulus and possible direction for the responses. But for feedback, the behavior of a system could take into account neither past experiences nor future contingencies. It could not learn from its own successes or mistakes.

If we consider first, a system that has a narrow range of responses, as

esses—will turn out to be central for a political system. It is for this reason that I interpret feedback as only one of a variety of response mechanisms for the generation of support and not as the central axis around which my whole analysis revolves. For references to the mode of systems analysis common in the communication sciences, see *A Framework for Political Analysis*, chapter VIII, footnote 6.

[2] For an interesting application to society as a whole, see A. Kuhn, *The Study of Society: A Unified Approach* (Homewood, Illinois: Irwin, Dorsey, 1963).

[3] N. Wiener, *The Human Uses of Human Beings* (New York: Doubleday Anchor, 1954 rev. ed.), p. 33.

can be found in many a physical system, we can see feedback in its minimal role. It enables the system, once it is set upon a course, to attempt to stick to it. This constitutes a simple error-regulating system. A speed regulator may exist on a motor so that if the motor passes beyond a desired, specified speed—its output—a unit will detect this excess as an error and activate a regulator that reduces the input of energy. The speed is reduced and the motor is kept within pre-set limits.

In this case we have response and control by simple feedback, one that holds outputs within fixed limits so as to keep a system operating at an established level. The responses to feedback information are restricted narrowly. Input of energy may be increased or decreased only. No alternate patterns of response are available for regulating the system other than the pre-determined range of fluctuations in energy.

Complex Feedback

But feedback plays a more significant role in those systems that are able to select from a broader range of alternative responses. We find such systems among those that are capable of learning from past experience, such as the human being viewed as a system, or social systems. Typically these systems are able to learn because they can store information through memory subsystems, selectively recall the stored information for scanning, and apply decision rules for evaluating it. These systems are then capable of responding by adopting new courses of action based upon these procedures. As we have already seen with political systems, they may modify themselves or their environment in order to achieve their goals.

Without being endowed with a complex set of feedback processes, a system of this kind—one that can choose and vary its responses—could not learn or redirect its behavior. Without being provided with an array of information about the consequences of present outputs, it could not add to its store of knowledge, its memory would forever remain static, and it would have no way of implementing its potentialities for learning and changing.

With feedback, however, the system is able to acquire some idea of how close it has come to its objectives and, if it desires to achieve a better approximation and has the capabilities for doing so, it is in a position to seek to modify its behavior with this end in view. Without feedback, each output would be completely independent of the other; with feedback, outputs may be highly interrelated, cumulative, and consistent. To phrase this in more usual language, the outputs may be purposive, rather than random and devoid of goal-direction. Returning information about the state of the system, its distance from desired goals, and about past and continuing effects of action already taken, enables the decision centers of the system to engage in any corrective action perceived as feasible and necessary to achieve the goals.

Each transaction with its environment in the form of an output, followed by the feedback of information about the consequences, adds to the knowledge that a system acquires through its decision centers. It gains information about the nature of the system itself, its environment, its resources and capabilities for imposing its will on the environment, and the resistances it may find there. Feedback enables the members of the system to learn to know themselves and the situation in which they find themselves.

Mere survival needs alone will give a distinct advantage to those systems that are sufficiently dynamic and flexible to modify their own behavior so as to cope with changes in their structure or in the environment. But beyond survival, feedback enables a system to explore and discover new ways for dealing with its problems. On the basis of information about present and past behavior, a system is able to select, reject, and emphasize one pattern in favor of another.

In personality systems, we would call this learning from experience, this storing up of a bank of wisdom, and this readiness to invent new strategies, part of the process of maturation. In social systems we are less likely to designate the same kind of results as social "maturation." But they do exist. This is why the history of social systems is vital for an understanding of how they are likely to meet new contingencies. The experiences they have learned tend to be stored in the folklore, traditions, prejudices, and socializing practices of the system. In modern systems, all forms of transmission of information—the oral and the written word, printed pictures, punched cards, and scored tapes—fulfill the same function. They can be used as a source for guidance about how new problems are to be met. Yet each system, within historically defined broad limits, finds its decision centers at least minimally free to adopt entirely new and innovative devices to handle any situation and even to create new goals.

More precisely, as we shall see in greater detail in Chapter 28, systems may be ranged on a continuum, with those at one pole bound relentlessly by custom from which they find it difficult to deviate except fractionally at any moment. At the other extreme would lie those systems in which uninhibited rationality dominates. At this pole there would be no constraints upon behavior at all except that, for the attainment of a desired end, outputs should be the most effective available. But systems could not locate anywhere on such a continuum without feedback information either to keep them within traditionally defined limits or as an essential condition for purposive innovations.

Goal Selection and Feedback

Feedback permits purposiveness of a different kind as well and this describes a further characteristic response of many systems. Goal-directed behavior may involve novelty or innovations of action so as to achieve predetermined objectives; but it may also refer to the capacity of a system to take advantage of information and respond so as to change the goals themselves and establish new objectives. We have already seen this in the form of action having in view the modification or fundamental transformation of a regime and political community.

Unlike mechanical or biological systems from the lower orders of life, social systems are not only error-controlled in the sense in which I have just been talking about the pursuit of set goals, but they may be purpose regulated, as Vickers has put it.[4] In the case of the motor with a governor, the regulator can control only within the pre-set limits. In social systems such as political life, the limits themselves may be broadened, narrowed, or fundamentally altered. The goals sought may be changed if the existing ones are found wanting or undesirable.

If, on the basis of feedback about current and past performance, a system is capable of reorganizing its behavior and if it can recommit its resources, it may also be able to modify its purposive patterns or goals. In this way, feedback may do more than help to "regulate" the flow of outputs; it may be the basis for periodic, even continuous modifications in the fundamental pre-existing objectives of a system, as incoming information about experience seems to dictate. Insofar as structure and processes are themselves dependent upon the nature of goals, they too may undergo profound transformations in the process.

Feedback can thus be seen as a central condition for all self-transforming or ultra-stable systems. Without the availability of returning information about experiences with goals, transformations of goals themselves could only be random and possibly quite disjunctive with current or past experiences. With feedback, such experiences can be related to the continuous revisions of future long-run hopes, anticipations, and possibilities.

[4] G. Vickers, *The Undirected Society* (Toronto: University of Toronto Press, 1959).

Feedback and the Political System

It is apparent that to attain any objectives related to the level of support in a political system, possession of a capacity to produce outputs would not be enough. The system must provide some means for bringing to the attention of its decision centers, the authorities, information about the state of the system and its environment and the results of any actions already taken. In this way, this information may be compared with what had been anticipated and it may be taken into account in any follow-up future action. Through such feedback, the authorities are aided in determining the extent to which their outputs are contributing to the alleviation of stress from loss of support and the extent to which they have succeeded in adding to the store of positive support.

The feedback may be completely ignored, of course. In that event, the effectiveness of the authorities in achieving their objectives would very probably be seriously impaired by their failure to find out what was in fact happening to the supportive frame of mind of the politically relevant members in the system. This would be particularly true where the authorities sought not just to maintain a minimal level of support for a given state of the system but decided to branch out in the search for new bases of support or to construct a fundamentally different kind of regime or community.[5] In political life as in other social systems, feedback can be shown to be fundamental both for error-regulation, that is, to keep a system pointed in an established direction—preservation of the *status quo*—or for purposive redirection, that is, to move off in search of new goals to conquer.

Varieties of Feedback Loops

Feedback is more than a logical necessity for political systems however. It represents part of the living reality of these systems. In preparation for an examination of the role that feedback processes play in the dynamics of a political system, we must look at their typical components.

Although I have been speaking about information feedback, it

[5] The conditions under which support is freed from an ascribed basis and made available to those who can win it (achieved support) form a main theme of S. N. Eisenstadt's volume, *The Political Systems of Empire.*

would be erroneous to assume from the singularity of the expression that there is only one feedback loop in a social system. It is true, in many physical systems this is usually the case. There may be one point at which error, from the point of view of the fixed objectives of the system, is detected, another point at which this error may be regulated and corrected, and a single pathway between the two through which contact is maintained. But in most social systems, even if they consist of only a few persons, there is a high probability that we can find a large number and variety of such loops through which output effects and related information are communicated to the authorities. The task will always be to distinguish and isolate those that are immediately most relevant to the purposes of the analysis.

A political system does not differ from other social systems in this respect. Especially in large scale systems, we can expect to find unlimited numbers and varieties of feedback loops. Diagram 5 depicts the flow of outputs and of inputs of support for a political system. Six basic types of loops are identified. These are only illustrative; they are by no means exhaustive. They could be quickly multiplied by connecting any two actors in the system wherever it appears plausible that mutual interaction would occur, based at least upon information feedback. The fact is that if we find any two subsystems within a political system or any subsystems within a system and outside a system that are linked together in such a way first, that the outputs of one become the inputs of the other and second, that thereby some effort at regulation of the relationship may take place, we can say that they are joined by feedback ties. Feedback is the dynamic aspect of this kind of coupling between systems or subsystems.

We can see this clearly represented in the diagram. Loop I indicates that among the producers of the inputs of demands and support, such a linkage may occur. One member (or group of members) in a system may express his political views to another; the other may respond critically or otherwise; in the light of the response, the first member may change his opinions or behavior. The illustration does not add much to an understanding of the relationship when stated so simply, without including the properties that a dynamic analysis will later bring out as associated with the feedback processes. I point to it only to show that there is a type of feedback process confined exclusively to the input sector of the system.

Loop II shows a loop that has sprung up between one of these two members who is receiving some benefits, let us say, from an interest group, as indicated by the broken line and its direction, and who returns support as his response. The shading on all lines may be ig-

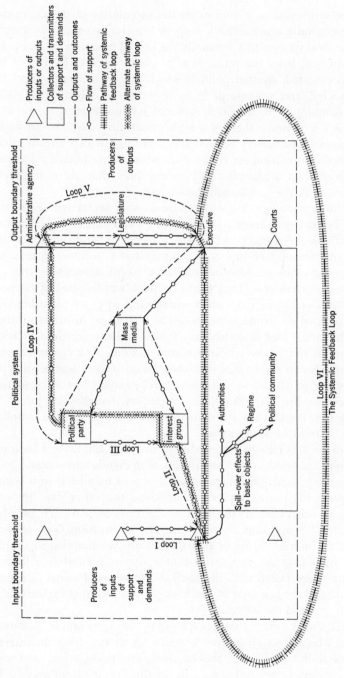

DIAGRAM 5 MULTIPLE FEEDBACK LOOPS OF A POLITICAL SYSTEM

nored for the moment. Although the diagram cannot show this, the behavior of the interest group could be influenced and controlled in the next round by this return of support and so on in a mutually interactive process.

Loop III describes the path that feedback follows between the same interest group and a political party. In return, presumably for benefits received, the interest group in its turn is provided with support by the party; the converse is usually equally true.

Loop IV is another boundary loop, but this time between the party previously mentioned and a unit that produces outputs for the system as a whole, let us say some part of the administrative services. This unit may itself be linked in a feedback process with the executive of the political system. In this event, as indicated by Loop V, the feedback of information about support is confined to the producers of outputs.

Finally, through the systemic feedback loop,—numbered VI—which is one of many possible loops, the outputs of the executive flow back to influence the behavior of the individual (or group) with whom we first began, a producer of inputs of support and demands. His (or its) reaction to these outputs, let us assume, are communicated directly back to the executive as shown by the cross-barred line of alternate dots and dashes. But it could just as easily have been diagramed as passing through several intermediary demand-collecting and, as we shall see, support-collecting agencies, represented here by interest groups, parties, or mass media. One such alternative path is indicated by the shaded line flowing from the producer of the inputs through the interest group, party, and administrative agency to the executive.

In each of these loops, the indicated output from a subsystem need not be in the form of positive support. It could introduce some disadvantage or danger for the member or subsystem affected by it. In this case it would invite a withdrawal of support. The lines on the diagram, therefore, may indicate the flow of effects and information that reflect either positive or negative support or some combination of both.

Furthermore, from the circularity of the loop, it may appear as though each output immediately sparks some proportionate increase or decrease in the flow of support or directly assures a continuation of the current level. As we shall see, to draw this conclusion would compel us to assume linearity in the relationships implied in feedback, a condition valid for many physical systems but utterly unlikely in most social situations. But I shall correct this misconception at a later point as the non-linearity of most social feedback processes is not relevant to the present discussion.

The Systemic Feedback Loop

Unity Out of Multiplicity

This cursory survey of easily differentiable loops serves two purposes. It introduces us to a sample, if only a small one, of the variety of loops. An exhaustive analysis would however ensnare us in a veritable morass of feedback loops. Out of them, some selection would have to be made if any coherent understanding of the part played by feedback was to be achieved. Criteria of selection that enable us to set most loops aside will be introduced in a moment.

Furthermore, and incidentally, this sampling of loops opens the first door to an appreciation of the contributions of feedback processes to the dynamics of a system as a whole. Through the interlocking chain of feedback loops, all of the participating members in any one loop may be coupled, if only loosely, with many other members in the system. To point this up, I have deliberately selected the participants in the various feedback diads so that an unbroken line could be drawn through the six different actors who make up the six pairs in the six different loops. If we look at each loop as a link in a continuous chain—which they indeed form pictorially and literally—we can appreciate that the interaction around any one feedback loop has the potential, if it is strong enough, to pass its influence down the chain to other units in the system.

At this preliminary stage in a theory of political systems, when we are still trying to get our general bearings, a detailed analysis of this kind cannot and need not be undertaken. It would add confusion where clarity and simplicity are desperately needed.[6] Rather, I shall focus attention only on the systemic feedback processes, those that link the outputs of the political system considered as a unit of analysis to the inputs of support and demands and in that way back again to the initial producers of the outputs, the authorities.

[6] The practicality of a more detailed analysis is beyond doubt, however. Although even the small chain of loops we have here seems very complex to the unaided mind, modern computer technology reduces the solution of the decision functions involved to a simpler matter. The vital task would be to construct an initial verbal and then mathematical model that took into account at least the central variables that influence decisions for each unit in a loop and to settle on plausible rules governing behavior.

Insofar as intrasystem or boundary-spanning feedback loops contribute to or in some way take part in systemic loops, I shall take them into account. But in that case, they will be considered not as components of other feedback loops but rather solely as unanalyzed components of the major networks. Whatever assumptions we make about their behavior may be due to their nature as part of subsidiary feedback structures. But as long as we can make reasonable assumptions about the way they will behave, for purposes of macroanalysis we do not need to push any more deeply.

Finally, even for purposes of exploring the systemic loop, we cannot risk the excessive complexity that would be involved, when trying to work out the main lines of analysis, if we forced ourselves to take into account each differentiated feedback loop in which a member of the authorities, as producers of outputs, might participate. The diagram indicates that the units producing outputs may be the point of origin of an infinite number of different feedback currents. Each administrator, legislator, or executive may produce outputs and may be perceived as doing so by an equal number of differentiated members of the system. The numbers involved here in a modern mass society might defy even modern computer technology. Fortunately, at no level of analysis would it be necessary to take into account separately each feedback loop. Averaging would prove possible.

But again, for our purposes, even this would be too refined. For the multiple producers of outputs and inputs, unless the context clearly requires otherwise, I shall at least begin as though the producers of outputs, the authorities, constituted a single, internally undifferentiated output unit that produced all outputs. Similarly, the numerous producers of inputs will be conceived as a single entity. This returns us to the simplicity of the earlier diagrams of a political system,[7] but this time with the flow of support particularly in mind. The systemic feedback loop, when expanded, can therefore now be represented as on Diagram 6.

By standing so far off from a system that we do not see the multiple component units at the points of inputs and outputs, we shall greatly simplify the processes, it is true. It is as though we were initially reconciling ourselves to using a telescope rather than a microscope because we are not yet sufficiently confident of the units and processes that we want to lay open to detailed analysis. But this is the very task of qualitative model construction, initially. In the process, we shall have the opportunity to concentrate our attention on only the basic

[7] See chapter 2.

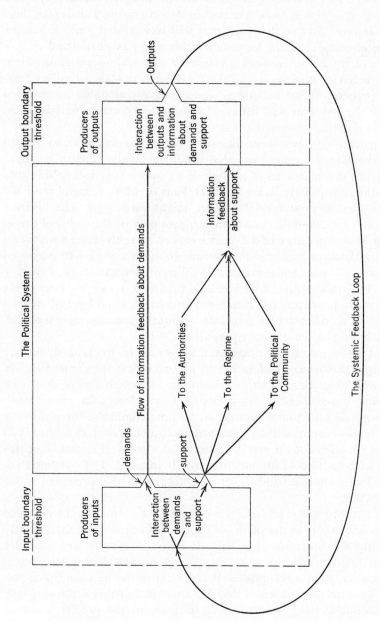

DIAGRAM 6 THE SYSTEMIC FEEDBACK LOOP

components that help to determine the effects of the feedback processes on the generation of specific support, our main task.

The Constituent Elements of the Systemic Feedback Loop

But even if we decide that we shall be concerned with the systemic loop, our decision could easily be mistaken for a kind of analysis that has appeared occasionally in the literature in which feedback plays an important part. In these cases, as in some studies of international relations,[8] of intrasystem behavior [9] and of decision-making in organizations,[10] the focus is on the decision-makers in the relevant system. The major problem of these studies has been: how do the decision-makers arrive at decisions about their objectives and effectively manage to attain these objectives or some substitute, if, in process, the initial objective needs to be modified or abandoned? How do decision-makers set a course, modify it as necessary but in any event, remain on target as long as one is available?

Most research, within the context of decisional and organizational theory at any rate, is normative in character. What is sought is an understanding of the conditions for the effective establishment and achievement of goals, where the criteria of effectiveness may range from unspecified efficiency to a postulated welfare function or maximization of profits. In each instance in the literature, where information feedback appears prominently, it acts as a mechanism to inform the decision-makers of the extent of deviation from the desired course of action. Depending upon the quality of the feedback as tested by distortion and time delays and upon their resources and skills, the decision-makers may adjust their behavior so as to increase the likelihood of attaining their objectives. However circuitous a path the effects of initial decisions may take in returning to the decision-makers, the touchstone of the analysis always is: has the decision led to the maximization of profit, the growth of the economy, the reduction of illiteracy, the increase in employment, the weakening of the enemy, or any other general or specific goal? If not, to what can this be attributed? If it is attributable to feedback processes, how can these be improved so as to contribute to the more effective attainment of the goals? The focus is on decision-makers and the role of feedback in linking the behavior of decision-makers to the desired state of affairs.

[8] See the writings of K. W. Deutsch.
[9] G. Vickers, *op. cit.*
[10] See chapter 2, footnote 3.

Although it is true that in analyses suggested by questions such as these, the producers of outputs must become a central focus, it would not be particularly helpful for us to follow this lead. Such an approach may be necessary and valid for a partial theory of decision-making or organizational behavior, especially one that is geared to a normative rather than a descriptive science. As such it is concerned with allocative problems within systems: what are adequate ways for allocating the resources and values of the organization so that it might most efficiently achieve its objectives? But such an approach would not contribute centrally to the development of a general theory seeking to explain the persistence of whole political systems in a world of stability and change. We are not concerned with the way in which systems may best organize themselves so as to attain their goals. We are interested in structures for goal attainment only to the extent that success or failure to achieve a goal reacts back on the input of support. Thereby allocative processes would be connected to the aggravation or alleviation of stress on the political system.

For this reason, the critical feedback loop for us does not confine itself to the output sector of a system exclusively. It is not defined by the relationships between the authorities and their specific goals. It includes, rather, the authorities, their goals *and* those politically relevant members in a system upon whose support the system must depend for its persistence over time. This is what I have designated as the systemic loop (Loop VI in Diagram 5). It is feedback that flows from the system as a whole and may return through the system to the point from which it started, spreading its effects in the system through the chain of feedback loops already described. The consequences that outputs have for the input of support will be shaped in considerable part by the extent to which information about outputs are conveyed along the feedback loop and, in an accurate and timely manner, to all those concerned with the outputs. It will also be affected decisively by the manner in which the members who form the links in the feedback loop respond and react to this information.

The systemic loop may be conveniently analyzed into three components or structural elements, each of which will merit some special consideration if we are to explore the various factors that constitute the "feedback function" in the mathematical sense. If we begin with the ouputs and their outcomes we shall find that these provide the stimuli for the members of the system, the behaving units whom they may affect or may be perceived to affect. We view the members at the input threshold of the system, as indicated on Diagram 6. These members may then respond to the stimuli by modifying their demands and varying their support for one or more of the basic political objects. We shall discover that it is here that outputs and inputs of both demands and support become dynamically inter-related. In continuation of the feedback flow, directly or indirectly the members communicate their sentiments to the authorities, another set of behaving units who were initially responsible for the outputs or who choose to do something further about these outputs. Finally, these authorities may then react to the response by follow-up outputs and this reaction may be considered the start of another cycle in the flow of effects and information along the systemic feedback loop.

In brief, the relevant phases, in one complete cycle around a feedback loop, that would be vital in any feedback function, are four in number: the outputs and outcomes as *stimuli,* the *feedback response,* the *information feedback,* in the strict sense, about the response, and the *output reaction* to the feedback response. We shall also be concerned with the relationship among these four sets of processes together with the behaving units that they affect. We shall examine each of these processes in turn. They represent modes of interaction between the units producing outputs, the authorities, and those varied units that produce inputs both of support and demands. These four phases are outlined on Diagram 7 and they correspond to and set out more simply the feedback loop as depicted in Diagram 6.

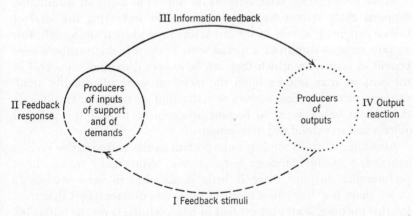

DIAGRAM 7   THE FOUR PHASES OF THE SYSTEMIC FEEDBACK LOOP

24

The Feedback Stimuli

IT DOES NOT MATTER WHERE WE BREAK INTO THE SYSTEMIC FEEDBACK loop to begin our analysis of it. Since I have been conceptualizing outputs as the mechanism through which authorities may succeed in generating specific support for the political objects, it is appropriate to begin by examining the way in which members of a system may be expected to react to such outputs. I have labeled this as phase I of the feedback loop diagramed in the preceding chapter. How do outputs act as stimuli in the feedback process so that they may lead members to increase or reduce their input of support?

Outputs as Stimuli

As we have already seen, outputs do not stand alone in stimulating support; every system has various means for increasing the level of diffuse support and may in the last resort turn to coercion as well. But outputs serve as stimuli of a special sort. They offer the members some benefit in return for which they can be expected to offer support; [1] or the outputs may impose upon the members some identifiable disadvantage, such as an onerous tax or restriction on function. In this case they might be expected to become antagonistic toward the political objects and to extend negative support.

Associated outputs are just as important as the authoritative type in generating specific support. For example, with regard to associated performance outputs, there is little doubt that in most systems in which there is a division of political labor and differentiated structures for this purpose, if all outputs had to rely exclusively on the authoritative kind, it would be impossible to meet the broad range of demands, actual or potential, among the members of the system. As we have seen earlier, attachment to a political system relies to some extent on the

---

[1] C. W. Mitchell, *op. cit.*, pp. 384–385, makes the point that in the United States regime changes have been avoided in part because demands could be met.

benefits and favors that those in authority find it in their power to distribute to the members of the system.

Associated performances of this kind perform the same kind of function that equity at first, and then administrative law had performed for the rigor of the law. They help to allow for the play of discretion in areas that cannot for one reason or another be successfully handled directly through authoritative outputs. Where these associated outputs violate the mores of the social group, they become stigmatized as corruption, nepotism or favoritism. But even in this unpalatable guise, there can be little doubt that the persistence of such forms of behavior testifies to the probability that if they were successfully and completely prohibited and prevented, the authorities in most systems would find it considerably more difficult to mobilize specific support.

But regardless of whether the origin of the specific support lies in authoritative or associated outputs, their capacity to foster negative or positive support will depend upon the kind of stimuli they constitute for the members. When we examine outputs from this point of view, we find that they are by no means uniform. They will vary along two dimensions at least. As stimuli, the impact they leave on the members and their ability, therefore, to generate (or undermine) specific support will depend first, upon whether they do in fact modify the circumstances surrounding the members of the system and the members react to this effect or second, upon whether they only act so as to modify the way in which the members *perceive* the outputs to modify the circumstances. Outputs examined from the point of view of their function as feedback stimuli acting upon the members and obtaining positive or negative supportive response, can therefore be classified into two types: circumstantial or perceived.These are really two possible aspects of the effects of each output but for purposes of analysis we can treat them as though they were two separate types of effects.

It may appear that to differentiate the actual impact upon circumstances from the perceived impact must draw us into making so fine a distinction, that we will end up in needlessly splitting hairs. But we shall quickly see that this is not the case. We shall be identifying vital differences in the way in which outputs may ultimately stimulate responses for the maintenance, withdrawal, or increase of support.

Circumstantial Feedback Stimuli

In serving as feedback stimuli, outputs may at times act in such a way as to be disconnected from the response. Members may vary their input of support and yet it may be impossible to describe their behavior as a specific and direct response to outputs. Nevertheless, for the objective observer, there may be no doubt that the supportive state of mind is a specific response to conditions or circumstances that have been shaped or modified by preceding outputs. In this event, the response is disconnected from the stimulus, at least in the subjective perception of the members themselves, even though the linkage may be apparent to an objective observer. If we failed to recognize and analyze feedback stimuli such as these, a kind that acts indirectly on members by changing the conditions under which they live, we would be neglecting an important means through which specific support is typically generated in all political systems.

Circumstantial feedback stimuli, therefore, will consist of those consequences of actions that modify the conditions in which a behaving unit, such as an individual member or group, acts and that lead the unit to modify or maintain its pattern of supportive activity. When the behaving unit becomes aware of the conditions created by the outputs—or what I have called the outcomes—or unwittingly reacts to them, even though it may not have been able to connect the consequences with the initial outputs that set them in motion, the unit has nevertheless been influenced, at least indirectly, by the outputs.

Allaying Present Discontents

Such disconnected stimuli are by no means rare; members do not have to perceive outputs as the source of their contentment or grievances for the effects of these outputs to regulate the input of specific support. One kind of situation occurs in which outputs may modify circumstances without the knowledge of the members and thereby conduce to supportive behavior that is not wittingly related to the outputs. Members may become dissatisfied with the circumstances under which they find themselves in society and demand their rectification. The authorities may undertake to produce outputs that correct these circumstances. With the disappearance of the offending conditions, the demands will presumably be satisfied, their continuance would no longer make sense, hence they disappear.

Yet it is not only possible but frequently quite likely that the members may have no awareness that the outputs created these favorable conditions and may even continue to condemn the existing authorities for never having taken appropriate action. But since the demands no longer have a realistic base, there would no longer be a sufficient sense of deprivation to withdraw support from the political objects.

As a concrete illustration of this, we can conceive of members eagerly seeking higher unemployment benefits or increased protection for industries, infant or senile, suffering from foreign competition. It may seem economically sound to the authorities that these demands not be met directly. The authorities may prefer to take measures to create new employment for workers, new investment opportunities for declining industries, and increased rates of economic growth in general. If we assume that such outputs were successful, the circumstances giving birth to the demands would clearly disappear and we could expect that the demands would follow suit. Yet the members might never link up the actions of the authorities to their resulting more contented lot. Indirectly and unperceived, the outputs will have served to maintain or increase the level of support.

Anticipating Future Discontents

A very similar situation occurs where authorities act to anticipate future conditions that might threaten the input of support and thereby succeed in averting future stress on the system. Yet the members may be entirely unaware that their positive attitudes toward the system have been influenced by prior outputs.

Part of the failure of ordinary members to show concern for future conditions frequently flows from the fact that they may not be sufficiently aware of what the future holds in store to be able to make demands with regard to them. They find it difficult to anticipate the occurrence of events that would create dissatisfactions and that may require present action in order to be avoided. In fact, as modern societies have become more differentiated and technical in their skills, it has become increasingly difficult for even informed social scientists to understand, let alone to attempt to predict the course of events.

Furthermore, even in those systems in which the ordinary member is able to get some sense of the emergence of such future sources of discontent, the division of labor in society may be such as to leave them with neither the time nor, for that matter, the interest to attempt to bear responsibilities for the future by formulating present demands concerning it. This is typically a task that the members may expect either the authorities or some leadership in competition with the authorities to undertake for them. Only *ex post facto* are the members likely to raise demands; they are apt to complain after they have suffered from the failure of the authorities to exercise what, through hindsight, is condemned as lack of adequate foresight.

Looked at from the point of view of how such future conditions are in fact met through present outputs, most systems create a suitable motivational structure in occupants of authority roles so that they feel the responsibilities for anticipating possible future sources of discontent and for acting currently so as to avoid them. Internalized cultural norms and, at times, pressures from competitors for the authority roles, will induce incumbents of these roles to take present action so as to avoid decline in support due to future contingencies.

Thus even if the membership may not anticipate future unemployment, a decrease in the standard of living, or future international losses, the authorities may act to increase the rate of economic development or to cement international alliances so as to avoid these future sources of grievances. Similarly, in anticipation of future large increases in population, the present authorities may plan for improvements in transportation and communications and the parsimonious use of natural resources to prevent any major dissatisfactions. Members of the present generation may have no demands in relation to such matters; future contingencies may not even have crossed their horizon or consciousness. Nor need they for that matter have any awareness of the implications for the future of the outputs being produced in the present.

If the conditions which the outputs are designed to bring about do in fact occur, at least in part, if not exclusively, as a result of the past outputs, we can expect that the members who benefit from the outcomes of the outputs will not be unfavorably disposed toward the system. By so affecting the future circumstances that the members respond in a positive rather than a discontented way, the outputs will have managed to prevent the erosion of support that might presumably have occurred if the authorities had not had the earlier foresight to take the action that they did. Yet at that earlier period we have assumed that the members were not in a position to understand that they ought to be demanding the kind of outputs that the authorities, on their own, undertook to produce. If the members are gratified by these outputs, their support for the system is likely to be assured. No membership has yet withdrawn its support from a regime or community toward which it felt no grievances. Yet we are assuming that the members are not able to associate their satisfactory circumstances with any prior outputs.

These two types of situations, in which outputs modify the circumstances in which the members find themselves, demonstrate that support can be generated or lost without the members being aware that outputs are the particular stimuli of their response toward the system.

The positive effects have been created indirectly by shaping the circumstances under which the members live and, therefore, may appropriately be termed circumstantial in character. What are fed back as stimuli to the members are the outcomes of the outputs and in the minds of the members these may remain permanently unassociated with the outputs.

In the realities of political life, there are few political systems in which the actual authorities responsible for the benefits, or their self-identified heirs, would fail to point out their part in producing the desired and beneficial circumstances. But taking the limiting case as a means of isolating the independent effect of circumstantial stimuli, even if such a linkage were not established in the minds of the members, the feedback process would provide a stimulus for response in the form of continued or increased support. For feedback stimuli to be effective in bolstering or in undermining support—since not all outputs and their outcomes work in a positive direction—they do not always require awareness on the part of those who are so influenced.

Perceived Feedback Stimuli

However effective unperceived outputs may be in generating specific support, one of three conditions may serve to link the members in some way to a perception of the outputs. Where it redounds to the advantage of the current incumbents of authority roles, they will seek to utilize the outputs in such a way that the members recognize what is being done on their behalf. Where the outputs may appear to work against their interest, competitors for the authority roles will be likely to draw this to the attention of the members. Finally, regardless of what the authorities or their competitors may seek to do, where there is any involvement of the general membership in the political processes, they will seek to interpret the meaning of the output for themselves. Thereby their perceptions of what is taking place in the way of outputs will have an opportunity to influence the extent of their supportive sentiments.

Once we begin to take into account the awareness that members have of outputs, it is apparent that a new and potent force is at work. However a community of objective observers might choose to interpret the consequences of a given output, the ability of the output to inspire or destroy support will be a function of the way in which the members themselves perceive the output. Outputs will act as phenomenological stimuli rather than as directly felt experiences alone; at least this will be another major dimension of their effects. Outputs will be screened through the perceptual apparatus of the individual or group. If the member sees the output as favorable, then even if it has primarily adverse consequences, unless he can at some stage be brought to perceive them as such, he will interpret the stimulus positively as it concerns support. The converse is of course equally true.

Perceptions constitute a central aspect of stimuli that need to be clearly distinguished from their disconnected circumstantial aspect. It is not what the outputs do in any objective sense but what the members perceive them as doing that forms the basis for subsequent responses or contributes to what might be called the decision function of the members at this point in the feedback loop.

Induced Misperception

Perception may lead to distortion of the reality as it might be interpreted by a set of objective observers; but it may also simply reinforce the objective facts about the effects of outputs. We can visualize a variety of alternative ways in which either of these results might occur, that is, in which perception may act as a feedback stimulus.

In the first place, the authorities may take no action to meet conditions of which members are complaining and are therefore putting in demands. Yet by virtue of interpretations offered through associated verbal outputs, the authorities may induce the members to perceive them as though they, the authorities, were in fact taking many and varied steps to meet the demands. At times, the authorities may be completely deceptive about this as a way of meeting a difficult political situation for themselves. If they are believed, support would also be forthcoming for the political system as a whole through the general overflow of specific support to all political objects. But at other times, it may be that the authorities genuinely feel that past outputs, whose outcomes or effects are still being felt, have in fact adequately taken care of the demands currently being made. If the authorities are able to persuade the members of this interpretation, they will be able to control perception of outputs and, thereby, the nature of feedback stimulus.

By their very nature, those intangible performance outputs, that I call services, have sufficient built-in ambiguity so that they readily lend themselves to the manipulation of perceptions. Services, it has long been recognized, present us with numerous difficulties in enumeration and measurement. As Gross has pointed out,[2] in the case of the output

²Chapter 22, footnote 7.

of governmental services, their amount and quality may be kept deliberately ambiguous. The wants and demands of the members of a system differ greatly. The competition for the commitment of the energies and resources of a system may be keen. Through the maintenance of ambiguity, it may be possible to give the services performed the appearance of meeting the needs of a broader spectrum of wants among the members. If it is difficult to determine what services are in fact being performed, who is offering them, and how long they continue—a not uncommon situation in the case of the outputs of administrative organizations in modern mass societies—it increases the degree of freedom that the authorities have for interpreting the services in ways that are most advantageous at the moment. In this way the authorities are able to enhance the benefits they derive in the way of gratitude, support or, at least, lack of discontent.

Autonomous Misperception

In the second place, if induced perceptions may lead the members to give the authorities credit for conditions that they did not create, uninduced or autonomously generated perceptions may be the mechanism through which the authorities acquire praise or blame without in any way being responsible for the circumstances in which the members find themselves. For example, a feedback stimulus may be spurious and yet just as real as though outputs had been the source. This is typically the situation when conditions occur for which no authorities can be held to blame in any rational sense. Yet they may be held to account for what has happened. The responsibility placed on Hoover for the Great Depression is a classic illustration. Given the available level of economic knowledge at the time, it is unlikely that there is anything he could have done, even with a cooperative legislature and court, to have turned the Depression aside.

But perception may also work in the other direction equally well. In the one case, it may lead members to see negative consequences where none exist. But in another case, because of what has been labeled the "halo effect," [3] having a generally favorable attitude to the particular occupants of the authority roles, a member may be inclined to see the authorities as acting in his interests or on behalf of his demands more frequently than any objective appraisal would reveal. Distortion may as easily lead to positive as to negative effects on support, even when it constructs benefits virtually out of the whole cloth.

[3] H. Guetzkow, *op. cit.*

Symbolic Gratification from Outputs

In the third place, perception may lead to the substitution of symbolic gratification for demands in place of any genuine fulfillment. It has been amply demonstrated that, at times, outputs meeting the expressed demand may not be required in order to stimulate the perception that the demand has been fulfilled. Symbolic outputs alone may offer sufficient gratification; appearances are equal to the reality.

A recent inquiry has significantly shown that in the United States when legislation passed in the name of small business is analyzed, it turns out that very little of it has actually been or could possibly be beneficial for small businessmen. Indeed, much of it may even be considered objectively to be inimical to their interests. Yet the associated verbal outputs accompanying such legislation, both from the legislators and the leaders of organizations presumably representative of small business, have helped to create and perpetuate the image of the legislation as highly advantageous to small business.[4] The mere symbols of benefits, in the form of outputs ritualistically produced in the name of small business, have been effective in shaping the nature of the output stimulus rather than the substance of what was accomplished through the legislation. Symbols rather than circumstances are the effective stimuli.

Although the cited research does not inquire into the psychodynamics of why symbolic gratification should displace tangible outputs, it may be that the rewards obtained from the outputs are purely psychic in nature. The legislation may not meet the material needs of small business for the control of monopolies or availability of investment capital at a low rate of interest, yet it may be that the small businessman is really contented with much less. The feeling that he is an object of attention and concern from the authorities and that efforts appear to have been made on his behalf, may be sufficient psychic reward to still demands and win supportive attitudes. Expressions of love here may well be enough.

If the criteria used to interpret the nature of the stimulus lead us to look for what the small businessmen are saying they want, we would have to conclude that the businessmen's perceptions are false. But if

[4] See H. Zeigler, *The Politics of Small Business* (Washington: Public Affairs Press, 1961); M. Edelman, "Symbols and Political Quiescence," 54 *American Political Science Review* (1960) 695–704; and O. R. Holsti, "The Belief System and National Images," 6 *Journal of Conflict Resolution* (1962) 244–252.

the criteria reflect the possibility that underlying the apparent demands are latent demands for expressions of concern and attention, then we would have to say that their perceptions are correct. But in either case, the nature of the stimulus and, consequently, its effect on the flow of satisfaction from the membership, will depend upon how the outputs are perceived.

How long symbolic gratification may endure as a satisfactory output is an entirely different matter. It may be a feasible state of affairs insofar as it is difficult to check the facts and to discover whether outputs asserted to meet demands, do so in fact. But if the need for the comfort of being an object of concern is the overriding consideration, there may be no real incentive to inquire into the actual nature of the output stimulus. This would seem to be the case with small business. Serious inquiry would presumably have shown that very little legislation passed in its name has proved materially valuable to it.

The significance of perception in relationship to output stimuli, whether they are symbolic or real, is signalized most visibly by the prominence of verbal statements usually associated with authoritative outputs, at least in large-scale political systems. Associated verbal outputs accompanying the authoritative outputs are a means of assuring the authorities that the desired construction will be placed upon their actions. In this way the authorities constantly seek to mold the perceptions of the stimuli so that they may be able to obtain maximal benefit by way of support for themselves. But as we know, this also has spillover supportive consequences for other objects in the system.

Conditions of False Perception

It is clear that if the authorities relied exclusively and naively upon the bare and uninterpreted effects of outputs to revitalize flagging support, they would soon be disappointed. At least they would have to assure themselves that correct rather than false perception of the outputs was occurring. But we may now proceed further and inquire into the conditions that make it possible, likely and even necessary for members of the system to rely frequently upon perception, untempered by experience or objective appraisal, as a means of interpreting the nature of the stimuli in the feedback processes. What predisposes members of the system to rely less upon an objective appraisal than on their perception of what takes place, subject to all manner of distortion and misinformation as it must be?

The Role of Causal Indeterminacy

Aside from any other consideration, the importance of perception in the feedback processes is multiplied to an extraordinary degree by the highly indeterminate character of the chain of cause and effect in social matters. Social causation is ambiguous and obscure for the professional students of society and necessarily much more so for the laymen in a system.

In some cases, where there is a specific and well-defined benefit sought, such as an increase in tariffs, decrease in income tax rate, or additional depreciation allowances, the connection between the outputs and the satisfaction of the demand may be unmistakable. But in an increasingly greater number of instances, especially in modern complex societies, it has become virtually impossible to trace through confidently the consequences that flow from an output or even a set of them. Nor is it any simpler to begin with any given social conditions and to link these in a backward flowing chain of causation to any individual output or series of prior outputs.

Trained observers and experts in the social sciences experience vast difficulties in following through any sequence of effects that may seem to have been set into operation by a series of decisions and actions on the part of the authorities. For the economy, we scarcely know what the overall effects of the outputs of government are as they ramify through the society; much less are we able to interpret the consequences of actions on other sectors of society. In the United States, do the laws actually protect against monopolies as they are designed to do? Does foreign aid achieve its objectives, assuming these are known? And if they are not, what consequences do they have for the sentiments on the part of peoples in foreign societies toward the United States? This is not to complain about the state of the social sciences which are far in advance of what they were only a few short decades ago. But it does suggest that our understanding of social phenomena is still at the stage that perhaps medicine was in the Middle Ages; we are undoubtedly still letting blood with the hope of curing the patient.

Under conditions of perceptual indeterminacy such as these, there is certainly little reason to suspect that the layman finds himself in a position *superior* to the expert in seeking to interpret the consequences of outputs. This difficult situation in which we all find ourselves, gives a wide range of free play to perception—one is almost tempted to say, to the imagination—as an instrument for interpreting the nature and adequacy of outputs. There is a great temptation for the effect of the outputs to be interpreted so as to bring them into harmony with the needs of political conflict and competition.

We may see demands as having been met when in fact they have obtained only nominal fulfillment through formal outputs; but whether the outputs meet the substantive content of the demand is another matter, inaccessible to the untrained mind and virtually even to the expert. Prejudice as through party or leadership identification, ideological predisposition, vunerability to persuasion by others, accidental bits and pieces of information, skill in evaluating such information, and similar factors may be more important in determining how a member interprets outputs as stimuli, than the actual impact of the outputs on the circumstances surrounding the members.

Delays in the Outcomes of Outputs

Other conditions relevant to output stimuli operate in exactly the same direction and compound the indeterminacy with which the member is confronted. In many cases, because of the time factor, a member cannot estimate whether an output has really met his demands. It may be necessary to wait for the implementation of the outputs. To establish whether a demand for action to spur the growth rate of the economy has in fact been adequately met, may entail years of waiting so that the outputs may have a chance to take effect. In this event, the members putting in the demands must take a lot for granted and be willing to make assumptions about the probable and possible future results of the outputs. They are compelled to hazard informed guesses about the adequacy of the outputs and, therefore, as to whether they can consider that their demands have been met. These are fertile fields in which conflicting perceptions may roam.

Furthermore, even where the output stimuli call for short-term effects so that it is reasonable to expect that members may wait until the outcomes of the outputs have become apparent, complications occur. Political life is not a laboratory for social causation even though it is metaphorically frequently described as such. When a given output is produced, all other actions are not held constant so as to determine how much of the variation in social behavior is attributable to the selected output. Even in small societies, outputs occur in a continuing stream. Each output follows on the footsteps of the next one so that the outcomes become quickly intertwined and inextricably so, at least to the eye unaided by powerful and technical analytic tools. Yet, out of this continuously tangled skein of events, members who are able to put in demands and support are called upon to make some kind of judgment of the decisions and actions of the authorities.

To some extent reality testing may be available. If more money is voted for education in the coming year, a member may check his educational tax rate, the quality of education in his school system, or the money that his school district gets, aside from the school tax itself. But there is no reliable way open for him, unless he is willing to expend an extraordinary amount of time and energy, to determine whether the effect of increased funds moves education in a direction compatible with his prior demands. He must fall back on his general perceptions of what is happening in education and hope that he is not in error.

In brief, the output stimulus that operates to influence the support response will frequently take the form of a perception. The accuracy of the perception will be shaped by the difficulties of interpretation imposed by the indeterminacy of discovering cause and effect in the social system as a whole.

Perceivability of Output Stimuli

Indirectly, outputs may become the stimuli for members and thereby generate specific support of a positive or negative sort. Unknown to the members, the outputs, as we have seen, may modify the circumstances under which they live. But if the outputs are to act directly in fostering such support, they must at least be perceivable to the members of the system. It may seem strange that I should raise this point so late in the analysis. I seem to have been taking it for granted that all outputs are to some extent perceivable even though they may not in fact be perceived. But this need not always be the case. Indeed, under modern conditions of government it may become increasingly less so.

To begin with, in the field of international affairs, a premium is placed upon secrecy, on presumed strategic grounds. There may be a deliberate effort to give the appearance of no decisions or actions where such outputs have in fact been undertaken. Alternatively, efforts may be made to distract attention from the true outputs to spurious ones.

In addition, even for domestic matters, the volume of outputs may be so great or its technicality may be so involved that effective secrecy may be maintained for some time either deliberately or inadvertently. Certainly in the case of nondemocratic systems, the possibility is greatly enhanced. But even in democratic ones, the intricacies of modern decision-making and administrative processes are so great that many outputs simply cannot be perceived.

It is true, where special groups seek to ferret out the decisions and actions that are taken, it may be that there is a time limit upon the concealment of any outputs. As the specific efforts to maintain control over atomic secrets about nuclear weapons have revealed, even where secrecy is approved by many members of the system, whether democratic or otherwise, attrition takes place according to well-known patterns. For most matters even in this highly sensitive area, it takes only about two years for the secrets to filter out through an entirely natural process.

Even though eternal secrecy may be impossible in the political sphere, the length of the delay in perception of the output stimulus is critical. Even two years or less may be sufficient to create a logic of events that cannot easily be reversed and will be recognized as such by politically relevant members. The delay will therefore have vital consequences for any kind of subsequent response. A member may be reconciled to accept as a *fait accompli*, an output that might have been opposed if it had been known at its inception. Furthermore, if an output remains concealed for a long enough period of time, its occurrence and effects may be purely of historical interest. Such outputs are at times discovered through memoirs and historical documents of political systems even though their numbers are probably far fewer than is commonly thought.

But whether the delay is for a short period or an indefinite one, whether it occurs by design or accident, the interruption of the flow of feedback stimuli at least postpones the response. As a result, much of what political authorities may do is perceived and acts as a feedback stimulus, but too late for the members to do anything about it.

Reality Testing of Outputs

If it were only perception that was at work, all political life would be but a battle of words or a massive exercise in persuasion. The authorities would just need to discover effective means for shaping the perceptions of the members and they could assure themselves of an unlimited flow of support for all levels of the system. Some students of politics have indeed arrived at just such a conclusion. With modern technological skills in the area of mass communication and persuasion becoming increasingly sophisticated, it is regularly suggested that it is only a matter of time when any regime will be able to perpetuate itself indefinitely.

The fundamental truth in this conjecture is that means of control through propaganda, education, persuasion, indoctrination, and communication, whichever vocabulary is most appealing, cannot be denied. Modern skills do increase the opportunities for perpetuating control. But two conditions constantly militate against outputs designed to regulate perception so as to maintain an undeviating flow of support for any given political objects.

In the first place, in those regimes that permit competitive appeals to the membership about the appropriate modes for interpreting outputs, the dialectic of perception so introduced frees the member's mind for independent judgment and evaluation, however difficult it may be at times.

In the second place, as I have already indicated, stimuli are not only perceptual in character; they also take a circumstantial form. Regardless of how the members may be led to perceive the flow of output stimuli and even if they do not see any outputs at all, they alone are able to measure their actual experiences of life against culturally developed expectations about what is desirable and possible. If the gap between what are perceived as the outputs or what become the actual outcomes, on the one hand, and what is culturally expected, on the other, increases, the disparity so created serves as a rough measure of possible discontent.[5] If perceptions of outputs and experiences move in directions opposite or even orthogonal to the goals set by cultural expectations, the net balance of effects of these two different kinds of stimuli will form the final stimulus in the feedback loop. It is the life-experience or basic reality testing that also operates to foster or erode support.

This is just another and fuller way of indicating that the ultimate stimuli are a composite of both dimensions in most outputs, the circumstantial, which calls upon experience as a source for evaluating the system, and the perceptual. As we shall see in the next chapter, it is the impact of this composite stimulus—the difference between what is experienced, what is perceived, and what is expected as outputs—that governs the feedback response.

[5] For an elaboration of this thought consult D. Easton, "The Perception of Authority and Political Change"; also chapter 25 for further discussion of such a measure.

Mediation of Output Stimuli

It may be argued that this line of reasoning violates much of what we know about political involvement, particularly in those types of systems, such as democracies, in which the expectations relating to political interest, concern, and participation are high. Even in these systems, the extent of political apathy is often dramatically widespread. If this is so, how can we argue that members are motivated to offer or withdraw support by stimuli about which they may know little or care less? Indeed all the evidence indicates that with the increasing complexity of governing, the highly technical nature of many decisions that have to be made, the large number and variety of matters that have to be settled through outputs, and the vast volume of affairs demanding the attention of members of a system, there is little likelihood that a member will have either the time, interest or resources to follow each output as it occurs or to react in any way at all, except on a very highly selective basis.[6]

We met this situation earlier and saw that, at one limiting extreme, we could conceive of members reacting by ignoring outputs entirely. In that case they would be confronted with a continuing set of conditions of which they might approve or disapprove as they experienced the outcomes. They would at least know when the shoe pinches and could cry out to whatever set of authorities happened to hold office.

But we can also see that a different alternative may exist. They may lean on others to mediate the interpretation of outputs. Unable to inform themselves about all or most technical and varied outputs, the members may be driven to rely on trusted leaders and experts to act as brokers between themselves and the perception of outputs. The leaders of a political party or interest group and the head of a locality, village, or lineage perform such services. The members will depend on others, such as these, in whom they have built up confidence, to help them make sense of what is happening in the political sphere. We have witnessed this with regard to mediated demands; here, therefore, we find that support too may be mediated. The member commits his support to this intermediary and takes his cues from such persons or groups about the way in which output stimuli are to be perceived or interpreted.

---

[6] A. Downs, *op. cit.*, argues that it would not be rational for members of democratic systems to do otherwise.

Everything that has been said about the role of direct perception by the member himself applies equally to mediated perception, except that another stage has been added. Here we have a second order level of perception at work. The member must now react to a stimulus as he perceives it to be perceived by a trusted leader or reference group. The subsequent flow of support will be regulated not by the impact of the stimuli on the member directly but by their effects on those who have become his *de facto* representatives or spokesmen. This is a kind of representation or substitution function that occurs in all kinds of large-scale systems, totalitarian or democratic, domestic or international, one that requires as close an empirical scrutiny as is currently being given to the formal representative structure in legislatures.[7]

As a case in point, outputs from the United Nations are considerable for the international political system. Yet outside of attempting to keep the peace, members of the national units perceive it to be doing far less than it is in fact doing. They do not perceive the role it and its agencies are playing in world health, population regulation, food supply, supervision of international communications and transportation, and the dissemination of basic economic social and political data.[8]

If the political leadership in each national system, such as the authorities, party leaders or publicists, perceived the varied outputs of the UN or communicated them widely to the membership, this mediated perception could be effective in building up new images of the extent to which the UN and its associated organizations are fulfilling the existing demands of some members and the possible demands of others. But lacking such mediated perceptions to inform the membership in the component subsystems of this international system, there is little likelihood that any perception of its outputs, much less an undistorted one, will be widely acquired.

In fact, the perceptions that do filter through the mediating structures of political leaders and the mass media tend to prevent the development of a public informed about the varied and numerous outputs with long range consequences produced by the complex of organizations that compose the UN. Awareness of the connection between

[7] A. Campbell *et al.* in *The American Voter* (New York: Wiley, 1960) demonstrate how the perceptions of issues and demands at a certain stage of development, in our conceptualization, are influenced by party and leadership identification, and derivatively, the way in which issues, or perceptions of who favors an issue, affect the input of support in the form of votes alone.

[8] W. A. Scott and S. B. Witbey, *The United States and the United Nations* (New York: Manhattan, 1958), especially Table 21, p. 39, and p. 252.

the international system and various international outputs is a central problem for that system. Because it relates in part to perception, it can be resolved only with difficulty as long as the national communication media and political leadership are not concerned to bring outputs of the international system to a level of easy and, perhaps, high visibility.

This reference to mediated perception does not imply that members are unable to perceive the outputs of authorities unaided by others. But in large-scale systems, neither will they be able to perceive all outputs without the intervention of the perceptions of others. Typically, therefore, the stimuli for most members will represent a combination of direct and mediated perceptions. When we add this to what I have said before about non-perceived kinds of stimuli, we can sum up by saying that the elements shaping the output stimuli to which members will react in the output loop are a tripartite composite of the reality testing of circumstantial evidence, direct perceptions, and mediated perceptions.

Particularity and Patterning of Output Stimuli

By treating each output as a particular and unique stimulus to which members respond, it has been possible to point up the various factors that help to determine the impact such a stimulus may have upon the members. But in doing so, the analysis has been somewhat misleading insofar as it has seemed that the support of the members is influenced by each output, taken in its particularity, or even the specific outcomes of the outputs as they percolate back to affect the experiences of the members.

In some instances, particular outputs may well act as the stimulus for a given input response. As I have indicated, in some cases the demand for decisions and actions may be quite well defined: a farm organization seeks a higher subsidy for identified products; a union seeks a specific modification in an existing labor statute; consumer organizations press for carefully spelled out supervision in the use of additives in food; riparian members demand flood control on their river system.

Furthermore, in some instances a demand may be highly dramatized in the system and, in the conflict for influence, a great deal may be contrived to hinge on a decision over a particular area of demands. Decisions about a declaration of war or suing for peace, action on behalf of conservation of resources, steps to bring a colonial disturbance to a conclusion, and similar visible issues may act as easily identified stimuli influencing the supportive feelings of the membership.

Aside from classes of cases such as these, in the normal course of events the stimulus cannot be a given output, each considered with respect to its particular and unique consequences for the members of the system. Indeed, in the case of democratic political systems under conditions of large-scale modern societies, in seeking to assess the role of the members, who of necessity must rely on expert counsel, the idea has frequently been advanced that although members cannot tell whether a given output is good or bad, they can at least tell over the long haul whether and when the shoe begins to pinch. As we have seen, this may well be the case. But the fact is that for long periods, members of a system may endure shoes that do not fit if they can be persuaded to perceive either that they really do not pinch or that they ought to be patient and wait for better shoes coming on an early freight.

Underlying this traditional democratic notion is the more general conception that applies to the politically relevant members of all types of systems, namely, that the stimuli consist of an aggregate of outputs over an interval of time. Feedback stimuli refer to such a pattern of outputs over time. One knows whether the shoe pinches, not through one trip to the corner store but as the result of a continuous experience under varying conditions. Through mediated or direct perceptions and through their own experiences with the circumstances in which they find themselves, the members are in fact able to accept outputs as stimuli. At any moment of time they may not and need not view outputs so rationally as to offer or withhold support on the basis of a single output or short series of them, or on the basis of a limited range of experiences. But we can expect that their sentiments toward the various objects in the system will be affected favorably or adversely by outputs and experienced outcomes as their impact accumulates over an interval of time.

Accordingly, as we move to the next stage of the feedback cycle, even though avoidance of circumlocutions compels me to speak as though members were responding to specific outputs and experienced outcomes, it should be borne in mind that the stimulus for a response consists of a pattern of outputs as it develops over time or an accumulated series of experienced outcomes. Outputs will be used elliptically to refer, therefore, to this pattern of outputs and outcomes over a period of time, unless the context indicates otherwise.

25

The Feedback Response

THE PRODUCTION OF OUTPUTS THAT ACT AS STIMULI FOR THE MEMBERS is only the first phase of the feedback process. The second phase, as we saw in Diagram 7 in Chapter 23, incorporates the responses of the members to these outputs. If anywhere, it is here that the amount of specific support generated by the outputs becomes evident. Hence we must examine just who it is that does the responding, what methods will help us assess the impact of outputs on the inflow of specific support and how the forthcoming support is related to the stimuli. Once we have been able to determine the conditions that shape the nature of the supportive responses to outputs and outcomes, we shall be able to move on, in the next chapter, to the various ways in which these responses themselves are communicated to those who are responsible for producing the outputs as stimuli in the first place.

The Responders to Feedback Stimuli

Who respond to the feedback stimuli and to whom are their responses communicated? It should be clear that there is no structural difference between those who introduce demands and those who react to outputs. The behaving units in this segment of the feedback loop, those who are responding to what the authorities have done, are also the demand-producing units whose activities we have already examined in detail when discussing the input of demands. In both cases, they are part or all of the politically relevant members in a system, those who can and do participate in the political processes. Insofar as we consider them producers of demands and of specific support, we are viewing them with regard to activities that appear at the input boundary of a system.

But to whom are the reactions of these members directed? As in the case of demands, we may expect that if fluctuations in specific support are, in turn, to lead to subsequent action to prevent support from falling below a critical level, information about such fluctuations must in some form find its way back to the authorities. At least, if it does not, it is not likely that the authorities will be able to act through outputs to attempt to cope with the problems so created. But we shall come to this matter of communication between the producers of support and the producers of outputs in the next chapter.

At the moment, the essential point is that in their roles as demand-makers and support-givers, the relevant members of the system stand at a critical point in the whole feedback loop. How they respond to the stimuli will determine the extent to which outputs have proved effective in maintaining a minimal level of support for the various political objects. Since they do stand across the feedback loop in this way, just as we have interpreted their activity as equivalent to that of gatekeeping with regard to the flow of demands, similarly we may view them as performing a gatekeeping function over the input of support. With them is located the capacity to open, close or leave ajar the sluicegates of support.

Assessment of Feedback Response

How are we to obtain even a rough assessment of the impact that outputs and their outcomes have upon the reaction of the members affected by them? What will determine the degree to which the responses to the stimuli are positively or negatively supportive?

Fluctuations in support as a response will be shaped by at least three different kinds of factors. First, where the stimuli are unperceived outcomes from the outputs, the level of satisfaction with experienced conditions will provide a measure of the support that the member is likely to feel for the various political objects. Second, where there is some perception of outputs, support can be expected to be forthcoming to the degree these outputs are interpreted as satisfying an unarticulated need, present or future, or as meeting a current demand. Variations in the input of specific support will at least be established by the total satisfactions obtained from these two basic sources. And third, such variations may flow from conditions, perceived or otherwise, that are largely unrelated to any activity on the part of the authorities. Changing economic conditions, for example, constitute a parameter that may stir up dissatisfactions or new hopes in the system even though they are a result of circumstances over which the authorities have no actual control.

At this point I am not concerned with measuring the total reservoir of support available from the members of a system. This is a problem that has already been dealt with as far as we need to go at our level of analysis.[1] Here my problem relates rather to the ways in which outputs by themselves may be conceived as a characteristic mechanism through which systems may bolster lagging support. We are holding constant other determinants of support so as to test for the independent effects of outputs. Our attention will be confined exclusively to the kind of stimuli discussed in the previous chapter. What we now need to inquire into is the possibility of indentifying the elements necessary for estimating the impact that these various output stimuli may have upon the appearance of specific support as a response.

Output Success and Output Failure

Meaning of the Concepts

The success or failure of outputs in winning the supportive response of members will depend upon the extent to which the outputs—viewed as the net effect of perceived outputs and experienced outcomes from unperceived outputs—are able to meet the current demands of the members or anticipate and abort possible future demands by preventing grievances from arising. Satisfaction derived from outputs that have met present or anticipated demands will serve as a major means for inducing the input of specific support. Feedback stimuli will consequently have a decisive effect on the succeeding inputs of demands as well as on the input of support; in this way both of these inputs become closely intertwined.[2]

Analytically, we have here a threefold interactional process. In the first phase, stimuli succeed in meeting current demands or in averting the emergence of future demands. The resulting reduction of demands reflects the satisfaction with the actions of the authorities or with experienced circumstances. This, in turn, in the second analytic phase, nourishes supportive attitudes which are communicated to the authorities. Finally, through the operation of spill-over effect, satisfaction with authorities or conditions in general, is likely to lead the members to remain contented with or to withhold hostility from the political objects such as the regime or community. Failure of feedback stimuli to meet demands or anticipate future circumstances will, of course, lead in an opposite direction.

[1] Earlier, in chapter 10 we went as far as we need to go in considering the general measurement of support and in chapter 17 we examined various general classes of support.

[2] See Diagram 6, "input boundary threshold," chapter 23.

Briefly put, output success as just defined will tend to stimulate support; output failure—the lack of a perceived or felt correspondence between outputs and demands or outcomes and the demand stimulating conditions—will tend to erode it. The feedback response will be a function of the relationship between output stimuli and demands, present or anticipated.

Millennial Ideals and Output Failure

The concepts "output success" and "output failure" seem simple enough at first glance but, in fact, they contain a number of obscurities, if not outright ambiguities, about the possible relationship between feedback stimuli and response. This returns to a point I touched on at the end of the last chapter. There we saw that the net effect of output stimuli was related to the difference in positive as against negative satisfactions received from the combination of perceived outputs and experienced outcomes. Now we can go further and demonstrate that not all stimuli that would seem to meet the definition of output failure, even if they are perceived to do so, need lead to a feedback response in the form of support withdrawal. The effect of feedback stimuli on the gatekeepers of support cannot be understood except as a function of the relationship of the outputs to the cultural expectations prevalent in the system toward such outputs.

As we have seen, earlier in the discussion of demands, members may at times voice demands that are clearly ideal in character. Very frequently they may appear in the form of ideologies spelling out millennial future states of affairs. These may not even represent long range expected goals but only targets to give direction and purpose for present action. In the normal course of events, no one expects that these broader ideals will be attained even in a distant future. They are symbols of solidarity and criteria by which to judge the appropriateness or justice of present outputs.

It is true, under some conditions, such long-range solidary and legitimating ideals may be taken more or less literally. In the case of many developing countries, with high illiteracy rates and understandable impatience to right the felt wrongs of many generations, social and economic egalitarian and humanitarian ideals have been interpreted as practical and immediate objectives, if not by the leadership, at least by large segments of the membership. Output failure here, when the Western ideals failed to materialize into realities, has led to bitter disappointment and frustration with the meaning of independence and freedom. In most systems it has brought a swift reaction from the new indigenous authorities to prevent the support for the new system, that had been raised to a high pitch during the struggle for independence, from being suddenly undermined by the predictable and unavoidable output failure. Theories of guided democracy and one-party systems quickly emerged as institutional devices to stem the threatened ebb in the tide of support. We have already seen that these mechanisms also served the purpose of helping to reduce the volume of demands, the so-called revolution in rising expectations, that accompanied political emancipation.

But in older systems, through the processes of political socialization the members have learned to discriminate between the solidary ideals and what are usually described as the practical realities, although even here many understandable differences of interpretation still occur. But the range of variation in interpretations is relatively narrow. Through a process of slow political growth over the years, as we saw in Chapter 7, a culture of political self-restraint has been nurtured, and undoubtedly similar attitudes must in due course take root in the developing nations. Under these conditions, the failure of ultimate ideals to materialize need not give birth to a feeling of output failure and its accompanying feedback response in the form of support withdrawal.

But even in systems in which the expectations of members are curbed by such cultural constraints, output failure might on occasion occur with regard to ultimate ideals themselves. Such failure might contribute to the erosion of support if the members are ever brought to feel that current patterns of outputs unnecessarily postpone or are likely to prevent for ever a closer approximation of these millennial ideals. To some extent the Negro in the United States since World War II has developed a sharp consciousness of the unnecessary slowness in moving closer to the professed ideals of equality. One may also speculate, in the case of the Soviet Union, on whether the reiteration of promises of vast future economic improvements, if grossly exaggerated, may not set in motion disappointments with outputs, the consequences of which may be seriously unstabilizing for the authorities and regime.

Culturally Expected Goals and Output Failure: An Index of Contentment

But if, in the usual course of events, failure to attain the ideal goals does not act as a feedback stimulus that threatens the input of support, output failure will occur, however, when the perceived outputs and outcomes do not measure up to the culturally sanctioned practical objectives. At the other extreme from the ideals are those demands that members voice because, in the context of the culture and circumstances, they consider it reasonable to seek their fulfillment. Where such demands are perceived as spurned or neglected, the probability is high that the members will deny their support to the authorities at least, and through spill-over, in time, to the basic political objects.

In effect what we could construct here is an index of political contentment. It would consist of the ratio between outputs and demands, where demands and outputs have been summed over an interval of time. Such an index would measure the probable degree of support that the members would be prepared to offer the political objects. It represents the imbalance between demands and perceived outputs. Thus, if the index formed by the number of outputs satisfying demands over the number of demands voiced were to exceed the ratio of one, it would indicate that the members felt they were getting more than they reasonably expected.[3] The farther it fell below one, however, the greater the likelihood that the outputs would be contributing in some degree to the accumulation or reinforcement of hostility toward the authorities and, if the process were to continue long enough, toward the regime or political community as well.

The Distribution of Contentment
Among Members in a System

As an estimate of the potential stress to which a system is exposed from the deterioration of support, even a calculus of individual gratifications or deprivations measured in this way would not necessarily provide a decisive indication of the state of the system. What would prove critical in determining the degree of output success or failure would be the distribution of such sentiments over the whole of the membership.

The outputs do not need to develop a net balance of satisfaction among all the members in a system. Some members usually count for more than others in the support that they offer. To obtain the support of what I have been calling the politically relevant members, it may not be necessary to offer all members positive output incentives. Only the most influential, whatever the reasons may be, need to be wooed.[4]

[3] The use of the term "reasonable" does not mean that the members may be acting rationally. It is employed here only in the sense that in the culture, the demand or underlying expectation is accepted as permissible by most members, however unreasonable it may be viewed either by a minority or if imported criteria are used.

[4] It has been suggested that if we assumed rational behavior, the optimal strategy of a set of authorities might be, not to seek to satisfy the demands of one's friends

The aggregate gratifications or deprivations experienced by these members as a result of outputs and outcomes will have greater impact on the persistence or change in support for a system than the fulfillment of demands for the remaining members of the system. Outputs do not need to satisfy all of the members or even most of them but only some of them, the most influential.

But even among these politically relevant members, to maintain an adequate level of support it may be sufficient to meet the demands of only a certain proportion. The critical variable lies in the distribution of satisfactions. Net gratification and deprivation may be so distributed among individuals and groups in a system as to create divisive and schismatic responses rather than to heal any pre-existing ones. Because support is a social phenomenon involving the relationship of groups and individuals, it is not enough to measure the aggregate satisfactions obtained by summing all individual satisfactions. Such a sum may be high, indicating that most demands are being satisfied for most members taken individually. Yet conceivably, the sytem might be under considerable stress from declining support.

For example, this might occur under conditions in which some segment of the membership is constantly excluded from enjoying any outputs. A stream of outputs and outcomes that consistently favored one large group over another smaller group might show up in any aggregate measure as providing a relatively high degree of collective satisfaction of demands. But if, in accord with the prevailing sense of equity, the disadvantaged minority group felt unfairly and regularly excluded and could anticipate no change in these conditions, the output stimuli might succeed in generating such cleavages as to destroy the possibility of all members working together in the same regime or community.

Minority nationality groups within systems typically find themselves in this position. Prior to the Civil War in the United States, the southern states were similarly roused by a feeling of past and anticipated continuing failure to obtain satisfaction for their future wants and current demands. The net balance of benefits (for individuals singly considered or for the whole aggregate of the politically relevant members) contributes less to the alleviation of possible stress from loss

or political supporters or to minimize hostility of one's opponents, but to pursue a course that will outsmart the enemy in competition for the support of uncommitted members of the system. See A. Downs, *op. cit.* This might work where the uncommitted are politically relevant members. But if they are not, any efforts to solicit their support would prove futile, unless they could be newly mobilized into an effective political group in the system.

of support than the nature of the distribution of satisfactions throughout the system.

The Distribution of Satisfactions over Time

It is also clear that not even these politically relevant members, in
proportions that do not stimulate cleavages, need to have their demands met all of the time if outputs are to succeed in avoiding stress.
Some of the time may be sufficient.

This enables us to inquire more closely into just what has been
meant when I have said that it is necessary to consider the impact of
outputs "over a given interval of time." The net balance, even for the
relevant members considered as a potentially divided group, is not a
calculation based upon gratifications and deprivations derived from
the opposing tendencies of outputs at a moment of time. Rather, as in
the case of individuals considered severally, it is these tendencies as
they work themselves out over a period of time. Politically relevant
members may be able to tolerate a considerable volume of unfulfilled
demands if, periodically and opportunely, some demands are met. An
astute set of authorities, in Machiavellian fashion, often meets just
enough, at least so as to still any critical accumulation of discontent.
In the language of practical politics, this involves offering sops or
conciliatory outputs at just the right moment to head off any brewing
storm of dissatisfactions.

The Linearity of Feedback Response

But regardless of the distribution of support in space or time, the
impact of perceived outputs and outcomes on specific support will also
depend upon the extent to which linearity exists between the two.
Must any drop or increase in support be directly proportional to the
apparent intensity of the stimulus?

The answer to this question is probably in the negative. The very
fact that, as we have seen, it may take a whole pattern of outputs or
unresponsiveness on the part of the authorities for the members to
begin to feel deprived, suggests that there is no necessary linear relationship. If it takes a great accumulation of disappointments and frustrations to disillusion members with an ongoing system, it would normally require an even greater series of deprivations to rouse them to
the kind of organized action required to transform a regime or destroy
a political community.

Various alternatives are theoretically and empirically possible. A large series of stimuli may produce only a small response as when outputs lag for extended periods and yet members maintain the input of specific support at the same level. But the converse may be equally true at other times. A small stimulus may trigger a massive response. A shot fired by the military during a rally to protest continued indifference of the authorities to the demands of members, may be the beginning of a revolution.[5] Small actions may set off a chain reaction that leads to the elimination of existing authorities, transformation of the regime, and even of the community. The capacity of the members in a system to tolerate frustration will vary but need not be typically proportional to the apparent provocations.

The determination of the degree of feedback response, in terms of negative or positive support for the objects of a system, is not a simple matter. Yet judgments about the effects of feedback stimuli are constantly being made in practical political situations. Predictions about the effects of outputs on the membership of a political system are the stock in trade of the practicing politician as well as of the scholar so that this theoretical need is not alien to empirical reality. What is clear from our discussion is that outputs do not need to satisfy all of the members all of the time or even most of the members most of the time. To maintain a level of support within its critical range, the feedback stimuli only need to satisfy some of the members, the politically relevant or influential ones in the system, some of the time.[6]

[5] Of course, a small action that does trigger a large revolt is an indication of underlying smoldering discontent. In the same way, a delayed reaction in personal emotions may be set off by a trivial incident, revealing a past history of dissatisfactions and grievances. The triggering incident is only the last in a series of stimuli, and the underlying factors contribute to the political "elasticity" of the situation.

[6] The reader may wonder whether this way of conceptualizing the connection between the feedback stimuli and the gatekeepers of support must commit or predispose this mode of analysis to excessively rationalistic assumptions about political behavior. It may indeed appear from discussion of the ratio of demands to outputs that the member who is putting in support must, in some neo-Benthamite fashion, calculate the advantage to himself in the light of how the authorities act. If he fails to get the expected benefits, then he must conclude it is wiser to withhold support from these authorities. With the continuation of this process, he might take stock of his feelings toward the whole way of ordering political relationships and decide to withdraw support from the regime.

Such a rational model of behavior might be useful if one wished to adopt the utilitarian assumptions that man knows his own interest and will pursue it. But for purposes of our analysis I have assumed no specific and dominant kind of motivation in political behavior. Whatever the extent to which political motivation is plural or monistic in character, intellective or affective, my only assumption in this area

We must remind ourselves, of course, that here we are considering only the support generated through outputs. But because outputs are only one source of overall support for the objects of a system, even complete failure in this respect need not necessarily lead to change. In fact, if failure of outputs to measure up to demands in a given time interval led to the collapse of political systems, there would probably be few that could survive under modern conditions. As governmental decisions become more complex, their results are less and less likely to be felt by a current generation. Judgment on the adequacy of the outputs would need to be postponed so long that they would scarcely be useful as a test for supporting any political object. Increasingly, political systems must tend to rely on diffuse support to tide it over particularly rough periods in its history.[7] As a last resort, a set of authorities may induce the minimal support it needs through the use of coercion and violence. Furthermore, as I emphasized at the outset of the discussion on support, a predisposition to withdraw support may be impeded in its actual expression by lack of organizational ability or resources on the part of the discontented.

is that the increase or reduction of support flows from perceptions of what the authorities have done or actual experience with the outcomes of their behavior. In other words, I am assuming that members respond to various output stimuli, as described, and fluctuations in the inputs of support are thereby linked to outputs in a meaningful and determinable way.

[7] This is a condition not unique to modern political systems but to other aspects of modern society as well. Compare the position of political authorities with that of the executive in corporate industry as described by J. W. Forrester, *op. cit.*, p. 8.

26

The Communication of Feedback Response

WE BEGAN OUR DISCUSSION OF THE FEEDBACK LOOP WITH THE IDEA that it identified a set of processes through which information about the impact of outputs was fed back to the authorities. Thereby they were able to make some effort to adjust and adapt their behavior to attain the level of support they sought for any of the political objects.

To this point we have inquired into the nature of the outputs, the variable ways in which they might affect the members of the system, and how these members might in turn respond to their input of support. We must now proceed further along the flow path in the feedback loop to discover how information about the input of support is itself communicated to the authorities and the way this may influence the level of specific support.

Information about Responses

If the actions of the gatekeepers of support are to have any consequences for the future behavior of the authorities, that is, for the outputs with which they may follow up their initial outputs, information about fluctuations in the input of support must get back to them in some way. Anything that stands in the way of the flow of this information, to block it entirely, to delay or distort it, will play a significant part in shaping the follow-up behavior of the authorities. It will also help to determine the probability of their being able to achieve whatever objectives they have for the continuation, cessation, or increase in the input of support.

Without such information, the authorities would have no inkling as to whether their prior outputs had achieved an effect, whether negative or positive, relevant to their own objectives; they would be left entirely in the dark as to what their next step should be. Uninformed guess work would have to prevail. With delays or distortions in feedback response, the effects would be almost as variable. Not that the consequences need be only negative in character; that is, they need not always serve to undermine support. As we shall see, delays, at least, may contribute to the capacity of the authorities to stimulate specific support in a positive as well as a negative direction.

The authorities must seek two kinds of information if they are to obtain clues about the extent to which they have succeeded or failed in maintaining what they conceive to be a desired level of support. They will require information about the general state of mind of the members concerning support and, in addition, some specific indication of the extent to which outputs have in fact managed to meet demands of the politically relevant members.

Information about Supportive Attitudes

With regard to information about the supportive frame of mind, we need not assume that the gatekeepers will respond to stimuli in some explicit or necessarily rational way as by saying: I withdraw support or present you with mine. Rather, as in most other kinds of social behavior, the growth or attrition of support can be detected from telltales which the authorities seek out or receive from the politically relevant members.

These telltales will vary with the nature of the regime and the specific circumstances. Where political conditions permit, for example, they may take the form of political criticism of the authorities in increasing proportions; hostile apathy, pacific demonstrations or deputations, refusal to pay taxes, outbreaks of violent opposition, the emergence of an active, hostile counter-elite to the authorities themselves, or a rise in acts of treason. The absence of such behavior, the acceptance of or acquiescence in the going political objects, or the presence of explicit actions expressing solidarity behind the political objects, would be manifestations of positive support. These are kinds of cues of which the authorities may take note and to which they may in turn respond in order to achieve whatever level of support they may deem appropriate.

Information about Satisfaction of Demands

But if specific support is in part also a function of the satisfaction of demands as held by politically relevant members, insofar as the information fed back to the authorities conveyed some idea about output failure and success along these lines, they would be in a better position to know the extent to which any increase in support might be contingent upon additional efforts to meet articulated or anticipated demands. Looked at from the inverse point of view, the failure to meet demands is not a demand problem exclusively; it does not only involve the volume or variety of demands and means of coping with them. It is a support problem as well; it concerns the capacity of the authorities to bolster support by meeting demands.

The authorities may be unwilling to meet some demands for one of two reasons. Either they might think that to do so would defeat the very objectives that the demand-making members would like to achieve; or they might see it as against their own interests or the interests of others to whom they are more sensitively responsive. But where the authorities do desire to meet demands, unless they acquire information about what demands have been met by past outputs, which ones are continuing to be voiced, who are voicing them and the like, with the best intentions in the world and all the necessary resources, the authorities might not be able to produce the required outputs. By communicating information about the effectiveness of past outputs in satisfying existing demands, aborting future demands, or arousing additional and new demands, feedback proves itself essential.

Accuracy and Distortion of Information

The effectiveness of outputs as a mechanism for generating specific support will be seriously affected by the accuracy of the information returning to the authorities about the general supportive state of mind of the members and specifically about the success or failure of past outputs and outcomes in meeting demands. Upon what factors in the political system does the accuracy of such information depend? [1]

In part, distortions or error will derive from the kind of lenses the authorities use to interpret the behavior of the members in the system. Factors influencing perception that we have already discussed as they affect the ordinary member, apply as well to the authorities, individually or as a group. Ideology, prejudice, indifference, and lack of skill and judgment will all contribute to the perceptual accuracy of the authorities.

In part, however, the length, complexity, and fidelity of the transmission belt along which information has to be carried, if it is to reach

---

[1] The literature on social disaster is instructive about some of the consequences of interference with information feedback processes. See, for example, H. W. Williams, "Some Functions of Communication in Crisis Behavior," 16 *Human Organization* (1957) 15–19.

the authorities, will contribute to the possibility and probability of error. In primitive systems, especially small ones, where face-to-face contact alone prevails and secondary groups, if they exist, are small enough to resemble primary groups, the flow of information about the supportive sentiments of the members would experience minimal loss and distortion. The chief or elders can sense fluctuations in antagonisms directly. But in large-scale, more differentiated systems, where complex structures stand between members and the authorities, as information about support moves along a flow network toward the authorities, it may be so reinterpreted that it no longer mirrors the true state of mind of the members.

In such large-scale systems a variety of mechanisms are available for informing the authorities about feedback response. But none of them has proved totally accurate, either singly or in combination. For example, in a democracy, direct communication between a representative and his constituency provides one source of information about the supportive frame of mind and satisfaction of demands. But a representative typically has been unable to command the resources or skill for taking adequate samples so as to obtain an accurate picture of the distribution of supportive feelings, assuming he desired to do so. Instead he must rely on one or another of a variety of channels for his information. Party structures in all mass systems, contacts between individual members and administrators, soundings taken by opinion leaders, reflection and refraction of sentiment through the mass media, expressions of opinions by interest groups, represent the variety of means through which information may be transmitted to the authorities.

Opinion polls stand as perhaps the latest addition, historically, to the devices useful for this purpose. But they have never been carefully developed for testing fluctuations in supportive sentiments toward the various political objects. At best, voting and opinion studies have been employed to provide data about supportive attitudes, under specific and narrow conditions, concerning alternative candidates for elected office. For non-democratic systems, such a tool of investigation is utterly inadequate for obvious reasons. Nevertheless, this technique has added to the repertoire of mechanisms which the authorities might use, if they saw fit or necessary, to acquire more accurate feedback information about support or the effect of outputs.

But all the means mentioned, including attitude polling, are in a sense competitive or at least not necessarily complementary. The greater the number of channels of communication available, the less likely it is that any one will dominate and thereby skew the feedback response typically in one direction. It might be argued, therefore, that competitive diversity in response channels maximizes the chances for accurate perception of feedback by the authorities.

But against this possibility we need to place the unreliability of any single channel in communicating feedback response to the authorities. Multiplying the number of channels also means that each channel will reflect the kinds of distortion specific to it and this puts the recipients of the information, the authorities, in a difficult position. If the information about response fed back through each channel is complementary or consistent, but erroneous, the authorities may be misled into accepting the weight of evidence so presented. They would be acting on misleading information about the state of support or degree of satisfaction with outputs. To the extent that the different channels return conflicting information—as where the party officials say one thing, mass media another, and personal random contact by the authorities still another—the authorities are once again thrown back on their own fundamental rules of interpretation as supplied and molded by ideology, prejudice, habit, or self-interest.

Even for a democratic system, Burke's admonition to the representative to pursue his own conception of what is desirable and necessary in the way of outputs, was partly gratuitous. Feedback processes are not sufficiently accurate or, under usual circumstances, sufficiently consistent, something that all practical politicians intuitively know. It is difficult for the authorities individually or collectively to be confident that information about the supportive frame of mind of the politically relevant members is even reasonably accurate. The pressure to fall back on one's own intuitive judgment is strong and universal.

It is usually equally difficult to know when past outputs have satisfied voiced demands in whole or in part. In large-scale political systems, a thick mist of doubt and ambiguity of necessity surrounds the effects of outputs on meeting demands and building support. Yet in seeking to penetrate this mist, the authorities are handicapped in their efforts to generate specific support, assuming they desire to do so, by their differing and often incompatible descriptive estimates of the same political situation.

This is one of the critical properties of all large-scale systems. The authorities must act in an atmosphere of partial ignorance, considerable misinformation, and consequently of great uncertainty.

Time Lags and Delays

I now propose to assume that a system has solved the problem of transmitting to the authorities correct information about the supportive attitudes of the politically relevant members and the effect of outputs on their demands. This assumption will enable us to search out the independent effects of time lags in the feedback to the authorities, a second major dimension of the communication process between authorities and gatekeepers of support. Such time lags, we shall see, seriously affect the capacity to use outputs as a mechanism for generating specific support; but peculiarly, they may also have simultaneous beneficial consequences. It is to these dual and opposing effects that my remarks will finally be directed.

If the initial outputs or outcomes have led to widespread discontent or a growing sense of deprivation on the part of the relevant members, the time it takes the information to get back to the authorities is clearly vital. Whether or not the authorities choose to correct the situation, at least knowing that it exists, enables them to take whatever action they may deem appropriate to cope with it. Most frequently time lag is not an all or none matter. It is rather a question as to whether the information, such as it is, has arrived in sufficient time to provide the authorities with the opportunity to achieve the best results for their objectives. Whether the authorities are wise enough to take advantage of the information obtained or have the will and resources to do so, are, as always, entirely different matters.

The Effects of Too Much Time Lag

Intuitively we can appreciate the stress inherent in excessively slow feedback of information about responses. How long the delay would have to be for it to have such adverse consequences on the input of support, would be an empirical matter varying with systems. But wherever the threshold might lie for any system, if the delay passes beyond it, any unfavorable effects set in motion initially by outputs may have a chance to take root and grow, until a small set of original grievances turns into smoldering resentment or, finally, open political rage. If time delay occurred in only a few isolated instances, its effect on support might not be serious. But if the typical pattern in the system, due to its structure or norms, was for feedback response to lag continuously, a grave erosion of support could occur.

For some subject matters, efforts on the part of the authorities to follow up past outputs on the basis of information feedback about present responses may not be affected by time delays, even if they are extended. But for other areas, too late may be equivalent to not at all. Thus, members in a system may not build up serious grievances if the authorities fail to meet demands for better educational or recreational facilities. But if such material matters such as economic welfare, unemployment, or the spread of disease really count in the culture, time would be a vital consideration in relation to supportive sentiments.

The Effects of Too Little Time Lag

The general effects of excessive time lag, especially in societies as time-conscious as modern ones, need little further elaboration. But what is not equally apparent is the fact that an excessively rapid feedback response may also have injurious effects on the input of support. Insufficient time lag may be as crippling to the ability of the authorities to utilize outputs to encourage specific support as the presence of an excessive time lag.

An illustration is suggested in cases where spontaneous grass roots movements express intense discontent over some output that has taken place or at the failure of the authorities to act where it is thought they should have. In these instances, the speed of the feedback may so overwhelm the authorities that they are driven into quick and often inadequately considered action. A moderate pause in the feedback response, under such circumstances, would give the authorities an opportunity to evaluate the alternatives more fully, to discuss the response with those contributing to it, and to examine the validity of the response itself. Outputs produced in reply to instantaneous responses to prior outputs or conditions may, in the long run, do more to undermine than to promote specific support.

In this light, we can see that time delays are not entirely negative in their impact on support. Time lag may serve a vital damping function to prevent hasty action by the authorities in coping with feedback response and thereby it improves their opportunities for acting more effectively in the pursuit of specific support.

The degree of time lag, it is clear, will influence both the form and consequences of feedback response. We need, therefore, to look at those factors in a system that affect the rate at which members are likely to react to feedback stimuli and the varying consequences of these different rates for the generation of specific support by the authorities.

Determinants of Delay: The Feedback Channels

The Nature of the Channels

One of the major sources of delay in the feedback response derives from the nature of the channels along which information travels.

These channels may be of two sorts; direct or mediated. In the first case, communication may be without benefit of mediators. Information will be relayed directly to the authorities by the individual members or groups themselves who thereby act as their own gatekeepers over their responses.

But it is apparent that in many other cases, the responses may be processed through a number of gatekeepers before reaching the authorities. A member of a system may not have a strong enough sense of efficacy to feel that he can do much on his own or the realities may make this obvious. He may complain to an interest group about the level of tariffs or high level of unemployment; or expressions of discontent may appear first in mass media as letters to the editors, soundings by opinion leaders, or even as news reports of the state of mind of the members in the system.

Alternatively, expressions of dissatisfaction or contentment with perceived outputs or circumstances may spread from an individual member to precinct captains, to higher party officials, and ultimately to party representatives who hold political office. These expressions of sentiment may be joined along the way by similar or conflicting views communicated to interest groups and by their leaders, in turn, to higher party officials. Simultaneously, individuals, groups, and party leaders may be informing administrative officials, legislators, and others directly of their state of mind.

These behaving units, when linked together, form channels along which communications about support flow; the units are the gatekeepers who, we have seen, are also active with respect to the input of demands. Although this uses a democratic system as a model, similar processes occur in all systems, at least among the politically relevant members, however varied the structures may be that act as channels of communication of supportive feelings.

Effect of the Quantity of Channels

Time lags in the transmission of feedback response will vary with the number of channels available for carrying information about support. We may hypothesize that the fewer the number of channels for carrying this information, the longer the time necessary for the responses to find their way to the authorities.

Without doubt, where the number of channels are few, it would help to concentrate great power in the hands of a limited number of gatekeepers. They would control the basis upon which the authorities arrived at judgments about what ought to be done, if anything, about the way members are perceiving and feeling about outputs. But aside from this important consideration about the location of power in the system, the reduction of channels for the communication of supportive sentiments would tend to delay the transmission of feedback response. Every social and political structure can carry only a finite amount of information in a given time interval, as we have already seen in our discussion of demands. If, in fact, all feedback response in large-scale systems could be confined to a limited number of channels, a great deal of information about the effects of outputs and outcomes might never reach the authorities.

One-party regimes typically tend in this direction today. The party stands not only as the major gatekeeper over the inflow of demands and their conversion to issues, as we have seen before; members are also expected to voice their grievances, within permissible limits prescribed by the regime, and other indications of supportive feelings, to the party leadership at each level of the system. They are not expected to create new structures to store or to relay their sentiments about outputs to the appropriate authorities.

But under conditions of modern mass societies, it is impossible for any regime to restrict the gatekeeping function over support to one structure alone, even where one party nominally and literally dominates the communication structure. Not only would it increase the hazards to the authorities of excessive dependence upon one source of information; it would so overburden the party that it could not fulfill its tasks with minimal adequacy.

In most single party systems, other channels along which feedback response can travel, tend to come into existence. They may take the form of presumed representative institutions at the local and most inclusive levels of the system; of semi-popular administrative organizations as in the USSR; or of specially created groups to offer members a controlled forum in which to vent their grievances, as in the case of supervised trade unions, peasant organizations, or other vocational groups. These form the eyes and the ears of the authorities for continuously taking the supportive pulse of the members in the system.[2]

[2] Such multiple channels along which feedback response may flow to the authorities do reduce control over the expression of supportive or hostile sentiments. Other controlling and social monitoring measures such as secret police, cultural norms, and partly lackeys are available, however, to keep the expression of supportive feelings within bounds manageable for the dominant members in the system. Yet apparently whatever risk is involved in this respect cannot be avoided. The advantage to the authorities by way of information about the attitude of the mem-

Determinants of Delay: Number of Receptors of Feedback Response

Delays in the communication of feedback response may also be incurred through the numerical insufficiency of receiving points in the system. The receptors to which feedback is directed among the authorities must be able to handle the volume of information embodied in the feedback if excessive time lag between the return of the information and any subsequent follow-up action is to be avoided. There may be an adequate number of communication channels but too few points at which the information is finally received and used as a possible basis for further outputs.

At the one extreme, we might visualize a system in which all responses must find their way back to a single person in authority; he stands as the sole receptor. He may take the form of a supreme monarch, a paramount chief, the Secretary of the Party, or a Prime Minister. Transparently, if any system could so confine the flow of responses to one individual, information overload would be overwhelming in a system of any size, as we have already seen in the case of demands. Queuing up of information about the condition of supportive sentiments, complete neglect of part of it, confusion or disorganization with their attendant delays, could not be avoided.

A number of methods typically arise to cope with such possibilities, identical with what occurs in efforts to handle a large volume of demands. The situations are quite comparable even though in this case the information relates to support rather than to demands alone. The receptors could be improved so that through more efficient processing they are able to handle a larger volume of information. Priorities could be established according to varying criteria which would control the order of handling feedback information, to the complete neglect of some. At its simplest, a monarch may refuse to give an audience to a supplicant if his support is considered unimportant. A representative may be relatively indifferent, in the press of business, to a small shopowner as compared to a powerful corporation.

We shall return to methods such as these, in the following chapters. But in addition, the number of receiving channels may be increased so that feedback response may move toward a greater variety of targets among the authorities. Members would be able to lodge their com-

bers toward outputs—and demands as well, as we have already seen—will usually outweigh any marginal loss of control over the expression of discontent.

plaints or expressions of approval at more than one point in the authority structure. This method will be examined here.

Typically, problems of possible delay in systems have been met by providing a vast number of feedback loops differentiated according to the persons in authority that are included in the loop and the subject matters with which such a person might be expected to deal. We have already seen this in our initial discussion of the multiple loops in each basic segment of the overall or systemic feedback loop. At that time, we had decided to conceptualize the output points as a single entity and to avoid breaking it down into its numerous differentiated subsidiary loops. Here, however, it is useful to cut through this conceptualization and lay bare again the large number of points at which outputs may be produced, each of which may be the target for different kinds of feedback responses.

Typically, all political systems, at least beyond the primary group type, seek to cope with potential delay through proliferating receptors of responses. All feedback does not flow to the chief of state, for example, or even to his immediate assistant, whether we are speaking about a Bantu bureaucracy or the United States. Members tend to complain to that point in the structure of authority where it is probable that they will obtain the most effective handling of their problems. They want the person in authority, perceived as most relevant, to know about their response. By providing differentiated means of access to the set of authorities, the system is able to handle a larger volume of feedback responses about support in a given interval of time, and time lag in dealing with such responses may be reduced. It helps to make it possible for the authorities, if they so desire, to adjust subsequent outputs in a way that takes into account the supportive state of the mind of the politically relevant members.

Determinants of Delay: Storage and Release of Feedback Response

Even if there were an unlimited number of channels and receptors available for communicating these sentiments, delay in feedback response might nevertheless be occasioned by the practices of gatekeepers in the feedback channels in collecting, storing, and discharging sentiments related to support. But whether or not delays for these reasons must hamper the generation of specific support is a matter we must explore.

The Storage of Responses

At the one extreme, we could visualize a delay of indefinite duration. This would be equivalent to saying that the gatekeepers along the communication networks completely blocked expressions of dissatisfaction. Presumably fear alone could result in such complete severance of communications between the members of a system and their authorities. But whatever the cause, the authorities would be put in the position of never knowing the reaction of the politically relevant members to their outputs. Whatever follow-up they introduced to their initial outputs could be nothing but random stabs in the dark, insofar as they were oriented to the problem of seeking to stimulate additional support for any or all of the basic political objects. They would become aware of the magnitude of any attrition in support only too late to be able to compensate for it. A situation such as this would introduce permanently unstable elements into the system.

But the complete severance of communications about the supportive state of mind among the relevant membership is a totally unreal condition for political systems. Few authorites could tolerate it. What is even more significant, in modern large-scale systems it would be virtually impossible, except perhaps under temporary emergency conditions.

But is the polar antithesis to an indefinite time lag any more realistic? It would take the form of a continuous flow of communications that reflected every change in the supportive frame of mind among the politically relevant members. Every time a member was dissatisfied, he would duly and directly communicate it to some person in authority. This is an equally improbable relationship to visualize, if only because it would presuppose that all members had more time for and interest in politics than has ever been typical of any system. If anywhere, it may perhaps be closely approximated in small non-literate societies. There, political involvement reaches a degree of intensity seldom if ever achieved in any large-scale system and certainly never in modern structurally differentiated ones. But even in such small systems, a member would soon wear out his welcome and find deaf or impatient ears awaiting him, if every grievance were freely and frequently expressed.

Complete and permanent storage of supportive sentiments and continuous and uninhibited expression of them as they arise, form logical possibilities that are equally improbable in empirical situations. Minimal storage and some delay in the discharge of these sentiments will take place. Systems will vary in the mechanisms through which collection of sentiments takes place and in the expected or endorsed rate of expression.

In small systems composed of primary groups alone, for example, such as a Bushman band or group of Eskimo, there is direct and immediate access to those who decide what the group is to do. Storage here would be completely within the locus of the individual himself, or at most in a small clique of kinsmen or friends. The release of the sentiments would be restricted only to what the conventions of politeness and strategies for maximizing influence might dictate.

But in systems of larger size, spatially and numerically, the mechanisms for the collection of supportive sentiments and the rules governing their delay or discharge are far more complex. Groups rather than individuals are typically the structures through which sentiments reflecting positive or negative support are combined and withheld until the time seems opportune to express them. Furthermore, the rules governing the collection and discharge of these sentiments may vary from the highly restrictive and controlling provisions of dictatorial regimes to the much more liberal ones associated with democratic regimes.

But aside from variations in the structures and norms relating to the storage and release of support, we need to explore the implications that the resulting time delays bear for the capabilities of the authorities in meeting stress from loss of support. From what I have already said, one consequence is transparent on the surface. Excessive delay will keep essential information from the authorities, and this point I do not need to argue any further. The only question here is whether delay attendant on storage and episodic release can ever have beneficial consequences for any efforts to increase the flow of specific support. What is the relationship between delay in the communication of negative or positive supportive sentiments and the ability of the authorities to react to feedback response?

The Smoothing Function of Support Storage

Delays resulting from the collection and storage of responses serve to protect the authorities from the constant perturbations that they would otherwise experience. By helping to space out the flow of communications about support, delays enable the authorities to appraise with greater deliberation the information coming back. It does not compel them to do so; but at least it provides the opportunity.

Storage of feedback responses acts for the authorities in much the same way that springs and shock absorbers serve the passengers in an automobile. They smooth out the infinite number of jolts and bumps on a road that would otherwise be directly and continuously transmitted to the passengers. Instead of being subjected to the constant pressures of individual, disjointed, and often episodic complaints or even expressions of approval, through storage and measured release, responses related to support may be fed to the authorities in a more evenly regulated flow.

We can understand this consequence of delay through storage by looking at democratic regimes. In such systems, aside from types composed of small primary groups, members are encouraged, in the prevailing ideology, to express themselves directly and freely to their representatives and public officials. Fortunately for the capacity of authorities to absorb, interpret, and deliberate on feedback information, the system has never really worked in this way. It is true, representatives and other authorities might well prefer to hear from the individual members directly, if there were no other costs involved. It would provide a most accurate source of information. But the costs would prove extremely high. The flow of information would be of such a magnitude as to overtax the facilities of any set of authorities. In addition, in the plethora of signals from members to authorities, many would be moving in opposite, conflicting, and incompatible directions, as we have seen. The authorities would be compelled to set up collecting and storing facilities of their own, if only to organize and regulate the flow within manageable limits.

In practice, interruptions in the flow of feedback response through storage take place, in all democratic regimes, in numerous ways. At the simplest level, a representative is frequently unable to read his large volume of mail; others read it for him, condense the information into convenient and meaningful categories, and have it on tap to be drawn upon when needed.

But a large amount of pre-processing of support and preliminary storage takes place before feedback response ever reaches the authorities. Gatekeepers such as interest groups, parties, political leaders, the mass media, lineages, and age-sets, which we have found to be central to the conversion of wants into demands and demands into issues, also play a vital role in the collection and discharge of support. They act as repositories, as it were, to which members may bring their complaints or expressions of approval and through which these feedback responses may be combined, synthesized, organized, reinterpreted and if necessary, temporarily held in abeyance.

An interest group, for example, may hear its own membership voice sentiments about a set of outputs relevant to the objectives of the group. It is then able to express some measure of the supportive feelings of its members. Where the leadership of such a group has lost direct and frequent contact with its membership—constituting a leadership rather than a grassroots organization—it would, of course, express only the presumed state of mind of its membership. But regardless of how representative an interest group may be of its followers, it does bank support, as it were, and feed it out in measured amounts. In delaying the flow of supportive sentiments it serves its own objectives in influencing the allocation of values in the system. But it has the additional systemic consequence of helping to protect the authorities from being inundated by a continuous flow of feedback responses.

The Expressive Function of Collection and Storage

This brings us to another central consequence of delay points in the transmission of feedback responses. Insofar as the collection and storage of feedback responses serve to delay them, the members at the response point in the loop may be aided in presenting their supportive feelings more effectively to the authorities. In thus helping to provide a better measure of the state of mind of the members, delay improves the opportunity for the authorities to achieve their own objectives. It gives them better information about the degree of resistance or support that they can expect to find for any action they decide to take in following up the reception of feedback responses.

But at the same time it works in an opposite direction. The delay may reflect the fact that individual feelings are being combined so as to make the feedback responses more effective as a means to change or maintain the outputs and outcomes of the system. In this event the authorities may be pressed in a direction that they might otherwise not have taken but one which, because it better mirrors the demands of the members as they are incorporated into the feedback, contributes more effectively to fostering specific support.

The structures through which collection and storage take place may contribute to this effect on specific support in two ways. Through such structures and organizations, the members are able to combine their various feelings about the feedback stimuli into a common and concerted program of action. Feelings of approval or hostility in varying degrees may be muted, heightened or fused with the sentiments of others in an interest group or party, for example, so that they may leave a greater impact on the authorities. The delay for purposes of combining forces increases the intensity and concentration of the response and its visibility.

Furthermore, the very notion of delay suggests that these structural gatekeepers of support—interest groups, parties, age-sets, and the like—not only collect support but they control its release as well. The fact that the politically relevant members combine and organize to express their supportive sentiments, negative or positive, indicates a common pursuit of objectives. Supportive sentiments will be expressed or withheld as the achievement of these objectives seems to dictate. Hence release of such sentiments is neither necessarily automatic nor continuous, nor is its form fixed. This regulation of the time and form of expression of positive or negative support enables the members to communicate their antagonisms, complaints, resentments, or approval in a manner that appears most appropriate for achieving the demands incorporated in their feedback response. In this sense it improves their chances of obtaining outputs of which they can approve.

It is clear, therefore, that in the feedback of responses, the time lags associated with the collection, storage, and strategic discharge of these responses may be quite functional to the purposes of the members themselves. Specific support will be encouraged. Furthermore, as indicated, by protecting the authorities from the unstabilizing effects of the constant and disjointed barrage of complaints that might otherwise occur, the same delay has equally significant consequences for giving the authorities time to absorb the information being communicated before acting upon it. It therefore also improves their opportunities for maximizing specific support, given the will and resources to do so.

Storage and Release in Varying Types of Systems

It may appear from what has just been said about delay that it applies only to democratic systems. It may even appear on the surface that I have carefully adopted a democratic model of a system in order to illustrate the analysis adequately. In non-democratic regimes, we can imagine that the capacity to control the storage and release, especially of negative supportive sentiments, through the domination of organized groups, would be of critical importance, but for reasons other than those already discussed above. We would expect the authorities to attempt to cut off and delay permanently the voicing of hostile feelings. The capacity to delay would constitute a central source of power and the authorities could not afford to allow this control to pass out of their hands.

But when we have acknowledged this fact, it does not exhaust what can be said about the function of storage and release of positive or negative supportive sentiments in non-democratic systems. What is not at all obvious is that even in these systems there must be some means for regulating the collection and discharge of responses critical of outputs and circumstantial outcomes. Otherwise the authorities would be driven to exhaust the resources of the system in efforts at coercive suppression of all discontent, if it should rear its head very high.

In dictatorial systems, for example, the norms and power relationships that exclude most members from effective participation in the political processes come into conflict with the inescapable requirement in modern systems to provide some means for aborting or regulating the accumulation of negative sentiments. It has been thought that totalitiarian regimes in particular have sought to handle this critical problem by atomizing the relationships among the members of the system, isolating the individuals so that they have no chance to group together for the collection and concentration of their hostilities, and suppressing their expression.

But even casual scrutiny of totalitarian systems demonstrates that in fact other methods for coping with negative support are typically used. Group life may at times take on even greater importance than under other systems, so much so indeed that members of the dictatorial system are either encouraged or compelled to join a variety of different and overlapping groups. If we consider the USSR as an illustration, members are expected to belong to a whole series of groups as they mature and take their place in the economic, political, and social life of the system. Children and youth groups, party, sports and social groups, vocational and directly governmental organizations provide a meeting ground in many different and overlapping settings for the members of the system. Far from isolating the individual so that he confronts the authorities or latent power structure as a lone atom, the individual is deliberately pressed into complex sets of relationships with others in society.

As in democratic systems, the authorities in dictatorial systems, under conditions of mass society at least, need information about feedback response. The sustenance of a group structure provides the necessary basis for it. As in democratic systems, such groups act as points for collecting and regulating the discharge of support or oppositional sentiments. They enable the authorities in dictatorial systems to inform themselves in a manageable way of the state of mind of the membership about support for all political objects.

To be sure, this knowledge will more likely be put to use in dictatorial systems to meet the objectives of the authorities rather than those of the membership. Any release of stored sentiments is subject to careful control as to timing, mode of expression, and object of criticism. But the discontent does express itself even if only as protestations in the name of the public good.

But here the matter is not this simple. Through the fact that storage takes place at all, subtle pressures may be exerted on the authorities by the knowledge that great pools of antagonism have been built up at one of these collecting points. In some modest way, therefore, the storing and timed release of supportive sentiments may, even in dictatorial systems, help to set the authorities on a path of action that serves to meet some of the deepest wants and demands of the membership. In this way, the time lag in the feedback of responses, through its smoothing and expressive functions, may help to bring about an increase in specific support. Here, of course, as in all systems, the extent to which this occurs will depend on the desire of the authorities to meet these demands and their skill in taking the appropriate actions to execute this desire.

What distinguishes non-democratic regimes from other types is not only that they provide mechanisms for delaying and regulating the flow of supportive sentiments. We have seen that such time lags are vital for the generation of specific support in democratic systems as well. The mark of democratic regimes in this respect is that their norms permit greater freedom of entry into the political market place for new organizations that seek to collect and transmit supportive sentiments. They also encourage a greater diffusion and competition among the collecting points and a greater decentralization of control over and timing of the discharge of discontent. Hence the number of storage facilities for gathering and synthesizing supportive sentiments is limited only by what is practical and possible.

Furthermore, the norms of democratic regimes encourage easy discharge of sentiments. On the one hand, the members themselves are encouraged to communicate freely and frequently with the authorities. On the other, the authorities operate within assiduously cultivated norms that all of them—representatives, administrators, even judges—ought to keep their ear to the ground for expression of popular sentiments. The channels of communication are to be kept open between members and the authorities as well as among the members themselves, so that they may join forces in seeking to obtain attention for their feedback response. The threshold for the discharge of these sentiments is low. Hence the gatekeepers of support tend to escape the control of the authorities.

But over and beyond these differences, democratic and non-democratic regimes participate equally in the benefits provided by delay and storage of supportive sentiments. In both systems, they make possible the encouragement of specific support.

In brief, when we examine the response phase of the systemic feedback loop, we find that it is not enough to know that the members do respond in one way or another to outputs and outcomes. Their estimates of the actions of the authorities and their general attitudes toward the political objects need to be communicated to the authorities if the latter are to be able to take any relevant action through outputs to increase the level of specific support. Distortion in the transmission of sentiments may interfere with the fidelity of the information received by the authorities. Delays due to a variety of causes may hamper the efforts of the authorities to deal with situations in time. But we have also seen that delays need not always place impediments in the way of the authorities; at times they may be a necessary condition to enable the authorities to absorb the implications of mounting opposition to the political objects and to take what they consider to be the appropriate action to allay it, if they so desire.

27

Output Reaction—I

THE IMPORTANCE OF INFORMATION FEEDBACK LIES IN ITS CONTRIBU-tion to keeping the authorities informed as to whether the objectives they seek are being attained, or at least about the extent to which they are falling short of their mark. It consists of two strands. One provides information about the general effects of outputs, such as the degree to which they have reduced unemployment, increased productivity, strengthened the country, where these are the relevant objectives; the other, about the state of mind of the members as it relates to these consequences, indicating how the members are reacting to them. As I have suggested, it is the long-run spill-over effects of outputs that influence fluctuations in support for the political objects.

Under conditions of relative stability in a system, as in the United States, the feedback of information about support for the political objects tends to be taken for granted and is implicitly favorable; little attention may be paid to it. But where a system is undergoing rapid change, as in transitional areas, or where fundamental instability is a major problem, authorities will be very much preoccupied with seeking to use feedback response to gauge the state of attitudes toward one or another of the political objects. Under such circumstances, the information carried along the response channels is likely to include explicit statements from the members about their attitudes in these areas. Less is left to implication and inference than in the case of stable systems.

If information feedback is to be minimally effective, however, it must not only enable the authorities to estimate their distance from their objectives but it must also suggest the kind of corrective actions that may be necessary to maintain a minimal level of support. The impact of the total feedback loop will therefore be more than just a function of the adequacy of returning information, its accuracy, or discontinuity in time. It will depend as well upon the likelihood that the authorities are able and willing to react to the information and upon the very ways in which they do decide to react. It is to this reaction of the authorities to information feedback about responses that we must now turn if we are to appreciate fully the factors that contribute to the growth or decline of support for the political objects. This will bring us to a discussion of phase IV of the feedback loop depicted on Diagram 7, page 381.

The Authorities as the Output Units

Outputs as a Stream of Events

Now that we have examined the first three major phases of the systemic feedback loop, we are able to look upon the authorities in a somewhat different light. We can obtain a more accurate picture of the part they play in the stimulation of specific support. To this point, in interpreting their function as the units in the system through which outputs are produced, I have left the impression that they are activated to do so through the input of demands. Such demands arose either from among the authorities themselves or from input units represented by other members in the system. The demands or situations leading to the production of outputs have seemed to be isolated from what the authorities had previously done, were capable of doing, or were willing to do. We have not yet inquired into the fundamental interrelationship of the authorities with the rest of the system.

With respect to the input units, for example, whether we are considering them in relationship to the input of demands or of support, we have already seen that it is quite artificial to attempt to divorce them from what happens elsewhere in the system. Politically relevant units do not put in demands or support unrelated to what has already been taking place. The inputs are part of an ongoing process; they are responses to the feedback stimuli and thereby are partly shaped by the way in which the feedback processes operate. By viewing inputs in this light, we were able to link the activities of the input units—the producers of inputs—to other parts of the system. They constitute one phase of a continuous flow of information and behavior, a seamless web of activities, that I have identified as the feedback loop.

In the same way, we have now reached the point in our analysis where we can place the output units in their natural setting as part of the complex interactions of a system. To do so, we shall have to examine the part that the producers of outputs play in this same set of dynamic feedback processes. We shall find that outputs just do not appear, as it were, in reaction to demands independently introduced by the input units. The outputs can now be seen as the *reaction,* by those who have the power to produce outputs, to the response segment of the feedback loop. They are an integral part of the continuing and unending flow of information and behavior with regard to support as well as demands.

Now that we are in a position to locate the output units more accurately, we shall be able to link the authorities more closely to the forces at work in the persistence and change of political systems. We have already seen the contribution that outputs and outcomes have upon the inflow of support and demands. We shall now look at the part played by the producers of these outputs in the whole feedback loop and at the way their actions may influence the generation of specific support.

Assumptions about the Producers of Outputs

As output units, the authorities form a critical part of the feedback loop. The nature of their continuing reactions will help to determine the flow of outputs available to mobilize specific support.

What properties of the authorities and what kind of circumstances will condition the way in which they take advantage of the information, coming to them from the feedback response, for purposes of producing further outputs? For this part of the analysis, it will be helpful to exclude any variability in the reaction of the authorities due to time lags or distortions in the communication of feedback response, although we shall shortly need to examine time lag at a different point, one where it will concern the tardiness of reactions from the authorities to feedback response. I shall assume, unless otherwise clearly indicated, that there is total and complete communication of information about the perceived consequences of prior outputs, including the feelings of the input units toward the authorities. However artificial and improbable this condition is, it will enable us to isolate and amplify for analytic purposes the separable consequences flowing from the behavior of the authorities. We can then relate these consequences to the likelihood that they, the authorities, will be able to promote the input of specific support.

Furthermore, we do not need to make any monolithic or inflexible assumptions about the motivations of the authorities in the production of outputs. They may act to satisfy a need or desire for power, to fulfill a detached principle of right and wrong, to express a socialized sense of responsibility to the community at large, or to gain a calculated advantage over their adversaries. We are concerned with the consequences for support, not the intentions behind outputs, although undoubtedly the two have an important relationship.

Thus, it is not necessary to conceive of the authorities as rationally viewing outputs in the way we have been interpreting their possible consequences. Subjectively for the authorities, the production of outputs may represent a matter of seeking to deal with unavoidable pressures in the system for action or with their own interpretations of how a major problem ought to be handled. Whether to agree to a treaty for nuclear disarmament free of requirements for on-site inspection or to conserve the natural resources of the country need not be conceived by the leadership in the system as outputs calculated to win the support of any or all segments of the membership. Here, as in other areas of our analysis, the subjective or rational intentions of the actors do not necessarily dictate the consequences of their behavior for the system. From a systemic point of view, all we need to consider is whether the outputs have positive or negative supportive results. However, where the intentions of the authorities appear to be an especially relevant or decisive determinant, there would be little point in not taking them into account.

Within the limits of these assumptions, the consequences for support of the way in which the authorities deal with or react to feedback response will be a function of a number of factors. It will depend upon the willingness, readiness, competence, resources and capabilities of the authorities for acting upon returning information and taking follow-up measures to attain their aims. Put in formal terms, these factors may be described as the degree of responsiveness of the authorities themselves, the time lags in reacting to the feedback response, the competence of the authorities, and the resources, internal and external, available to them. This and the succeeding chapter will be devoted to an exploration of these elements in the fourth and last phase of the systemic feedback loop.

Responsiveness to Feedback

Meaning of Responsiveness

The reaction by the authorities to the information coming to them about feedback response will depend initially upon the degree to which they are responsive to the wants and expressed demands of the input units. *Responsiveness,* to give additional meaning to a concept used by K. W. Deutsch, S. A. Burrell et al.,[1] will be interpreted to mean first, that the authorities are willing to take the information into account and give it consideration in their outputs and second, that they do so positively in the sense that they seek to use it to help avert discontent or to satisfy grievances over the initial outputs or some unfulfilled demand.[2]

Responsiveness of authorities will vary from extreme sensitivity to stony impermeability to the wants and demands of the politically relevant members of the system.[3] In the one case, the authorities could be expected to react very elastically so that a small expression of dissatisfaction from the input units might trigger massive action to adjust conditions in their favor. In the other, massive complaints and grievances might lead to minuscule modifications in previous outputs without any real desire or intention to accommodate the dissatisfied members.[4]

[1] Op. cit.

[2] Not that the substantive content of the demand always needs to be met. As we have already seen, even though some outputs may not succeed in meeting demands, knowledge that efforts have been made on behalf of producers of inputs and that they are not being neglected or ignored will, in itself, help to reduce frustrations and discontent and thereby either prevent the withdrawal of support or positively stimulate it. In this sense, even unsuccessful efforts to match outputs to wants and demands may be interpreted as a form of responsiveness. For the authorities to have tried and failed is better than not to have tried at all, as long as the members so perceive the situation.

[3] In his examination of interest groups in India, my former colleague, Myron Weiner, adopts *responsiveness* as a central concept, blending it fruitfully with his use of demands as a major variable. See *The Politics of Scarcity*, p. 200. This volume offers an excellent case study of the additional understanding obtained through putting these kinds of concepts to work in the analysis of developing systems.

[4] We have already seen that outputs are not the only sources of support. Under some conditions, the need for outputs to bolster support may be reduced to the vanishing point. Compare the observations of L. W. Pye, *Politics, Personality and Nation Building* (New Haven: Yale University Press, 1962), p. 19: "*The character of political loyalty gives political leaders a high degree of freedom in determining policies.* The communal framework of politics and the tendency for political parties to have world views inspire a political loyalty which is governed more by a sense of identification with a concrete group than by identification with its professed policy goals. The expectation is that the leaders will seek to maximize all the interests of all the members of the group and not just seek to advance particular policies.

"As long as the leaders appear to be working in the interests of the group as a whole, they usually do not have to be concerned that loyalties of the members will be tested by current decisions. Under such conditions it is possible for leadership to become firmly institutionalized within the group without having to make any strong commitments to a specific set of principles or to a given political strategy.

"Problems relating to the loyalty of the membership can generally be handled more effectively by decisions about intragroup relations than by decisions about the

What conditions will determine the point at which any specific set of authorities might fall along such a scale of responsiveness? What qualities of the authorities will make it likely that they will or will not respond to the demands of the members and orient themselves to the supportive frame of mind of these members as relayed through the feedback processes?

Sanctions or Power as Means for Compelling Responsiveness

The way in which the authorities will react to feedback response will in part hinge on the kinds of sanctions that the politically relevant members might be able to exercise in pressing their points of view upon the authorities. These sanctions will be heavily dependent upon the nature of the regime. Control of votes, wealth, prestige, or other values of the society, or the ability to threaten physical coercion will serve as sources of influence for impelling the authorities in the direction sought by those who hold such power. A considerable part of political research in the past has gone into the exploration of the sources of political power over the formulation and execution of policies. Responsiveness will be a function of the extent to which the persons in positions of authority feel they have no alternative, if they wish to maintain their position, but to meet the wants and demands, explicit or implicit, in the feedback response.

That the power relationships in the system are in the long run central for determining the responsiveness of authorities and the nature of their outputs cannot be gainsaid. This is just another way of stating that unless the authorities are receptive to the wants and demands of the politically relevant members, they will not for long have enough support behind them to be able to continue to allocate the values in the society.

But this proposition about the relationship of responsiveness of authorities as a function of the locus of power in a system is not quite so definitive as it may appear. In the first place, the distribution of power in a society is not always clear-cut and unambiguous. In the competition for power there is great room left for doubt among the contenders goals or external policies of the group. As long as harmonious relations exist within the group, it is generally possible for the leaders to make drastic changes in strategy. Indeed, it is not uncommon for the membership to feel that matters relating to external policy should be left solely to the leadership, and it may not disturb them that such decisions reflect mainly the idiosyncracies of their leaders." (Italics in original.)

themselves, and certainly for the authorities, as to who is more or less influential in any controversy. In the resulting ambiguities, it is at times possible for the authorities to obtain considerable independent control over the political allocative processes. No combination of groups may be naturally strong enough to dislodge them or they may be able to pit one group against another and artfully prevent any combination from emerging as dominant. The Bonapartist dictatorship is the classic illustration of a "divide-and-rule" domestic strategy.

Hence, the authorities have ample opportunity to escape the sanctions of powerful groups in the system, at least temporarily, by design or accident. If so, they will constantly be confronted by the question as to whether their outputs have been sufficient to hold the support of the politically relevant members, or of an adequate combination of them, not for themselves alone but for the regime and community with which they are identified.

In the second place, even members with considerable power in the system are not always certain of the influence that they hold or of the ultimate persuasiveness of their sanctions. Persons who hold power typically are reluctant to test their strength any more frequently than is absolutely essential; every failure in its use chips away at its future effectiveness. In the many cases of doubt as to the extent of influence held by a set of members, there is room for the authorities themselves to decide whether they should yield to the demands of the members or pursue an independent set of objectives. Under some conditions, the authorities may even refuse to budge from their unwillingness to meet the demands of those whom, *ex post facto,* we can see had become the politically powerful members of the system. Especially in a situation where the bases of power have been shifting, a deep fissure may separate the authorities from the powerful groupings in the system. This was apparently the case between the authorities of the Fourth Republic in France and important sections of the military staffs. Authorities are not always aware of shifts in the power potential of members in the system. Nor is it always clear which groups are the most influential at a given historical moment.

In the third place, authorities are not infinitely flexible and adaptive; they may not be willing to move with the tides of power and ideologically, they may be incapable of doing so. Authorities act within traditions and frames of reference out of which they often find it difficult to extricate themselves. Although the English squirearchy could adjust to the outlook of a commercial and industrializing society, the French aristocracy found itself unable to cope with the demands of the rising middle classes in the late eighteenth century. At least for limited periods of time, it may be possible for authorities to resist the pressures of feedback response even from those with considerable and growing power in the system. In the long run, they may thereby be inviting social or palace revolutions; but in the short run, they may be able to stave off catastrophe by a calculated policy of granting minimal and timely concessions to feedback response from the politically powerful members of the system.

In short, from the general proposition that the authorities tend to be responsive to the politically relevant members in the system, we cannot safely infer the extent to which the authorities will in fact meet the wants and demands of these members. Many special historical and social circumstances intervene that offer the authorities the opportunity to escape, at least temporarily and often for what may turn out to be very long periods, from their ties to the dominant members of the system. The fact that the input units may represent powerful groups in the system is no guarantee that under all circumstances the authorities will be responsive to their feedback. It does, however, enormously increase the likelihood.

The Social and Political Distance of the Authorities

In the relationships between the authorities and different combinations of the membership, the power of the members to impose sanctions and compel conformity to their feedback response is only one general way in which the authorities may be induced to act responsively. The sympathies of the authorities, their capacity to understand and appreciate sensitively the problems and demands of others, their intuitive ability to foresee emerging wants of members, and their general attunement to the perspectives and ambitions of various parts of the politically relevant members in a system will help to establish the kind of attention they pay to feedback response from such members. It will lead them to listen and react selectively to the information coming from the members and thereby it will influence the concern and attention paid to feedback response.[5] The biased sensitivities of the authorities will enlarge or narrow the degree to which, through their reactions, they will be able to foster or discourage specific support.

In some measure, lack of responsiveness need not be due to any

[5] For the selective responsiveness of authorities, see R. Bauer, I. Pool and L. A. Dexter, *op. cit.*, p. 415 under the significant heading "A Congressman Determines What He Will Hear."

calculating design or desire to thwart those putting in demands. It may simply be a product of the inability on the part of the authorities to comprehend what those voicing demands really want. Channels of communication may not exist. This has been found to be the case in India, where, due to lack of organized and alert interest groups, the authorities are unable to react effectively to the demands of various segments of the membership.[6]

But aside from structural considerations such as these that impede the communication processes, a major influence shaping the nature of the selective listening and reaction to feedback response will be found in the social and political distance separating the authorities from the input units. Channels of communication exist but the messages are not fully and subtly understood.

In part, class, status, or caste differences between authorities and sections of the membership may give birth to divergent psychological sets characterized by different ideological, ethical, and perceptual predispositions. Authorities may be relatively incapable of becoming aware of and responsive to cues fed back from members other than those who resemble their own class, status, or caste categories or with whom they identify.

Although no political event can be attributed to a single cause, the attrition of support for the feudal monarchy in the latter days of the *ancien régime* in France can be traced in part to the vast gulf that had developed between it and the growing commercial and small industrial classes. Similar lack of sensitivities to the wants and needs of newly mobilizable middle and lower class segments of the membership in many Latin American systems today threatens to undermine support for the wealth-oriented military dictatorships and their associated regimes.

The impact of socio-psychological distance on selective and empathic listening and attention looms large historically in connection with ethnic, racial, and nationality groups. Typically the leaders of these groups have complained about the lack of responsiveness of the

[6] "One consequence of making policy in such a rarefied atmosphere (where farmer organizations are non-existent) is that it is exceedingly difficult to implement. Scholars and journalists have referred often to both the Indian penchant for elaborate planning and their lack of skill in implementation. Deficiencies either in Indian administration or in the Indian character are among the most popular explanations. But one must remember that the very ease with which Indians—and foreign experts—find it possible to experiment with new programs is a function of the relative distance separating those decision-makers from the citizenry and from popular political pressures." M. Weiner, *op. cit.*, p. 149.

authorities who do not share their values, perspectives, and background. They have felt the lack of an attentive and sympathetic audience for their grievances.

Before they attained their independence, the Irish had felt that they could never get a fair hearing or insightful consideration of their complaints from the English parliament and administrative apparatus. Whatever formal rights of political participation the French-Canadians may have and whatever their influence in the federal parliament, they nevertheless continue to feel a deep sense of political inefficacy; they cannot trust the Anglo-Saxon authorities to display an intuitive appreciation of their wants and demands. They watch suspiciously every move of the authorities to protect themselves from any disadvantage that need not be intended by the authorities but that flows from a lack of genuine appreciation of French-Canadian values and perspectives. Similarly, in the United States, the Negro has suffered not only from the reluctance to give him equal legal and social recognition, but from the absence of informal consideration of his wants and demands with an equal degree of subtlety, sympathy, and understanding normally expected by and given to the white membership.

In terms of the political structure, such selective responsiveness frequently manifests itself through constraints on the circulation of the leadership into positions of authority. Where the authorities listen with empathy to feedback response from varied social classes, ethnic or racial groups, it will probably reflect this through the fact that among the authorities, in position of influence, will be found members drawn from these demographic groupings.

But the converse is not equally true. Not all representation of excluded groups among the authorities need be accepted as unquestionable evidence that responsiveness has been built into the structure. Frequently, if vertical mobility may be permitted some members of a neglected social segment, it is likely to be available only to those leaders who are ready to share the points of view and objectives of the relatively inaccessible host political stratum. The "Uncle Tom" Negro in the United States symbolizes, in an epithet adopted by the Negroes themselves, the continuing lack of sensitive listening to the wants and demands of the Negroes as a group, even where some of their numbers succeed in ascending to positions of authority.

To some extent, this kind of selective listening and responsiveness, a kind of silent communication, goes on in all political systems. It is just aggravated where fundamental social or other significant differences in the society separate the authorities from part of a membership who have expectations of being able to express their demands and have them listened to. But beyond this, even if such visible demographic differences did not exist, silent communication would nevertheless interfere with the way in which the authorities handle feedback response.

Through their internalized value systems, all authorities "represent" the outlooks of differing segments of a political system and this is true in democratic regimes as well. Some among the authorities may attune themselves to the feedback response of agriculture, others to business or labor, and still others to the consumer. Conservative authorities may entertain an image of themselves as speaking for the conservative elements in the system and may feel particularly responsible for perceiving and acting on their needs and demands. Each set of authorities may be, if not deaf to the pleas and blind to the conditions of others, at least less concerned about their needs.

This intangible quality of empathy and rapport is a largely neglected factor in research about political relationships, primarily because of the difficulty of sorting it out as a separate dimension for purposes of empirical research. Yet it is vital for understanding the way in which authorities handle feedback response and, therefore, for their capacity to arouse specific support. It is often indeed, the source of antagonism toward a system, as in the case of the sentiments of oppression that it breeds even where members may have formal access to positions of authority.

The situation of the American Negro is again a case in point. Cultural and color differences frequently mean that the white authorities are less attuned to the subtle cues regarding the wants and demands of Negroes as a group. It leads to a high degree of non-linearity in the relationships between the white occupants of authority roles and the Negroes in all parts of the system. A vigorous display of discontent has appeared necessary in order to obtain a small favorable reaction from the authorities. More than any other single factor, this relative inelasticity in the reaction of authorities to feedback response from the Negroes helps to account for the dramatic, angry, and at times violent political style of the Negro in the presentation of his grievances about the political and social situations in which he finds himself.

Hence, even under conditions of instantaneous, complete, and accurate information feedback, the capacity to generate specific support would depend upon the readiness and ability of the authorities to orient themselves sensitively to the general values and perspectives of the input units from which this information comes and to empathize with the members.

Negative Reactions

We must bear in mind that in this sense, unresponsiveness to information feedback is no proof that the authorities are failing to acquire and take the information into consideration in their own planning for future outputs. They may well rely extensively on such information as a source of intelligence about the sentiments of the input units so that they, the authorities, may be in a better position to circumvent the demands of the members. Unresponsive authorities may be very efficient at accumulating feedback response and utilizing it; but if they are unresponsive as defined here, they will not seek to stimulate support by reacting so as to satisfy the feedback demands. Rather, they may devise ways to ignore them without unnecessarily endangering the input of support.

In this way feedback may provide even relatively impermeable authorities with information essential for the more effective attainment of their own objectives as against those of other members in the system. Where this occurs, of course, feedback response may be used for purposes that in the long run undermine the confidence of relevant members in their authorities, and ultimately, through spill-over effect, in the regime and community as well. But this situation may also enable the authorities, through astute manipulation of the feedback knowledge, to postpone such a day, if not indefinitely, at least for politically rewarding periods of time.

However, we do not have to pursue this line of discussion further. Where the authorities do not seek to use outputs to bolster support, we can ignore their negative reactions to feedback response. Outputs will not serve to alleviate stress caused by the decline of support but to aggravate it. Our primary task in this section of the analysis is to understand the way in which outputs are a coping mechanism for reducing the dangers from insufficient support for the political objects. But to the extent that the authorities do use outputs to generate specific support, we must continue to probe into the characteristics and qualities of the authorities. Thereby we may be able to shed further light on the conditions that will impede or promote their efforts.

Output Lag

Responsiveness involves time as an essential ingredient. Not only must the authorities show a concern for the feedback response of at least the politically relevant members, if they are to activate specific support. This concern must also be expressed tangibly within a time limit when it can do some good. In the production of outputs, it is often a matter, not of too little too late, but of quite enough not soon enough.

I shall continue the basic assumption adopted earlier, however unreal it may be: that there is perfect information about feedback response. I shall now introduce an additional and more plausible assumption: that the authorities desire to meet the wants and demands of the input units either because these units are powerful enough to compel such attention or because, whatever the reasons, the authorities choose to react positively to the demands. Clearly, we need not think of these assumptions as artificial conditions consistent only with a democracy. Theoretically, there is no reason why they could not occur in autocracies or any kind of dictatorial system in which, because of declining support, the authorities feel the need to shore up their position by offering specific benefits to the politically relevant input units.

In any event, regardless of the structural types to which these assumptions might apply, delays by the authorities in producing outputs to meet feedback response represent a further condition that would interfere with the development of specific support. Here, as at all other points in the feedback chain, time lag frequently proves to be crucial.

Time lags may occur for two fundamentally different reasons. On the one hand, they may be a product of resistance by the authorities to the demands contained in the feedback response or the necessary outputs implicit in it. On the other, they may occur as an inescapable element of a situation in which there is simply insufficient time to deal with the number and range of problems demanding the attention of the authorities. We shall examine these two situations in turn.

Output Procrastination

Although the authorities may be willing to meet feedback response at some future time, they may deliberately refrain from dealing with feedback response at the time it occurs. They may keep on postponing it or perhaps make half-hearted efforts to cope with it in the hope that the need to make the concessions called for will disappear. But such postponement may push the withdrawal of support beyond a point of no return. Output procrastination continued over a sufficiently long period of time may be the equivalent of output failure. It can rouse such antagonisms that resolution of differences within the context of the given regime or even community may become virtually impossible. Responsiveness has a time dimension that adds an independent effect to efforts to meet feedback response.

For example, in many recent African and other colonial areas, the postponement of efforts to meet indigenous demands and transparent growing wants in due time, created political crises basically irremediable within the context of the imperial regimes and communities involved. Support had fallen too low and could not be revived after World War II even if all the earlier demands for greater self-government and a greater share of the local wealth being produced through foreign capital were to be met. If efforts in this direction had been made far earlier, however, as a way of coping with feedback response to colonial rule, the strength and irresistibility of the post-World War II drive toward complete political independence might have been considerably weakened, if not made superfluous in many instances.

But by the fifties the time lag at this late date had become too great. Too long a time had elapsed between the pressures for reform and the actions which the imperial powers became willing to take after World War II. Offers of greatly increased self-government, easier access to income and wealth created in the dependent areas, and important symbols of responsibility and dignity came too late. Yet these measures probably represent more in the way of output concessions than would have been required if more serious efforts had been made, before World War II, to keep the support of the colonial areas for some form of imperial regime and community.

The Lack of Time to Process Outputs

In addition to time lag in fulfilling or otherwise coping with demands, that is deliberately created through the unwillingness of the authorities to meet the feedback response, there is another kind of delay which is forced upon the authorities. This delay occurs as a result of the lack of time to attend to all matters at once.

Not all societies require the same speed of reaction to feedback response. Societies vary significantly in their sense of time. In traditional systems, the pulse of social life is slow and the sense of urgency behind demands may on the average be low. Especially in those traditional systems where popular involvement is low, members simply expect that in due course, as custom dictates, the authorities will act. In modern systems, where the rate of social and political change over given intervals of time, as well as the rate of social interaction within any one interval of time are greater, time emerges as a central consideration. Time delays are, therefore, less likely to be tolerated readily.

But regardless of variations induced by the role that time plays generally in a society, in all political systems where the authorities have a number of matters to deal with at one time, some kind of priorities must be assigned. The lack of adequate resources will, of course, move in the same direction but we shall come to that. Here the only resource under consideration is that of time itself.

Because of the simple fact that there is a limit to the number of matters that can be dealt with simultaneously, priorities in the production of outputs must occur. Some criteria for regulating the order must be utilized, if only implicitly. These will effectively determine the priorities, in turn, that the authorities will give to the various parts of the feedback response as they process these parts into outputs, if we assume, as we do, that the authorities do in fact seek to satisfy such feedback response.

The criteria that establish the place in the queue for the demands arising out of the feedback response will vary for different authorities and for the same ones at different times. The internalized norms and values of the authorities may themselves dictate the order in which feedback responses will be met. The pressures, varying in the intensity and and scope of support accompanying the feedback, may compel the authorities into a given pattern of selection. Those who clamor the loudest, who are perceived to represent the most influential members of the system, or who are able to gain the ear of the authorities in one way or another, may command the earliest outputs. The dramatic urgency of some circumstances, such as a natural catastrophe or crisis in international security that rouses the conscience of the whole system, may force a matter upon the authorities for consideration and action.

But whatever the criteria dictating the order of selection in a time period, the unavoidable need to allocate time, energy and attention results in output lags. This is the output side of what previously we had considered under the category of demand input overload. As a result of an excessive volume, each matter demanding attention must take its place in line.

Such unavoidable delays will have two different kinds of consequences. On the one hand, there may not be enough time to consider some matters at all, at least during the period of time when action might have done some good. Once the situation to which the outputs are applicable have occurred, the outputs will have lost their value in fostering support. Measures to abort or avoid an economic depression would be of little use if they were postponed and in the interval the expected depression occurred.

On the other hand, some demands may ultimately be met in time. Yet, due to the basis of priority, these demands may not be met as soon as its sponsors would have wished. As queuing up to wait for outputs takes place, members may object to the positions their demands hold in the line. The agenda for legislation sketched in the message of the President of the United States on the State of the Union, or the Speech from the Throne in the British sphere, represent statements of proposed priorities in dealing with outputs. Such a queuing process itself becomes the source of additional grievances as indicated by the fierce struggles over the location of an issue on the timetable of a representative legislature and by similar contention over a proposed agenda for discussion that we can assume takes place in the inner circles of dictatorial systems.

The huge backlog of unprocessed bills found toward the end of the session in many modern legislatures testifies to the reality of the output lag. The frustration of the interests represented in these bills that fail to get the early attention of the authorities indicates the consequences that this lag has for support. To find one's demands satisfied later than desired or expected will serve to diminish the specific support evoked, at least as compared to what might have been obtained at an earlier time. Overdue outputs may sour the satisfactions obtained.

Positive, Damping Effects of Time Lag

Not all delays in outputs need lead in the direction of reducing the expected benefits for the system in the form of specific support. On occasion, as we saw before with regard to feedback response itself, time lags may serve a damping function. They may enable the authorities to take stock of the feedback responses, to give them more mature consideration and reflection and, thereby, to act more rationally than would otherwise have been possible. Delay also provides the politically significant members an opportunity to intervene in the decision process. It helps to bring outputs into conformity with their demands and to reduce the hostility that the outputs might otherwise arouse in them. Where damping has such consequences, it serves to keep up the level of specific support.

This kind of function has frequently been ascribed to second chambers in representative systems. In most cases, undoubtedly, as has been demonstrated frequently enough, these structures may delay in the interests of powerful minorities rather than on behalf of a broader public. To that extent, however, they do succeed in sustaining specific support for the regime among these powerful minorities. No better proof could exist of the consequences of this kind of damping for the input of support. From the point of view of the democratic ethic or of any specific goals, such results may not be desired. But this is a matter of evaluating the consequences, not describing and understanding them. Whether we so desire it or not, every system will tend to have some kind of mechanisms for preventing precipitous action and to permit at least the dominant forces in the system the opportunity to bring their point of view to bear.

Norms of the regime stand as another general type of mechanism that serves this damping purpose. Norms emerge in all systems to regulate the processes through which outputs are produced. Typically, they provide for delaying periods so that due consideration may be given to the wisdom of the proposed course of action and so that the interested and politically relevant members may be consulted or may be allowed to present their views. Custom and law, for example, may require royal commissions to investigate whole new areas for government action, as in Great Britain. Standing committees may arise in legislative bodies to provide more detailed and prolonged attention to proposals for outputs. There may develop rules such as the requirement for three readings of a bill, to control the speed with which it may be considered. These represent well-known delaying devices in democratic systems.

Although less attention has been paid to similar procedures in non-democratic regimes, we can predict, on a *priori* grounds, that they must exist in some form. Even so simple a fact as that a decision must await the calling of a meeting of the ruling committee of the dominant political party or must await the traditional assembly of the lineage elders in the field of an evening, ties outputs to time. It provides at least one opportunity to regulate the flow of outputs so as to prevent hasty, ill-considered, and by definition, possibly support-endangering actions.

As we have typically found to be the case in estimating consequences, few social processes contribute wholly in a positive or negative way to the stimulation of specific support. We must always search out the net effects that result from the process acting simultaneously in both directions. This is similarly the case for time lags. Their net effect on the input of specific support will depend upon the balance struck by the simultaneous contributions of delays in two directions. On the one hand, they may bring about grievances because of the failure of the authorities to meet feedback responses in time. On the other, they may create satisfactions by providing the authorities with time to consider the wisdom of their outputs and to appraise the wants of a more inclusive proportion of the politically relevant members.

28

Output Reaction—II

THE EFFECTIVENESS WITH WHICH AUTHORITIES WILL BE ABLE TO EN-
hance support through their reaction to feedback response will
be a function of more than just their responsiveness or the time lags in
the production of outputs. The kinds of resources they have at their
disposal will impose additional constraints upon follow-up outputs.

For purposes of this analysis I shall conceive of resources in the
broadest sense. They may be classified into two basic types: external
and internal. External will refer to the material means for achieving
goals where the source of these means can be assigned to the environment of the system, as in the case of various kinds of goods, services or
money. Internal will reflect the kinds of means that the system itself
provides in the form of its own political structures, organizations or
rules of behavior.

Unless otherwise indicated, I shall retain the assumptions that the
authorities possess quick and accurate feedback about the responses to
their actions and decisions, and that they desire and seek to satisfy
the demands embodied in these responses. By doing so, we continue to
eliminate all problems concerning responsiveness and misinformation.
This will free us to explore the extent to which variability in the
reactions of the authorities is due to the nature of the resources alone.

External Resources

Absolute Limits on Resources

The social and physical environment external to the political system [1]
may impose insuperable burdens upon authorities who are seeking
to meet feedback response. The systems in the environment of the political system may fail to provide the physical means for catering to the
wants and demands of the members even where there is a serious effort
to do so.

[1] For a full description of the environment of a political system, see *A Framework
for Political Analysis*, chapter V.

This is so transparently the case that little needs to be said about it. The economy may not provide the material resources. The society may not produce the personnel or skills to measure up to the calls being made upon the political system. Thus, large, well-equipped and modernized standing armies are impossible where the social system provides only a low level of organizational skills, communications technology, medical science, or economic productivity. If the revolution in rising expectations, which corresponds to a sharp rise in the volume of Western-type social and economic demands, could readily be met through the available resources, the stability of any developing system might more easily be assured. But lacking this means of developing specific support, such systems have typically fallen back on other devices: the indirect or outright suppression of groups voicing such demands or the intensification of diffuse support.

Relative Limits on Resources

But a system is not confined to the resources with which it finds itself endowed or which are wanting at any moment. Political systems, because they are self-directing feedbacks systems, are able to operate on their environment so as to make them more tractable or hospitable to the kinds of demands the members are voicing. Carefully designed programs of economic and social development will enable the authorities to maximize the advantages of whatever resources they do have. But even here, the capacity to create the resources necessary to meet feedback response is severely restricted. The economic and social level from which a system starts may be so low that it cannot introduce any significant measure of change into its environment without aid from outside the system.

This is the well-known condition of many developing systems today. Such social systems require assistance until some indeterminate take-off point is achieved. At this time a system may be able to spur its own economic and social growth with diminishing special assistance from the outside. But the need to seek external aid itself imposes limits on the extent to which feedback response may be met. Furthermore, where political systems are a part of developed societies, lack of economic or other kinds of social resources may simply set boundaries to what can be done and frequently these cannot be easily altered.

But these limits are not known in advance in all cases and there may be large margins of doubt as to just what can be done. Hence the authorities of a system may hold out the expectation that demands can be met. But here as elsewhere, if we are to understand the impact on specific support of efforts to manipulate and transform the available resources in the environment, we must once again raise the question of time. Can the authorities introduce the necessary modifications in time to meet demands that are being made? Reaction to feedback response is seldom exclusively a matter of adequacy of external resources; it usually involves the ability to handle the feedback within a time interval.

In face of the growth of Western type demands, few developing systems can be made over into highly industrialized societies in a decade or two. As the United States is currently discovering, even the rate of economic development in modernized societies cannot be quickly modified. This suggests that important aspects of the parameters of a political system may prove relatively intractable within the time limits available for meeting feedback response and thereby for stimulating specific support.

Allocation of Resources over the Long-Run

But resources are not usually just present or absent. More frequently there are limited quantities available to the system. The task is to allocate their use over time so that the limited resources may be exploited to best advantage from the point of view of their impact on specific support. Even though I have adopted the assumption that the authorities are willing to meet feedback response as a way of building such support, this does not imply that the authorities can best achieve this goal under all circumstances by converting feedback demands forthwith into outputs. At times, the very strategy of avoiding additional stress from loss of support due to dissatisfactions with perceived outputs may require that the members be denied fulfillment of their feedback response either temporarily or permanently. The fact that members complain that their shoes pinch is no evidence that a new pair of the kind the system can afford will do any better.

If the authorities sought to meet all the grievances over past outputs, greater discomforts might well be in store for the members. The authorities would thereby be creating future conditions militating against the growth of specific support.

This is just one way of formulating the short-run instead of the long-run problem that must constantly plague all political authorities. Response to demands for increases in expenditures in any areas, as for arms or welfare, for foreign aid or new expressways, must all be balanced against probable wants, demands and grievances of members in the future. The authorities cannot discount the future entirely; to do so would at least expose them to the possibility of future incapacity to meet demands. In most practical political circumstances, it would also bring down upon their heads the ire of those in the system who are future-oriented or who are prone to invoke such an orientation in the competition for positions of influence and authority.

Internal Resources: Talent of the Authorities

Internal resources fall into two classes: the organization, skills, and general competence that characterize a set of authorities and the rules available to them, in the culture, for deciding how to react to feedback response. Incompetence in the application of decisions and inappropriate rules for the selection of the knowledge available to meet feedback response are kinds of sources of output failure, in reaction to feedback response, that are as important as excessive delays or lack of external resources.

Talent and Ability of the Authorities

We may interpret the talent of authorities as being composed of two parts: personal ability and organizational skills. Personal ability reflects the native insight and intelligence of the individuals occupying positions of authority as reinforced through education and training. The capacity of the system to handle feedback response in such a way as to strengthen the supportive attitudes of the members will hinge in significant part on the success in attracting to positions of authority persons with adequate wisdom and education. The timeliness and effectiveness of outputs are related to the level of education, experience, and good judgment to be found in the specific occupants of authority roles at any moment in history.

Most modernized societies, virtually by definition, will have taken steps to establish and maintain minimal criteria for recruitment to positions of authority. Although this applies particularly to the administrative and judicial services in various systems, indirectly it also affects the political leadership itself. Leadership tends to fall into the hands of those who have better than average education and the process of competing for positions of authority in itself trains the leadership in many of the competences required by the system. Although the problem of obtaining administrators who, in their personal talents and skills, measure up to the exigencies of the day, can never be said to be solved, over the ages routines have been devised and maintained at least to provide persons with minimally qualified administrative and judicial expertise. It has only been with the sudden emergence after the second World War of the newly developing political systems that the serious dependence of political systems on the quality of the authorities, both of administrative and leadership types, has forcibly impressed itself upon the world.

Organizational Capabilities

Over and above the native talent of the authorities lie what we may call their social and organizational resources or capabilities. To what extent do the authorities possess or display skills in constructing structures for the general tasks of governing? Intelligence, education, and native talent are by themselves insufficient. The authorities must be able to build or maintain structures that can contribute to the level of support by encouraging the adequate satisfaction of demands.

Although in this analysis I am not concerned with the varieties of structures as such, or with understanding their modes of operation, structural strains or incompatibilities may contribute independently to output failure even where all other conditions seem to be met. The presence of adequate structures and organizations in the system for the integration or coordination of outputs in the fulfillment of demands stands as a necessary resource.

This is the obverse of the questions we discussed earlier with regard to direct structural regulation of support through modification of the regime.[2] There we discussed the measures that might be taken. Here we address ourselves to the capacities of the authorities to devise such measures.

To illustrate this through a single and yet typical example, we need only to reflect on the critical problems created by the existence of multiple producers of outputs. Since this condition is primarily relevant to structural devices for overcoming it, we have been able to neglect its presence. We did so, it will be recalled, by deliberately assuming for purpose of our analysis that the producers of outputs are unified and undifferentiated, just as though there were only one voice through which the authorities spoke. As we have had occasion to do before, here I shall again temporarily abandon this assumption for a more realistic appraisal of the circumstances surrounding the producers of outputs and recognize the presence of multiple feedback loops.

The plural authorities characteristic of most political systems exist

[2] Chapter 16.

in what I previously referred to as multiple environments.[3] The environment in which the authorities operate consists of many parts and any single person, group or entity among the authorities sees through his or its lenses only a limited segment of this environment. Each unit among the authorities will be especially sensitive to the feedback signals and cues in the form of facts, demands, or expressions of support from the part to which it feels related. Each unit will be part of a separable feedback loop as indicated on Diagram 5, page 374.

In fact, in modernized societies, it is of the very nature of the division of labor at the level of authority that outputs should be particular to that area of the environment that is a matter of concern for the given output unit. We find Departments of Labor, Agriculture, or Foreign Affairs that concern themselves with the outputs particular to their subject matter. Even in representative legislatures, specialization of interest regarding outputs occurs in a high degree; some representatives undertake to familiarize themselves intimately with limited areas of policy-formation and become specialists in military matters, foreign affairs, taxation, agriculture, and the like.

The fact and responsibility for production of outputs rests, therefore, in more than one set of hands, increasing as a function of the numerical size of the authorities and reflecting a proliferation of differentiated output structures. This diversity in the producers of outputs increases significantly the probability of heterogeneity of outputs, even under conditions of a tight dictatorship. Such heterogeneity means that the outputs may conflict at least over subgoals and frequently over their primary objectives as well. If this is so, the effectiveness of outputs in meeting demands and generating support cannot remain independent of their complementarity, coordination, or incompatibility.

Where there are numerous producers of outputs, the ability to meet the feedback response from any one segment of the system will be seriously hampered if the outputs from different producers have contradictory or conflicting effects. In the United States, there has been little real success in handling what has become a nagging and virtually insoluble problem of hydraheaded government. Under highly differentiated authority structures, one branch of government may encourage mergers of firms so as to develop efficiency and economy while another branch expends great efforts in combating such efforts on the grounds that they tend to create monopolistic conditions with administered and inflated pricing practices. Scholarly panaceas, from minor juggling with the powers of the President to radical transformation of the party and Congressional structures and relationships, as well as the proposals

[3] See chapter 3, footnote 12.

of commissions on administrative reorganization, have not succeeded either in being accepted or where applied, in coordinating the outputs of the varied and numerous branches of government.

What is aggravated for various reasons under the American political structure, with its separation of powers, finds its counterpart in greater or lesser degree in all political systems. Where the various output units possess the organizational capabilities to achieve complementarity in their outputs, this will immeasurably strengthen the possibility for the authorities to pursue a successful course of action in meeting feedback response, assuming as we have that the desire to do so is present.

Internal Resources: Decision Rules

There is another aspect of organizational skill and competence in achieving objectives that refers, not to the direct execution of outputs, but to the preliminary processing of data that precedes the actual outputs. In considerable part, the rules by which these preliminary activities are conducted will shape the kind of outputs that occur. However much the authorities may hope to be able to meet the demands and wants of the members, without the requisite means for obtaining, processing, storing, and selectively recalling the necessary knowledge, they will not be able to handle the problems raised in the feedback response.[4]

The Function of Social Storage and Retrieval

To understand the basic importance of the processes for storing and recalling information, we shall have to turn once again to the intricacies of social causation and the persistent difficulties we have with understanding them, given the level of development of the behavioral sciences today.

In the context of actual political situations, political behavior is, in the present state of knowledge, highly unpredictable, except for a few selected areas. We cannot expect that advance estimates of the ade-

[4] The actual means and structures employed for these purposes in different systems will vary enormously. A consideration of the effect of different structures, organizations, and procedures would, however, be a matter for microanalysis. At our level of analysis, we shall be concerned with exploring the general processes that must be present and would have to be fulfilled through some kind of structural facilities. As usual, we are interested in the processes taking place, not in types of structure except as illustrative means.

quacy of an output for providing the expected satisfactions for feedback response will prove particularly reliable.

Aside from any other consideration, factors largely outside the control of a given set of authorities may unexpectedly interfere with the anticipated outcomes. Some unaccountable fluctuations in the international market, a war scare, or a sudden change in consumer spending or saving habits may quickly upset any prior calculations. Depending upon the technological level of development in a system, experts may be available to help map the probable course of events flowing from each set of outputs. Yet here, in spite of the rapid strides made by the social sciences in modern society, their capacity to understand and handle the numerous complex variables involved in the attainment of specific goals in a live setting is more noteworthy for its failures than its successes, however spectacular a few in the latter category may be. Forecasting is still a risky business for the specialist in the social sciences, outside of a few limited areas; predicting, an almost impossible one. For the occupants of authority roles, informed and judicious guessing is still the rule.

The need to make decisions and take action cannot wait upon the development of expertise. If all the authorities had to choose between were reliable knowledge from the social sciences on the one hand and their own random guesses on the other, they would indeed find themselves in an awkward if not impossible situation. But as has been observed,[5] authorities and members seek to cope with their low predictive powers in social life as a whole not through reliance on random choices but through the adoption of working rules of thumb. These are the products of experience, tempered and adjusted in many cases by the advice and wisdom of experts.

Through the use of such precepts, authorities may hope to estimate and interpret the probable cause of events and the probable outcome of policies and decisions. The authorities are able to make their way through the morass of variables even if their way is poorly illuminated by their imperfect understanding of social life. In the face of great uncertainty about how and why members of political systems behave and institutions function as they do, these precepts act as guides or decision rules to help the authorities appraise their problems and take action to meet them.

If each generation of authorities had to start from scratch in building up a body of precepts upon which they could depend, they and the system with which they were associated might well succumb before they could accumulate enough such rules of thumb; they would have

[5] G. Vickers, *op. cit.*, pp. 59–60.

to rely exclusively on improvisation. But the fact is that except for the authorities in entirely new systems, they are able to draw upon a bank of past practices in the system. These are stored in the traditions of the system and handed down to each succeeding generation through the normal socializing processes. In effect, past experiences, as encapsulated in the traditions of the system, form a social memory bank or repository that is a critical source of guidance for helping any generation of authorities in coping with feedback response.

The Storage of Social Know-How

The way in which the authorities may be expected to cope with feedback response will in part be a function of the kind of experiences transmitted to them through their culture. Past ways of handling similar problems at the very least provide a point of departure for considering other alternatives, as may be the case in a rationally oriented society. In a traditional society, they may be decisive in establishing the current choice.

But not all systems have the same reserve of experiences upon which to draw nor are they all qualitatively of equal utility in guiding the authorities through the labyrinth of contemporary problems. Systems will vary with regard to the degree of their success in achieving their objectives in the past and will, accordingly, leave different traditions and experiences upon which future generations may call.

Although comparisons among systems along these lines may seem difficult and impressionistic, as they undoubtedly are at our present level of empirical research in this area, nevertheless we do constantly make some kinds of qualitative judgments in these matters. We speak of the different measures of success that systems have consistently had in handling their severe crises, or the greater frequency of crises which some systems seem to find themselves in as a result of the kinds of past decisions that were taken. The great "ifs" of history are our ways of asserting that alternatives were available to the authorities; if some other decision had been taken, the outcome might have been significantly and valuably different.

Systems are known to build up patterns of response to situations that influence succeeding generations. In part, the whole and somewhat premature study of national temperament or national character revolves around the effort to trace out continuity in this respect. The French, for example, have developed rules of thumb for solving social crises that seem to encourage a challenging leadership to take to the barricades more readily than is the case in other political systems, or that tempt the leader of strength to seek sole power in apparent emergencies.

But perhaps the function that precepts selected from the past play in political systems may best be pointed up if we turn to those systems in which a sizeable store of experiences has not been accumulated. This is the case in systems that have little or no past as continuing entities. We could expect them to be severely handicapped in handling their problems.

Systems of this kind are to be found today in those many new political systems that have been entering upon the international political market place at a hitherto unknown rate. They are being called upon to make complex and novel domestic and international decisions without, however, having had the time and opportunity to build up a backlog of traditions and experiences upon which to draw or even against which to react. Each complex of events calls for a decision that is utterly novel; the authorities cannot even intuitively associate it with any prior similar situations for whatever suggestive guidance that might be teased from them.

To some extent, what distinguishes old from new systems, is the opportunity that old systems have had to grow and mature. Not that thereby they necessarily become better according to any moral criteria. Rather, the significant fact is that through the course of history, the authorities have been confronted with a large variety of events and happenstances. Each performance of the authorities has given added knowledge about the nature of the systems, its constraints, and capabilities and helps to clarify for the authorities the apparent limits of action for the attainment of objectives. Through the various means for storing experiences, as in the literature, folklore, and documents of a society, the past becomes encoded in a way that makes it readily available to each succeeding generation of that culture. This becomes the system's memory bank from which the members may selectively draw as they confront present experiences. Political culture embodies this lore and tradition of experience, interpretations, and precepts that have withstood or succumbed to the trial and error of the ages.

By definition, new systems are short on experience and long on current critical problems, at least with respect to themselves as political units in their present form. If expertise were sufficiently developed in the social sciences to be able to offer reliable advice about possible outcomes of varying outputs, the lack of a body of experiences upon which to draw would not be so significant. But where not only old systems, but new systems as well must rely on informed rules of thumb, the lack of a period in which to grow and mature before being confronted with major crises, domestic and international, handicaps the newer systems in establishing and achieving objectives.

Rules for the Retrieval of Stored Experiences

But the mere presence of a social memory bank containing traditional methods for handling problems upon which to call, and even the existence of a rule that legitimates the appeal to or use of such traditions, in and of itself does not point the way in which the bank should be utilized. Such a bank and rule represent only a potential resource for the authorities. Members could not possibly recall the whole of history transmitted to each generation, even if it were desirable or necessary. Retrieval is always selective. What a person recalls will hinge on those rules governing the ways in which he scans his memory, the criteria of appropriateness used to make selections from the information retrieved, and the rules regulating the way he goes about separating, synthesizing and reorganizing the knowledge recalled for immediate use. What applies to the individual holds with equal force for any group of authorities. The rules themselves constitute part of the available resources necessary for handling feedback response.

A temperamentally conservative person in authority will interpret the meaning of the past for future actions differently from one who is innovative and experimentally inclined; a politically conservative person in authority as against a liberal one will choose a different aspect of past experience to amplify and examine and may interpret it differently, especially with regard to its import for present purposes. What this means is that the rules of recall, assessment, and application may themselves derive from and be shaped by varying strands in the political culture.

Hence the way in which the authorities seek to use experience will depend on two factors: the general reliance in the culture upon past methods as against contemporary innovations; and the particular strand of the past that the authorities, through their predispositions, are likely to recall and emphasize. But whatever strand the authorities may choose, they are never so devoid of knowledge about the past, so freed from dependence upon it, so confident of their capacities to meet each new situation in an entirely novel way, or sufficiently possessed of time, that they can ignore entirely the lessons of past experience, as they intepret them, as a resource for helping with current outputs.

The Flexibility of Retrieval Rules

The range of alternatives open to the authorities as they search for ways to meet feedback response will depend significantly on the restrictive or expansive nature of the norms governing the way in which and the extent to which past experiences are handled as a guide to present action. The decision rules may free the authorities to explore the widest range of alternatives in meeting feedback or they may confine the authorities to a narrow and unchanging spectrum as inherited from the past. There may be no escape from the old compromises that had worked in the past; or a new crisis may permit the authorities to consider new alternatives.

The varying extent to which systems show such differences in the degree of specification about the way in which problems are to be met, will have transparently vital consequences for the capacity of the authorities to adopt outputs and take actions that will be likely to generate specific support. Frequently, in the face of pressing crises, authorities or leaders who seek office will find it necessary to reinterpret goals of the system, to propose reorganization of the political structure, or even to displace an old one entirely. Not that the leaders need to conceive themselves as being inventive and innovative; indeed they may well want to give the appearance that they are simply continuing past traditions. But the capacity to maintain a minimal level of specific support may depend on seeking out new bases for this support by meeting the demands of new or emerging segments of the systems, such as a new social class.

From the point of view of the internal resources, and setting aside the matter of the native intelligence and skill of the authorities, what kind of culturally-determined decision rules limit the range of choices open to the authorities in selecting among alternatives? We might visualize plotting systems on a continuum according to the degree of restriction on choice of outputs. We might locate at the one hypothetical extreme, those systems in which the political culture narrowly specifies the way in which each problem is to be met. At the other pole we would put those systems in which no prescriptions are laid down at all; the authorities are completely unrestricted as to choice of outputs. In a moment we shall see that close approximations to this end of the continuum can be found today in the new or developing political systems. But at the more restrictive pole of the continuum, no system, not even the most highly traditional, could possibly survive for long if the culture compulsively and inflexibly spelled out in detail each choice permitted to the authorities. Such a system might persist, but not in a world of change, however slow the change might be. It would prove fragile and brittle.

Tradition as a Limiting Criterion of Choice

Within the limits of the two hypothetical extremes represented on such a continuum, however, systems do show vast differences in the degree of restriction on the choice of alternatives open to the authorities. In non-literate systems, for example, where traditionalism has deep roots, it provides for most contingencies in environments the cycles of which are relatively stable. The range of choice is narrow. If extended drought occurs, the norms may call for scanning traditions to determine which among a variety of alternative rituals are to be performed. In highly rational systems, on the other hand, the range is thrown wide open through the rule that the best means available, traditional or novel, as evaluated by technical experts where possible, ought to be used. In both cases, however, the political culture has provided guides in the form of norms of behavior to aid the authorities in selecting alternatives.

This is not to say that the norms restricting alternatives to the scanning of past experiences alone, as in traditional systems, freeze the authorities inescapably into an inherited mold. Even in traditional systems there is seldom if ever a requirement calling for the wholesale and unmodified transfer of past methods to present problems. The chief, medicine man, or gardener as the case may be, finds some room for choice by virtue of the fact that every rule has its associated circumstances under which it may be appropriately applied. Through the necessary identification and interpretation of these circumstances, alternative rules may be invoked out of the traditional repertoire, at least within culturally recognized or tolerable limits. This keeps the door ajar for some variation in outputs to accord with the changing wants and circumstances.

Nevertheless, the operating rules or routines for scanning and selecting from past experience are quite restricted, especially but not only in traditional societies. When confronted with a problem, it is as though the authorities are expected to match situations and to behave according to relatively set patterns once the matching pair has been found. If a catastrophe occurs or is so defined, no further scanning of experience for ways of handling the matter need take place; the outputs must call for the known specific ritual at least. The choice of alternatives is severely restricted.

Rationality as a Limiting Criterion of Choice

Although inflexible rules that prevent the synthesis of past information into new patterns of behavior are readily identifiable for nonliterate and other traditional systems, we may be somewhat less aware of their presence in modern and presumably rationally oriented systems. As a norm, rationality itself specifies that where a method can be found that, for the achievement of an end, is more efficient than one used in the past, it should be adopted. Yet modern systems in fact can be ranged along a continuum of traditionality characterizing their predisposition to generate and accept new ways of reacting to feedback response or attacking any kind of problem.

Some systems will show a greater propensity to confine themselves to the habitual practices of the past; others will act according to rules that permit them to scan and recombine past experiences into novel outputs. Innovation and creativity in contriving political outputs for handling both initial and feedback demands is as rare a quality among sets of authorities as it is among the individuals who compose them. Every system constantly borders on the danger of falling into ruts or smug routines. However strong the norm of rational efficiency in handling outputs may be, they need to be reinforced by specific routines to detect and break away from outmoded prejudices and habits.

Dictatorial systems are particularly hard pressed. The very nature of their regime, by imposing narrow limits on freedom of discussion and severe penalties for political failures, reduces the range of alternatives that can be scanned. In part, the handicaps on outputs so encountered are compensated for by secrecy and less interference with rapid action.

Democracies tend to maximize the search of the memory bank of alternatives, especially by operating with rules that encourage the competition of ideas. But in spite of this, even in rationally oriented democratic systems, traditional patterns in producing outputs do exert strong attractive powers. In the United States, for example, after the stock market collapse of 1929, Hoover did begin to take some steps to meet the oncoming depression. But even the rule of rationality—that each situation is to be examined for the most efficient way of solving it—did not lead to extensive scanning of modes for meeting unemployment and poverty, alternative to those that were already prevalent in the system. It took a massive upheaval in social and political sentiments to permit the authorities, in the early Roosevelt period, to break open new methods for handling economic depressions. The decisive

stage involved driving the Supreme Court itself outside of its habituated substantive rules of interpretation into new patterns compatible
with an age in which the rate of change was rapidly increasing.

The new rules relating to outputs for handling depressions and
economic cycles have now been built into the structure of the American political system and have succeeded in creating their own ruts.
The range of alternatives still has difficulty in fluctuating very far out
of the neighborhood of outputs dictated by conservative economic
standards. If we contrast this situation with the novelty permitted in
European democratic systems, economic practices which in 1950 were
considered highly experimental are today part of the accepted ways for
coping with low rates of economic growth. Such innovations in Europe
in the way of outputs are still viewed as beyond the range of experiment in the United States. The scanning rules in the United States
with regard to possible political outputs in the economic sector, therefore, remain confined to semi-traditionalistic norms. There is a tendency for these rules to read, in effect: "we must stick to the older ways
of doing things"; or "what was good enough for our immediate forefa-
thers is good enough for us."

The Absence of Choice Criteria and of
Stored Experiences

If we turn our attention to the new political systems, we find that
they are in an anomalous situation with regard to innovation in the
face of change. In one respect, in many cases where new systems have
come into being, the lack of a storehouse of past experiences must
handicap the authorities in looking for rules of thumb by which to
handle current problems. But in another respect, this offers such systems a distinct advantage. They are not weighted down by past bag-
gage and, within the limits of resources and internal resistances, they
are free to let their imaginations roam in the choice of methods for
coping with feedback. In the older systems, to achieve the same results,
it would be necessary to have strong decision rules that encourage the
authorities to neglect or forget part of inherited political experiences.
In this way they might partly free themselves from bondage to their
past.

But the increased degrees of freedom for innovation made available
in new systems, through their very newness, has to be heavily discounted not only against the value of a bank of stored experiences but
also against the accompanying lack of norms to suggest the relevant
rules in scanning and selecting alternatives for outputs. Where a sys-

tem is newly born, by definition it has had little time or opportunity to learn extensive operating rules for meeting new situations. Where, in addition, the rate of social change intruding through the society into the political system is high, the authorities have little chance to absorb and reflect upon the lessons of each new experience and to incorporate them into norms of the political culture as guides for future members. Each set of authorities is left somewhat on its own, in a sense, with all the doubts, insecurities, and anxieties that go with the lack of some prototypical and respected examples, at least as initial guidelines against which to react in looking for a course of action.

It may be that, not unlike human beings as individuals, who after all constitute the acting members of the system, systems require some "gentling" during their early learning stages if they are not to be severely handicapped in the pursuit of their objectives. Experiments have at least suggested that the capacity of human beings, in their individual capacities, to adapt to change depends on their being exposed to gradual and regulated, specific and non-specific changes as they mature.[6] Through a relatively slow and ordered rate of learning, a system may incorporate into its political culture, rules about ways for deliberating over and evaluating stress on support and ways for regulating and implementing outputs. In this way the system may hope to maximize the likelihood that its goals will be achieved. Where, however, systems with a brief past undergo rapid change in which authorities have little chance to delay decisions or to call on whatever expertise there is, the resulting inadequate operating rules may contribute to erratic and unstable behavior.

From a practical point of view, this might call for extraordinary efforts to utilize expertise where possible and to build in structural delays for outputs so that more time than may be customary in older systems is devoted to deliberating on alternatives. Absence of such regulatory mechanisms increases the difficulty of avoiding sharp swings of outputs from one extreme to another. Examination of both foreign and domestic policies of many of the new nations reveals considerable indecision and pendular fluctuation. If highly traditionalistic norms may be destructive of creativeness in outputs, the relative absence of such traditions may leave the door open to erratic output behavior. It leaves the authorities with insufficient guidance in the way of past experiences for meeting current feedback response as well as other kinds of demands being imposed upon them. This situation must

[6] E. Horvath, "Psychological Stress: A Review of Definitions and Experimental Research," *General Systems: Yearbook of Society for General Systems*, Vol. IV (1959), 203–230.

therefore interfere with their efforts to utilize outputs as a way of reinforcing support for the political objects.

To sum up, then, as the producers of outputs, the authorities represent the last link in the feedback loop. It is through their reactions to the continuous flow of information and actions through a system and its environments that a system may seek to control, regulate, modify, or fundamentally transform the situation in which it finds itself. As we have seen, this is intrinsic to the properties of an open system.

By virtue of the feedback patterns that it possesses and of the presence of authorities who are responsible for and capable of reacting to the feedback, a political system is able to adapt to the circumstances in which it finds itself. But as we have seen before, it can go further. It has the capacity to invent new modes of behavior, set new goals for itself, and rearrange both its environment and its own internal structure and rules. Thereby, regardless of the intentions of the authorities, a system is able to assure the persistence of processes for allocating values and obtaining compliance.

In our discussion of the various components of the feedback loop we have analyzed the way in which these processes work. The role of the authorities in the stimulation of specific support, the last two chapters have brought out, is critical. It will vary with the extent of their own responsiveness to fluctuations in demands and support as fed back from the input units, with time lags in the flow of information around the loop, with the availability of external resources, and with the kinds of native talents and organizational capabilities they possess and the storage and retrieval procedures that they pursue. By filling in the values for each of these variables in any given system, we have the opportunity of assessing the ways in which the authorities in the system may, through their outputs, foster or undermine the growth of specific support.

Outputs and Diffuse Support

A final point may be made. Although I have been restricting my remarks about outputs to their effect for fostering specific support, it is clear that outputs may also be discussed in the light of their consequences for diffuse support. The authorities may become aware of the role that sentiments and beliefs about legitimacy, the common good, or the community play in the input of support at the regime and community level. Where information feedback alerts them to the fact that the state of mind of the members in the system is such that diffuse support is on the wane, positive and deliberate counteracting efforts may be taken.

With this possibility in mind, we can readily appreciate the fact that a separate analysis might be undertaken, parallel to the one just completed on specific support, that would demonstrate the relevance of outputs for the growth of diffuse support. In this instance the authorities would be acting to create a general sense of good will, not through the spill-over effects of offering tangible benefits of some sort, but through direct efforts to create a more favorable state of mind.

Whether or not appeals to a populace to display greater loyalty to their system, to make greater sacrifices in the name of a higher welfare for all or for the nation, actually do help to arouse stronger sentiments binding the members to the system, may be accepted as a moot point. But it is clear from the behavior of the authorities in all systems undergoing stress that at least they do strongly believe this to be the case. Members are typically exhorted to display greater evidence of patriotism and loyalty. And even in the daily course of events, in anticipation of any future possible stress, laws are passed to teach the history of one's country, to require various kinds of ritual to be performed such as saluting the flag, to display the appropriate symbols of authority on ceremonial occasions, or to teach the doctrines associated with the regime.

Outputs such as these could not be interpreted as rewards to bolster favorable sentiments. They represent frontal attacks of a different sort. Nevertheless, after each succeeding round of actions taken by the authorities to promote diffuse support, the flow of information back to these authorities would be as important as comparable information is with regard to the effects of those outputs designed to produce specific support. Time lag in the receipt of information and in the responses undertaken, the availability of resources, internal and external, and many of the other factors we have already discussed with respect to the feedback processes and specific support, would be equally important here. But the nature of their relevance is sufficiently evident to relieve us of the need to undertake a separate analysis of the role of feedback in the case of outputs that deal with diffuse support. The reader will be able to draw the necessary inferences himself.

However, one additional consideration does need to be mentioned. If specific support is to be generated, the authorities alone are in a position to distribute benefits to the members of the system, at least of the kinds available through authoritative outputs. It is the authorities who are the key figures in bolstering specific support.

But if diffuse support is to be encouraged, the matter is considerably different. It is open to any member or group in the system to take actions, even if they are not authoritative, to build up sentiments favorable for the persistence of the regime or community. Typically, a decline of diffuse support may arouse reactions among the non-authoritative members of the system who for one reason or another strongly identify with the political objects and feel impelled to bring others to share their attitudes. Opinion leaders, the mass media or patriotic organizations may take it upon themselves as a civic duty to bolster up any flagging diffuse support.

In many instances such responses on the part of the members of the system may be even more significant for the level of diffuse support than any action that the authorities could possibly take. In this sense, the provision of sufficient diffuse support for the political objects is not exclusively dependent upon authoritative outputs as is the level of specific support. This is an additional reason for not inquiring into the relationship between the outputs of the authorities and the input of diffuse support with the same detailed attention that we paid to their role in building up specific support. Nevertheless, to the extent that the authorities are active with regard to diffuse support, feedback here too is a basic mechanism that permits a system to cope with possible stress.

Reprise of the Function of Support

Persistence, we have seen, depends upon understanding what it is that may threaten to prevent a system from continuing to make and implement decisions and actions and from getting them accepted as binding. Inputs of various sorts, we discovered, constitute a way of pinpointing the source of such stress. Demands represented one of these potentially stressful inputs. Their numbers and variety may so overwhelm a system as to incapacitate it entirely if it were not for the presence of structural and cultural mechanisms that regulate the conversion of wants to demands and the flow of these demands through the system to decision-making points. Fluctuation in support was identified as another major source of stress.

But from the perspectives of systems analysis, the support that has become of primary significance is not the kind for which members compete in their search for power or office in a system, although, as we had constant occasion to note, what happens in day-to-day politics regularly and necessarily spills over into the arena of systems support.

Rather, we were driven to consider support that is extended to or withheld from the basic political objects: the political community, the regime, and the authorities as a generalized set of role incumbents. In seeking to understand the way in which the lack of sufficient input of such support may stress a system and the typical patterns of response in coping with it, we were drawn into a discussion of the complex function of feedback in political life. But in undertaking an analysis of this aspect of the political system, we have also discovered that this enabled us to bring together and reveal the intimate and intricate interrelationship of all the analytic components of this system.

Support for the basic political objects, we have seen, may be diffuse in character. Specific mechanisms of regulation, as in the stimulation of legitimacy, a sense of common interest, or a bond of political community, arise that may permit a system to maintain an adequate inflow. But where these break down or operate ineffectively, or where, as is typically the case, they are by themselves inadequate, additional means are available to all systems through the production of outputs. It was in an effort to account for the effectiveness of outputs as generators of specific support that we turned to the feedback processes.

In doing so, we arrived at the central processes through which a political system is able to act in a dynamic way to adapt and regulate its behavior as a set of interactions for authoritatively allocating values. Of even greater significance, through feedback a system acquires the necessary means through which to seek a more creative relationship to its potentially stressful environment than is traditionally implied in the idea of social adaptation. It is able to grapple actively, aggressively, and constructively with its environmental or internal influences. The outputs represent a major way in which a political system interacts with the influences bearing upon it.

To recapitulate the dynamics of the feedback processes, outputs act as stimuli that breed satisfactions or discontents, depending upon the impact they have on the circumstances surrounding the members or on the way they are perceived. Whether or not the outputs lead to an increase or decline in support will depend, however, on more than the extent to which they satisfy demands or create conditions that alleviate future demand-provoking conditions. If stress from inadequate support is to be averted, the nature of the distribution of satisfactions in the system, their effect upon the members who are politically powerful, and the patterns of satisfaction over time are all of equal importance. The inflow of support for the various political objects is a product of a rather complex equation.

But aside from the actual effects that the outputs have upon the members, for the authorities to be able to modify the supportive conditions under which the system is operating, they must have information fed back to them about two things: the general state of affairs in the system as they affect supportive attitudes, and the specific consequences of their own outputs, past or current. We have traced out the variety of factors that typically interfere especially with the accuracy and speed of information feedback and thereby with the capacity of the authorities to react in a way they consider appropriate to cope with the conditions they perceive.

Part Six

Conclusion

29

The Goals of Systems Analysis

THERE WAS A TIME IN THE HISTORY OF POLITICAL SCIENCE WHEN IT was possible to master the facts essential to the available level of understanding of political phenomena. But as in all other areas of life, the increasing specialization of labor in scientific inquiry has proceeded at such a pace that today the absorption of known facts has passed beyond the capacity of any individual or small group. The belated recognition of the function of theory is itself a response to what would otherwise be an impossible situation. It is a means of rescuing the student of political life from the need to be the master of all the facts that he might possibly wish to survey. As we know, empirically oriented theory supplies analytic tools that seek to bring order, economy, and stability to the effort to understand an everchanging phenomenal world.

It may seem that our choice is between some kind of macrotheory, such as systems analysis, or no theory at all. But nature does not really give us this degree of freedom. Whether or not we wish it, we do depend on broad theoretical orientations to guide us into narrower empirical paths. The real choice before us is always between an inarticulate set of assumptions, unrelated concepts, and poorly integrated generalizations as against explicit efforts to obtain greater theoretical self-awareness and tighter logical coherence.

But even if the social scientist were free to choose freedom from theory, in terms of the ethical presuppositions of his vocation it is doubtful whether he could justifiably neglect to make explicit his theoretical orientations. Explication of the goals of scientific understanding and the rational defense of choices are imperatives that the code of science imposes upon the student of political life. Theory enforces such responsibility upon the scientist. Without it, he would not have to account for any particular selection of facts as against another; as long as he could bring some restricted order out of the crude data of social life, he would have attained his end. But by compelling the scientist to prove the relevance of his research for the broader goals of understanding human phenomena, theory forces him ultimately to warrant his selection on more imposing and convincing grounds than intellectual whim, intuition, tradition or accident.

For the individual scientist, it is true, random search for data, unconstrained by formal theory, may periodically be an optimal strategy. The choice of this strategy will depend upon many factors such as the preceding level of understanding, the number of clues already available for answering unresolved problems, or the extent to which the research worker is groping in the dark for some first illuminating idea. But for a discipline as a whole, to continue to forego or ignore general theory is to renounce that which gives it a disciplined character and to reduce it at best to a poorly ordered array of diverse pieces of information or partial theories.

Criteria of Theoretical Adequacy

Political science cannot escape at least implicit, unsynthesized theoretical assumptions of some sort. Yet the fact that some kind of theoretical presuppositions lurk in the interstices of even crudely empirical research does not signify that somewhere there is waiting a single correct general theory or even a more limited conceptual framework. Political science would provide an extraordinarily powerful instrument of analysis indeed if it could discover a solitary set of concepts and propositions that were equally instructive for the investigation of all and every manner of problems in the discipline. But if the experience of the other sciences has been any kind of guide, it would be futile to expect that a single overarching theory is anything but a remote ideal.

Each theory pierces the gloom from a slightly different angle and highlights somewhat different problems. In the hardworking realities of research, we must be grateful if we are fortunate enough to be able to discover or invent tools of analysis that will be best for the special purposes we have in mind, always trying to broaden the scope of insight and understanding that a theory will give us but content if it can do well what it is designed to do. In the physical sciences, the alternative cloud and orbital models of atomic structure make it possible to present different facets of the properties of matter; [1] quantum and wave theories of light are equally valid for understanding diverse aspects of the behavior under investigation.

Unfortunately, as a result of the traditions of classical political theory, we are frequently led to believe that somehow or another there

[1] An illustration drawn to my attention by Stephen T. Easton.

must be one theory and only one, that can be right. By the very hortatory nature of moral inquiry, of which traditional theory is largely composed, this must be the case. It would be a poor ethical theorist who was not convinced of the exclusive wisdom of his moral objectives and who did not believe all others ultimately to be half-truths at best or utterly false. Ethical theorizing has emerged not so much to analyze and understand the sources of ethical judgments—although this is an important part of its task—as to make them, to persuade others of their merit, or to warrant them in some manner. But this traditional habit that leads to commitment to a single point of view need not be transferred automatically to empirically oriented general theory. New tasks require new criteria, new ways of looking at theory itself.

If we cannot say that we ought to expect that any one theory is the right one, how are we to evaluate and select among alternatives? Need all theories be of equal merit? Numerous general tests for selection among theories are well known. Elegance in formulation, economy of expression, simplicity, internal logic and rigor, fertility of insights are qualities that can be readily recognized as desirable. But the ultimate key, of course, is the adequacy of explanation and understanding offered by the theory.

Here two criteria may be advanced, particularly with regard to the kind of systems analysis we have just been developing. First, to what extent may the problems posed by the theory be considered relevant and necessary for theoretical analysis? Are there alternative ways of asking questions that are superior or take higher priority? Second, even if the puzzles that the theory seeks to solve are conceived to be intriguing and inescapable ones, can we say that the actual structure of categories does the job? Have the questions been answered in an adequate way?

The second criterion need not be discussed further since the whole of this volume stands as an effort to meet it. But now that we have traced out the intricacies of a systems approach as a proposed step toward developing a general theory, it will be helpful to reconsider the matter as to whether, after all, in the light of what we now know, we have really been asking the most profitable kinds of questions.

An Alternative Theoretical Question

To deal with this criterion, it is true that entirely different kinds of questions could have been posed and these would certainly have led to the construction of a conceptual framework quite remote from, although not entirely alien to the one that has been presented. How are decisions made? Who influences whom about the kinds of inputs that are made or the outputs that are produced? How is power distributed and put to work in selecting policies and implementing them? How are optimal strategies for attaining objectives assigned and pursued? Who shares in the benefits derived from political activities? What are the conditions under which popular control of rulers may be maximized? Each of these questions would have led to different although probably somewhat overlapping sets of categories for the analysis of political systems and would have brought to light different aspects.

But all of the ways of looking at political life implicit in these questions do have one thing in common. They impinge directly on the allocative consequences of political interaction. To the extent that they lead to theoretical inquiry, we may classify them generally as theories of allocation.

Many partial theories of political allocation have been suggested although they are not normally perceived in quite this light. Theories of party politics, interest groups, legislative behavior, political leadership, administrative organization, coalitions, voting behavior and the like seek to understand varying parts of the allocative processes. They deal with those structures or practices through which the outputs are influenced, formulated, and implemented and that thereby determine the way in which the valued things of the society are allocated. They are concerned with the determinants of what has been called "achieved" as contrasted with "ascribed" support.[2] Even though an overarching allocative theory has still to be proposed or formulated as a guide to the study of political processes,[3] there can be little doubt that this kind of orientation has at least implicitly dominated the theoretical interests of most political research. "Who gets what, when, and how" most simply and succinctly phrases this latent theoretical outlook.[4]

[2] S. N. Eisenstadt, op. cit., p. 25 and numerous other places dispersed through the volume.

[3] Efforts to construct general theories of power come closest to providing us with a general theory of political allocation. But with respect to these, see J. G. March, who has begun to doubt the wisdom of even posing what I have been calling "the allocative problem" in this way. "The Power of Power," a paper presented at the annual meeting of the American Political Science Association, New York, September, 1963.

[4] H. D. Lasswell, Politics, Who Gets What, When, How (New York: McGraw-Hill, 1936).

But what these allocative theories take for granted—the actual and continued existence of some kind of political system—I have here questioned and subjected to theoretical examination. How is it that a political system as such is able to persist through time? What is there in the nature of the system itself and the conditions under which it may typically find itself that would stand as a possible threat to its continued existence, whether in one form or another? Persistence and change of systems, or rather, persistence through change as is more often the case, has seemed to be the most inclusive kind of question that one might ask about a political system.

To put it in colloquial and perhaps, therefore, in more expressive terms, a systems approach draws us away from a discussion of the way in which the political pie is cut up and how it happens to get cut up in one way rather than another. There is a *status quo* bias built into allocative research when it is untempered with an appreciation of the systemic conditions under which the allocations are taking place. It leaves the impression that the pie must always remain the same and even that the allocative processes change for reasons that are explicable solely in terms of the system itself. To escape this bias, we need a theoretical framework that helps us understand how the very pie itself comes into existence and changes in its basic content or structure.

To leave this limited analogy, where the system itself is threatened with destruction, as in highly unstable systems, allocative theories, although relevant, no longer suffice. We need to turn to the basic forces—here described as stress—if we are to understand the processes through which political systems are able to fulfill their characteristic task, that of allocating values authoritatively for a society. We must engage in an attack on the broadest theoretical front. If we know how systems manage to cope with stress, how they manage to persist in the face of either stable or changing environments, other theories or sets of ideas aspiring to theoretical status that deal with various aspects of political life—decision-making, coalition strategies, game theories, power, and group analysis—all fit into place. They are no longer alternative or competing modes of analysis; they represent partial theories of allocation, referring to and explaining some special part or aspect of a political system.

However, just because they are narrower in scope, this does not in any way imply that they are thereby lower in importance. Yet, because they are narrower, what they all leave out of consideration is the system as a whole. We lack efforts at the construction of a theory that is oriented to the system, regardless for the moment of the form that such a theory might take. Systems analysis seeks to close this gap in one way. It offers a context within which partial theories of allocation may obtain greater meaning and significance without in the least seeking to deny the independent value of each in particular. If at some date a general theory of allocations should become available, at the very least it would complement a systems analysis; at most, it might be integrally woven into a systems approach.[5] To put the matter in another way, partial theories of allocation are not competitive because they are operating at a different level of analysis.

But the reader may well have some residual doubts about this interpretation of the linkage between partial allocative theories and a general "systems persistence" theory. After all, if we recall the discussion of support in the last several chapters, it may seem peculiar, at the very least, that I should now be asserting that a theory of political allocation would differ from that undertaken through systems analysis. Support does seem to turn on the way in which members may mobilize others in the pursuit of objectives and thereby it does seem to influence the way in which the valued things in a society are authoritatively divided and distributed. Indeed, in the very way in which I have described political life generally, as those interactions through which values are authoritatively allocated, one might be forgiven for inferring that allocation is central to a general theory formulated in this kind of context.

However, it should be clear by this time that my introduction of support as a central variable, for example, flows not from an interest in the part that it plays in helping to determine the way in which values are authoritatively allocated among the members. Rather, I was compelled to turn to it because of some central systemic problems that could not have been understood otherwise. Support has been analyzed in systems rather than allocative terms, as it concerns stress on a system and the capacity of the system to cope with it. Support did not enter our frame of reference because of the way in which its use and distribution might influence the various processes through which values are authoritatively allocated, a purpose that it serves in research on voting behavior, parties, interest groups, legislative behavior and the like.

Alternatively, by implication I have been arguing that insofar as political analysis and research have been attempting to explain and understand allocative functions within a system, the system within which the allocations take place has been consistently overlooked. Yet, without the existence of the system of behavior, we would be unable to discover those allocative processes, the variations in which require ex-

[5] For example, see the relationship as indicated in chapter 23.

planation. There would be no decisions to be taken or implemented. In short, research about allocative processes has always assumed what here we have been raising for explicit attention.

The Dynamic Character of Systems Analysis

The general image here of a political system is far removed from the narrowly dynamic one that must be a product of any effort to discover who shares in the values allocated by a system, how power is distributed and used, or the part that various kinds of structures play in implementing various presumed functions that sustain political life. Although all these approaches to political analysis cannot help but draw attention to the interactions among political actors, whether they are individuals or groups, interaction is only one form of dynamics. Unfortunately it may easily be mistaken for an entirely different type of dynamic theory, one that interprets political life as a set of processes through which work is accomplished and through which information and behavior are transformed into something new and different.

In one sense, even a theory of a static system will also reveal the interactions among the parts of the system. It is as though we had a movie film of a system at a given moment of time. Members would be hurrying about each interacting with others. In this sense, a static analysis, peculiarly enough, exposes a dynamic aspect. It would depict processes at work.

But in suggesting that systems analysis signalizes the dynamics of a system, I mean much more than this. Unless we were alerted to look for it, such a movie would fail to reveal the kind of work, not that individual members or groups in their particularity get done, but that the system as a network of interrelated actions itself manages to perform. No film could ever literally show this of course; but it is as though we could see what the outcome of all this activity was at each moment of time. The interesting and theoretically vital consideration about political life is that it does do work, and we can discover this by recognizing that through its outputs it may find a way to persist in a potentially stressful environment. As we have seen, when confronted with stress, whatever the source, it can go out to meet it and typically, what happens in a system can be meaningfully interpreted in this light.[6]

---

[6] On occasion, analysts of my publications have sought the source of my systems conceptualization in the input-output approach of economics. In fact, there is neither a historical nor a logical connection. It is one of the shortcomings of eco-

One part of this kind of systems dynamics, I have sought to show, consists of the fact that a system is a means whereby the inputs of demands and support are converted into outputs. This is the allocative aspect of the system behavior. It creates the basic political problem, as it were. How can a political system keep such a conversion process working and provide a social structure through which the work can be done? It was this question that ultimately forced us to inquire into the further one: what is it that stands in the way of such a conversion process? The existence of extreme variations in political structures in political systems, ranging from the most democratic to the most totalitarian, does not prevent the operation of this process. Conversion of inputs to outputs is not peculiar to any one kind of political system; it describes the processes underlying all systems. Our analysis had to be cast in far broader terms than those required for a theoretical framework designed to explore one class of political systems.

But if, for purposes of analysis, we accept as our jurisdiction every kind of system, we have been able to see that it makes sense to think of the conversion process as being threatened by stress from the inputs themselves. Excessive volume and variety of demands, or insufficient support may threaten to drive the essential variables of a system beyond their critical range. If a system is to persist, we have postulated, it must be able to devise methods for coping with existing or potential stress.

In the process of describing varying ways for doing this, we have in effect been witnessing the second kind of dynamics to which I have just referred. The members of the system are able to work on the system itself or its environment so as to transform or modify them and thereby assure the continuance of the essential variables. To put it in other words, through the coping mechanisms members of the system are able to provide for the conversion of inputs into outputs, that is, for the authoritative allocation of values for the society. In the preceding chapter, the discussion of concepts for analyzing the operation of the feedback loop brought to the fore the full complexity of this capability of the political system. It revealed the complicated relationships among all parts of a system. They form a continuous flow of action and reaction, from production of outputs as stimuli to feedback response, to information feedback about the response, and to output reactions on the part of the authorities in a truly seamless web of activities.

nomic theory that it remains at a lower level of dynamic analysis; it does not explicitly view an economic system as an open and constructively adaptive one. See the Preface of *A Framework for Political Analysis* for a statement of the most immediate influences that helped to shape my thinking in its present direction.

It is commonplace in political research to say that at one level of analysis, everything seems to be related to everything else. And even though typically we must chop off a segment of reality for specific research, it is always with the knowledge that somehow we are violating reality. For empirical purposes this is unavoidable and does little damage as long as we are sharply aware of what we are about. But from a theoretical point of view, it is crucial that we devise a set of perspectives and parallel categories that permit us to formulate the basic analytic questions in such a way as to take the interrelationship of political phenomena into account, and not in any trivial sense. We must do more than give passing recognition to the continuous flow of the interrelated activities through which a political system persists. A systems analysis does just this. It encourages us to interpret political life as a dynamic system of behavior, both as an interacting set and as a body of activities which, in their totality, are able to do work by converting inputs into outputs.

In this second and more inclusive sense of dynamics, we give new content and meaning to the idea so familiar in political research, that of political process. The study of political systems embraces an understanding of the processes through which authoritative allocations take place. But it does more. It needs to be extended to the analysis of the processes underlying system persistence through time. And persistence, we have already recognized, is intricately connected with the capacity of a political system, as an open, self-regulating, and goal-setting system, to change itself. The puzzle of how a system manages to persist through change if necessary, forms a central problem of the analysis of political life.

General Theory and the Long View

We have been interpreting political life as a system of behavior set in an environment and open to the influences stemming from that environment, as well as from internal sources. In this light, the identification of a political system is a way of referring to those processes through which authoritative allocations are provided for the unit under analysis, which, for our purposes, is the society at its most inclusive level.

Our central task has been to inquire into the way in which such conversion processes are able to endure at all, given the many dangers that beset them. We have pinpointed some of these threats as stresses that take the form of excessive volume and variety of demands or a decline in the level of diffuse and specific support below some empirically undetermined but theoretically specifiable minimum. We have seen that it is the peculiar capacity of any social system, including the political system, that it can cope with influences operating on it through positive, constructive actions. A system may change itself so as to incorporate or absorb the effects of such influences, the responsible members of the system may anticipate and ward off the stress, or, once the impact has been felt, they may take measures to prevent any further action that might imperil the system. The numerous and typical patterns of response have been examined generally, yet with sufficient detail to indicate the kind of research that would be appropriate for understanding the fundamental coping behavior of political systems. Finally, it has also become apparent that the members of a system would be hard put to respond if feedback processes were not available through which they might acquire the necessary relevant information about what was happening in the system and about the effects of their own actions.

During the previous discussion, I have taken advantage of the opportunity as it arose to emphasize that this mode of analysis tells us little about the way in which any particular type of system, such as a democracy, might persist. But it is a point worth re-emphasizing. I have carefully and deliberately excluded this from among my objectives. I am not unaware of the fact that it conflicts so prominently with the very considerable pressures today to devote our energies at once towards an understanding of the conditions surrounding the persistence of democratic systems. Yet if we had succumbed and had accepted a study of the conditions and operation of democracy as our immediate purpose, our attention would have been seriously diverted from a general theory to a partial theory, one relating to democracy alone. It would thereby have defeated our main goal.

On the other hand, the fact that I have opted in favor of considerably broader theoretical objectives, does not in the least imply that such a theory of democracy would not be useful or that it is not urgently needed, especially when we see how easily newly founded nations tend to slip into non-democratic molds. But even in face of the undeniable current urgency of the matter, it has seemed vital, for a fundamental understanding of political life, to pose a logically prior question, one that inquires into the way in which any or all political systems are able to continue to fulfill their characteristic function, the conversion of inputs into authoritative outputs. I have been arguing that if we can obtain some relatively reliable answers to this question, we will have taken a gigantic stride toward exposing the conditions for the operation and persistence of particular types of systems, including democracies. On this premise the study of democracies would recede logically to a second order position and it would raise a whole range of ancillary questions to which we have not found it necessary to address ourselves.

Yet we need not conclude from these remarks that a systems analysis as developed here is irrelevant or unsuited for pursuing the study of democratic systems. It is perfectly feasible—more than that, I would argue that it is necessary and revealing—to apply the present mode of analysis to any specific class of systems. With respect to democratic systems, for example, we would need to supplement our general questions with others that are, however, couched in a similar language. How do democratic systems, as defined, manage to persist under conditions of stability and change? Over and above the normal kinds of stresses to which all political systems are subjected, are there any special kinds that impinge upon democratic systems? Have democracies devised typical ways, other than those described for most systems in general, for coping with the kinds of stresses to which they are exposed? Is there anything special about the feedback processes in a democracy that impairs or improves the chances of such a system for coping with normal or system specific types of stress? General questions such as these, specific for system types, would take priority over a logically still much lower order of question, namely, those dealing with the special conditions surrounding the persistence of a system in the circumstances of a given kind of time and place, as under conditions of modern industrialism and mass society or of recent emergence from colonial subordination. Yet it is largely at this level of analysis that most contemporary studies of democratic systems are cast.

I am very much aware of the fact that it is not easy to take the long view and focus on any and all systems as such, especially when all the pressures of the world are toward immediate answers for immediate problems. Nor is it easy to declare openly that it is indeed possible to conceive of the survival of democracy, say, to be a second order problem logically, at the theoretical level, even though it is a first order problem ethically, at the practical level.

For political scientists it is doubly difficult to make the kind of choice that seems to be required. Political scientists constantly live in double jeopardy in this respect. Like all other social scientists, we are being driven to give whatever help we can for the solution of contemporary issues and this inevitably diverts considerable energy from what would be longer range considerations, not so closely bound to current policy needs. But in addition, as students of political life, we cannot help but be exposed constantly to the urgent issues of the day. They stand at the heart of the political process, as we have seen; they are the demands over which conflict arises in any system. It is not strange, therefore, that political scientists in democratic systems should feel more keenly than others the immediacy and urgency of the difficulties in which democratic systems may find themselves and that they should be even more aware than others of the need that the authorities have for whatever help is possible, in the short run. It is no less strange, therefore, that so many in political science should construe the central tasks of political research as the giving of advice or of developing policy proposals and regularly passing judgment on issues.

But if twenty-five hundred years of experience in political inquiry teaches us little else, it does suggest that the quickest way to obtaining solutions may well prove to be the slowest and least effective. Reliable knowledge does not come easily and is certainly not a product only of a sense of urgency. The wish here is not father to the product. In the long run we may hope to obtain a more reliable understanding about democratic systems and about ways to meet current issues if we are prepared today to direct our energies in some significant measures, as a discipline at least, to an understanding of political systems in general. The task of general theory is to guide us in this direction.

Paradoxically, empirical theory is imbued with the highest of ethical purposes—the discovery of knowledge for the application to human problems—but *en route,* by the nature of the case, it conveys the lowest sense of ethical immediacy. Fundamental knowledge in political science will have the opportunity to measure up to the demands that are increasingly being made upon the discipline once we become universally convinced of the validity of this proposition. Under the pressure of a culture that has never quite been persuaded of the utility of scientific scholarship in the social sphere, an awareness of this proposition is more vital than ever. It helps to ease the anxieties that many social scientists, as responsible members of a political system, must feel when they appear to "withdraw" in the face of insistent crises. It asserts what the ancients knew only too well, that they also serve who only stand and think.

Illusions about Theory

Although there has been considerable discussion about the tasks of theory in the social sciences, and to a lesser extent in political science, we have still not come to terms in other ways with what we are to expect from theoretical inquiry. Until we do, there is the great and constant danger that we may ask either too much or too little and in the process we may reduce the benefits currently available. Unless we are prepared to cast off some illusions we may have about the function of theory in research, the criteria we use in judging the theoretical efforts that do arise may be quite inappropriate to the objectives sought.

The Fragmentation of Theory

One illusion not usually identified as such, is to be found in the pervasive presupposition that somehow or another we are perpetually doomed to developing theories that apply to different sectors of political science. Theories must appear in bits and pieces. We have efforts at theories oriented toward comparative politics or international relations, as well as a host of less ambitious efforts directed toward domestic politics, what we might call theories of intranational politics. These have taken such forms as equilibrium analysis, at least latently present, group theories, and theories of power and of decision-making.

If these efforts at theory construction had been undertaken on the explicit assumption that they were only partial theories that some day would have to accommodate themselves to a more general theory of politics, there would be little with which to cavil. But usually there is the distinct impression that the objective is to establish them as independent and self-contained entities, as though political science will of necessity have to be satisfied with a loosely connected aggregate of theories, at best covering separately such fields as comparative politics, international relations, and national political systems. It is as though the accident of specialization of labor within political research predetermines the possible range of theory.

The weight of the analysis in the present volume has been pulling us firmly and forcefully away from a conclusion such as this. Implicit in my conceptualization has been the notion of a unified theory of politics. It is no longer appropriate to allow ourselves to become victims of presuppositions that lead us to think of general theories that are uniquely and permanently comparative, international, or intranational in origin or in scope.

The continued cleavage between intranational theories and hoped-for comparative theory is transparently untenable. All science is of necessity comparative; there can be little basis for circumscribing a theory by virtue of its national or comparative referents. It has only been the proximity to and identification with one's national political scene that has lent intranational research any special significance. This alone does not permit us to impute to it any special theoretical status. Indeed, research in national politics is itself comparative. In American political research, we compare state politics within the political system, voting behavior in different regions, party organizations as they vary in time and space, or local community political processes. Normally, the relatively higher degree of cultural and linguistic homogeneity and structural integration in a single society can be expected to reduce many of the problems involved in intranational as against international comparative political research; but not even this proposition is universally true. Within some societies, such as India or Indonesia, the parameters of political behavior may frequently show greater variations than those between two separate political systems.

But even though cross-system research may add to one's problems, intranational theories of power, decision-making, or group behavior are no less comparatively derived than any theory that might conceivably emerge from the subfield of comparative politics. The kind of subject matter considered, whether it lies within the boundaries of only one political system or cuts across two or more, is of significance only for the enrichment and enhancement of the reliability of a theory, not for its intrinsic nature.

But this point need not be fully argued. Today, when political science has become so sharply cognizant of the existence of non-Western systems and the role that exotic societies play in shaping political behavior, the comparative base of all theory formulation is quickly coming to be taken for granted.

But the case for the unity of theory seems to be less applicable to the field of international relations. Indeed the tendencies have gone in just the opposite direction. There has been considerable pressure for the organization of this subfield into an entirely independent discipline, not only on the grounds of administrative necessity but of theoretical uniqueness.[7] Some of the theories that have grown up have seemed peculiarly applicable to the interactions of the large aggregates that the modern political system represents, as illustrated in game theories and their various derivatives.

One way of seeking to overcome the apparent disjunction between

[7] Q. Wright, *The Study of International Relations* (New York: Appleton-Century-Crofts, 1955).

the main body of political science and international relations would indeed be to separate them and to search out intellectual bridges at a later time. Another way might be to insist that foreign affairs are just an extension of domestic politics and that they can be appropriately included in any general theory that is applicable to national systems. But neither of these alternatives offers either an appealing or valid solution. In the one, great diseconomies are involved; the social sciences are sufficiently fragmented without introducing another separate intellectual enterprise except under the most urgent necessities. In the second, we all know that although international affairs do represent an extension of domestic politics, they also involve something more. They can be conceptualized as a system of behavior, the international system, with numerous subsystems ranging from functional organizations of members drawn from national units, to organizations of such groups as NATO, the UN or SEATO, as well as the national systems themselves.

If we aspire to a general theory of politics, as we do in this volume, we may even go somewhat further than this. Not only is there an international political system, but it may in fact be usefully interpreted as just another type of system, to be analyzed, described, and compared with all other systems. It is not any more atypical or unique than other classifications of systems each of which, for special purposes, may be distinguished from the other.

We may validly adopt an international political system as our object of reference, within the systems framework that has already been developed, because, as I have earlier indicated in passing, international life itself may be designated as an international society. It contains a culture of its own and this is more than the sum of its component national cultures. International law and custom are just one manifestation of this culture. There is an international economy that is already being independently studied and the trends of which may deviate from trends in any single national economy. There is even a social structure to the international society as can be seen in the stratification of nations according to wealth, prestige, power, and the like, as well as the more obscure and ambiguous stratification that develops among individual members of different societies who meet in the international arena.

Our concern is not with these social systems for their own sake. But their presence does help us to appreciate that it is equally feasible to conceive of political life at the international level as an international political system, one among numerous aspects of the international society. The international political system possesses a theoretical status that is equivalent in every respect but one with the political systems of national societies. It differs only in the fact that the component units of the international system consist of large and powerful subsystems that we call national political systems, and regional groupings of them.

These create special problems of compliance but *theoretically*, even here, the differences are not so great as they may appear to be. In national systems we have large geographic units in the form of provinces, states, or departments. To be sure, there are differences in power among the subsystems of the international system. But this is equally true of national systems depending upon the legitimacy of the authorities and upon the looseness or tightness of the coupling among subsystems, ranging from the confederal type of system represented by the relationship among clans in many primitive tribes to the unitary systems of modern political systems.

This interpretation of the international political system as just another kind of political system cognate with any national system creates no theoretical hardships, at least with the systems conceptualization developed here. Indeed, it offers us an opportunity to expand our idea of the nature of the international system so that it includes more sensibly the actual actors in this area of politics. Although most current theories of international politics systematically take into consideration the presence of national units, regional groups, and functional organizations as subsystems, they tend to ignore the development of new kinds of actors. With the shrinking of the world, individual members of these component subsystems have become increasingly oriented to world affairs; they respond to world events and the nature of their responses helps to condition the way in which the sub-unit of which they are part participates in the international system. We would be forced to neglect an important kind of actor if we did not accept such members individually considered, as direct rather than derivative components in the international system.

If the argument is offered that the individual member is often unaware of the international sphere, as in the case of some members in modern systems and of many members in large-scale traditional ones, such as peasant societies, the answer is simple. It is true that in such systems members may be scarcely alive to the existence of an international system; in some cases, where an elite dominates, the individual member may be totally ignorant and disinterested in what occurs beyond the distant hills. But this need not exclude these members from the system. It would only indicate that they are peripheral and lack consciousness of their role. But it would not reduce the utility of including them as direct components of an international system. Even in the most advanced national system, many members are equally apathetic to political life; they become exclusively objects of outputs and not participants in their formation. In international systems this condition is just more likely to prevail today; in future generations, however, changes may well occur.

The international system is comparable in all respects to any other kind of system, at the theoretical level, although the values for the relevant variables will clearly be different. That is to say, we can identify in the international system all of the basic variables that we have already discussed for political systems in general. But as any close inspection would show, the international system reflects a condition more akin to many kinds of segmentary lineage primitive systems than to modern ones, although a comparison along these lines would carry us far afield.[8]

Nevertheless, in the international system, the members of the international society seek to resolve some of their problems through the authoritative allocation of values. As we have already seen, the lack of strong or universal feelings of legitimacy with regard to authorities or structures need not prevent us from recognizing the existence of a political system; legitimacy is only one basis upon which authority may be established and accepted. Members of the international system put in demands and seek to have them converted into outputs. The authorities in this case are considerably less centralized than in most modern systems, less continuous in their operation, and more contingent on events, as in the case of primitive systems. But nonetheless, historically, the great powers and, more recently, various kinds of international organizations, such as the League of Nations and the United Nations, have been successful, intermittently, in resolving differences that were not privately negotiated and in having them accepted as authoritative. It is they who have acted in the role of authorities.

The international system also has a regime. The relationships among the component actors are not random nor are their interactions entirely without constraints. Rules and expectations prevail, even though they may be less regularly complied with than in the many national systems.

[8] See D. Easton, "Political Anthropology"; R. D. Masters, "World Politics As a Primitive Political System," Yale University, unpublished manuscript, 1963; C. F. Alger, "Comparison of Intra-national and International Politics," 57 *American Political Science Review* (1963) 406–419, especially pp. 414 ff.

Finally, in addition to authorities and regime, there is an international political community, as the term was defined before. It certainly is not a community in which its problems of living together are solved through peaceful means with the regularity we have come to expect of modern systems. And, in addition, the sense of community may fluctuate from zero to a slightly higher point on a scale. But we know that there is a difference between the mere existence of a group that shares its division of political labor and the sense of mutual identification or sense of community that it may have. The one can and does exist without the other.

But we do not even have to push our argument that far. It is extremely doubtful that a sense of community is entirely absent. If the fictional and improbable were really to occur, and we were faced with an imminent, massive and hostile invasion from some distant planet, there is little doubt that the sudden and intimate cooperative action on the part of all members of the international system would quickly lead future scholars to the discovery that after all there had been vague, ill-defined but nonetheless real ties upon which to build the necessary military and political defenses.

Without pursuing the analysis any further, however, the main point is that we need to begin to conceive of a unified theory of politics that embraces national, comparative, and international approaches to systems. Theoretically, each system, including the international, would undoubtedly be subdivided into various types. For any class of them special subtheories would undoubtedly be required, just as we now think in terms of special subtheories about democracies or dictatorships. But at one level, propositions could be made that apply to them all, and certainly the underlying body of major categories of analysis would not need to differ. As presented here, a systems analysis aspires to this level of generality and comprehensiveness. It represents the search for a unified theory of politics.

As long as we operate with the illusion that each subfield of political science can and ought to formulate an exclusive theory for its own subject matter, we cannot help but continue to believe that a general theory is impossible. There will be no incentive for an effort to break out of the narrow ring that such a presupposition places around the construction of theory. If we conceive the situation to be otherwise, there will be a need both for reaching out systematically across the subfields and for open and avowed efforts to break completely out of the old patterns and establish new and unified approaches to political theory.

Theoretical Simplicity

There is another illusion that has been equally hard in dying: that a theory suffers because it is only an extreme simplification of reality. If one argues, for example, that the political analysis in this work does not do justice to the complex richness of political events, that political life is far more subtle and involved, that major areas of political interaction have merely been mentioned but hardly elaborated, such observations would be perfectly correct. This objection would reveal, however, that the general antipathy in all the social sciences toward theory, a product of the dissatisfaction with the grand designs of traditional social philosophy, has led only too slowly to a recognition of the fact that every theory, by its very nature, is defective. The task of theory is above all to simplify and in so doing, much of the intuitive and empirical texture of political behavior is lost, in the first step. To deal with complexity by an equally complex theory would result in thwarting, not in aiding understanding.

At most, a theory is only a distant approximation to the apperceptive mass of the world as we come to know it in experience. The task of theoretical development is to add complexities as we become increasingly proficient with the limited models initially developed. If we are searching for a model that will duplicate a political system, the most accurate one is the political system itself. It is the very effort to get away from this conception that leads to a theoretical model based on a judicious selection of those variables that will most economically yield an understanding of the system. It is no criticism to suggest only that the systems theory presented here is an oversimplification; it is merely an invitation to introduce additional elements to bring the theoretical picture of the system closer to the empirical system.

But if we still feel somewhat uneasy in the presence of theoretical models unburdened by detail, at least one other illusion has been finally and irrevocably shattered. We no longer expect the theoretician to search for the massive substantive theories such as were contrived by the great social and political philosophers of the past, all-embracing in their scope and definitive in their presumed validity. Even though some still nostalgically strive for it, the day of the single grand design for the interpretation of political life is past. The requirements of a rigorous science have finally chastened political inquiry until it has come to know its realistic limits. It must begin by searching for the appropriate variables to expedite the tasks of research, a set of logically coherent categories in terms of which to identify these variables, and generalizations that put these concepts to use in explaining the functioning of political systems. From these formal beginnings, it is to be expected, substantive theories of politics will begin to emerge.

What has been and could only be attempted here is a modest and small step, a slow inching forward toward a distant horizon on which, some day, we may hope that there will appear a reasonably helpful macrotheory about political and social behavior. The appropriate question to ask about a theoretical analysis today is not: does this fully explain the functioning of political systems or does it offer a fire-proof set of concepts toward that end? At this stage, to ask that question is to predetermine the answer. This systems analysis does not, could not, and ought not to be expected to do so. The appropriate question is: does this approach help us to take a small step in the right direction? If so, it accomplishes its objectives. By an accumulation of such steps, we shall slowly build up the collective wisdom, courage, and stamina to take increasingly larger ones with less hesitation or faltering along the way.

Index